BMC Control-M 7: A Journey from Traditional Batch Scheduling to Workload Automation

Master one of the world's most powerful enterprise workload automation tools – BMC Control-M 7 - using this book

Qiang Ding

BIRMINGHAM - MUMBAI

BMC Control-M 7: A Journey from Traditional Batch Scheduling to Workload Automation

First published: October 2012

Production Reference: 1041012

Published by Packt Publishing Ltd.
Livery Place
35 Livery Street
Birmingham B3 2PB, UK.

ISBN 978-1-84968-256-5

www.packtpub.com

Cover Image by Anvar Khodzhaev (cbetah@yahoo.com)

Credits

Author
Qiang Ding

Reviewers
Bentze Perlmutter
Robert Stinnett

Acquisition Editor
Dhwani Devater

Technical Editor
Lubna Shaikh

Copy Editors
Brandt D'mello
Insiya Morbiwala
Laxmi Subramanian

Project Coordinator
Vishal Bodwani

Proofreaders
Lesley Harrison
Lynda Sliwoski

Indexer
Rekha Nair

Graphics
Nilesh R. Mohite
Manu Joseph

Production Coordinator
Arvindkumar Gupta

Cover Work
Arvindkumar Gupta

About the Author

Qiang Ding (Melbourne, Australia) has been working within the Control-M space for more than a quarter of his life. During his early days at BMC Software, Qiang resolved countless number of critical technical issues for Control-M customers around the world from Fortune 500 companies to government organizations. In recent years, Qiang has travelled hundreds thousands of miles around Australia and the North AP area to help many organizations to design, manage, and optimize their batch workload automation environment and to extend his passion to others by delivering Control-M trainings to end users and BMC Partners.

Currently Qiang is temporary living in Sydney and working on a enterprise wide Control-M migration and Consolidation project for a major Australian bank. He enjoys working with other experts in the field and is constantly involved in finding ways for making improvements to the batch environment that he works on.

Acknowledgement

There are many people that I would like to thank for their contribution to the creation of this book and to those who have reviewed, proofread, commented, and provided quotes.

On a greater scale, I would like to thank Bentze Perlmutter and Graeme Byrnes, who originally taught me every technical detail of Control-M, followed by Bruce Roberts, who in the recent years embraced my Control-M knowledge from a pure technical level into business level. I also would like to thank people who I worked for and worked with in the past few years, those who had a faith in me and gave me the opportunity and trust, including Allen Lee, Amy You, Angel Wong, Bao Ling, Louis Cimiotti, Chris Cunningham, Craig Taprell, Curtis Eddington, David Timms, Digby Pritchard, Doug Vail, Ian Jones, Jason St. Clair, Jeffrey Merriel, Jim Darragh, Matthew Sun, Min Yuan, Moshe Miller, Rabin Sarkar, Rick Brown, Shaun Kimpton, Stephen Donnelly, Tom Geva, Tristan Gutsche, Xianhua Peng, Yuan Yuan, and Ze'ev Gross. Last but not least, I would like to thank my friend Mike Palmer who inspired me and guided me in every aspect of my life.

For all those who have provided support and guidance over the years and if I have yet to mention your name, I sincerely apologize.

About the Reviewers

Bentze Perlmutter has 15 years of IT experience, working in various companies and holding positions in operations, QA, technical support, engineering, systems management, and production control.

His main area of expertise is batch and workload automation using tools such as Control-M and AutoSys. He has worked on complex projects requiring evaluation of solutions, design and planning, implementation, administration, and on-going support within large organizations, mainly in the financial industry.

Robert Stinnett has worked with automation systems on various platforms from mainframe to distributed since 1992. He has been using Control-M since 2003 when he was the lead for bringing it to CARFAX, the leading provider and pioneer of vehicle history reports, where he has worked for the past 10 years.

Robert is active in many Control-M communities, has given presentations at various conferences on the capabilities and cost-benefits of using an automated workload management platform, and has written a number of open-source utilities to help take advantage of and extend Control-M's capabilities on the distributed side.

One of the next big things he sees for automation systems is their integration with Cloud. He is currently working on projects that explore how Cloud can be used for providing capacity on demand as well as providing redundancy and scalability to existing automation and scheduling implementations.

Robert is also an active member of the Computer Measurement Group where he sees the role of automation in IT as one of the major reasons to have a sound performance and capacity management program in place to help manage the continuing technological evolution taking place in businesses.

He can be reached at Robert@robertstinnett.com.

www.PacktPub.com

Support files, eBooks, discount offers and more

You might want to visit www.PacktPub.com for support files and downloads related to your book.

Did you know that Packt offers eBook versions of every book published, with PDF and ePub files available? You can upgrade to the eBook version at www.PacktPub.com and as a print book customer, you are entitled to a discount on the eBook copy. Get in touch with us at service@packtpub.com for more details.

At www.PacktPub.com, you can also read a collection of free technical articles, sign up for a range of free newsletters and receive exclusive discounts and offers on Packt books and eBooks.

http://PacktLib.PacktPub.com

Do you need instant solutions to your IT questions? PacktLib is Packt's online digital book library. Here, you can access, read and search across Packt's entire library of books.

Why Subscribe?

- Fully searchable across every book published by Packt
- Copy and paste, print and bookmark content
- On demand and accessible via web browser

Free Access for Packt account holders

If you have an account with Packt at www.PacktPub.com, you can use this to access PacktLib today and view nine entirely free books. Simply use your login credentials for immediate access.

Instant Updates on New Packt Books

Get notified! Find out when new books are published by following @PacktEnterprise on Twitter, or the *Packt Enterprise* Facebook page.

Table of Contents

Preface

Control-M is one of the world's most wildely used enterprise class batch workload automation product produced by BMC Software. With a strong knowledge of Control-M, you will be able to use the tool to meet ever growing batch processing needs. However, there is no book that can guide you to implement and manage this powerful tool successfully until now. With this book, you will quickly master Control-M, and be able to call yourself "a Control-M" specialist!

This book will lead you into the world of Control-M, and guide you to implement and maintain a Control-M environment successfully. By mastering this workload automation tool, you will see new opportunities opening up before you.

With this book, you will be able to take away and put into practice knowledge from every aspect of Control-M implementation, administration, design, and management of Control-M job flows, and more importantly how to move into workload automation, and let batch processing utilize the cloud.

You will start off with the history and concept of batch processing and how recenty it got evolved into workload automation, and then get an understanding of how Control-M fits into the big picture. Then we will look more in depth at the technical details of the tool - How to plan, install, use, as well as manage a Control-M environment, and finally look at how to leavage the tool to meet the already sophiscated and ever growing business demand. Throughout the book, you will learn important concepts and features of Control-M through detailed explainations and examples, as well as learn from the author's experience, accumulated over many years. By the end of the book, you will be set up to work efficiently with this tool, and also understand how to utilize the latest features of Control-M.

What this book covers

Chapter 1, Get To Know the Concept, gives a good understanding of the concept of batch processing and centralized enterprise scheduling – what were the challenges and why they exist today. Besides that, it also provides an overall view of the latest concept – workload automation.

Chapter 2, Exploring Control-M, gives an overview of the features of Control-M, important concepts, and reviews the architecture of Control-M.

Chapter 3, Building the Control-M Infrastructure, introduces the concept of the "Three Ages" to archive workload automation, and then looks at the different requirements and challenges at each stage. It also talks about the sizing and the technical considerations that are necessary for building a solid batch infrastructure. Finally, it shows how to get started into the technical details and prepare machines and the environment for the Control-M implementation.

Chapter 4, Creating and Managing Batch Flows with Control-M GUI, looks at the important job scheduling concepts of Control-M in depth and applies them by defning some simple jobs in Control-M Desktop, and manages them using the Control-M/EM GUI client. Then it goes one step further by defning a complete batch fow to meet a scheduling requirement.

Chapter 5, Administrating the Control-M Infrastructure, starts with installing the additional Control-M components – BIM and Forecast, followed by discussing the tasks involved in expanding and updating the Control-M environment. It talks about the different methods of performing regular installation tasks, such as applying fix packs and installing Control-M/EM GUI clients, as well as demonstrates how to define Agentless remote hosts in both Linux and Windows environments. Towards the end, it explains how to perform some must-known administration tasks, including stop/start Control-M components, define Control-M/EM user authorizations, and customize the GUI.

Chapter 6, Advanced Batch Scheduling and Management, shows to add more jobs to Control-M by bulk load jobs from the crontab. It explains how to transform file processing job flow from time-based scheduling into event-driven scheduling, and improve some part of the job flow by using additional Control Modules. After defining the jobs, it revisits the Control-M/EM GUI client to discover more GUI features, such as advanced functionalities offered in ViewPoints and archived ViewPoints. It also gives an overview of how to use BIM and Forecast to proactively monitor jobs and estimate potential impacts, by creating What-if scenarios. Towards the end, it visits the Reporting Facility, takes a look at each available report type, and discusses how to automate reporting.

Chapter 7, Beyond Everyday Administration, focuses on the administration side of Control-M but in more depth. It starts with looking at the command-line utilities that can be used to affect the active environment. More importantly, it reviews the different security options provided by Control-M, as well as a demonstrates the Control-M mirroring and failover. After having secured the environment, it took us to the new level by perfecting the Control-M environment.

Chapter 8, Road to Workload Automation, makes a number of improvements to the file processing job flow from both the integration and performance aspects, by using the cutting-edge Control-M add-on features. These include enabling the job fow to have exposure to external applications, by using the BPI web service interface, integration with ESB with BPI web service and message queue jobs, rendering the processing truly parallel, and implementing load balancing. Towards the end, it turns our processing flow into workloads, and taps into the power of cloud computing to for limitless processing.

Who this book is for

This book is suitable for professionals who are beginning to use Control-M, but who also have some general IT experience, such as knowing the concepts of computer system architecture, operating systems, databases, basic computer networking. Some entry level skills in scripting languages will be of help along the way.

Also for those who are from the mainframe environment or moving from other schedulers to Control-M, you can use this book as a starting point.

Conventions

In this book, you will find a number of styles of text that distinguish between different kinds of information. Here are some examples of these styles, and an explanation of their meaning.

Code words in text are shown as follows: "By 12:00am, there are ten orders generated in total. Program PROCESS_ORDER is set to trigger at this time of the day to process them".

A block of code is set as follows:

```
<soapenv:Envelope xmlns:soapenv="http://schemas.xmlsoap.org/soap/
envelope/" xmlns:sch="http://www.bmc.com/ctmem/schema630">
   <soapenv:Header/>
   <soapenv:Body>
      <sch:request_order_force>
```

```
            <sch:user_token>?</sch:user_token>
            <sch:force_it>yes</sch:force_it>
            <sch:control_m>CTM_LINUX</sch:control_m>
            <sch:table_name>TEST</sch:table_name>
            <sch:odate>ODAT</sch:odate>
        </sch:request_order_force>
      </soapenv:Body>
    </soapenv:Envelope>
```

Any command-line input or output is written as follows:

```
# pwd
 /usr/java/jboss-6.0.0.Final/bin
 # ./run.sh -Djboss.as.deployment.ondemand=false -b 0.0.0.0
```

New terms and **important words** are shown in bold. Words that you see on the screen, in menus or dialog boxes for example, appear in the text like this: " One to one relationship simply means the jobs run one after another, for example, when **Job A** is completed, then **Job B** starts.".

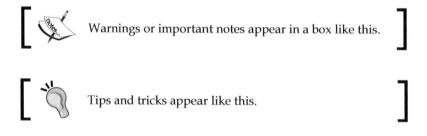

Warnings or important notes appear in a box like this.

Tips and tricks appear like this.

Reader feedback

Feedback from our readers is always welcome. Let us know what you think about this book—what you liked or may have disliked. Reader feedback is important for us to develop titles that you really get the most out of.

To send us general feedback, simply send an e-mail to feedback@packtpub.com, and mention the book title through the subject of your message.

If there is a topic that you have expertise in and you are interested in either writing or contributing to a book, see our author guide on www.packtpub.com/authors.

Customer support

Now that you are the proud owner of a Packt book, we have a number of things to help you to get the most from your purchase.

Errata

Although we have taken every care to ensure the accuracy of our content, mistakes do happen. If you find a mistake in one of our books—maybe a mistake in the text or the code—we would be grateful if you would report this to us. By doing so, you can save other readers from frustration and help us improve subsequent versions of this book. If you find any errata, please report them by visiting `http://www.packtpub.com/support`, selecting your book, clicking on the **errata submission form** link, and entering the details of your errata. Once your errata are verified, your submission will be accepted and the errata will be uploaded to our website, or added to any list of existing errata, under the Errata section of that title.

Piracy

Piracy of copyright material on the Internet is an ongoing problem across all media. At Packt, we take the protection of our copyright and licenses very seriously. If you come across any illegal copies of our works, in any form, on the Internet, please provide us with the location address or website name immediately so that we can pursue a remedy.

Please contact us at `copyright@packtpub.com` with a link to the suspected pirated material.

We appreciate your help in protecting our authors, and our ability to bring you valuable content.

Questions

You can contact us at `questions@packtpub.com` if you are having a problem with any aspect of the book, and we will do our best to address it.

1
Get to Know the Concept

Before we dive deep into the concept of Control-M, let's relax a little bit by beginning with a brief lesson on the history of batch processing. In the first chapter, we will be looking at the basic fundamentals of batch processing and the ever growing technical and business requirements, as well as related challenges people are facing in today's IT environment. Based on that, we will look at how can we overcome these difficulties by using centralized enterprise scheduling platforms, and discuss the features and benefits of those platforms. Finally, we will get into the most exciting part of the chapter, talking about a brand new concept, that is, workload automation.

By keeping these key knowledge points in mind, you will find it easy to understand the purpose of each Control-M feature later on in the book. More importantly, adopting the correct batch concepts will help you build an efficient centralized batch environment and be able to use Control-M in the most effective way in the future.

By the end of this chapter, you will be able to:

- Explain the meaning of batch processing and understand why batch processing is needed
- Describe the two major types of batch processing
- List the challenges of batch processing in today's IT environment
- Outline the benefits of having a centralized batch scheduling tool
- Name different job roles and responsibilities in a centralized batch environment
- Understand why workload automation is the next step for batch scheduling

Introduce batch processing

We hear about hot IT topics everyday, everywhere. Pick up a tech magazine, visit an IT website, or subscribe to a weekly newsletter and you will see topics about cloud computing, SOA, BPM/BPEL, data warehouse, ERP—you name it! Even on TV and at the cinemas, you may see something such as an "Iron Man 2 in theatres soon + Sun/Oracle in data centre now" commercial. In the recent years, IT has become a fashion more than simply a technology, but how often do you hear the words "batch processing" mentioned in any of the articles or IT road shows?

The history of batch processing

Batch processing is not a new IT buzz word. In fact, it has been a major IT concept since the very early stage of electronic computing. Unlike today, where we can run programs on a personal computer whenever required and expect an instant result, the early mainframe computers could handle non-interactive processing only.

In the beginning, punched cards were used as the media for storing data (refer to the following). Mainframe system programmers were required to store their program and input data onto these cards by punching a series of dots and pass them to the system operators for processing. Each time the system operators had to stack up the program cards followed by the input data cards onto a special card reader so the mainframe computer could load the program into memory and process the data. The execution could run for hours or days and it would stop only when the entire process was complete or in case an error occurred. Computer processing power was expensive at that time. In order to minimize a computer's idle time and improve efficiency, the input data for each program was normally accumulated in large quantities and then queued up for processing. In this manner, lots data could be processed at once, rather than frequently re-stacking the program card multiple times for each small amount of input data. Therefore, the process was called **batch processing**.

This is a file from the Wikimedia Commons. Commons is a freely licensed media file repository (`http://en.wikipedia.org/wiki/File:Blue-punch-card-front-horiz.png`).

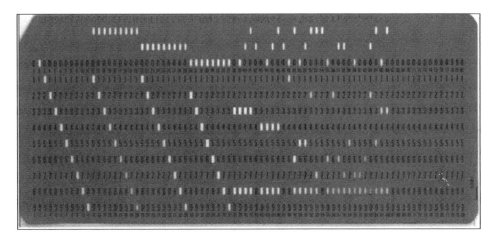

With time, the punched card technology lost its glory and became obsolete and it was replaced by much more advanced storage technologies. However, the batch mode processing method amazingly survived and continued to play a major role in the computing world to handle critical business tasks. Although the surrounding technology has changed significantly, the underlying batch concept is still the same. In order to increase efficiency, programs written for batch-mode process (a.k.a batch jobs) are normally set to run when large amounts of input data are accumulated and ready for processing. Besides, a lot of routine procedure-type business processes are naturally required to be processed in batch mode. For example, monthly billing and fortnightly payrolls are typical batch-oriented business processes.

 The dictionary definition of batch processing: (Computer Science) A set of data to be processed in a single program run.

Traditionary Batch jobs are known to process large amounts of data at once. Therefore, it is not practical to expect the output to be given immediately. But there is still a predefined deadline for every batch processing, either it is set by the business requirement (also known as **SLA – Service Level Agreement**) or simply because it needs to finish so that the dependent batch processing tasks can start. For example, a group of batch jobs of an organization need to generate the payroll data and send it to the bank by Monday 5am, so the bank can have enough time to process it and ensure the funds get transferred to each of the organizaiton's employee's account by 8am Tuesday morning.

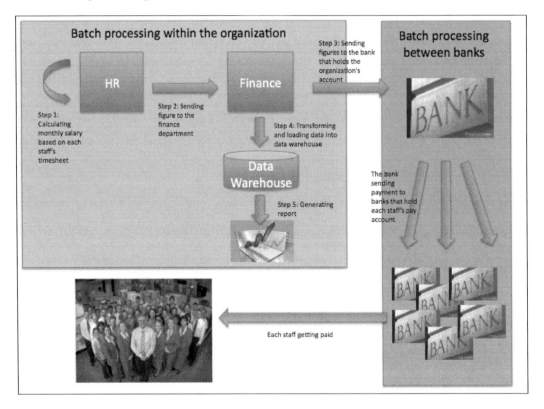

The rules and requirements of those business processes that require batch processing are becoming more and more sophisticated. This makes batch processing not only very time-consuming, but also task intensive, that is, the business process is required to be achieved in more than one step or even by many related jobs one after another (also known as job flow). In order for the computer system to execute the job or a job flow without human interaction, relevant steps within a job or jobs within a job flow need to be prearranged in the required logical order and the input data needs to be ready prior to the runtime of the job's step.

Batch processing versus interactive processing

As the time goes by, computer systems got another major improvement by having the ability to handle users' action-driven interactive processing (also called **transaction processing** or **online processing**). This was a milestone in computing history because it changed the way human minds work with computers forever, that is, for certain types of requests, users no longer need to wait for the processing to happen (only in batch mode during a certain period of time). Users can send a request to the computer for immediate processing. Such requests can be a data retrieving or modifying request. For example, someone checking his or her bank account balance on an ATM machine or someone placing a buy or sell order for a stock through an online broking website. In contrast to batch processing, computer systems handle each of the user requests individually at the time when it is submitted. **CICS** (**Customer Information Control System**) is a typical mainframe application designed for handling high-volume online transactions on the other hand, there is personal computer started to gain popularity which designed and optimised to work primarily in interactive mode.

In reality, we often see that batch processing and transaction processing share the same computing facility and data source in an enterprise class computing environmnet. As interactive processing aims at providing a fast response for user requests generated on a random basis, in order to ensure that there are sufficient resources available on the system for processing such requests, the resource intensive batch jobs that used to occupy the entire computing facility 24/7 had to be set to run only during a time frame when user activities are low, which back at the time is more likely to be during night, that is, as we often hear a more seasoned IT person with mainframe background call it nightly batch.

Here's an example of a typical scenario in a batch processing and transaction processing shared environment for an online shopping site:

- 7:00am: This is the time usually the site starts to get online traffic, but the volume is small.
- 10:00am: Traffic starts to increase, but is still relatively small. User requests come from the Internet, such as browsing a product catalog, placing an order, or tracking an existing order.
- 12:00pm: Transaction peak hours start. The system is dedicated for handling online user requests. A lot of orders get generated at this point of time.
- 10:00pm: Online traffic starts to slow down.
- 11:30pm: A daily backup job starts to back up the database and filesystem.
- 12:00am: A batch job starts to perform daily sales conciliations.

- 12:30pm: Another batch job kicks in to process orders generated during the last 24 hours.
- 2:00am: A multi-step batch job starts for processing back orders and sending the shop's order to suppliers.
- 3:00am: As all outstanding orders have been processed, a backup job is started for backing up the database and filesystem.
- 5:00am: A batch job generates and sends yesterday's sales report to the accounting department.
- 5:15am: Another batch job generates and sends a stock on hand report to the warehouse and purchasing department.
- 5:30am: A script gets triggered to clean up old log files and temporary files.
- 7:00am: The system starts to hit by online traffic again.

In this example, programs for batch mode processing are set to run only when online transactions are low. This allows online processing to have the maximum system resources during its peak hours. During online processing's off peak hours, batch jobs can use up the entire system to perform resource-intensive processing such as sales conciliation or reporting.

In addition, because during the night time there are fewer changes to the data, batch jobs can have more freedom when manipulating the data and it allows the system to perform the backup tasks.

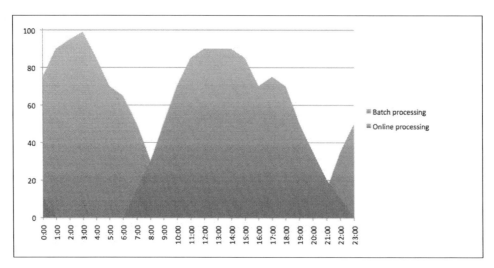

Time-based batch- and event-driven batch

What we have discussed so far – Batch processing defined to run during a certain time is traditional time-based scheduling. Depending on the user's requirements, it could be a daily run, a monthly run, or a quarterly run, such as:

- Retail store doing a daily sales consolidation
- Electricity companies generating monthly bills
- Banks producing quarterly statements

The timeframe allocated for batch processing is called a **batch window**. The concept sounds simple, but there are many factors that need to be taken into consideration before defining the batch window. Those factors include what time the resource and input data will be available for batch processing, how much data needs to be processed each time, and how long the batch jobs will take to process them. In case the batch processing fails to complete within the defined time window, not only does the expected batch output be delivered on time, but the next day's online processing may also get affected. Here are some of the scenarios:

- Online requests started to come in at its usual time, but the backend batch processing is still running. As the system resource such as CPU, memory, and IO are still occupied by the over-running batch jobs, the resource availability and system response time for online processing are significantly impacted. As a result, online users see responses given slowly and get timeout errors.

- Some batch processing needs to occupy the resource exclusively. Online processing can interrupt the batch processing and cause it to fail. In such cases, if the batch window is missed, either the batch jobs have to wait to run during the next batch window or online processing needs to wait until the batch processing is completed.

- In extreme cases, online transactions are based on the data processed by the previously run batch. Therefore, the online transactions cannot start at all unless the pervious batch processing is completed. This happens with banks, as you often hear them say the bank cannot open tomorrow morning if the overnight batch fails.

A concept called event-triggered scheduling was introduced during the modern computing age to meet the growing business demand. An event can be as follows:

- A customer submitted an order online
- A new mobile phone SIM card was purchased
- A file from a remote server arrived for further processing

Rather than accumulating these events and processing them during the traditional nightly batch window, a mechanism has been designed within the batch processing space to detect such an event in real-time and process them immediately. By doing so, the event initiators are able to receive an immediate response, where in the past they have to wait until the end of the next batch window to get the response or output. Use the online shopping example again; during the day, orders get generated by online users. These orders are accumulated on the system and wait to be processed against the actual stock during the predefined batch windows. Customers have to wait till the next morning to receive the order committed e-mail and back order items report. With event-triggered batch processing, the online business is able to offer a customer an instant response on their order status, and therefore, provide a better shopping experience.

On the other hand, as a noticeable amount of batch processing work is spared during event time, the workload for batch processing during a batch window (for example, a nightly batch) is likely to be reduced.

Is this the end for batch processing?

There have been talks about totally replacing time-based batch processing with real-time event-driven processing to build a so called real-time enterprise. A group of people argue that batch processing causes latency to business processes and as event-driven solutions are becoming affordable, businesses should be looking at completely shifting to event-driven real-time processing. This approach has been discussed for years. However, its yet to completely replace batch processing.

Shifting the business process into real-time can allow businesses to have quicker reaction to changes and problems by making decisions based on live data feeds rather than historical data produced by batch processing. For example, an online computer store can use a real-time system to automatically adjust their retail price for exchange rate sensitive computer components according to live feed currency exchange rate.

The business may also become more competitive and gain extra profit by having each individual event handled in real time. For example, mobile phone companies would rather provide each SIM card as soon as it is purchased, than let the customers wait until the next day (that is when the over-night batch processing finish processing the data) and lose the potential calls that could be charged during the waiting time.

Case study: Commonwealth Bank of Australia shifting into real-time banking

"In October 2010, Commonwealth Bank of Australia announced their future strategy in IT, that is, progressively upgrading their banking platforms to provide real-time banking for customers. Real-time banking is the ability to open and close an account, complete credit and debit transactions, and change features immediately. Real-time banking removes the delay we experience now from batch processing, where transactions are not completed until the next working day. Real-time banking will gradually replace batch processing, as our new banking platform replaces existing systems over the next few years."

Reference from Commonwealth Bank of Australia Website.

However, real-time processing is not a silver bullet. Although purchasing real-time solutions is becoming cheaper, moving the organization's entire batch processing into real-time processing can be an extremely costly and risky project. Also, we may find that current computing technology is still not powerful enough to handle everything in real time. Some IT professionals did a test during a project. They designed the system to process everything in real time and when the workload increased, the entire system just collapsed. We know hardware is becoming cheaper these days, but machine processing power is not the only limitation. When we talk about limited computing resources, it also can be the number of established sessions to a database or the availability of information for access. In case of a large request, such as generating a report, it may require exclusive access to the database. During the processing of data within the table, it is not available for other requests to modify. Therefore, such requests should be considered as batch processing and configured to run at an appropriate time.

The bottom line is not all business processes are required to be completed in real time. For example, a retail store only needs to generate purchase orders once a week. The store has no reason to transfer this business process into real-time processing, because they want to accumulate individual stock requests over a period of time and send it to the supplier in a single order. In this case, the shop can receive goods in bulk and save shipping cost, and at the same time there is a possibility to receive special offers that are given based on large order quantity.

ZapThink's Ron Schmelzer wrote:

Batch processing, often thought of as an artifact left over from the legacy days, plays a vital role in systems that may have real-time processing upfront. As he observed, "behind the real-time systems that power the real-time enterprise are regularly-updated back office business systems. Batch processes remain essential for one key reason: it is simply not efficient to regenerate a complete forecast or business plan every time the business processes a single event such as an incoming customer order."

Reference from ZapThink: http://www.zdnet.com/blog/service-oriented/soas-final-frontier-can-we-should-we-service-orient-batch-processing/1439

Either running the business process in real time or batches, the system designer should take many factors into consideration, such as:

- Is the business process required to be running in real time?
- What will the cost be to run the business process in real time?
- What are the negative impacts on others, if running the business process in real time?
- Will the benefit justify the cost and impact?

Moving IT into real time should be driven by actual business needs rather than the technology. The person who is going to design the system needs to carefully consider what needs to be processed in real time and what can be processed in batch to meet the business requirements and balance the system utilization. As a fact, large orgnisations today are still investing in batch processing and continuously trying to figure out how to make it run better.

Running batch processing tasks

To understand batch processing further we need to begin from it's father - the mainframe computers. **Job Control Language** (JCL) was introduced as a basic tool on the mainframe computers for defining how a batch program should be executed. A JCL is considered to be a job, also called a **job card** (inherited the name from punched cards). A job can have a single step or multiple steps (up to 255 steps in each JCL), and each step is an executable program or a JCL procedure (frequently used JCL statements are define into procedures for reusability). In JCL, a user needs to specify the name of the job, the program, or procedure to be executed during each step of the job, as well as the input and output of the step. Once the job is submitted for execution, the **Job Entry Subsystem** (JES) will interpret the JCL and send it to the mainframe operating system (MVS or Z/OS) for processing (refer to the next diagram).

The system will read the submitted JCL to figure out what application to run, the location of the input, and where the output should go to.

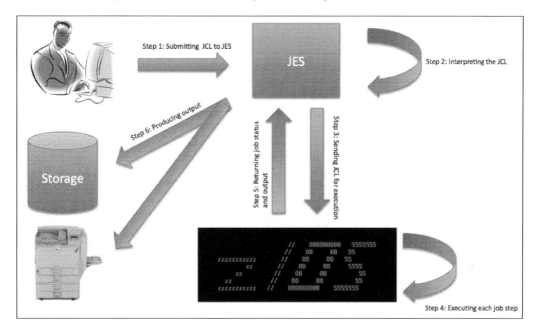

Batch processing can be a standalone task, but in common cases business processes require many steps to deliver. Technically, all these steps can be combined within one processing unit (for example, steps with a JCL), but if a step fails during the processing, rerunning that specific step can be challenging. There are third-party products provided on the mainframe computers just for managing rerun JCL steps.

On the distributed systems, it is up to the program designer to design their own way in the program to detect the error and handle such rerun action. In most cases, we have to restart the entire process from the beginning. In order to have flexibility and ease of management in batch processing, these steps are normally broken down into individual processing units (also known as jobs) and are set to be executed in sequence. By doing so, when a step fails in the middle of the processing or towards the end of the entire processing, a rerun can be allowed from the point of failure easily by rerunning the problem job.

Here is a Hello World edition of batch processing. `imagamingpc.com` is an online computer shop specialized in build-to-order gaming computers. The owner implemented his own order processing application to handle online orders. The system works in the following way:

1. During the day, customers visit the site. They choose each PC component to create a customized machine specification.

2. Once the customer submits the completed customized machine specification, a flat file gets generated in the system and tells the customer that the order has been received.

3. By 12:00am, let's say there are ten orders generated in total. A program is set to trigger around this time of the day to process these orders. For each order, the program first will check and make sure the parts the customer selected can be built into a complete working computer, whereas the order gets rejected if the components are incompatible with each other or some essential parts are missing. It is followed by sending an e-mail to the customer for correcting the order. For orders that passed the check, the program will scan the inventory to make sure each item is in stock, and sends an order confirmation e-mail to the customer. The program also generates and prints a daily build list. Sometimes there are orders that cannot be built due to missing parts, such as a specific graphics card being out of stock. In this case, the program will generate and print a backorder list and send the pending build e-mail to the customer to confirm their parts are being ordered and the system build is pending.

4. The next morning, the technician comes in and builds each machine according to the printed daily build list. At the same time, the person in charge of purchasing and procurement will place orders to each supplier according to the backorder list.

This is a very simple batch processing example. It's not hard to figure out that step 2 is an interaction processing and step 3 is a batch processing.

One of the very early challenges was that the order processing program often fails somewhere during processing. Sometimes it fails during generating the daily build list and sometimes it fails to send out e-mails to customers for pending build notification. No matter at which step the program fails, the program needs to be re-run right from the beginning, even if the problem was at the last stage only. As a result, every time when a re-run happens, the customer will likely be getting two confirmation e-mails. Also, when the number of orders is large on a given day, rerunning the entire thing can take a lot of time.

The owner of the business realized the problem and requested an IT person to come up with a better way to run this problem. Pretty quickly, the IT person came up with an idea, that is, break down each processing step into a separate program. In this case, if any stage failed, you would only need to re-run the failed task. As an outcome, the batch processing became the following:

- By 12:00am, there are ten orders generated in total. Program PROCESS_ORDER is set to trigger at this time of the day to process them. For each order, the program scans the inventory to make sure each item on the order is in stock and create the file called `daily build list`.

- According to the `daily build list`, the program MAIL_CONFRIMED_ORDER sends out an e-mail to each customer to confirm if his or her order is ready to be built.

- Another program called PRINT_DAILY_BUILD_LIST prints the `daily build list` for the technician who is going to build the machines on the following day.

- Program GENERATE_BACKORDER_LIST will create a list of orders that cannot be built due to missing parts, the list also gets stored in a file called `backorder list`.

- According to the `backorder list`, the program MAIL_BACKORDER sends out an e-mail to each customer to notify them that their order has been backordered.

- Another program called PRINT_BACKORDER_LIST prints the `backorder list` for the purchasing and procurement officer.

By now, we have a series of programs linked together and executed in sequence to handle the business process, as opposed to having one program that does everything. In this case, if the processing stopped half way through, the IT person can easily re-run that particular step followed by the rest, rather than executing the entire process from the beginning. Therefore, duplicate e-mails are no longer sent and the time required for re-processing is significantly reduced.

Batch processing is about making the best use of computing resources to process data and deliver result on time. Schedule jobs so that they can run imminently one after another, and keep the computing resource occupied without idle time. But this may not be considered as highly efficient with today's high processing power machines that have the ability to handle multi-tasking. Dividing steps into jobs provides a possibility of parallel processing for job steps that are not inter-dependent, as a result, maximizing the system resource utilization as well as shortening the end-to-end processing time. Use our online computer shop example by breaking down processing into tasks and running tasks that are not interdependent in parallel, we can significantly shorten the processing time.

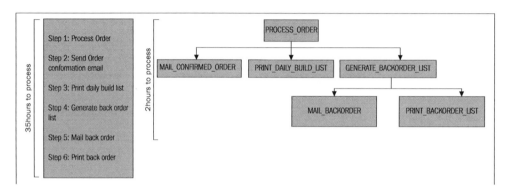

Another objective of batch processing is about delivering the processing result with minimal manual intervention. Technically, batch processing can be initiated by humans. In fact, back in the old days, companies employed operators on shifts to submit job streams at a set time of the day, check each job's execution result, and initiate restarts. However, running batch manually can be extremely challenging due to the nature of batch processing that it is complicated and detailed. The number of tasks for a business process can be large, and each task may require a complex input argument to run. Depending on the characteristics of the task an execution can take anything from minutes to hours.

In an environment that requires hundreds or thousands jobs to be scheduled each day, people who run the batch job not only need to work long hours to monitor each execution and ensure the right batch job gets triggered with correct input arguments at the correct time, but they also need to react to job failures, handle the complicated logic between jobs to decide which job to run next, and at the same time, keep in mind parallel processing, as well as ensure that each job is triggered as soon as its parent job(s) is/are completed to minimize machine idle time. Making mistakes is an unavoidable part of human nature, especially in a complex environment where everything is time-constrained. Businesses would rather invest in a batch automation tool than take the risk of having critical business problems due to batch processing delay and failures by human mistakes.

Automating batch processing

As the modern computing batch processing is far more complicated than just simply feeding punched cards in sequence into the mainframe as it was in old days, a lot more factors need to be taken into consideration when running batch processing due to its time consuming and task-intensive nature. Batch scheduling tools were born to automate such processing tasks, thus reducing the possibility of human mistake and security concerns.

There were home-grown toolsets developed on the mainframe computers for automating JCL scripts. Modern age distributed computer systems also came with some general ability to automate batch processing tasks. On a Unix or LINUX computer, CRON is a utility provided as part of the operating system for automating the triggering of executables. The equivalent tool on Windows is called **task scheduler**. With these tools, the user can define programs or scripts to run at a certain time or at various time intervals. These tools are mainly used for basic scheduling needs such as automating backups at a given time or system maintenance.

These tools do not have the ability to execute tasks according to pre-requisites other than time. Due to the limiting feature and unfriendly user interface, users normally find it challenging when trying to use these tools for complex scheduling scenarios, such as when there is a predefined execution sequence for a group of related program tasks.

Over the years, major software vendors developed dedicated commercial batch scheduling tools such as BMC Control-M to meet the growing needs in batch processing. These tools are designed to automate complicated batch processing requirements by offering the ability to trigger task executions according to the logical dependencies between them.

Basic elements of a job

Similar to CRON, users firstly are required to define each processing task in the batch-scheduling tool together with its triggering conditions. Such definitions are commonly known as "Job Definitions", which get stored and managed by the scheduling tool. The three essential elements within each job definition are:

- What to trigger – The executable program's physical location on the file system
- When to trigger – the job's scheduling criteria
- Dependencies – the job's predecessors and dependents

What to trigger

From a batch scheduling tool point of view, it needs to know which object is to be triggered. It can be a JCL on the mainframe, a Unix shell script, a Perl program, or a Windows executable file. A job also can be a database query, a stored procedure that performs data lookup or update, or even a file transfer task. There are also application-specific execution objects, such as SAP or PeopleSoft tasks.

When to trigger (Job's scheduling criteria)

Each job has its own scheduling criteria, which tells the batch scheduling tool when the job should be submitted for execution. Job scheduling criteria contains the job's execution date and time. A job can be a daily, monthly, or quarterly job, or set to run on a particular date (for example, at the end of each month when it is not a weekend or public holiday). The job can also be set to run at set intervals (running cyclic). In such cases, the job definition needs to indicate how often the job should run and optionally the start time for its first occurrence and end time for its last occurrence (for example, between 3pm to 9pm, run the job every five minutes). Most of the job schedulers also allow users to specify the job's priority, how to handle the job's output, and what action to take if the job fails.

Dependencies (Job's predecessors and dependents)

Job dependency is the logic between jobs that tells which jobs are inter-related. According to the job dependency information, the batch scheduling tool groups the individual, but inter-related jobs together into a batch flow. Depending on the business and technical requirements, they can be defined to run one after another or run in parallel. The common inter-job relationships are:

- **One to one**
- **One to many** (with or without if-then, else)
- **Many to one** (AND/OR)

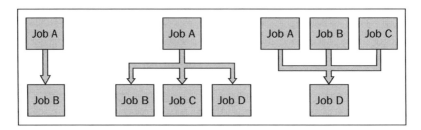

A **one to one** relationship simply means the jobs run one after another, for example, when **Job A** is completed, then **Job B** starts.

A **one to many** relationship means many child jobs depend on the parent job, once the parent job is completed, the child jobs will execute. Sometimes there's a degree of decision making within it, such as if job A's return code is 1, then run **Job B**, or if the return code of **Job A** is greater than 1, then run **Job C** and **Job D**.

A **many to one** relationship refers to one child job that depends on many parent jobs. The dependency from parent jobs' completion can be an AND relationship, an OR relationship also can be AND and OR mixed, for example, in an AND scenario, **Job D** will run only if **Job A**, **Job B**, and **Job C** are all completed. In an OR scenario, **Job D** will run if any of **Job A**, **Job B**, or **Job C** are completed. In a mixed scenario, **Job D** will run if **Job A** or **Job B** and **Job C** is completed.

During normal running, the batch scheduling tool constantly looks at its record of jobs to find out which jobs are eligible to be triggered according to the job's scheduling criteria, and then it will automatically submit the job to the operating system for execution. In most cases, the batch scheduling tool can control the total number of parallel running jobs to keep the machine from being overloaded. The execution sequence among parallel jobs can be based on individual job's predefined priority, that is, the higher priority jobs can be triggered before the lower priority ones. After each execution, the job scheduling tool will get an immediate feedback (such as an operating system return code) from the job's execution. Based on the feedback, the job scheduling tool will decide the next action such as to run the next job according to the predefined inter-job dependency or rerun the current job if it is cyclic. Batch scheduling tools may also provide a user interface for the system operator to monitor and manage batch jobs, which gives the ability for the user to manually pause, rerun, or edit the batch job.

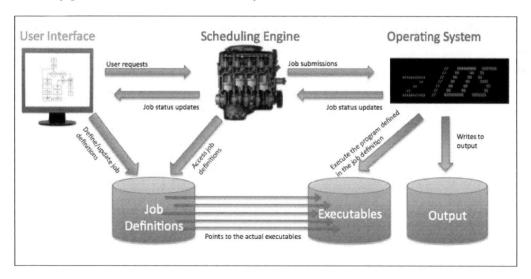

More advanced features of scheduling tools

Driven by business and user demand, more sophiscated features have been provided with modern scheduling tools apart from automating the execution of batch jobs, such as:

- The ability to generate an alert message for error events
- The ability to handle external event-driven batch
- Intelligent scheduling – decision making based on pre-defined conations
- Security features
- Additional reporting, auditing, and history tracking features

Ability to generate notifications for specified events

By having the ability to let notifications be generated on specified events, operators are freed from 24*7 continuous monitoring and only need to monitor jobs by exception. Users can setup rules so a notification will be sent out when the defined event occurs, such as when a job fails, a job starts late, or runs longer than expected. Depending on the ability of the scheduling tool, the destination for the notification can be an alert console, an e-mail inbox, or an SMS to a mobile phone. Some scheduling tools also have the ability to integrate with third-party **IT Service Management (ITSM)** tools for automatically generating an IT incident ticket. Job-related information could be included in the alert message, for example, the name of the job, the location of the job, the reason for failure, and the time of the failure.

Ability to handle an external event-driven batch

Even-driven batch jobs are defined to run only when the expected external event has occurred. In order to have this capability, special interfaces are developed within a batch scheduling tool to detect such an event. Detecting a file's creation or arrival is a typical interface for event trigger batch. Some batch schedulers also provide their own **application programming interface (API)** or have the ability to act as a web service or through message queue to accept an external request. The user needs to prespecify what event to trigger, which job or action within the batch scheduling tool, and during what time frame. So during the defined time frame, the scheduler will listen to the event and trigger the corresponding batch job or action accordingly. External events can sometimes be unpredictable and this can happen at any time. The batch scheduling tools also need to have the ability to limit the number of concurrent running event-triggered batch jobs to prevent the machine from overloading during peak time periods.

Intelligent scheduling – decision-making based on predefined conditions

Besides generating notifications for events, most of the advanced batch scheduling tools also have the ability to perform intelligent scheduling by automatically deciding which action will be performed next, based on a given condition. With this feature, a lot of the repetitive manual actions for handling events can be automated. Such as:

- Automatically rerun a failed job
- Trigger job B when job A's output contains message Processing completed or trigger job C when job A's output contains message Processing ended with warning
- Skip job C if job B is not finished by 5pm

This feature avoided the human response time for handling such tasks and minimized the possible human mistakes. It significantly contributes to shortening the overall batch processing time. However, this is not a one-size-fits-all approach, as there are chances that the events rather need a human decision to take place. This approach can free the user from repetitive tasks, but can also increase maintenance overhead, such as each time when the output of a program is changed, the condition for automatic reaction more likely needs to be changed accordingly.

Security features

For information security concerns, files that reside on the computer system are normally protected with permissions. A script or executable file needs to be running under the corresponding user or group in order to read files as its inputs and write to a file as its output. In the case of a database or FTP job, the login information needs to be recorded in the script for authentication during runtime. The people who manage the batch processing require full access to the user accounts to trigger the script or executable, which means they will also have access to the data that they are not allowed to see. There are also risks that the people with user access rights may modify and execute the executables without authorization. Batch scheduling tools eliminated this concern by providing additional security features from the batch processing prospective, that is, provide user authentication for accessing the batch scheduling console, and group users into different levels of privileges according to their job role. For example, users in the application development group are allowed to define and modify jobs, users in the operation group are allowed to trigger or rerun jobs, and some third-party users may only have the rights to monitor a certain group of jobs.

Additional reporting, auditing, and history tracking features

While the batch scheduling tool provides great scheduling capability and user friendly features, tracking historical job executions and auditing user actions is also available. This is because all jobs runs on the same machines are managed from a central location. By using the reports, rather than getting logs from each job's output directory and searching for relevant system logs, the user can directly track problematic jobs, know when a job failed, who triggered what job at what time, or create a series of reports to review the job execution history trend. Apart from being handy for troubleshooting and optimizing batch runs, the information can also become handy for the organization to meet the IT-related regulatory compliance.

Centralized enterprise scheduling

Looking back 20 years, technology has grown beyond imagination, but the needs for batch processing haven't been reduced. According to Gartner's Magic Quadrant for Job Scheduling 2009 report, 70 percent of business processes are performed in batch. In the same report, Gartner forecasted a 6.5 percent future annual growth in the job scheduling market.

Challenges in today's batch processing

In the recent years, IT is becoming more and more sophisticated to meet the ever-growing business requirements. The amount of information to be processed in batch is scarily increasing. At the same time we are also in a trend of batch window shrinking. As a consequence, the system's in-built scheduling functionality or homegrown scheduling tool can no longer handle the dramatically increasing complexity. Let's first have a look at the evolution of surrounding technologies, which affected the way batch processing runs today:

- The mixture of platforms within IT environment
- Different machines and applications are inter-related. They often have to work together to accomplish common business goals

From running batch on a single machine and single application, we ended up with an IT environment with hundreds or thousands of machines. Some of these machines are acting as a database server or data warehouse running Oracle, Sybase, and MS SQL Server. Some other machines may purely be used for running ETL jobs from Informatica or Datastage. There are also machines that are dedicated file servers for sending and receiving files according to a specific event. Then there are backup applications running data archiving tasks across the entire IT environment. Besides these, we still have mainframe computers running legacy applications that need to integrate with applications in the distributed environment.

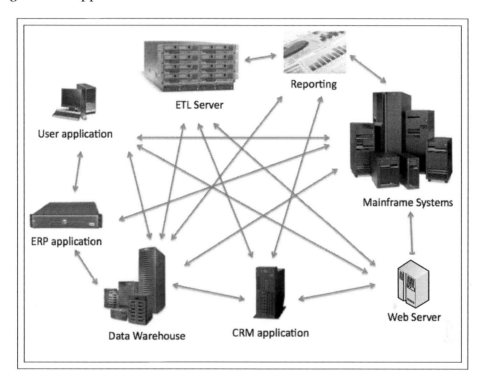

More or less these machines will have their own batch jobs running to serve a particular need. Not only that, applications that are specialized in a particular area may also require batch processing. Some of these applications such as PeopleSoft Finance and SAP R/3 had to come with an in-built batch scheduling feature to meet its own batch processing requirements.

These platforms and applications can rely on a built-in scheduling feature to handle basic batch processing requirements without a problem. Issues arise when business processes require cross platform and cross application batch flow. These islands of automation are becoming silos of information. Without proper methodology, interrelated jobs on different platforms simply don't know when the parent job will finish and the finishing status, thus not knowing when it should start. There are different approaches in order to allow each step of a cross platform job flow to execute in the correct order. The most common one is the time matching method.

With the time matching approach, we first need to know roughly how long a given job takes to run in order to allocate a reasonable time frame for it to finish before the next job starts. The time allocated for each job has to be longer than its normal execution time in case the processing takes longer than normal.

Let's revisit the `imagamingpc.com` example:

As the batch processing got broken down into individual tasks, the quality of customer service began to improve and the site became busier and busier. After six months, the average number of orders per day increased to 300! The business owner was happy, but the IT person was a bit worried; he summarized the following issues to the business owner:

- Currently everything is running from one machine, which is presenting a performance bottleneck and some degree of security concern.
- Sometimes if there are too many orders generated, the batch jobs cannot complete execution within the designed batch window. In an extreme case, it will finish the last step at 11:00am the next day. During this time, the CPU is constantly hitting 100 percent, thus the system cannot process new order requests coming from the web.

At the moment, the IT person only gets to know that the batch flow failed in the morning after he gets into the office. It was ok when the amount of data was small and he could just re-run the failed step and run the rest of the flow. But as the number of daily orders starts to increase, re-running some of the stage can take a lot of time. Sometimes it takes the whole morning to re-run the `PROCESS_ORDER` step, so the technician cannot build any machines until the `daily_build_list` is finally generated. During this time, the rerun will also take up most of the CPU resources, which again affects the system processing real-time customer requests from the web.

After research and consulting with other similar businesses, the IT person came up with the following solution:

- Move the inventory database into a new machine (machine B), separate from the web server (machine A) to reduce its resource utilization.

- Instead of populating an individual build list into flat files on the webserver, create a new database on a separate machine (machine C) dedicated for storing an individual build list. In this case, PROCESS_ORDER can run quicker and cost less disk IO. Therefore, hopefully it can complete within the designed batch window and not affect the online processing during business hours.

- To keep the data secure, once all the processing is completed, backup all data onto tape.

The business owner agrees on the approach. During the implementation of the new environment, the IT guy ran into a new problem. Now the batch jobs are divided to run on different machines. There's a synchronization issue, that is, when inter-related jobs are not on the same machine, how do the downflow jobs know their parent job(s) is finished? The IT guy took the time matching approach, that is, defined a timeframe for each step to run. The sequence of the job's execution is as follows:

1. 12:00am to 1:00am: FTP order is generated during the day from **Machine A** to **Machine C**.

2. 1:00am to 1:30am: **Machine C** populates a build list into the database.

3. 1:30am to 2:00am: Run "PROCESS_ORDER" on **Machine C**.

4. 2:00am to 2:15am: MAIL_CONFRIMED_ORDER gets executed from **Machine C**.

5. 2:15am to 2:30am: **Machine C** runs PRINT_DAILY_BUILD_LIST.

6. 2:30am to 3:00am: UPDATE_INVENTORY gets triggered by **Machine C**.

7. 3:00am to 3:30am: **Machine B** triggers GENERATE_BACKORDER_LIST.

8. 3:30am to 4:00am: **Machine B** runs MAIL_BACKORDER.

9. 4:00am to 5:00am: **Machine D** runs RUN_BACKUP to backup data on machines B and C.

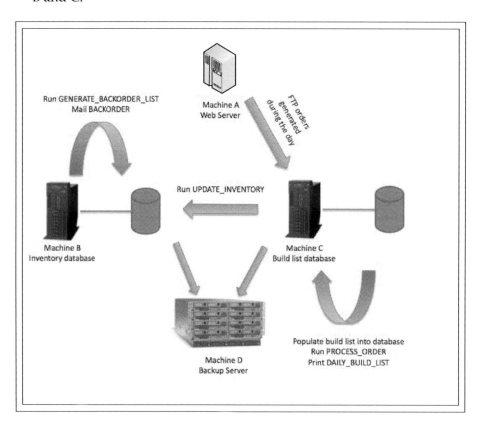

In this example, each processing step is spread across different machines and applications, rather than running off a standalone server (refer to the previous diagram). Each step depends on the previous one to finish before it can start, so it can continue on the work based on what the previous step has done. Obviously, there would be a problem if the confirmed order e-mails got sent out before the order data is fully generated. Sometimes the job may take longer to run due to the increased amount of input data or insufficient amount of computer processing power. Therefore, an extra time window needs to be allocated for each job by taking into consideration the worst case scenario to avoid overlap.

The time matching approach can allow cross platform and application batch flow possibly to run in its designed order, but there are still challenges present in the following areas:

- Processing time
- Batch window length
- Batch monitoring and management
- Cross time zone scheduling
- Resource utilization
- Maintenance and troubleshooting
- Reporting
- Reacting to changes

Processing time

With the time matching approach, the entire batch flow will take longer to run due to the time gap between job executions. Child job(s) will not trigger until the scheduled time comes, even if the parent job(s) finished early or at the average finishing time. In extreme cases, a parent job(s) may run over its allocated time, which means the child job(s) will get triggered according to the predefined time while the parent job(s) is still running. This can cause a serious failure and may require data rollback and reset the overlay job(s) to go back to its initial state. As a consequence, the total duration of the batch flow execution will increase with the risk of running longer than the pre-agreed batch window. This is extremely unfavorable under the current trend where the processing time is increasing and batch window is shrinking.

Batch window length

In a traditional scenario, batch window is allocated at night when online activity is low. The system has plenty of time to run the batch jobs and recover from error before the online activity picks up again next morning. As the Internet became popular, organizations have become able to expand their businesses by offering product and services globally. This requires the computer system to be almost 24 hours available for processing online requests from different time zones, and therefore leaves very little room for batch processing.

Batch monitoring and management

When jobs are running on different platforms, they can be monitored as per machine basis only. The user can see which job completed and which job failed, but unable to see everything as a complete business process flow. Many business processes today require thousands of jobs to complete and these jobs may be spread on hundreds of machines. It is not practical for operators to track each step of the batch flow by logging on every machine that is involved in the processing. Not only because this approach is labor intensive, but also because different skill sets are required for people who are in charge for batch jobs running on each different environment. Also, it is difficult to find out what the consequences would be if one job needs to be started late or if some jobs need to be disabled for a given day.

Cross-time zone scheduling

In the trend of globalization, it is common to see that a business has operations set up in many different countries. Sales offices located in North America and Europe, manufacturing offices located in Asia, and customer support centers located in South America. Each of these locations doesn't operate on its own and it is more than likely they need to share large amount of data between them, consequently there will be business processes that require batch processing within different regions to be executed one after another. Due to the different operation time and different geography, cross-time zone scheduling is found to be extremely hard to achieve by the time-matching approach. It also increases the challenge for batch monitoring and troubleshooting.

Resource utilization

In the time-matching approach, if some batch jobs' execution often exceeds their allocated time frame, the application owners either have to resolve the long running job problem or delay the next job's start time to allow more execution time for the problematic job. This will ensure that the long running job is completed without having overlay issues, but will also unnecessarily increase the overall execution time of the batch flow when the problematic job does not overrun. This time gap makes the system idle, and brings more difficulty to the batch processing when the entire batch window is already small.

Maintenance and troubleshooting

In a multi-platform environment, each system or application is likely to be managed by individual teams that are specialized in their own areas. As each batch job resides on different machines across departments, it can take hours to track down the failure point. For example, at 2:00am, a reporting job gets triggered and fails immediately. The person in charge for reporting quickly checks the cause of the problem, and discovers that the parent job failed at 1:50am too. The parent job was a database script that inserts data from CSV files, which were meant to arrive at 1:30am. So the DBA checks with the person who is in charge for the creation of the file, it goes on and on, and may even turn out that the job failure is caused by someone on the other side of the world. By the time they find out the original problem, it is already too late to allow the rerun to complete within the SLA.

Just think from the maintenance point as well, all these failures were caused by a rename to the CSV files. Without seeing the whole picture, the person who made the modification did not know there's a downflow reporting job, or many other parties outside his department may rely on these files for further processing.

Reporting

Batch running report is important information for analyzing the behavior of the batch flow. Job execution information collected on each machine may not represent a cross-platform business process because the individual machine is only running a portion of the entire business process. To report on the job execution status of a cross-platform batch flow, we need to collect data from each involved machine and filter out any job information that is not related to the batch flow definition. This process can be complicated and time-consuming and may require modification each time the batch flow is changed.

Reacting to changes

The business environment does not stay the same all the time. Changes made to the business can dramatically affect how IT works. Think about situations such as company mergers. Without an overall view of the entire batch environment from a business process point of view, plus a lack of standardization and documentation, IT will become a resistant of the business transition. Even with business events as small as a marketing campaign, batch jobs may require longer than normal to run in order to process the extra amount of data. For example, when a national retail store is opened for 24 hours during the Christmas period, the machine needs more resources to be capable of handling the online transactions. With batch jobs residing across many platforms, a lot of manual modifications will be needed to cater to the temporary change.

Costs for computer hardware are reducing, but sometimes adding more machines and technical staff may not be enough to effectively face the challenges we talked about so far, but can even complicate the situation further. If the IT components do not work together very well, the business will face serious problems. Just think about suffering from currency exchange rate increases due to failure in processing an order on time, penalties for batch processing missing its service-level agreement, and security risks. IT risks can cost the business a huge amount of profit and even potentially affect the company's share price and public image.

The solution

The computer networking technology allows machines to communicate with each other freely. Based on this technology, batch scheduling tools are able to expand their ability to schedule jobs on multiple platforms and provide users with a single point of control instead of running a standalone batch scheduling tool on each individual machine and using the time-matching method to schedule cross-platform batch flow.

During runtime, the centralized scheduling platform examines each job's scheduling criteria to decide which job should be running next, each time it sends a job execution request to the remote host that was predefined in the selected job's definition. A mechanism on the remote host needs to be established to communicate with the centralized scheduling platform, as well as to handle the job submission request by interacting with its own operating system. Once the job is submitted, the centralized scheduling platform will wait for the response from the remote host and, in the mean time, submit other jobs that are meeting their scheduling criteria. Upon the completion of each job, the centralized scheduling tool will get an acknowledgment from the remote host and decide what to do next based on the execution outcome of the completed job (for example, rerun the current job or progress to the next job).

Let's re-visit some of the challenges mentioned earlier that are related to cross-platform batch processing and analyze how to overcome them by using the centralized scheduling approach:

- Processing time and resource utilization
- Batch monitoring and management
- Cross-time zone scheduling

- Maintenance and troubleshooting
- Reporting
- Reacting to changes

Processing time and resource utilization

Centralized scheduling approach effectively minimizes the time gap between the executions of jobs, thus potentially shortening the batch flow's total execution time and reducing system idle time. Cross-platform jobs are built into a logical job flow according to the predefined dependency, the centralized scheduling platform controls the execution of each job by reviewing the job's parent job(s) status and the job's own scheduling criteria. In this case, jobs can be triggered imminently when its parent job(s) are completed. If the parent job(s) takes longer to run, the child job will start later. If the parent job(s) completed early, the child job will also start earlier. This effectively avoids job overrun, that is, the child job will not get triggered unless the centralized scheduling platform received a completion acknowledgement from the parent job(s).

Batch monitoring and management

We often hear from more senior IT people talking about their "good old days" - batch operators has a list of all jobs expected to be executed on the day, together with a list of machines where these jobs are located. They had to manually logon each machine to check the perivous job's completion state, then logon another machine to execute the next job, Centralized scheduling allowed users to monitor and manage cross platform batch jobs from a single point of control. Users no longer need to estimate which job should run next by looking at their spreadsheet, because jobs that belong to a single business process are grouped into a visualized batch flow. Users can see exactly where the execution is up to in the batch flow. Centralized scheduling also provides a uniform job management interface. The people in charge of managing the batch jobs no longer need to have in-depth knowledge of the job's running environment to be able to perform simple tasks such as rerun a job, delay a job's execution, or deploy a new job.

Cross-time zone scheduling

The time-matching approach requires each job defined to match each other's scheduling time. For example, if a job is located in Sydney Australia (GMT +10), its child jobs are located in Hong Kong (GMT +7), Bangkok Thailand (GMT +7), and LA USA (GMT -5). If the parent job is set to run between 2pm to 3:30pm Sydney local time, the child jobs need to start at 12:30pm Hong Kong local time, 11:30am Bangkok local time, and 8pm LA local time. The schedule of each child job needs to be changed every time the parent job's scheduling is changed or when day light saving comes. It is much easier to manage cross-time zone batch flows when job scheduling does not rely on the time-matching approach. Jobs without additional time requirements are defined to run immediately once the parent jobs are completed, regardless of which machine they are at and what time zone the machine resides on.

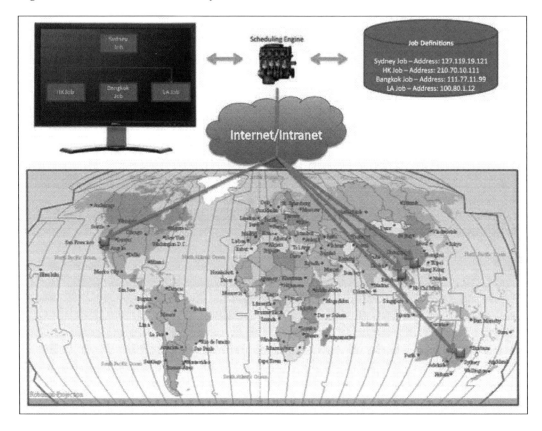

Maintenance and troubleshooting

When an exception occurs, centralized batch scheduling platform allows the users to clearly see where the problematic jobs are located in the business process. Therefore, it is easier for them to estimate how it is impacting the down flow jobs. Operators who manage the batch processing can easily take actions against the problematic jobs from the central management console without the need of logging onto the job's machine as the job owner to perform tasks such as rerun or kill the job. In case a failure needs to be handled by the application owner, the operators can easily identify the job's owner and escalation instructions by looking up to the job's run book, which also can be recorded within the scheduling platform. From a maintenance point of view, before a job scheduling criteria needs to be modified, such as its execution time, the user can clearly see the job's child jobs from the central management console to find out the impact of such a change.

Reporting

As jobs are managed and scheduled from a central location, it is easier for the centralized scheduling platform to capture each job's scheduling details, such as its start time, end time, duration, and execution outcome. The user can extract the information into a report format to analyze the batch execution from the business process point of view. It saves the need for collecting data from each involved machine and filtering the data against the batch flow definition.

Reacting to changes

A centralized batch scheduling approach provides IT with the ability to react to business changes. In a centralized batch scheduling environment, batch jobs are managed from a single location and more likely follow the same procedure for deployment, monitoring, troubleshooting, maintenance, retirement, and documentation. During a company merger, it is much easier to consolidate two batch platforms into one, to compare dealings between each machine on an application basis.

The centralized scheduling approach speeds up batch processing and improves computing resource utilization by overcoming the cross platform and multi-time zone challenge in today's batch processing. From the user point of view, batch jobs are managed according to business processes rather than focusing on job execution within each individual machine or application. As a result, the cost and risk to the business is reduced. IT itself becomes more flexible and able to react to the shifting of business requirements, helping to improve the agility of the business.

A centralized enterprise scheduling platform would have the following common characteristics (some commercial product may not necessarily have these characteristics or are not limited to them):

- It can schedule jobs on different system platforms and provide a centralized GUI monitoring and management console, such system platforms are (but not necessarily) mainframe, AS/400, Tandem, Unix, Linux, and Microsoft Windows.

- It can schedule jobs based on its scheduling criteria, such as date and time.

- It has the ability to execute job flows according to predefined inter-job logic regardless the operating system of the job.

- It is able to automatically carry out the next action according to current job's execution status, the job's execution status can be its operating system return code or a particular part of its job output (for example, an error message).

- It has the ability to make decisions on which job to schedule by reference to its priority and the current resource utilization (that is, limits the number of concurrent running jobs and allow jobs with higher priorities to be triggered first).

- Handle event-based real-time scheduling.

- Some degree of integration with applications (for example, ERP, Finance applications).

- Automated notification when a job fails or a pre-defined event occurs.

- Security and auditing features.

- Integration with ITSM (IT service management).

From batch scheduling to workload automation

Today batch scheduling has evolved from single platform automation to cross platform and cross application scheduling. The rich features provided by the tools effectively reduced the complexity for batch monitoring and managing. It seems everything needed for batch scheduling is available and the users are satisfied. However, history tells us that nothing stays the same in IT; technology needs to grow and improve, otherwise it gets replaced by other newer and better technologies, and batch scheduling is not an exception.

In Gartner's Magic Quadrant for Job Scheduling 2009 edition, it stated right at the beginning "Job scheduling, a mature market, is undergoing a transformation toward IT Workload Automation Broker technology."

Reference -Gartner's Magic Quadrant for Job Scheduling 2009.

Based on what we know so far, this section we will be looking at where batch scheduling is going in the very short future.

Batch scheduling: Static scheduling

As discussed earlier in this chapter, for all these years, batch scheduling was primarily static scheduling. Even in an advanced centralized batch scheduling platform, jobs are set to run on a certain day according to the calendar definition and during a certain time on a predefined destination host. This is absolutely fine if each time the computing resources are available for batch processing and the workload doesn't go beyond the board. But it seems too good to be true in the trend of shrinking batch window and increasing demand for event-triggered scheduling.

During a defined batch window, machines are working extremely hard to run batch jobs one after another. It is common to see these machines fully utilized during the entire batch window, but still unable to complete the processing on time. But at the same time, there are other machines that are not part of the processing just in idle state. Even these idle machines are allowed to be used for temporary batch job execution; it is not worth the effort to re-configure the batch jobs to run on these hosts only as a one off thing.

Recall what we have discussed about event triggered scheduling. With this type of scheduling, job flows are waiting for the external event to happen by listening on the event interface, such as a file's arrival or web service request. Once the request arrives, the job flow will be triggered on a predefined host. These job flows are normally defined to allow some degree of parallel processing so multiple user requests can be processed at the same time. This feature is largely limited by the resource of the physical machine, whereas in some extreme cases large amount of requests are getting triggered within a short period, but cannot get processed straightaway due to the limitation of the computing resource, so the new requests have to be queued up for previous requests processing to complete. This issue ultimately will reduce the level of end-user experience and cause business losses.

Simply allocating more computing resources to handle the additional workload is not the most effective solution for this problem, because:

- Most of these workload peaks or activity sparks are unplanned. It is not cost efficient and environmental friendly to have the additional IT resource stay in the idle state during off peak hours.

- Due to the static nature of batch jobs, routing job execution onto additional processing nodes requires modification to the job definition prior to the job's runtime. For a large amount of jobs, it is not practical and human errors may occur during frequent job modifications.

- It is hard to pre-allocate the workload evenly among all available processing nodes, especially for event-based scheduling. Dispatching workload prior to execution can be an option, but requires some degree of human decision, which defeats the original purpose of batch processing automation.

- Adding more computing resources will complicate the already overwhelmed IT environment even further.

More computing resources may temporarily accommodate the grown batch processing demand, but in long term, it will increase the IT's **total cost of ownership (TCO)**. The business will also get lower **return of investment (ROI)** on IT due to the expenses of additional computing recourse and the increasing number of technical staff required for managing the environment.

The Workload Automation concept

IT Workload Automation Broker (ITWAB) technology was originally introduced by Gartner in 2005. It was born to overcome the static nature of job scheduling by allowing batch jobs to be managed as workloads according to business policies and service agreement. By following this standard, batch scheduling should become more flexible, and therefore, be able to take advantage of the virtualization technology and become resource aware to be able to dynamically assign the workload based on runtime resource utilization. Batch processing should also expand its ability on top of the existing event-triggered batch processing by adopting the **service-oriented architecture (SOA)** approach for reusability and offer a standard integration interface for external systems.

Dynamic batch processing with virtualization technology and Cloud computing

Virtualization technology has become common in the organization's IT environment in the recent years. With this technology, users are able to convert underutilized physical machines into virtual machines and consolidate them into one or more larger physical servers. This technology transformed the traditional way of running and managing IT. It improves existing hardware resource utilization, at the same time provides more flexibility and saves datacenter's physical space. Because virtual machine images can be easily replicated and re-distributed, system administrators are able to perform system maintenance without interrupting production by simply shifting the running virtual machine onto another physical machine.

Cloud computing took the virtualization technology one step further by having the ability to dynamically manage virtual resources according to real-time demand. When IT moved towards cloud computing, the workload automation approach enabled the batch scheduling tool to tap into the "unlimited supply" of computing resources. With this approach, instead of defining jobs to run on a static host, jobs are grouped into the workload which is to be assigned to any job execution node without the need to modify the original job definition. By doing so, the batch scheduling platform can freely distribute processing work onto virtual resources in the cloud according to runtime workload. Under scenarios where existing job execution nodes are hitting usage limit, the scheduling tool can simply request new virtual resources from the cloud and route the additional workload to them. For time-based batch processing, this approach will always ensure that sufficient computing resources are available to allow the batch processing to complete within its batch window. For event-based batch processing, batch requests generated by random external events can always get processed immediately without queuing.

The benefit is significant when batch processing needs to handle unexpected workload peaks or unplanned activity sparks, that is, computing resources are no longer a bottleneck. IT people are also able to manage processing sparks caused by temporary business changes without physically rearranging computing resources.

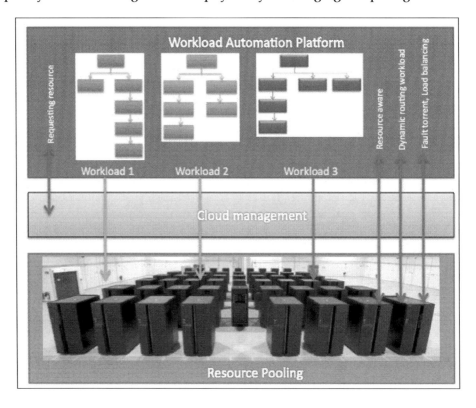

Energy saving is another major benefit of the workload automation approach. During off peak time, batch processing workload is automatically routed and consolidated to fewer machines. The unutilized virtual resources are released back to the cloud. The cloud management tool will decide how to consolidate the rest of the running virtual machines onto fewer physical servers and shut down physical machines that are left idle, whereas with traditional physical resources, it is not practical to shut down each time the utilization is low. Once the machine's role is defined, it cannot be easily reused for other purpose.

In order to achieve this so called end-to-end workload automation, the scheduling tool is required to be aware of real-time resource utilization on each job execution host and should have the ability to integrate with the cloud management tool.

Integration with real-time system, workload reusability

In the earlier part of this chapter, we discussed whether or not a real-time system could completely replace batch processing. Batch processing can justify its existence because of its high performance nature when it comes to processing large amounts of data. There has always been a gap that exists between the batch processing and real-time processing. Event-triggered scheduling was designed to bring this gap so batch processing can get triggered by real-time requests. But due to the static nature, event-triggered scheduling is struggling to keep up with today's dynamic demands of IT.

Organizations often see batch processing's static nature as their biggest road block when integrating with real-time systems, because real-time systems deal directly with business rules and business rules change all the time. As a workaround, they try to avoid batch processing as much as possible and implement the entire solution on the real-time system and achieve cross-platform processing by wrapping processing steps into a standard interface such as web services. The system may well enough to allow rapid changes to be made, but users are more likely to suffer poor performance when it comes to processing large amounts of data at once.

In the workload automation approach, batch processing is defined to be policy-driven, becoming a dynamic component of an application to serve real-time business needs. By adopting the **service-oriented architecture (SOA)** design principles, a batch flow can be triggered on-demand as a single reusable service and loosely coupled with its consumers.

> SOA is a flexible set of design principles used during the phases of system development and integration in computing. A system based on SOA architecture will provide a loosely-coupled suite of services that can be used within multiple separate systems from several business domains.
>
> Reference to Wikipida - Service-oriented architecture.

With good batch design practice, programs for individual jobs can possibly be reused by other business processes. For example, convert an FTP file transfer processing method into a standalone job and then convert its hardcoded source and destination value into a job's runtime input arguments. This allows the program to be reused in different file transfer scenarios. Same idea can also be applied to a data backup process. Once it is converted into a job, it can be used for backing up data from different sources or perform the same backup in different scenarios. This approach can effectively reduce the number of duplicated functionality jobs to be defined and managed.

By defining batch flows as reusable services, the details of batch processing are encapsulated. A request can be sent to trigger the batch processing through web services or messaging queue when needed, then let the batch scheduler run the batch processing in black box and return the desired outcome to the requester.

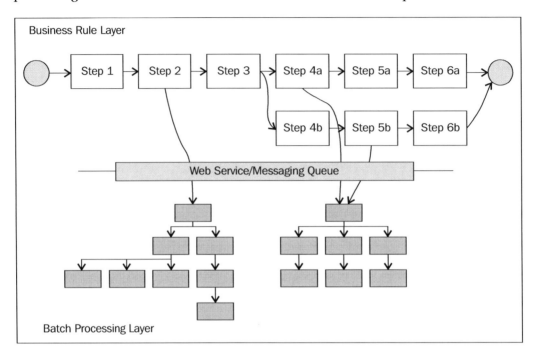

With minimal changes required, the batch processing that is made can be reused in a number of real-time processing scenarios. In this case, the system designers do not need to carry the risk of reinventing the wheel and at the same time the processing performance is maintained.

Summary

Well done. We have completed the first chapter! This has been an interesting trip through history back to the future, that is, from the beginning of batch processing all the way to today's latest technology. As people always say, for everything there is a reason, the best way to understand its purpose is to understand the history. By now, you should have a good understanding of the concept of batch processing and centralized enterprise scheduling – what were the challenges and why they exist today. On top of that, we also had an overall view of the latest concept – workload automation.

Later on in this book, you will see how the challenges are addressed and how the ideal workload automation cocept is achieved in the amazing feature of Control-M. Stay tuned! We are just about to let the real game begin!

2
Exploring Control-M

This chapter is an introduction to the BMC Control-M workload automation solution for distributed system environments. We will start with a brief history of Control-M, followed by a walkthrough of the components and features offered by Control-M version 7 and introduce the important concepts behind its three-tier architecture. We will also look at how organizations normally work with Control-M, different job roles, responsibilities, and the process involved in managing and monitoring the running of batch jobs.

As I mentioned in the introduction that a batch scheduling related career will be challenging and rewarding, we will also introduce Control-M certification education and touch points on career-related topics towards the end of this chapter and talk about how to find Control-M online communities.

By the end of this chapter, you will be able to:

- Have a good understanding of the history of Control-M
- Describe the general features of Control-M
- List key components of Control-M and its features
- Explain the Control-M three-tier architecture
- Understand how Control-M is used in real environment, different job roles, and responsibilities
- Know how to get technical help for Control-M from different sources
- Effectively select Control-M related educations and certification offered by BMC software

Control-M overview

In *Chapter 1, Get to Know the Concept*, we introduced the concept of batch scheduling and workload automation in general terms. More importantly we discussed the challenges with batch processing and the reason for having an enterprise workload automation tool. Now, it's finally time to start the real journey to explore one of the world's most popular and powerful workload automation platforms – BMC Control-M version 7.

This book's focus is on the distributed system part of Control-M, but in order to let you understand the batch concept and history of Control-M, previously we had to bring mainframe into a number of our topics. From this point onwards, you can assume that everything we discuss is under a distributed system context, unless specifically addressed.

Control-M road map

Control-M was a batch-scheduling tool originally developed for scheduling jobs on mainframe computer systems, by an Israel-based company New Dimension Software (the company was originally called 4th Dimension Software and later renamed to New Dimension Software). In the early 90's, Control-M also became available on the distributed environment (for example, Windows and Unix). Users can use Control-M either in a distributed/mainframe only or mixed environment. There are a number of other mainframe-focused products within the same product line such as Control-D, Control-M/Tape, Control-O, Control-V, and Control-M/Links. BMC software acquired New Dimension Software in 1999 and continued the product line. In the recent years, BMC software made Control-M to become part of its BSM strategy by integrating Control-M with BMC Atrium **Configuration Management Database (CMDB)**. Today Control-M is one of the most widely used enterprise batch scheduling software on both mainframe and distributed environments, with customers around the world from every major industry.

The following are the milestones in the Control-M history:

- 1985: Innovated the integrated approach for batch processing automation (mainframe)
- 1993: Provided single focal point of control of the heterogeneous batch environment – Enterprise Control Station (later on, the name changed to Control-M/Enterprise Manager)

- 1993: Release of control modules to extend Control-M's scheduling capability into external applications
- 1996: Enabled event-based scheduling
- 2000: Release of new control modules - integration with ERP applications
- 2004: Added the support for SOA approach – Business Process Integration
- 2004: Link batch scheduling with business SLAs – Batch Impact Manager
- 2006: Release of Agentless technology - part of Control-M 6.3.01
- 2007: Integration with BMC Atrium CMDB – BMC Batch Discovery
- 2008: Workload Lifecycle Management - within Control-M 6.4.01
- 2010: Workload automation – Control-M 7

BMC software introduces a new version of Control-M approximately every two years. The major releases in the past were Control-M/Server 2.2.4, Enterprise Control Station 500, Control-M/Enterprise Manager, and Control-M/Server 6.1.x/6.2.1/6.3.01/6.4.01 and the latest version 7. The popular versions we see in today's real-world production environments are 6.2.01, 6.3.01, and 6.4.01. By the time the book is published, there will be users considering a move or those that have already moved onto Control-M 7, but at the same time unsurprisingly we might find that there might be some users still partially running unsupported versions such as 2.24, 6.1.x. In between version releases, **Fix Packs** may be released for problem fixes and enhancements. There are also **Patches** released to address urgent problems.

Key features

Control-M is a true cross-platform workload automation solution with ability to integrate and execute batch workloads across the organization's entire IT environment. From the traditional time-based scheduling to event-triggered batch processing, Control-M provides a secure, fault-tolerant, and highly scalable dynamic workload automation environment that allows users to monitor batch execution by exceptions, and manage an entire organization's batch workload according to business policies and service-level agreement from a single point of control. In addition, Control-M offers comprehensive auditing, reporting, and workload lifecycle management features. In the evolutionary release of version 7, Control-M enhanced its features by adopting the workload automation concept to become more resource-aware and gain ability to manage dynamic workload in real-time and take the advantage of virtualization and cloud computing.

The following is a summary of Control-M's key features (some of them are specific to the version 7 release and may not be offered as a part of the base package):

- Ability to schedule cross-platform batch flow.
- Allows real-time batch monitoring and management from a single point of control.
- Supports calendar-based scheduling and event-trigger scheduling. Meets complex scheduling requirements.
- Dynamically manages the execution of workload according to real-time CPU resource utilization.
- According to the predefined rules, to automatically perform actions when a job execution event has occurred (for example, a job failed with a certain return code, or the job didn't run at the expected time).
- Allows batch execution history lookup.
- Automatically generates an alert when a job fails or a predefined condition is met.
- Security enhancements – User profiling and authentication against LDAP or Microsoft Active Directory, run-time job filtering (for example, reject job submission if matching keyword found in job definition), SSL-enabled communication between internal components, and auditing of user actions provides various types of reports against the live or historical batch environment.
- Job version control and built-in change management facility.
- Integration with ITSM and IT management software.
- Ability to relate batch jobs to business services.
- Forecasting capabilities for planning changes in the batch environment.

Are you surprised, or should say, excited to see a world class workload automation platform that provides rich features to cover every aspect of running complex batch workload in an enterprise-wide IT environment? We will cover each key point in the preceding list in this book through explanations and examples.

Supported platforms

As an enterprise-level cross-platform workload automation tool, Control-M supports job scheduling on a wide range of systems in the distributed computing environment. BMC software's Control-M R&D team has done an excellent job to keep Control-M up-to-date to support the release of new operating system's versions and technologies. From time-to-time, they have also dropped support for some legacy platforms and old versions of operating systems that are being phased out.

At the time the book is written, Control-M version 7 supports job submission on the following systems and versions:

- Microsoft Windows 2003/2008 (Standard and Enterprise Edition), XP Professional, and Vista/7 (Professional, Enterprise, and Ultimate) running on 32 or 64 Bit Intel/AMD processors.

- Oracle Solaris 8, 9 running on 32 or 64 Bits SPARC processors and version 10 running on 32 or 64 Bit SPARC or Intel/AMD processers.

- IBM AIX 5.2, 5.3, 6.1, and 7.1 running on 32 or 64 Bit power processors.

- HP-UX 11.11,11.23, and 11.31 running on 32 or 64 Bit PA-RISC processors or 64 Itanium processor (11.31 and 11.23 only).

- Red hat Enterprise Linux Server AS/ES 4 and RHEL Server 5 and 6 running on 32 or 64 Bit Intel/AMD processors or IBM zSeries (except ES 4).

- Oracle Enterprise Linux Server 5 running on 32 or 64 Bit Intel/AMD processors.

- Suse Linux Enterprise Server 9, 10, and 11 running on 32 or 64 Bit Intel/AMD or IBM zSeries processors.

- iSeries (AS/400) V5R4, V6R1 and V7.1 (Control-M/Agent for iSeries 7.0.00).

- OpenVMS 6.2, 7.1, 7.2, and 7.3 (Control-M/Agent for OpenVMS 2.25.01).

- Tandem Guardian G06.xx and H06.xx (Control-M/Agent for Tandem Guardian 6.3.02).

- UNISYS 2200 ClearPath OS 2200 9.x and 10.x (Control-M/Agent for UNISYS 2200 6.4.01).

 For an up-to-date list, please see the latest Control-M product release notes or visit the **Product Availability Compatibility** page on the BMC support website `http://www.bmc.com/support` (login required).

Control-M natively supports execution of jobs on distributed system platforms by having an agent application that resides on the job execution machine to interact with the operating system directly. Jobs running on each platform are the executables that are compatible with the operating system itself, such as running Shell scripts on Unix or Linux environment, running `.bat` or `.com` executables on Windows platforms, running Perl code, or a Java program running in a machine's JVM environment. On the main-frame side, Control-M for z/OS version 7 supports job scheduling on IBM z/OS v1.9, v1.10, v1.11, v1.12.

Agentless technology was introduced in the release of Control-M 6.3.01. With this feature, users can run jobs on a remote host without preinstalling Control-M's agent application. This feature allows rapid job deployment – you no longer need to wait to create a user account, allocate disk space, open firewall ports, install, and configure agent application, and so on. This feature also allows Control-M job scheduling on operating systems that are not natively supported by Control-M agent application, such as CISCO OS, FreeBSD, SCO Unix, and so on.

More importantly it can dynamically save the ongoing maintenance effort of patching and version upgrading for each Control-M agent application—reduces the TOC of Control-M dynamically over a long run. By saying that, it doesn't mean Control-M/ Agents are no longer needed. In the next chapter, we will talk in depth about when it is a good idea to use Agentless and when Control-M/Agent is required.

The Control-M way

Different centralized batch scheduling tools have similar ways of scheduling batch workload—trigger jobs to be running on the destination machine from a centralized scheduling engine, but the concepts within each tool and the ways they manage jobs internally are rather different. Let's beging with understanding some basic Control-M concepts and terms.

Control-M job

In Control-M, each **job** represents one execution step of a batch flow. The job definition records what to execute, to be executed under which user, on which machine, on which day, under what conditions, required resources, how does it run (run once or cyclic), the time frame (from/to time), job's time zone, under what conditions it runs, and the post-actions upon job's completion.

Jobs are grouped into two logical viewing hierarchies in Control-M—datacenter/table /job and Application/group/job. From a job point of view, a **datacenter** represents the scheduling engine where the jobs are stored and triggered from. Within each datacenter, related jobs are stored into table or layers of tables (sub-tables). In the second hierarchy type, jobs are logically grouped together according to the actual application and group that they belong to.

Job conditions

As we discussed in the previous chapter, most of the batch jobs are not stand-alone. A number of jobs may be logically related to each other, together to represent a business process and required to be executed in a pre-defined order. The dependencies between jobs are called **job conditions** in Control-M.

For each job, a user can define what preconditions are required for the job to run (**IN conditions**) and in what condition the job will be produced once it's finished (**OUT conditions**). A job will get submitted by Control-M if the IN conditions are met (given that all other prerequisites are already met). Upon a job's completion, it will produce OUT conditions for whoever needs it. Control-M/Server keeps a track record of all existing conditions, in order to decide whether the down-flow jobs can be submitted or not.

Resources

Within each job definition, a user can define logical resources that are required for the job's execution. It is another prerequisite for job execution, normally used to limit concurrent number of executing jobs or limit the access to an exclusive resource. A resource can be a **quantitative resource** or a **control resource**. Quantitative resource represents resources that can be measured in quantity, such as number of concurrent database connections or percentage of CPU usage. Control resource is used to isolate a resource when exclusive access is required for one job, such as job A requires exclusive access to file F, while job A is running, other jobs who also need access to file F are not allowed to run until job A is completed.

Submitting jobs

Once the jobs are defined, they are stored in Control-M as static job definitions. At a certain time each day, Control-M will review these job definitions and decide which jobs are eligible for execution on that day. Selected jobs are made active and get stored into the scheduling engine's set of database tables and are together called **Active Job File (AJF)**. Jobs become active does not mean they will be submitted for execution imminently. Instead, the Control-M scheduling engine will check each job in the AJF constantly throughout the day and submit the job when all prerequisites are met. Control-M cyclically examine each job's pre-requisite in the following order:

1. Check the job's submission time (for example, right now it is 6:01pm and the job is defined to run between 6 to 9pm. In this case, Control-M will continue to the next check).

2. Check the job's pre-requisite condition (for example, job B requires job A to be completed and therefore release JOB_A-OK condition. Control-M looks up in its record and finds the condition, and therefore continues to the next check.)

3. Check the job running host to make sure communication wise it is available for job submission.

4. Check if the required logical resources are available and make sure there are no other logical restrictions.

If all these requirements are met, the job will be submitted for execution.

Post processing

Control-M is famous for its powerful, post processing ability. In Control-M, post processing activities are the tasks to be performed automatically right after a job's completion. It is predefined in each job as part of the job definition. Post processing is triggered when the predefined conditions are met, for example, a trigger of a notification after the job's failure or delay, a trigger of job rerun, or other events upon detection of a specific string appeared in the job's script or its previous run's output (for example, an error message string).

From the user's perspective - Control-M/ Enterprise Manager

Control-M/Enterprise Manager GUI Components are a set of desktop applications that provide users with complete monitoring, management, and reporting of cross-platform batch processing environment in a standardized and simplified approach. The complicity of the heterogeneous batch environment is encapsulated to the people who manage the batch jobs, that is, without having platform-specific knowledge the user can define, monitor, and manage job executions on any of the supported systems through the centralized GUI front end in a uniformed way.

 Before the release of Control-M/Enterprise Manager, the GUI representation of Control-M was called **Enterprise Control Station (ECS)**.

Control-M/Enterprise manager GUI front end has four components:

- Control-M Enterprise Manager Client
- Control-M Desktop
- Control-M Configuration Manager
- Reporting Facility

Control-M/Enterprise Manager GUI Components are Microsoft Windows-based applications. Users can choose to install the application manually or use Control-M's automatic GUI client deployment technology (Control-M/EM Web Launch – available since Control-M/Enterprise Manager 6.3.01 FP3). Authentication is required for accessing each GUI components, username and password can be defined and stored within Control-M/Enterprise Manager or letting Control-M/Enterprise Manager to authenticate against LDAP.

Control-M Enterprise Manager GUI Client

Control-M Enterprise Manager GUI Client is the central point for graphical batch monitoring and control. Within the GUI, active jobs that are running across the IT environment can be presented in flow diagram according to the logical order between them or in list format. This allows the user to monitor and manage batch flows purely according to business process and lessens the unnecessary worry about the job type, and what OS environment it is executing on. By default, the GUI group jobs in datacenter/application/group/job hierarchy, but this can be customized according to the user's personal preferences. The display of jobs can be dynamically filtered according to user defined filter rules. Control-M uses 6 colors to represent the job's different statuses for the ease of human monitoring, for example, green means the job has completed successfully, red means the job has failed, gray means the job is waiting for its submission condition. Each active job's color gets updated in real time as its actual status changes. Users can easily track any job's running status as events are happening. Alternatively, users can manage jobs by exception, by using Alert Window provided as part of the GUI Client.

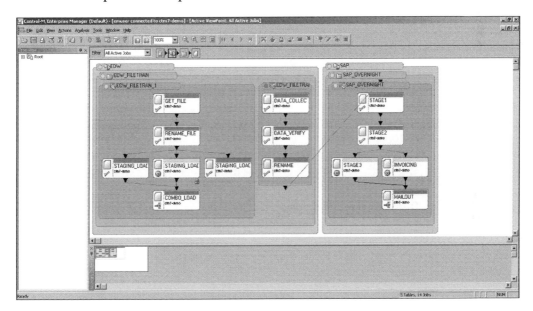

With the right privileges, users are able to perform manual interventions to jobs through the GUI, such as pausing the job flow, forcing a job's execution, modifying a job's runtime definition, deploying a new job into AJF for execution, or rerunning a particular job. Each user action gets sent to the Control-M backend in real time for immediate effect. A user can view the job's output with a simple click on the GUI rather than logging on to the job's actual running host. More advanced features are also available on the GUI, such as viewing a job's critical path, manually assigning a job's precondition, modifying job's priority, or even doing a playback of batch job execution from a previous day.

Control-M Desktop

The Control-M Desktop is the user working space for defining and modifying job definitions, working with job calendars, and viewing job forecasts (optional component). It provides a uniformed job editing interface to define and modify job definitions regardless of what operating system it is going to be running on. For each job, users are required to define which executable or command the job is going to trigger. A number of special job editing forms are provided for application specific job types, such as database job, SAP job, Peoplesoft job and so on. Again, the created job definitions can be presented in flow diagram or list format.

Users can define jobs from scratch or mass create jobs from predefined job templates. Users are also allowed to perform, find, and update on existing jobs.

The jobs defined in Control-M Desktop can be saved in Control-M job draft format (.drf) on the user's local computer. As version 6.4.01, Control-M Desktop allowed job definitions to be saved in .xml format. In comparison to the .drf format, the .xml format offers much more flexibility, it is human readable, and allows users to directly mass-update the job draft by using a text editor's "find and update" feature without loading into Control-M Desktop.

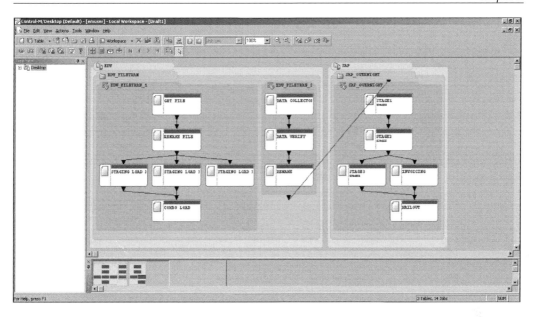

Since Control-M/Enterprise Manager 6.4.01 fix pack 1, Control-M Desktop added the capability to handle Unix crontab job conversion user can directly import a crontab file through Control-M Desktop. Control-M Desktop will then convert the input file into Control-M job definitions. Apart from defining new jobs, the user can also view changes to jobs/tables and restore the definition to an earlier state by using the Version Manager tool that is build-in Control-M Desktop, again since version 6.4.01.

Job calendar is another important element of Control-M. It allows jobs to share a common scheduling pattern. For instance, a calendar includes all working days or a calendar includes all public holidays. A user can select the right calendars during job definition and assign them to the job, therefore saving the effort of repeatedly defining the same scheduling days for jobs which have the same scheduling pattern. These calendars are also defined and managed through Control-M Desktop.

Control-M Configuration Manager

Control-M Configuration Manager is the central place for managing Control-M components within the batch environment. In Control-M/Enterprise Manager 6.2.01 and earlier versions the equivalent was called Control-M Administration Facility. Back then, features offered by Control-M Administration Facility only provided functionalities for managing server components of Control-M/Enterprise Manager and some basic administration utilities. Since the release of 6.3.01, **Control-M Configuration Manager (CCM)** added the ability to manage the scheduling engines (Control-M/Server) and job execution hosts (Control-M/Agent), as well as many other functions around the administration aspect.

In order to monitor and control components, firstly users need to define the manageable components into CCM and set the **Desire State** for each of them. Once the component is defined, Control-M/Enterprise Manager will then be able to automatically start or stop the component according to its desire state. If the process state is changed (went down due to error or came up), CCM will display the real state of the process on the GUI and at the same time set the state of the process back to its desired state. This feature allows the user to manage Control-M components from the central GUI front end rather than logging onto each machine for checking, starting, or stopping the services.

Other management functionalities within CCM include a menu option for performing maintenance tasks to the Control-M/Enterprise Manager database, changing system configuration parameters, and modifying security related configuration items. In version 7, users can even turn on debugging for Control-M/Server and Agent through the CCM menu options.

Reporting Facility

The Reporting Facility is the key tool for extracting batch related informaiton from Control-M and analyzing the batch environment therefore supporting future decision making such as forcasing batch processing volume or planning on optimising batch processing duration. It provides a user interface for generating reports against the data collected by Control-M/Enterprise Manager while the system is running.

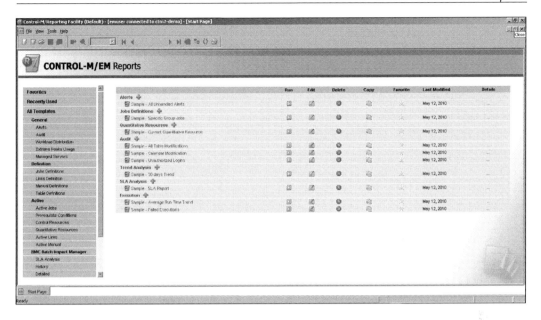

A user can create customized reports based on the provided report types and save them as templates for further use. Report types are grouped into three basic categories plus two additional categories. The basic categories include reports that are related to static job definitions, active jobs, as well as general report types such as alerts and auditing. The two additional report categories are available when Batch Impact Manager and Control-M Forecast are installed.

The report can be saved in the Crystal Reports format or exported into other common formats. The available formats are: comma separated values (`.csv`), tab separated values (`.ttx`), Acrobat (`.pdf`), Excel (`.xls`), Word (`.doc`), HTML 4.0 (`.html`), and XML (`.xml`).

Apart from generating report interactively, a user can also produce report from reporting command line utility. This feature allowed pre-defined reports to be produced automatically via Control-M when the pre-defined command line is scheduled as a job. Since Control-M/Enterprise Manager version 6.4.01, a new job type, reporting is provided in Control-M Desktop to allow users to specify reporting arguments from GUI, which is more user-friendly and an alternative way to schedule reporting jobs.

Control-M's Optional Features

There are optional components developed by BMC software to enhance the features of Control-M and extend its scheduling capability. These add-on components are:

- Control-M Control Modules
- Control-M BIM and Forecast
- Control-M Batch Discovery

Control-M Control Modules

As we discussed in *Chapter 1,Get to Know the Concept*, today's batch environment not only has become a cross platform scheduling within different applications, but there is a huge amount of processing that is also required to be done in batch mode. These systems need to work together with a number of databases, data warehouses, file transfers, and other applications such as Peoplesoft Finance or SAP to deliver the expected end result.

For FTP/SFTP file transfers, we can write scripts to handle the authentication and perform the transfer. For retrieving or inserting data into databases, we can embed queries into shell scripts for the batch scheduling tool to trigger. Some of the applications provide command line interface for execution, such as IBM Datastage's dsjob command for triggering ETL projects. The available tools are enough to get things rolling, but users often find challenges in a complex environment. The most common challenges are:

- Defining a script for file transfer or database access requires special scripting skills and users often find it hard to troubleshoot the problems when faced with hundreds of lines of code.

- Constructing the command line execution for a particular application requires sophisticated arguments, some of these arguments are only determined at run time, for example, locate and process a randomly generated file.

- Handling of event triggered scheduling and integration with external systems has to be developed in house, therefore there is a lack of standards and quality control.

As an enterprise wide centralized scheduling platform, apart from scheduling standard jobs on the systems listed in supported platforms, with additional software package's support (Control-M Control Modules), Control-M can automate special job types such as file transfer, web services, messaging, java applications, as well as able to expand its schedule capability into major applications such as SAP, Oracle E-Business Suit, Informatica, and PeopleSoft.

The purpose of Control Modules is to make application specific job scheduling become easy, therefore necessary parts of the processing that run in those applications can be integrated with the traditional type batch jobs as much as possible to allow the end-to-end business process to be presented in Control-M. On the other hand these jobs can utilize the standard Control-M job features and provide users with a unified job management interface across different scheduling scenarios. By using these Control Modules, we can effectively reduce the time required for creating batch jobs and the users do not need to be experts in each application, but still can deliver high quality batch job flows that represent the end-to-end business processes.

The available Control Modules are:

- Control-M/Control Module for SAP
- Control-M/Control Module for PeopleSoft
- Control-M/Control Module for Oracle E-Business Suite
- Control-M/Control Module for Advanced File Transfer
- Control-M Business Process Integration Suite
- Control-M for Database
- Control-M for Informatica
- Control-M for Cloud
- Control-M for IBM Cognos

In this book, we will cover the detailed features of Control-M/Control Module for Advance File Transfer, Control-M Business Process Integration Suite, Control-M for Databases, and Control-M for Cloud.

Control-M/Forecast and BMC Batch Impact Manager

Control-M/Forecast and BMC Batch Impact Manager are the two add-on components of Control-M/Enterprise Manager. The reason we group these two add-on features into the same section is because users normally use them in conjunction to achieve proactive management for their batch workloads and the actual business services.

Control-M/Forecast

In life we see forecasting everywhere. We watch daily weather forecasting to determine what to wear the next day, financial advisers perform forecast on our superannuation to determine the investment strategy, businesses are based on sales forecast to measure resource allocation for each customer account. Forecasting is a critical part of planning in almost any occasion. There is no difference when it comes to managing batch workload. Under complicated batch scenarios, it is extremely challenging to manage and plan a batch environment without having an estimation of what will happen.

For example, an overnight batch flow consists of more than 15000 interrelated jobs. The operators who manage the batch workload maybe interested to know:

- What will be the total duration of this over night batch flow during the coming weekend?

- What if the batch window needs to be reduced by 1 hour to accommodate other processing tasks on a special day?

- For a group of jobs that are defined to run on a workload balancing cluster, what will be the impact on the entire batch workload, if one or two machines within the cluster need to be taken offline for 3 hours during the coming Friday's processing peak hours?

Control-M/Forecast does the hard job in the background by calculating the job's statistical information that is collected by Control-M/Enterprise Manager during batch job running. The forecast result is presented at per-job level in a GUI view. Users can not only see a given job or batch flow's estimated start, but also the ending time for a given day. They can also apply what-if scenarios to proactively analyze how an event can impact the batch workload.

BMC Batch Impact Manager

Control-M's rich workload automation features allow the user to manage batch processing by exceptions. However, as business requirements are becoming more and more sophisticated, the number of jobs required for each processing is increasing and the dependencies between jobs are getting even more complicated. Reacting to each individual job failure with the same approach without seeing the bigger picture may not be the most effective way to ensure critical services to meet their SLA.

Reuse the example we mentioned in the *Control-M/Forecast* section, now the 15000 interrelated jobs are designed to deliver 80 different business services. In the event of a job failure or delay, operators will be notified immediately through SMS, e-mail, or ITSM ticket by Control-M (if event notifications have been presetup in the jobs). The job failure or delay message normally includes the severity of the failure as a reference for the users who are going to restore the job. If many jobs fail or are delayed at the same time, it is extremely hard for the user to figure out whether the actual business services will be impacted or not, and if so, which business services out of the 80 are impacted, and which problematic jobs are having the most impact on the more critical business services.

BMC Batch Impact Manager enables batch processing monitoring at the service level. It allows users to focus on services that are directly impacted during events of job failure or delay, so they can be more focused on letting each business service to meet their SLA rather than just fixing problematic jobs one after another without seeing the bigger picture. Batch Impact Manager also can trigger alert and work in conjunction with BMC Remedy ITSM to automatically trigger incident ticket.

Batch Impact Manager uses job statistical information in reference to the sequence of job execution within the batch service to calculate how much a job's delay (or completed quicker than usual) can affect the completion time of the business service, as well as suggesting how quickly a failed job needs to be fixed in order to ensure the business service completes within its SLA.

Batch Impact Manager provides its own batch service focused GUI view on top of the normal Control-M/Enterprise Manager GUI Client for users to monitor real time batch running at the service level. User can also run the batch service in simulation mode and apply what-if scenarios for the near future – a mini Control-M/Forecast, that is, focusing on the near future.

BMC Batch Discovery

When is the good time window to schedule an outage change on a production machine that will bring minimal impact to critical batch services? What is the actual business impact if the outage change did not finish within agreed change window? These are the type of questions regularly asked by the change management. Given that business processes today commonly require task intensive and cross platform complex batch processing, it can be very challenging to provide an accurate answer to these kinds of questions. By performing an outage change without knowing these facts, the organizations are at the risk of suffering business loss and getting a penalty for missing the SLA.

BMC Batch Discovery integrates Control-M with organization's **Business Service Management (BSM)** big picture by automatically discovering batch services and the associated computer resources as related **change items** (CIs) for the organization's **configuration management database (CMDB)**.Once all the batch services CIs and associated computer resources CIs are imported into the CMDB, the people who do not have visibility to the batch environment (for example, the change manager) can look up the CI of the computer resource that requires the outage to find out if there are any batch service CIs associated with it, and therefore able to estimate potential impacts to the business services.

By knowing the associated batch services, the users who have access to Control-M can use Control-M/Forecast to find out the best time window for such outage that will bring no impacts or minimal impact to the business service. The users can also apply what-if scenarios to the batch service to see the worst-case scenarios, such as what if applying a change took longer than agreed outage window or what if an extra outage window is required to rollback a failed change.

In order to use this tool, the Control-M environment has to have BMC Batch Impact Manager installed on top of Control-M/Enterprise manager. The organization also has to use BMC Atrium CMDB and BMC Remedy AR System as the foundation of their BSM strategy.

Control-M Architecture and Components

Control-M is well known for its three-tier architecture. By utilizing networking technology, Control-M components among the three tiers can communicate with each other freely, therefore work together to provide cross platform job submission and tracking, and at the same time allow batch workload to be monitored and managed from a centralized location.

Control-M/Enterprise Manager sits at the top layer. It provides the backend of graphical user interface and administration facilities. The middle tier—Control-M/Server is the schedule engine that performs the actual job submission and tracking. And the bottom tier is Control-M/Agent that runs on different machines to handle job submission requests from Control-M/Server. Control Modules and Agentless hosts are also part of the bottom layer, but just under Control-M/Agent. This is because Control Modules are only to be installed as add-on components of Control-M/Agents and Agentless hosts are managed by Control-M/Server through selected Control-M/Agent(s).

The combination of the three tiers is considered as a complete Control-M environment. Each environment can have exactly one Control-M/Enterprise Manager connecting with one or many Control-M/Servers, and each of the Control-M/Server can connect with hundards or thousands of Control-M/Agents as well as optionally some CMs attached or Agentless remote hosts.

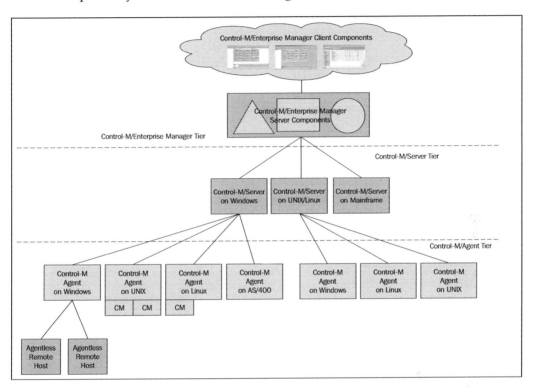

With this highly scalable architecture, users can choose to run their batch environment a single scheduling engine or divide the workload onto multiple scheduling engines, but still have the ability to monitor and manage the jobs within a single GUI—as long as every Control-M/Server configured to communicate with the same Control-M/Enterprise Manager.

Control-M/Enterprise Manager

There are two sub-layers within the Control-M/Enterprise Manager layer—Control-M/Enterprise Manager GUI Client components which have already been introduced and Control-M/Enterprise Manager Server components. Unlike the GUI client components which can only be installed and running on Windows based machines, Control-M/Enterprise Manager Server components can be installed and run on Windows, Linux, or Unix based machines.

Control-M/Enterprise Manager Server Components

Control-M/Enterprise Manager Server relies on database for storing information such as, static job definitions, active job's execution information, historical job execution information, as well as information required for Batch Impact Manger and Forecast. In the previous versions, prior to 6.4.01, BMC shipped Control-M with Oracle and Sybase databases (database licenses inclusive). The user can choose to use the BMC supplied database or their own Oracle or Sybase. For Control-M/Enterprise Manager running on Windows machines, users also have the option to install it with their own MS SQL database. Since version 6.4.01, BMC added support for BMC supplied PostgreSQL database and excluded Sybase from its software supply, but Control-M/Enterprise Manager was still allowed to install with user owned Sybase. In version 7, only PostgreSQL is supplied, which means for users who wants to run Control-M/Enterprise Manager on an Oracle or Sybase database, they have to provide their own.

Control-M/Enterprise Manager Server components are a set of processes that play different roles at the back end. These processes are:

- Naming Services
- Control-M Configuration Server
- Control-M/Enterprise Manager Configuration Agent
- GUI Server
- Gateway process (GTW)
- Global Condition Server (GCS)
- Global Alert Server (GAS)
- Control-M Web Server

Naming Service

The Naming Service provides the foundation for the majority of communications between Control-M/Enterprise Manager components. It is in fact an embedded TAO (The Ace Orb) naming service— an open-source C++ implementation of CORBA (Common Object Request Broker Architecture) protocol. It is a middleware in between Control-M/Enterprise Manager components allowing the components to communicate with each other over the network by using the same interface.

> From Wikipedia: The **Common Object Request Broker Architecture** (CORBA) is a standard defined by the **Object Management Group** (**OMG**) that enables software components written in multiple computer languages and running on multiple computers to work together (that is, it supports multiple platforms). CORBA is useful because it enables separate pieces of software written in different languages and running on different computers to work together like a single application or set of services. More specifically, CORBA is a mechanism in software for normalizing the method-call semantics between application objects residing either in the same address space (application) or remote address space (same host, or remote host on a network).

Control-M Configuration Server

Control-M Configuration Server component was introduced in Control-M/Enterprise Manager 6.3.01 as a background service to support CCM GUI front-end and perform backend administration tasks like cleaning hysterical data from the database on regular intervals.

Control-M/Enterprise Manager Configuration Agent

The role of Control-M/Enterprise Manager Configuration Agent hasn't changed much since the earlier versions. It manages the states of a number of Control-M/Enterprise Manager Server components. Those managed components are: GUI Server, Gateway processes, Global Condition server, and Global Alert Server. Control-M/Enterprise Manager Configuration Agent does the start-up, shutdown, and recycle for these components according to the **process Desire State flag** that is set by the user in CCM.

Control-M/Enterprise Manager Configuration Agent also constantly checks each managed component's real status and records it into Control-M/Enterprise Manager database. Control-M Configuration Server will read the information and present it on each active CCM GUI client session.

GUI Server

Unlike other Control-M/Enterprise Manager Server components, GUI Server has a lot more responsibilities. For GUI clients, it does most of the heavy lifting part of displaying jobs (reduce the workload on each GUI clients) as well as handles user requests that come from each active GUI client session. For Control-M Desktop, GUI Server handles user actions on job definitions, such as loading job definitions from EM database and writing job definition modifications to EM database. It also handles other tasks such as EM security (GUI client authentication), EM command line utility requests, and collecting GUI client auditing data.

Gateway process (GTW)

As we already know, Control-M/Enterprise Manager does not handle the actual job scheduling, the actual scheduling engine that submits jobs and tracks job execution statues is Control-M/Server. Gateway process enables the communication between the two layers so jobs can be displayed on GUI clients in real time and user actions can be immediately passed to Control-M/Server.

Dedicated gateway process is required to be defined for each Control-M/Server to handle the communication. Within the Control-M/Enterprise Manager layer, each gateway process has direct access to the EM database. On the remote side, a connection is permanently established to the target Control-M/Server.

Global Alert Server (GAS)

The Control-M/Enterprise Manager GUI Client provides an alert window for the user to track exceptions in the batch environment. Such exception can be a job's failure, a job has been running too long, or Control-M/Agent has gone unavailabe. The alert information gets transmitted from Control-M/Server to Control-M/Enterprise Manager by the gateway process. Global Alert Server is in charge for processing and presenting these alert notifications.

Global Condition Server (GCS)

In a multi Control-M/Server environment, jobs resided in different Control-M/Servers might be related and to be executed in a pre-defined logical order. the Global Condition Server handles the job dependencies between jobs running on different datacenters (Control-M/Servers).

In Control-M, a job condition is a string defined as part of the job definition, the Global conditions are distinguished from normal conditions by global condition prefix. User needs to predefine the condition prefix, as well as its source datacenter and destination. During runtime, the Global Condition Server recognizes conditions that are newly generated by jobs in the source datacenter (Control-M/Server) and distributes them to the destination datacenters (Control-M/Servers) according to the condition prefix definition.

Control-M Web Server

Control-M Web Launch (that is, web deployment of Control-M/Enterprise Manager GUI) and Business Impact Manager web interface. During late 2011, BMC released a new Control-M add-on product - Control-M Self Service. It is a web-based GUI that presents the batch workload in services view for the business level users. Those users can focus on business critical batch at service level without requiring a Control-M/ EM GUI installation.

The web-based GUI has also been optimised to be displayed on mobile devices such as iPhone or iPad.

Control-M/Server

The Control-M/Server is the heart of Control-M Workload Automation. In the background, it submits jobs onto job execution hosts according to their dependencies and priorities and tracks their status until the execution completes. Just the same as Control-M/Enterprise Manager, Control-M/Server for distributed systems stores information in its own database. (The reason we specifically stated distributed systems here, is because Control-M for mainframe stores information in data files rather than a database.) The stored information includes static job definitions, active jobs (AJF), job execution statistics, job logs, and so on.

Control-M/Server for distributed systems can be installed on Windows, Unix, or Linux machines. Control-M/Enterprise Manager and Control-M/Server can share the same machine and same database, but users normally separate the two for production environment to get better performance and in case of increase in load in the future.

Without Control-M/Enterprise Manager, Control-M/Server can still submit jobs automatically according to schedule. Basic menu driven tools and command line utilities are provided within Control-M/Server for users to monitor and manage jobs, but it is very unlikely to see a real life Control-M environment without having Control-M/Enterprise Manager installed. Control-M/Server's built-in command line and menu driven utilities can be used as alterative for job monitoring and management when Control-M/Enterprise Manager is temporarily unavailable.

Control-M/Server processes

Control-M/Server is a collection of 9 core background processes, plus 1 configuration agent process (introduced since version 6.3.01). Each process has its own role, such as being in charge of internal communication, communication with Control-M/Enterprise Manager, communication with Control-M/Agents, or handling job submission, tracking, and logging. Each process also generates its own log file for error diagnosis and monitoring. These processes are:

- **SU**: Supervisor
- **SL**: Job Selector
- **TR**: Job Tracker
- **NS**: Network Services
- **CE**: New Day and EM Communication Process
- **CS**: Client Service Process
- **LG**: Logger
- **WD**: Watch DogRT – Internal Communication Router
- **CA**: Control-M/Server Configuration Agent (Additional)

SU: Supervisor

As we can see within Control-M/Server there are another 8 core processes (excluding SU and CA) and each of these processes are required for Control-M/Server's normal functioning. Instead of letting users manually start or stop these processes one by one and monitor their running, Control-M/Server provides the supervisor—SU process to manage these processes. During a Control-M/Server start-up, the SU process gets started first and it brings up the other 9 processes. While the Control-M/Server is running if any process is exited for any reason, the SU process will detect the absence of the process and try to bring it up again. There is a max retry parameter to determine how many times the SU will re-try to bring up the exited processes if the processes keep on failing. Once the max retry is reached, SU will stop trying and bring all other processes down. It will shut down the entire Control-M/Server (SU process certainly knows the true meaning of Insanity: doing the same thing over and over again and expecting different results). During a normal shut down of Control-M/Server, the shut down request gets sent to the SU process, and the SU process will then stop all other active core processes and follow by exiting itself.

SL: Job Selector

SL process is one of the most critical processes in Control-M/Server (in my opinion). As we can tell from its name, SL process selects the right job for execution. It allocates resource for jobs that are eligible to run and releases the resource after the job is completed. It also handles part of the post processing work for each job. Since Control-M/Server 6.2.01, SL process became a multi-threaded process for performance improvement. As you can imagine, if SL process fails, all jobs that are waiting to be scheduled in Control-M will be in a hung state even if all prerequisite conditions for the job are met.

There is a lot more to talk about the SL process. We will take up the whole chapter if we go into every detail. Luckily, the internal algorithm of SL process is well designed, therefore, Control-M/Server can handle thousands of job submissions concurrently without us worrying about how it works internally.

TR: Job Tracker

The TR process is also a very important process. It tracks the states of all submitted jobs. Without TR process, we simply don't know what happened to a job after it got submitted. TR process gets job status update from Control-M/Agent in real time and updates the job's status in Control-M/Server database. By doing so, the SL process can perform post processing for that finished job and continue submitting new jobs as the down flow jobs' prerequisites are met.

Apart from relying on Control-M/Agents to provide job updates in real time, TR process also performs a Track All periodically to all running jobs. This feature is to prevent in events of job status updates were not received due to connection with Control-M/Agent was temporarily lost or TR process (or Control-M/Server) was down just at the time when the original job status updates were sent from Control-M/Agent.

NS: Agent Communication Process

Again, this is another critical process that is related to job submission and status tracking. In saying that, the NS process doesn't have either of these two roles, in fact it handles all communications between Control-M/Server processes and Control-M/Agent. It also maintains the communication with Control-M/Agents — check if they are available or not, and update the status into Control-M/Server's job execution node availability record.

CE: New Day and EM Communication Process

The CE process is newly introduced for version 7, in fact it is the combination of 2 processes (CD and CO) from the previous versions.

Firstly, it is in charge of generating information to be sent to Control-M/Enterprise Manager to reflex active batch workload status changes happened in the Control-M/Server. On the other hand, it also passes the request from Control-M/Enterprise manager such as the user requests initiated from GUI Clients or a global condition has been newly created.

Secondly, the CE process is in charge of Control-M/Server's daily refresh – **New Day procedure** (**NDP**). We will introduce NDP in detail when reviewing life cycle of a job during *Chapter 4, Create and Manage Batch Flows with Control-M GUI*.

CS: Server Process

The CS process handles GUI requests, such as holding a job, killing a job, and reruning a job. Up to 10 CS processes are allowed for handling multiple requests at the same time. The number of active CS processes can be hardcoded by the user or left to Control-M/Server to manage. From the user's point of view, they may feel a better response time during peak usage when multiple CS processes are presented. We will look at how to change the value of this parameter in *Chapter 5, Administrating the Control-M Infrastructure*.

LG: Logger Process

The LG process does event logging for the Control-M/Server. In additional, it handles utility requests from Control-M/Agent—there are a number of Control-M/Server command line utilities that are allowed to be invoked from Control-M/Agent. We can imagine those Control-M/Server processes on Control-M/Agent as soft links rather than performing the real task. LG process handles these request by triggering the actual process residing on the Control-M server and sends the execution result back to Control-M/Agent through the NS process.

WD: Watchdog Process

The WD process can do many different things, but these things are all optional.

Firstly, the WD process monitors Control-M processes and raises an alert when there's a problem. This feature can be turned on or turned off through configuration parameters.

Secondly, the WD process monitors Control-M/Server related resources (Control-M/Server's disk space and database usage) by invoking existing Control-M/Server utilities—ctmdiskspace and ctmdbspace.

Thirdly, the WD process performs Control-M/Server User Exists. We will introduce "User Exists" in *Chapter 6, Advanced Batch Scheduling and Management*.

RT: Internal Communication Router

The RT process is also one of the most important processes within Control-M/Server however hardly requres our attention. It acts like a network router to reduce the number of communication channels between Control-M/Server processes, therefore reducing the complicity of Control-M/Server inter-process communication. It listens on an **Internal Process Communication (IPC)** port that allows all the Control-M/Server processes we talked about to connect with each other.

CA: Configuration Agent

The CA process was introduced in Control-M 6.3.01. Its job role is similar to Control-M/Enterprise Manager Configuration Agent—to set the Control-M/Server **Up** or **Down** according to the desired state set by user in CCM. Of course it only communicates with the "master" - SU process and lets it to do the work of bring other processes up or down. It also retrieves Control-M/Agent status and sends the information to Control-M/Enterprise Manager to be displayed on CCM. It allows users to recycle Control-M/Agents and change their configurations through CCM.

Control-M/Agent

Control-M/Agent is a collection of processes that are constantly running on the job execution host to act on job submission requests from **Control-M/Server**. Control-M/Agent submits the actual executable program to operating system for execution, monitors the program execution, and provides the execution result back to **Control-M/Server**. Control-M/Agent is also the base of Control Modules, as well as handles the communication between **Control-M/Server** and Agentless remote hosts.

Users can choose from two connection options for the communication between Control-M/Agent and Control-M/Server—transient and persistent. With transient connection method, a new connection is created each time when Control-M/Server needs to talk to Control-M/Agent or vice versa. With persistent connection mode, a permanent connection is maintained between Control-M/Server and Agent. Persistent connection option was provided since version 6.2.01 to allow Control-M/Server and Agent connecting over a firewall that only allows communication from one side. It turns out that persistent connection also offers better performance when Control-M/Server and Agent are communicating in SSL mode.

Core processes within Control-M/Agent are:

- AG: Agent Listener, Request Handler
- AT: Agent Tracker
- AR: Agent Router
- UT: Utility Process

AG: Agent Listener, Request Handler

The AG process is a permanently running process that listens on a TCP port for requests coming from Control-M/Server (Control-M/Server NS process connects to AG process's listening port for sending job submission requests). Upon a job request's arrival, the AG process will decode the job request and spawn a child process to trigger the actual command or executable for execution.

Before version 6.2.01, Control-M/Agent on the Unix/Linux systems relies on operating system's INETD daemon for listening on server-to-agent communication. For each request that comes from Control-M/Server, the INETD process will create a new instance of the AG process to handle it.

AT: Agent Tracker

We can tell the purpose of this process from its name—tracking job status. During jobs running, a record for each job is created within Control-M/Agent. The TR process is in charge for monitoring the actual job process and updates the status record. For completed jobs, the TR process will acknowledge Control-M/Server and mark the corresponding status record as completed on the Agent side.

The TR process also performs post processing related to job's output file, by scanning the file and searching for required strings that Control-M/Server will later trigger post processing events for.

AR: Agent Router Process

The AR process is activated only when persistent connection mode is used. In a persistent mode, the AR process listens on the Server-to-Agent port and maintains the connection with Control-M/Server. Once a request is received, AR will route the request to the AG process. It also listens on requests from the AT process and routes them back to the job request's source— the Control-M/Server.

UT: Utility Process

As we mentioned while introducing Control-M/Server's LG process, there are a number of **Control-M/Server** command line utilities that are allowed to be invoked from Control-M/Agent. UT process is in charge for processing and submitting such utility requests from Control-M/Agent to **Control-M/Server**.

Agentless Technology

Job Submission to a remote host without Control-M/Agent installation is achieved by utilizing existing technologies that come with operating systems— **Secure Remote Shell (SSH)** and **Windows Management Instrumentation (WMI)**. Control-M/Server submits jobs to remote hosts through appointed Control-M/ Agents, then the Control-M/Agent opens the **SSH** or **WMI Connection** with the remote host and forwards the job submission requests. Multiple Control-M/Agents can be defined for submitting jobs to the same **Agentless Remote Host** for the purpose of workload sharing and high availability.

From the user's point of view, defining and monitoring jobs running on an **Agentless Remote Host** has very little difference as compared to working with Control-M/ Agent hosts. From a management point of view, the connection status of **Agentless Remote Host** can be monitored from CCM. Control-M also allows users to convert a Control-M/Agent host into an **Agentless Remote Host** or vice versa.

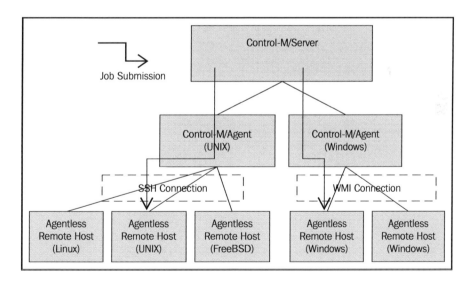

Control-M/Control Modules

We briefly introduced optional Control-M/Control Modules from the functionality aspects. There are two types of **Control Modules (CM)** — OS CM and Application CM.

In fact, all jobs submitted are handled by CMs. Normal jobs such as executing a command or running an executable are handled by the **OS CM**, which is came as a part of **Control-M/Agent**. The Control Modules we discussed earlier are the application CMs — CM for SAP, CM for Oracle E-Business Suite, CM for PeopleSoft, and so on. Application CMs are extensions of Control-M/Agent, therefore has to be installed on top of Control-M/Agent. In other words, Agentless remote hosts cannot handle application CM jobs.

How do Organizations Work With Control-M?

In an ideal environment, Control-M should be used as a centralized batch scheduling tool across the entire organization. These organizations are more likely to have a noticeable amount of complex batch processing running across multiple machines. To some extent, we could say that higher the number of jobs that are running, the more complex they are (that is, dependencies, scheduling rules, and number of execution hosts involved), and the more RIO Control-M will be present. That's why we see so many Control-M customers that are banks, insurance companies, large manufacture companies, or telecommunication service providers.

In many organizations, people around the world who belong to different departments are involved in batch processing and may have access to Control-M, but with different access levels depending on their job roles. The common job roles that could be related to Control-M are:

- **Developers**: Develop applications that requires batch processing.
- **Schedulers**: Define the batch jobs to be running in production.
- **Operators**: Monitor and manage production batch jobs running.
- **Application Owners**: Keep track of their batch job running at service level.
- **Administrators**: Monitor and manage the batch platform.

Like other enterprise-level software platform, organizations normally would have development, production, and testing Control-M environments. The developers normally would have access to the development environment to create jobs—utilize Control-M scheduling feature to meet batch requirements within their development project. After the jobs are created, they will create a request (perhaps, an ITSM request) and pass the job definitions to the schedulers to make the jobs go-live in production. Schedulers will then review the job definitions and make sure they are defined according to best practice or at least are not causing any errors or impacting the performance of production. Schedulers will also request the that developers provide runbook a for each job. A **runbook** is a general description of the job—what the job does and what the business priority and SLA are, as well as a set of instructions to tell the operator what to do when the job fails. So if any errors occurr while the job is running in production, the operators can perform a series of manual actions to the job or escalate the problem according to the instructions. Once the verification is done, the schedulers will raise change request and schedule these jobs in production. Operators on the other side will monitor and manage these jobs according to their severity and perform actions on failed jobs according to their runbook.

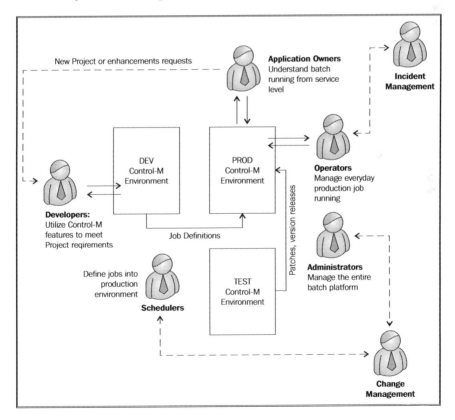

Administrators perform administrative tasks around Control-M such as installation, patching, troubleshooting, and tuning. Fresh version installations or new patch releases are normally tested on the test environment before rolling into development and production environment. Because generally they would have more experience with the product, they are often used by the **Developers** and **Schedulers** for expert advice. For failed jobs, the **Administrators** may have to work with the **Developers** and **Schedulers** for **RCA** (**root cause analysis**), fix the problem, and provide summary to **Incident Management** and the **Application owners**.

In a smaller environment, the job roles of scheduler, operator, and administrator could come down to one person or a small group of people in the operations team.

Where to Start?

Unlike open source software, it is not so easy to find Control-M related topics on the Internet simply by doing a Google search. It is also impossible to download Control-M installation from a third party website or purchase it from a shop. The primary location for Control-M-related information is BMC software website and some online communities. In this section, we will look at each of these places as well as discuss a little bit about Control-M related jobs and careers.

General Product information

On BMC software's website we will be able to find Control-M related marketing material, customer success stories, datasheets, and user interview videos. BMC divided the Control-M product into two groups based on platform—mainframe and distributed environment. From these pages, we will also find links to related products, such as Control-M for SAP, and Control-M/CM for Peoplesoft. Under the BMC website's Events section, we are also able to find Control-M related live events and webinars. However, we will not be able to find any detailed Control-M technical information from these pages because they are only avaiable under secured website which requires sign up with company support ID.

There are other ways to get help on Control-M. Initially there were two active technical related Control-M online forums. In recent years, Control-M was also brought into social media websites.

- Control-X Yahoo group: The Control-X Yahoo group is the most famous Control-M discussion group. It was founded in Nov 5, 1998. By the time this book is published, there will be over 1000 registered members. In order to join the group, we have to be a Yahoo member first then request access to the group. It normally takes two to three days for a new member's approval. URL: `http://tech.groups.yahoo.com/group/Control-X/`

- Scheduler Usage group: A user group available in both English and French language. Apart from discussion forums, the website also offers download links to Control-M related Fix Packs. URL: `http://www.scheduler-usage.com/`

- Facebook groups: There are two Control-M related groups on facebook — Control-M Users and BMC Control-M. Activities are relatively low when compared to the above two user groups, but you still should be able to meet people within the area and may even see some job offers from time to time.

- LinkedIn groups: There are a number of Control-M related groups on LinkedIn. We will find that a lot of members are either working in BMC software or working at a Control-M customer site. There are also recruitmentpeople who have joined these groups and they occasionally make job related posts.

Official Education and Certification

BMC Education Services offers various Control-M related courses and certification. There is a great chance that the training information has already been updated on the BMC site by the time this copy of the book is sold. Since the basic ideas and fundaments are always the same, going through these courses will help us choose the right education path.

There are five courses and one certification currently listed on the BMC Website at the time when this book is published. The following are the listed courses:

- BMC Control-M/Enterprise Manager 6.x: Scheduling — Part 1 (WBT)
- BMC Control-M/Enterprise Manager 6.4: Scheduling — Part 2
- BMC Control-M/Enterprise Manager 6.4: Scheduling — Part 3
- BMC Control-M/Enterprise Manager 6.4: Administering
- BMC Control-M for Distributed Systems 6.4: Certification Book Camp
- BMC Control-M 6.4: What's New (WBT)

BMC only offers one Control-M related certification — BMC Certified Administrator — BMC Control-M for Distributed Systems 6.4. Certification is not a prerequisite for getting a Control-M-related job, but obtaining this certification will increase our career prospects and help us become more competitive in the field, especially if we are looking at working for a BMC partner company in some foreign countries. To prepare for the certification exam, we need to attend a BMC Education instructor-led training course first. The required courses for the exam are:

- BMC Control-M/Enterprise Manager 6.x: Scheduling — Part 1 (WBT)
- BMC Control-M 6.4: Certification Boot Camp

The Boot Camp course is a five day instructor led course. It is well and truly a high-intensity course—9 to 11 hours a day, five days straight in a classroom with reading assignments for each evening. The class covers topics in the scheduling and administering courses plus hands-on labs for implementation related exercises. The certification exam is inclusive in the book camp course. It is an online multiple choice exam, but it can only be taken at the local BMC training center. Students can take the exam twice within three weeks after the Boot Camp course, of course retests are only for those who failed the first time.

Reading this book and doing the exercises throughout the book is definitely a great starting point in the future career path around Control-M and could also make the exam much easier to pass.

Getting a Job in Control-M

It is good to learn something new, but it would be better to be able to apply what we have learnt and get paid for what we enjoy to do. Similar to other software products, there are pretty much three career avenues we can go down with Control-M:

1. Work at a customer site, as a Control-M administrator, job scheduler, or operator.

2. Work at BMC software, as a technical support person or a software consultant.

3. Work at a BMC partner as a technical consultant to do pre-sale and/or professional service.

With every BMC Control-M customer, there will be potential for a Control-M related position. The role might focus more on the functionality side such as schedulers and operators, or could be more towards the administration side or doing project work. I have seen some of the companies do not have a dedicated Control-M administrator or scheduler/operator. The administration role maybe handled by a DBA or Unix/Windows system administrator. In this case if we are looking for a DBA or system administrator role with some Control-M skill on the side it would be really helpful.

When doing a job search, we often find that Control-M related jobs require the following knowledge and skill points:

- Understanding of Control-M architecture. Able to install and configure Control-M in different operating system environments.

- Experience with job scheduling. Able to define jobs with complex scheduling requirements.

- Able to convert and migrate jobs into Control-M, such as converting from Unix CRON jobs, migrating from an earlier version of Control-M or another scheduling platform.

- Leveraging Control-M utilities. Able to use Control-M utilities to meet scheduling requirements.

- Shell and Perl scripting skill and debugging skill.

- Understanding of operating systems, such as Windows, Unix, and Linux.

- Knowledge with databases (database to host Control-M), depending on what the company is currently using or planning to use with their Control-M. It can be Oracle, Sybase, MS SQL, or PostgreSQL.

- Some of the companies are mainframe and distributed systems in a mixed environment. When these kind of companies listing a job, the probability that they will expect you to have some degree of knowledge with using Control-M on a Mainframe and the ability to write JCL is high.

A lot of people who are working on Control-M today are from mainframe background. These people may not have the best knowledge about midrange environmnet or scripting language, but they would have a good understanding of the Control-M concept. Since they have been working in the field for a long time, they also have a good relationship and connections within the field to get the help they needed. On the other hand, there are fresh men who come for the Linux/Windows or DBA background. This group of people are good at getting their way around the system with installations and much more confinable with writing scripts, but may find it hard to use the Control-M concepts and terminologies at the very beginning.

On the positive side, there is a reasonable amount of large organizations around the world who use Control-M and they treat Control-M as a very critical application. But this may create a problem too. It largely depends on our physical location. In some countries and cities there are more Control-M customers therefore more chance for a job vacancy. Whereas if someone lives in a city that has no Control-M customers at all, or only a very small number of Control-M customers, re-allocation needs to be considered. Final words for this topic are: just understand our own strength, be flexible, go with your passion and the job will come.

Summary

We went through a lot of knowledge points during this chapter. In this chapter we looked at the features of Control-M, important concepts, and reviewed the architect of Control-M. I hope you are not overwhelmed. As you start using and managing Control-M, you will become more familiar with the concepts and the architectural side of the things. And you might find it useful to re-visit this chapter later on during the installation of Control-M and troubleshooting issues.

We will cover detailed information on a numbers of topics as we discuss them later on during the book. When you are ready, let's move on to the next chapter – *Building the Control-M Infrastructure*.

3
Building the Control-M Infrastructure

Unlike ordinary desktop applications, Control-M is an enterprise-level large-scale batch workload automation platform that handles the execution of end-to-end business processes potentially across the entire organization. Therefore, it is essential to properly plan the batch infrastructure in advance to fully utilize the benefits of Control-M and allow it to fulfill the future growth of the organization's batch needs.

In this chapter, we are going to look at important factors that need to be taken into consideration for building a complete batch infrastructure. We will start with introducing the "Three Ages" towards workload automation. This will be followed by discussions of pre-implementation-related topics, such as batch environment sizing considerations, choices of high availability solutions, storage space requirements, firewall configuration requirements, user experience-related performance concerns, and so on. Once we have the environment planned, we focus on the technical aspects by building a complete sandpit Control-M batch infrastructure.

By the end of this chapter, you will be able to:

- Understand the potential challenges of implementing a batch scheduling infrastructure, which is able to overcome those challenges by taking the right approach at the right time to achieve enterprise-wide workload automation.

- Analyze batch requirements and design an efficient batch environment by using the right Control-M technology at the right place to meet complex technical needs.

- Perform Control-M installation on Windows and Linux-based systems and carry out Control-M post installation tasks to ensure installed components are running and working with each other properly.

Three ages to workload automation

Enterprise-wide workload automation does not happen overnight. Converting non-standardized batch processing into a centralized workload automation platform can be time consuming and risky. We need to gain full understanding of the existing running batch jobs before moving them into the new platform, that is, how the jobs are currently scheduled? What are the relationships between these jobs? Which are the higher priority ones? Then based on the amount of jobs and the complexity, we can decide the method of the migration process, which either can be performed automatically or manually. Once jobs are migrated, a series of test needs to be performed before moving into production. Each production cutover is preferably to be transparent to the business' normal operation as much as possible or to be performed within the agreed outage window.

Apart from the technical challenges, "people issues" can be the next road block. First of all, users need to be educated about the tool. It can take a lot of time for users to accept and get used to the new way of operation. The bigger challenge is to let the application developers take in and apply the "centralized workload automation" concept. So during each IT project's development phase, they can utilize built-in features provided by the workload automation platform as much as possible rather than reinventing the wheel.

Forcing users and developers to fully take in the centralized workload automation concept and change their ways of working with batch processing straightaway could lead the project to an ultimate failure. Instead, different areas of approach and actions should be taken in stages according to the actual IT environment condition. We can group these different approaches and actions into three "ages", that is, the stone age, iron age, and golden age.

Stone age

Unless we are building an IT infrastructure from scratch, for any reasonable size organization, they should have a noticeable amount of batch jobs running already to serve different business needs. Such processes are either running by OS/application's inbuilt batch features or scheduled from homegrown scheduling tools (sometimes they can be manual tasks too). For example, these tasks can be:

- **End of day (EOD)** reporting jobs
- ERP application's overnight batch
- Housekeeping jobs, for example, database backup and log recycling jobs

Depending on the organization's business requirements, the number of batch jobs required to achieve the outcome can start from a few hundred and go up to tens of thousands across a large number of different job execution hosts. As we discussed in *Chapter 1, Get to Know the Concept*, in a heterogeneous environment it is extremely challenging to run cross-platform batch processing by using different tools, especially when the number of tasks is large and the batch window is small. Therefore, these batch processings are the most essential and critical ones to be consolidated into a centralized scheduling platform. On the other hand, these types of processing tasks are the "low hanging fruits" - relatively easy to identify and migrate, simply because they have already been clearly defined and scheduled by existing batch scheduling mechanisms, which means it is more likely that the job scheduling information can be extracted from these sources.

At the end of the day, it all comes down to the question of how to migrate the jobs into a centralized scheduling platform and how are they going to be triggered in the new environment. "How to migrate", as in, how the jobs should be extracted from the existing batch scheduling mechanism and how they should be imported into the new environment. It can be done by using a job migration program, if it is available, or else someone has to manually redefine the jobs from scratch. "How jobs should be triggered", as in, should the job directly trigger the script/command or use scheduling tool's extended features (that is, Control-M Control Modules) for batch processing within a particular application?

The bottom line is – this stage is all about standardizing the way the existing batch jobs are executed and managed by consolidating them into a centralized tool. The migration process should be relatively straightforward and should not require major modification to application codes as well as each application's architecture. However, this will change the way users manage and monitor batch jobs forever. It is the initial step for standardizing batch management and batch optimization, therefore we call it the "stone age".

The successful implementation of "stone age" will benefit the organization without a doubt. After a while, users will realize how easy it is to manage cross-platform batch flows from a centralized GUI. They no longer need to look at different screens to trigger jobs or monitor a job's execution. Instead, batch jobs are triggered automatically and are to be managed by exceptions.

Iron age

A lot of organizations stop improving and stop extending their centralized batch environment once they have completed the stone age. As the business rules are becoming more and more complex, it is common to see silos of batch processing existing in different applications that are related but not linked together, that is, they do not know about other processing taking place and how they relate. Plus on top of that, we have business process steps that are being "patched up" by mechanisms outside the centralized scheduling tool. As a result, batch flows within the centralized scheduling tool are commonly unable to present an end-to-end business process.

One possibility is that these organizations believe that they have already got everything that the centralized scheduling tool is capable of – triggering executables at a fixed time on a predefined day. Rather than someone taking the lead to discover and try other features within the batch scheduling tool, people in different parts of the organization always try to develop their own ways to handle more advanced requirements such as event triggering processing or inter-application file transfers.

In late 2010, I was involved in an EAI development project. During my meeting with some JAVA developers, I noticed they still think batch processing (in Control-M) is all about triggering some program to run at a fixed time and nothing more. Unless they change their views on batch processing and understand what "workload automation" is about, they won't be able to fully utilize the features provided by a workload automation tool for the applications they develop. As a result, after the application goes live, there will be a large amount of processing to be done by inbuilt or self-coded scheduling mechanisms while the other half is running in Control-M.

Iron age is about changing how batch processing is initially designed, that is, improving it by fully utilizing the capabilities of the batch scheduling tool. This requires ongoing education and letting application designers and developers accept and use features that are already available in a centralized scheduling tool rather than reinventing the wheel. This is a lot more challenging than simply extracting and importing batch-processing data from one tool to another during the stone age. Also, the benefits we get from the iron age are not as easy to measure as what we can directly see during the stone age. In the stone age, the users instantly get the benefits of managing batch from a centralized scheduling tool.

In reality, application development teams may rather write their own code to meet the processing requirements so that they can have total control of the application they have developed. Application developers may think "Why should we learn a new tool when we can simply write a few lines of code to achieve event-driven triggering?" or "In the future, if we want to change the way my application works, we might have to log a change request for the scheduling team to modify the batch job in Control-M, whereas having everything done in the code, we will have full control, therefore saving us a lot of hassle."

A certain degree of politics can also be involved. For example, the management of the application development team may think "If half of our work is done by the scheduling tool, where is our value?" or "We want to be more important to the organization's IT in front of the IT directors!" Another scenario with organizations is that they outsource their application development. Instead of building a new system from scratch for each project, the outsourcing companies try to modify what they have already implemented in other organizations for a similar project. In such cases, the outsourcing companies, most of the time, will refuse to do any major modifications to the application just to fit into the centralized scheduling tool. They might believe that by doing so, they can ensure that the project gets delivered with minimal time, cost, and risk. But in reality, the result always turns out the opposite.

In order to avoid falling into one of the categories mentioned above, the person who is going to promote "iron age" within an organization should work on people rather than expecting everything to turn out fine by only focusing on the technology. At the same time, higher-level management in the organization should provide a level of assistance by enforcing an organization-wide scheduling standard so the organization's IT can get the most out of the centralized batch scheduling platform and therefore maximize the business' ROI on it.

The definition of a successfully-implemented iron age is that the organization should see that batch flows are becoming more meaningful at the business service level (that is, presents the complete business process) and is optimized to process within a shorter batch window by using features provided with the batch scheduling tool (for example, percentage of processing is moved into the event triggered batch, which can happen outside the batch window). From an ongoing maintenance point of view, there are less homegrown tools to manage. The total time and effort required for application development may also reduce if the developers are familiar with the batch scheduling tool and know how to leverage the available features properly.

Golden age

Golden age refers to the full implementation of workload automation. It is not as easy to achieve as it sounds, because there are a number of prerequisites that need to be met before the organization even considers it.

First of all, the centralized scheduling platform needs to be upgraded to a more up-to-date version that provides the workload automation ability, such as Control-M version 7. Secondly, in order to get the true value from workload automation, the organization needs to have both the stone age and the iron age successfully implemented, that is, jobs in the centralized scheduling tool need to be well defined and presenting the actual business processes. Furthermore, it depends on how far the organization wants to go down this road in order to reach the pinnacle. The IT environment may look at providing the foundation to allow the batch environment to become more dynamic by using resource virtualization and cloud computing technologies.

Once all prerequisites are met, implementing the golden age requires the batch environment designer to work closely with a system architect and application developers. They need to transform the existing bath to become more flexible (moving away from batch jobs' static nature), so the workload automation tool can schedule them according to business policies and route the workload according to runtime load to the best available virtual resource for execution. The batch job should also be designed by following the SOA design principles for reusability and should be loosely coupled.

In the golden age, batch workloads are managed according to the business policies and service agreement. The limited machine resource bottleneck of batch processing is not much of a concern because resources can be acquired whenever needed. In this case, the system can handle a sudden spark of processing requests, while still ensuring the process to complete within its agreed batch window or SLA.

Planning the Batch environment

The foundation of the golden age centralized workload automation is a well-designed and properly configured batch software infrastructure. Although the technical aspect of installing commercial batch software such as Control-M is fairly straightforward, implementing a complete batch environment is not only about finding a server and installing the software. Building a batch environment without proper planning can turn out to be costly for the organization over the long run (for example, the penalty of constantly missing SLA due to an unstable batch environment, cost of modifying the infrastructure, and cost of additional licensing due to poor planning). It is also very challenging to make major structural modifications to the production batch environment without interrupting the business once everything has gone live and while working closely with each other.

A well-designed batch environment should be reliable, secure, and scalable. In order to properly plan such a batch environment from the beginning, the system architect needs to have an overall picture of the organization's IT environment, knowing the business requirements, technical challenges, and technical resource availability, as well as keeping in mind the technical requirements that come from the batch scheduling platform itself, that is, Control-M.

Control-M sizing consideration

Let's assume that we are at the beginning of the stone age. We start with interviewing each application owner to find out which batch processing they currently have and how they are running them at the moment. Based on this we are able to figure out which processing scenarios are suitable to be migrated to Control-M, their priority, and difficulty level. Once we have an estimation of the total number of existing tasks to be consolidated, we should be able to roughly figure out:

- What is the total number of batch jobs run per day (average and peak)?
- How many machines are involved in executing these batch jobs?
- Who are the users currently managing these batch jobs and how many of them are going to directly interact with the Control-M GUI frontend for job management and monitoring?

Total number of batch jobs run per day

When we talk about the total number of batch jobs, it really depends on how the processing tasks are grouped. We can have a single Control-M job to perform multiple tasks, such as to begin with reading information from a file, filter it, load the output into the database, and then send an e-mail notification for completion. Or we can split these tasks into individual jobs. Dividing tasks can make troubleshooting easier and reduce the time required when rerunning a particular task, but at the same time, this approach increases the amount of jobs to be managed. Such decision should be made on a case-by-case basis in reference to a standard rather than using a one size fits all approach.

It is important to have an estimation of the maximum number of actual Control-M jobs run per day. This information might be related to Control-M licensing costs (depends on the licensing agreement) and will affect some Control-M database configuration parameters. Control-M components are stateless; all job-related information and active environment state changes are stored in its database. Therefore, Control-M needs to know this information during installation in order to configure the database to provide the capacity and performance. There are three levels to choose from – small (less than 2,000 jobs/day), medium (between 2,001 to 10,000 jobs/day) and large (more than 10,000 jobs/day). With mdern databases the database tablespace can be set to `auto extend*` to accommodate job and data growth. Multiple Control-M/Servers should be considered to ensure best performance and stability if the estimated maximum number of batch jobs run per day is higher than BMC Software's recommended figure.

 When BMC-provided PostgreSQL database is used, the tablespace is set to auto extend by default.

Control-M does not support load balancing at the Control-M/Server level. It means that the jobs are predefined to permanently belong to a specific Control-M/Server. Control-M/Agents on job execution hosts are also preconfigured to communicate with a specific Control-M/Server. Partitioning jobs into multiple Control-M/Servers need to be carefully planned, because moving existing jobs from one Control-M/Server to another requires many manual actions, such as, a number of fields in each job definition need to be modified in order to shift the jobs from one Control-M/Server to another. Also the Control-M/Agent on the job execution host may need to be re-configured to accept a job submission from the new Control-M/Server.

Partitioning jobs into multiple Control-M/Servers is more than just dividing the total number of jobs by the recommended value and evenly distributing them into different Control-M/Servers. One of the biggest things that needs to be taken into consideration is the dependency between interrelated jobs. As we introduced in *Chapter 2, Exploring Control-M*, Control-M has a built-in functionality to support cross-datacenter job dependency, that is, global conditions. In order to use this feature, global conditions prefixes the need to be defined for those cross-datacenter dependencies in order to connect inter-related jobs that reside on multiple Control-M/Servers. Large amount of global conditions can increase complexity and processing overhead. Therefore, related jobs will be grouped into the same Control-M/Server as much as we can to reduce the needs for global conditions, unless some of the jobs in the flow have to run on a totally different environment. For example, mainframe jobs have to be scheduled in a mainframe Control-M/Server, and for global organizations, they often have multiple Control-M/Servers to handle jobs in specific geographic regions.

Total number of job execution hosts

The total number of job execution hosts managed by individual Control-M/Servers also needs to be taken into consideration during planning. Control-M/Server needs to concurrently maintain communication with every connected Control-M/Agent at all times, regardless of whether there are jobs scheduled on the Agent or not. Although Control-M/Server has no hard limit on the number of connected Control-M/Agents, managing these Control-M/Agents more or less creates overhead for Control-M/Server, especially when the number of Control-M/Agents is high. In a multiple Control-M/Server environmnet, we would balance the number of connected Control-M/Agents per Control-M/Server if there are thousands of hosts involved with batch processing.

Choosing which job execution hosts are to be grouped to the same Control-M/Server should be based on job relationships. Hosts that are likely going to execute inter-related jobs should be grouped into the same Control-M/Server to minimize the use of global conditions. The decision should be made in conjunction with the total number of jobs, as the total number of jobs running on these hosts can still exceed the recommendation of the maximum number of jobs run per day for each Control-M/Server.

Control-M/Agent itself is light-weight and really hasn't got a limit for the number of concurrent running jobs. The real limitation comes from the job execution machine's processing power and the operating system's maximum number of running processes. It is common to see that additional machines are added down the track to share the increasing processing workload. In this case, the additional Agents need to be added to the Control-M/Server that currently schedules the processing, so the additional Agents can be added as part of the job submission group, that is, node group. By doing so, Control-M/Server will be able to use its round-robin-based load balancing feature during job submission time to determine the best agent machine for job execution. This should be kept in mind during initial planning to allow each Control-M/Server with room to grow additional Control-M/Agents in order to share workload for a particular application's potential future batch processing needs.

Number of datacenters

Each running Control-M/Server needs to be defined into Control-M/Enterprise Manager as a datacenter along with an active gateway process in-between to handle the communication. When planning for the Control-M/Enterprise Manager server component machine, we need to take this factor into consideration to make sure the machine's CPU and RAM will have the capacity to handle those additional gateway processes running. On the other hand, the Control-M/Enterprise Manager database table will also require extra space to store the job definitions and active/archived job information to be presented in the GUI.

Smaller environments which are unlikely to have additional Control-M/Servers may choose to install Control-M/Enterprise Manager and Control-M/Server onto a single machine. However, for a larger environment, it is important to make sure the Control-M/Enterprise Manager machine has the extra capacity from both a, processing power and a storage point of in order to handle the future growth of the batch environment.

Amount of concurrent GUI users

Consolidating jobs into a centralized location changes the way jobs are managed. Users no longer manage and monitor jobs through different systems. Instead, they perform all these tasks from Control-M/Enterprise Manager GUI Clients. As we discussed in *Chapter 2*, *Exploring Control-M*, all GUI Clients are connected to the Control-M/Enterprise Manager server component – GUI Server. The GUI Server does most of the work to allow job information to be displayed in graphical form on each client.

Multiple GUI server processes can be defined to share the workload, but there's no real guideline to decide how many GUI server processes are needed to handle the number of concurrent GUI client sessions because it depends on the frequency of GUI actions, type of GUI actions, the machine's processing power, and so on. GUI server processes can be added at any time without any major impact to users as well as to the batch environment, but additional GUI server processes will also increase CPU and memory usage to the machine. Additional GUI server processes can also be defined on another machine where a full Control-M/Enterprise Manager server components installation is installed.

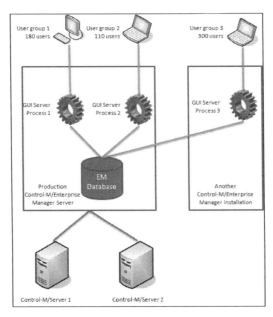

After an increased number of GUI server processes, users may still experience slow response when performing mass job actions in the active environment (for example, hold or free a job, view job sysout, rerun a job). Remember we talked about the Control-M/Server's CS process in *Chapter 2, Exploring Control-M*. The CS process handles EM to Server GUI user requests (for example, hold/free/rerun a job) on the Control-M/Server side. The number of CS processes can be increased according to the demand. Again, there's no accurate guideline for how many CS processes are needed; CS processes can be increased or decreased at any time or set to dynamically increase/decrease. We will demonstrate how to define a max/min number of CS processes in *Chapter 5, Administrating the Control-M Infrastructure*.

Use Control-M/Agent or go Agentless

Control-M Agentless Technology provides rapid job deployment by avoiding the needs of the Control-M/Agent installation on the job execution host. It can reduce the TCO of the Control-M application because the user no longer needs to worry about patching and upgrading the Control-M/Agent installation on each remote job execution host. At the same time, it can potentially allow first day support on new application rollouts. Control-M Agentless Technology is perfect for the following batch processing scenarios:

- The total number of hosts involved in batch processing is large, but some of them do not usually run many jobs, and therefore hardly justify the effort of installing and maintaining the Control-M/Agent on these hosts.

- Between the remote host and Control-M/Server, the Control-M/Agent communication ports are blocked by the firewall and cannot be opened due to security reasons.

- Control-M/Agent cannot be installed on a remote host (that is, the host is owned by a third-party vendor).

- The O/S and Platform of remote host is either very old or very special, and no Control-M/Agent is compatible with it.

Of course, Agentless Technology is not a one size fits all approach, simply because there are a number of limitations with the technology. Here's a list of things to be considered before deciding on Agentless Technology:

- Are there any jobs needed to be scheduled through Control Module? Control Modules are installed on top of Control-M/Agent. In order to install and use Control Modules, Control-M/Agent has to be installed first. By saying that, CM can be installed on other hosts and still be able to communicate with the application installed on this host.

- Is Control-M filewatch facility going to be used on the job execution host? Control-M filewatch facility is a file detection feature provided as part of Control-M/Agent. Therefore, in order to use it, Control-M/Agent has to be installed. Alternatively, we can use Control-M CM for AFT to perform filewatch on a remote host, but it may cost extra to get the Control Module software license.

- Are there any Control-M utilities which need to be triggered from the job execution host? As we introduced in *Chapter 2, Exploring Control-M*, there are a number of Control-M/Server utilities which can be invoked from Control-M/Agent. It is relying on Control-M/Agent's internal mechanism to accept the request and pass it to Control-M/Server.

- Will the jobs produce large sysout (output)? If so, will the users need to view these sysouts from Control-M/Enterprise Manager GUI? With Control-M Agentless Technology, the output of each job execution always gets transferred back to the Control-M/Agent that sent the original job execution request. Frequently transferring large sysouts between hosts can cause significant network overhead. In such cases, either the sysout should get deleted right after job execution, or simply install Control-M/Agent on the job execution host, so the sysout gets generated on the host and stays on the host for users to view from the GUI.

- Will the job execution host be running a large number of jobs in a high frequency manner? Is the job submission a part of a time-critical real-time system that requires imminent response? In such cases, Control-M/Agent installation is recommended for performance guarantee. This is because with Agentless Technology, jobs are submitted to the remote host through selected Control-M/Agent; time delay is unavoidable when opening the connection to a remote host through WMI or SSH for job submission and tracking.

Agentless Technology allows rapid job deployment. For applications that are just starting to move batch processing into Control-M, users can always set up Agentless job submission to fulfill the initial request and convert the host into Control-M/Agent in the future if needed. Control-M allows users to freely switch a job execution host between real Control-M/Agent and Agentless Technology, and it is transparent to job execution and management.

Production, development, and testing

Regardless, the batch jobs are migrated from an existing scheduling platform or developed together with new applications; these jobs need to be tested before going into production. Organizations have to build extra Control-M environments to separate development and testing from production. These development and testing Control-M/Server environments are often very similar to production or at least running the same version, so once the jobs are developed and tested, they can be transferred to production without significant modifications.

In smaller environments, the production, development, and testing are more likely to be separated only at the Control-M/Server level, that is, the organization will have a single Control-M/Enterprise Manager instance with all production, development, and testing Control-M/Servers defined and connected (we can call it **"All-in-One"**). User access is given according to the person's role in the organization; for example, an application developer may only be able to access jobs that reside in the development and testing environment, whereas production operators may have full permission to access jobs from all three environments.

In larger environments, the organization may have hundreds of GUI users from all around the world, running multiple Control-M/Servers with tens thousands of jobs in production, development, and testing. Sure enough, Control-M/Servers are running by themselves without interfering with each other and each user's access privilege can still be defined from Control-M/Enterprise Manager. The concern is that because the Control-M/Enterprise Manager's components, such as the GUI server, database, and global conditions, are shared between production and non-production, a possible usage spark from the development and testing environment could overload the Control-M/Enterprise Manager components, thus affecting the production system running. If this is a concern, it is common sense to completely separate the production from the development and testing environments (we can call it **"Split"**), that is, production Control-M/Server(s) are connected to the **Control-M/Enterprise Manager** which is dedicated to production. Development and testing Control-M/Servers are connected to their own **Control-M/Enterprise Manager**. This is a good way to make the production system's performance much more consistent and predictable; at the same time it reduces the complexity of the environment.

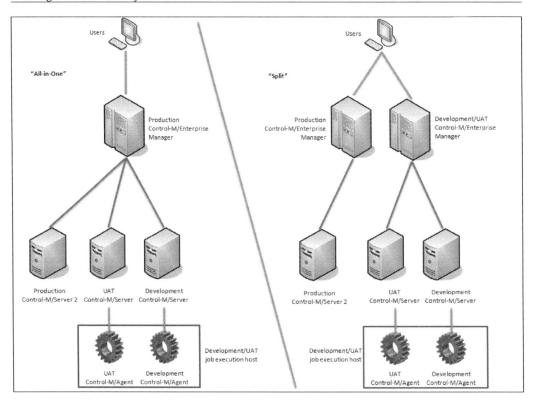

Control-M/Agents are to be installed on production, testing, or development job execution hosts, and connected to the corresponding **Control-M/Server** accordingly. Each **Control-M/Agent** is designed to interact with only one **Control-M/Server** at any given time. User can manually re-configure **Control-M/Agent** to talk to a different **Control-M/Server** (for example, moving a Control-M/Agent from UAT to production), or install additional Control-M/Agents on the same hosts if job submission is required by multiple Control-M/Servers concurrently.

Control-M high availability requirements

Prior to implementing the batch environment, how to ensure high availability should be taken into consideration as part of the planning phase to ensure that the future batch environment can offer continuous operation during special events such as outages for server maintenance, machine hardware failure, data corruption, power outage, or even flood, fire, and earthquakes at the server location.

News Paper Article: Floods take down CUA net bank (Australia)

By Luke Hopewell, ZDNet.com.au on January 12th, 2011

Credit Union Australia (CUA) has shut down its internet banking services because of the Queensland flood disaster, leaving customers nationwide high and dry.

The services have been shut down because CUA operates out of head offices in the flooded area of the Brisbane central business district. It apologized to customers via its website today.

"Customers can be assured that all data and accounts are secure" it said on its front page, adding that customers can still make withdrawals at branches and ATMs outside the flooded areas.

"Customers can be assured that all their personal data remains secure and CUA is working to restore services as soon as possible. However, we do ask for their patience at this time as we work through the issues" CUA said.

IT outages can cost a lot for the business; it is important to at least have a high availability (HA) strategy for the batch environment and consider disaster recovery (DR) if the required resources are available. In general terms, HA means the application can offer uninterruptable computing during a hardware failure or other issues, whereas DR means the application can offer recovery at a foreign site during a disaster, such as fire or earthquake, at the current running datacenter.

In Control-M, there are two aspects around the topic, that is, HA/DR of Control-M components and continuing batch processing on job execution hosts.

Control-M in a clustered environment

Some organizations may have invested into operating system-level clustering and associated hardware in their IT infrastructure to achieve HA and DR. We are talking about the traditional clustering technology here, such as **Microsoft Cluster Server (MSCS)**, **VERITAS Cluster Server (VCS)**, IBM PowerHA, Oracle Solaris Cluster, and so on. All components of the three tiers (Control-M/Enterprise Manager, Server, and Agent) can be implemented on most common types of Windows/Unix/Linux clusters to achieve high availability. It is essential to have the required hardware resource and operating system clustering fully configured prior to Control-M installation. Installing Control-M in a clustered environment requires additional configuration as compared to a normal standalone installation, but it offers nearly transparent failover to batch running and Control-M users.

In a clustered environment, Control-M applications need to be installed on the shared filesystem that can be accessed by each machine (cluster node) within the cluster. These nodes can be located in multiple datacenters in different cities or countries as long as they are able to communicate with each other and are able to access the shared disk through the TCP/IP network. As Control-M applications only support clusters in active-passive mode and not active-active mode, the shared filesystem is to be mounted to the cluster node, whichever is active. The active node has a virtual service IP assigned for other machines on the network to access. In the event of the active node's failure, the cluster management software imminently detects it and switches the Control-M application together with the service IP to the available **Standby**. In theory, the entire process does not require modifications on either the **Failover** component itself or the machines which are accessing it.

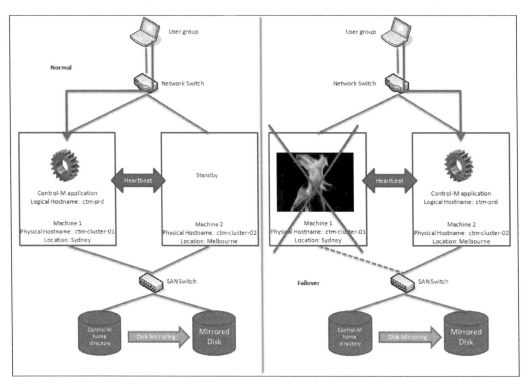

Because this method offers transparency and no interruption during **Failover**, it is considered to be one of the best methods for Control-M high availability. However, organizations should always bear in mind the cost of acquiring and maintaining the clustering infrastructure.

Control-M/Server mirroring and failover

Operating system-level clustering requires purchasing of additional software and special storage hardware, as well as technical experts to implement and maintain it. Some organizations may not have the budget and the expertise to do so. As an alternative, users can consider Control-M's built-in capability to achieve mirroring and failover at the Control-M/Server level with minimal additional cost.

Control-M/Server database mirroring

Control-M/Server database mirroring offers real-time data duplication to a secondary database purely at the application level – done by mechanisms within the Control-M/Server. During the normal operation of mirroring mode, the Control-M/Server executes each database update query in both the primary and secondary database to keep them consistent. Because the two databases are always holding the same information, in the event of primary database failure, Control-M/Server can be manually switched over to the secondary database for continuous operation.

Database mirroring can be implemented on all types of Control-M/Server supported databases, that is, Sybase, Oracle, MSSQL, and PostgreSQL. The method requires an additional machine to hold the secondary database. The secondary machine should have similar (preferably identical) hardware specifications and capacity to the primary database machine to avoid performance bottleneck. The primary and secondary machines can reside at a different location, as long as the network connection in-between is consistent. Configuring the mirrored database is straightforward and does not require specific database knowledge, as every step of the configuration is done by utilities provided with Control-M/Server.

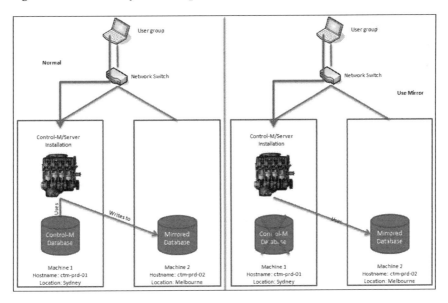

Control-M/Server failover

The database mirroring offered by **Control-M/Server** can only handle failures at the database level. The batch environment will still be interrupted if a disruption is beyond the database to the entire machine level that holds the **Control-M/Server installation**. **Control-M/Server** failover is another built-in mechanism that works together with database mirroring to allow a complete switch over to a standby **Control-M/Server installation** in the event of the primary site's total failure. When a failover is required, the users need to manually shutdown the primary **Control-M/Server** and start the secondary **Control-M/Server**, as well as update the Control-M/Server's communication details in Control-M/Enterprise Manager.

Again, the secondary machine that holds the standby Control-M/Server and mirror database installation should be identical to the primary to ensure performance. It can be running in a remote location, as long as there's a communication link between itself and the primary and the network performance is consistent. Unlike the operating system clustering solution, with the built-in Control-M/Server failover mechanism, both the primary and secondary Control-M/Server operates with the local machine's hostname rather than a virtual hostname. Due to this reason, each Control-M/Agent need to be configured to be able to communicate and accept job submission requests from both the Control-M/Servers.

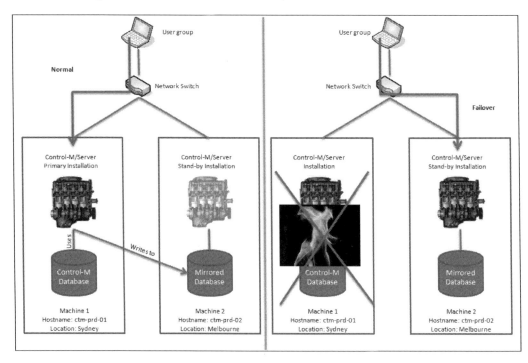

The limitation of Control-M/Server mirroring and failover is that a manual switch over to secondary is required in the event of a failure, as well as a manual switch back to the primary after the service is restored to normal. However, these manual steps can be fully automated and triggered by a monitoring solution such as BMC's ProactiveNet Performance Management solution. This is because the mirroring and failover actions are command-line utilities driven, which can be called by a third-party application in a non-interactive way. Technically, the switch over should take less than 10 minutes, but if it is going to be performed manually, additional delay may occur as it takes time for someone to respond to the event. During the switch over process, Control-M/Server needs to be completely shutdown, therefore no jobs can be scheduled until the switch over is complete. If such a delay is not acceptable at the business level, other high availability solutions might be worth considering even though this requires additional cost.

Control-M mirroring and failover could be the perfect solution for those small and medium size batch environments that have a more flexible batch window to achieve high availability without massive investment on clustering software and additional storage technology. The other thing that should also be kept in mind is that even though the Control-M/Enterprise Manager server components do not offer the same mirroring and failover mechanism, to some degree, HA is still possible through some simple backup and restore processes that can be done manually or automatically through a third-party application.

Control-M node group

As we mentioned in the earlier part of this chapter, multiple Control-M/Agents can be grouped together into a node group for round-robin-based load balancing job submission. Node groups can also provide continues batch processing when one or more job execution nodes in the node group are unavailable. During such events, Control-M/Server will automatically skip the problematic nodes and perform load balanced job submission on rest of the available Control-M/Agents. Once the failed node(s) are restored, Control-M/Server will automatically take them back into consideration again during the next job submission.

Node group technology is used to achieve continuous batch processing as an alternative to configuring Control-M/Agents with operating system clustering. In order to use this technology, each machine within the node group needs to pre-set up with similar characteristics to handle the submission of jobs, such as being able to access the common database, having the same user defined operating system for job execution, and being able to read and write a shared disk drive for the job's input and output. On the other hand, the batch jobs need to be **MSA (Multi-Server Architecture)** compliant so they can be executed on any of the machines within the node group to produce the consistent outcome.

Control-M does not have a limit for the number of nodes defined in a node group. It is a good practice to create a node group even for a single node and define jobs to be scheduled to the node group name. By doing so, the user can add, change, or remove job execution nodes to the node group without the need of modifying the job definition.

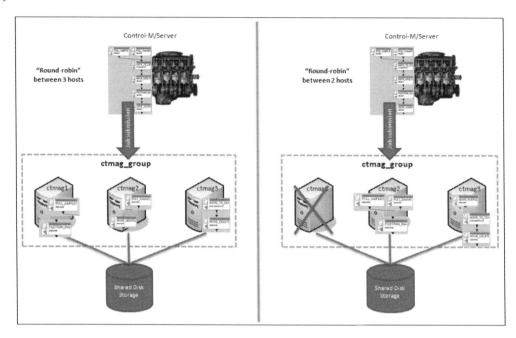

High availability by virtualization technology

Virtualization Technology offers a simple and cost-effective high availability solution, and at the same time, it dynamically increases the IT environment's hardware utilization. As organizations are starting to transform their physical servers into virtual machines, it is worthwhile to consider implementing the Control-M applications on virtual machines to save physical machine cost and at the same time achieve cost-efficient high availability.

If the virtualized environment is configured properly, Control-M components are no longer required to be installed on two or more machines for each instance. Instead, a virtual machine image holds the Control-M installation that will be stored on a shared storage and gets activated on a physical machine's virtual environment. In the event of the physical machine's failure, the machine image imminently gets restarted on the next available physical machine. The entire restart process is done automatically by the virtualization management software, which does not require going through complex failover steps and can be totally transparent to the end user or its client machines.

New features offered by the virtualization technology could even offer live migration of a virtual image from one physical machine to another without impacting the Control-M applications running. For example, by using VMware's VMOTION technology, users can schedule maintenance to the hardware at any time without worrying about interrupting the batch environment. It is also useful when virtual image migration is required because a potential problem or capacity issue is detected with the current physical machine.

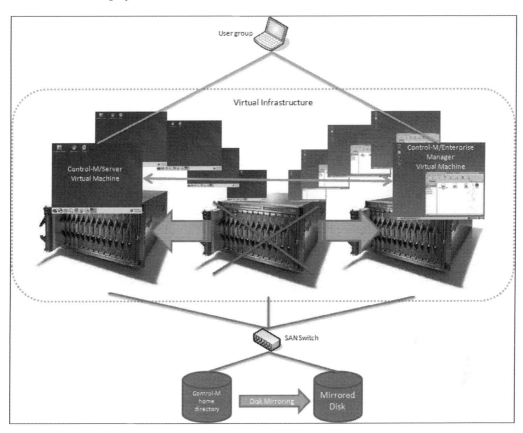

Virtualization technology offers a similar high availability standard as traditional operating system cluster, but with much less cost and more flexibility. However, before we decide to implement Control-M into a virtual environment, load simulation testing should be performed to ensure that the **Virtual Infrastructure** can produce similar performance as if running it on a physical machine and the storage shared across many virtual machines should provide a sufficient and consistent performance for Control-M application.

Pre-installation technical considerations

By now, we should have a rough idea about what the future batch environment will be like – estimated amount of jobs, how many Control-M/Servers, how many Control-M/Agents, Agentless Technology that will or will not be used, which high availability solution will be selected, and so on. It is necessary to document everything and keep it as a standard for future expansion of the environment, but before the actual installation starts, we also need to make sure the machines are meeting the Control-M pre-installation technical requirements.

Environment compatibility

Control-M components are designed to be installed on a wide range of computer system environment. Choosing the right operating system type, version, and machine architecture is the first step in building a stable Control-M batch environment. It is good to utilize the latest technology, but we must check the compatibility information listed on each product's release note or visit the **Product Availability Compatibility** (**PAC**) on the BMC software website for the latest supported operating systems, versions, and machine architecture before allocating system resources for any Control-M installation. In regards to Control-M products, BMC's website tends to be accurate and up-to-date and therefore can be well trusted.

Because the nature of Control-M/Agent is to maximize the scheduling capability of Control-M into diversified environments, it was made to support a much wider range of operating systems in comparison to what Control-M/Enterprise Manager and Control-M/Server can be running on. In case the operating system is not supported by the Control-M/Agent, a user can still consider the Agentless technology for remote job execution, as long as the remote host can support either SSH or WMI.

In most cases, Control-M installation script will detect the unsupported environment and exit with an error. Sometimes the installation may complete successfully on an unsupported environment, but that still doesn't mean the Control-M application will be running properly in the future. Installing Control-M components onto unsupported environments can cause unexpected behaviors during its running and voids the technical support from BMC Software for that installation. This is not a situation we want to end up with for a production system.

BMC Software provides a prerequisites verification program (`check_req` script) with each version of Control-M releases for checking Unix and Linux operating system compatibility for Control-M/Enterprise Manager and Control-M/Server. The script will verify the operating system's version, patches, kernel settings, hardware requirements, and user limit requirements and produce a compatibility report. It is compulsory to run the latest version of the script prior to each Control-M/Enterprise Manager or Control-M/Server installation and make sure that the script passes all its checking before starting the installation. For Windows platforms, the Control-M installation itself will perform the necessary checking prior to running the actual installation and will exit with meaningful messages if anything does not meet the requirement.

Choices of database

Control-M/Enterprise Manager Server Components and Control-M/Server can be installed on a BMC-provided database or a supported third-party database provided by the user's organization. With earlier versions of Control-M, Oracle and Sybase are shipped as part of the installation package. Many users chose to use them because they do not require additional licencing and they are designed to be easily installed together as part of the Control-M installation. In version 6.4.01, Sybse was no longer shipped with Control-M, instead PostgreSQL was introduced. Although, users still can use their own Sybase as long as the verison is supported. Again in verison 7, PostgreSQL is the only database shipped with Control-M installation package. The installation, by default, will install a new PostgreSQL database along with the product. With custom installation, the user still can choose to install the product with a database owned by the organization. Such third-party databases can be Oracle, Sybase, or MSSQL. User can aslo choose to install the product with an existing BMC-provided PostgreSQL database – as in sharing the database with another Control-M installation.

 For PostgreSQL databases, users must use the installation package supplied by BMC software as PostgreSQL versions that come with the operating system or are downloaded from the Internet are not supported by Control-M.

BMC software provides technical support to the databases that are supplied with Control-M and installed from the Control-M package. In case we are using a third-party database, we should always check the latest product release notes to make sure the desired database type, version, and OS platform combination is supported by Control-M. And, of course, the organization's DBAs will be in charge for the database's ongoing support and maintenance.

BMC software officially released a number of performance benchmark testing results based on different databases and OS combinations. In the report, PostgreSQL database in fact performed very well. However, it is still recommended to perform a number of tests to simulate the real production workload with different database combinations to compare the performance before making the decision.

 The report can be requested from BMC software technical support or the software consultant who is in charge of the region you located.

Sharing database between Control-M/Enterprise Manager and Control-M/Server can reduce maintenance overhead and at the same time improve machine utilization. For smaller environments, sharing a database between Control-M/Enterprise Manager and Control-M/Server may not be a bad idea, especially for users who would like to have Control-M/Enterprise Manager Server Components and Control-M/Server running on the same machine. However, for environments with large amount of jobs that require high throughput, it is sensible to have a database dedicated for each Control-M installation. When making such decisions, we should always take the batch environment's future growth into consideration.

System configuration requirements

The version 7 Control-M/Enterprise Manager, Control-M/Server, and Control-M/ Agent have their own specific requirements on how the system should be configured to accommodate them. In the past, there were significant numbers of users who missed out or simply ignored some of those requirements at the pre-implementation stage; they would be able to manage the Control-M application installed and running at the beginning, but ended up with obvious production problems a few months down the track.

Later in this chapter, we will be installing Control-M on both the Linux and Windows environment, so let's have a look at the requirements for each environment.

The up-to-date computer hardware and software requirements are listed in each product Release Notes which can be accessed from BMC securied website. For Unix and Linux machines apart from the usual requires, we also need to look at the kernel parameter settings and Control-M user account's user limits.

 In this section, the Control-M/Enterprise Manager is referring to the Control-M/Enterprise Manager server components.

 Control-M/Enterprise Manager GUI client components are Windows applications only.

Linux Kernel parameters

Below are the recommended kernel parameters for running Control-M applications in a Linux environment (with one instance of PostgreSQL database server). The recommendations for AIX, HP-UX, and Solaris are different, so please refer to the Control-M Installation guide if you are planning to install Control-M on those systems.

Shared memory

- SHMMAX (max shared memory segment size system wide): 600000000 bytes
- SHMMNI (max number of shared memory segments system wide): 800
- SHMALL (max number of shard memory pages system wide): >ceil(SHMMAX/PAGE_SIZE) or set it to 600000000, as recommended by BMC software

Semaphores

- SEMMNS (total number of semaphores system wide):
  - Control-M/Enterprise Manager with PostgreSQL: ≥800
  - Control-M/Enterprise Manager with other databases: Current value + amount required for database + 20
  - Control-M/Server with PostgreSQL: 800 + number of connected Control-M/Agents and Agentless remote hosts + number of connected Control-M/Agents with non-default configuration

- ○ Control-M/Server with other databases: Current value + amount required for database + 20 + number of connected Control-M/Agents and Agentless remote hosts + number of connected Control-M/Agents with non-default configuration
- ○ Control-M/Agent: Current value +1 for each instance installed

- SEMMNI (max number of semaphore sets system wide):
    - ○ Control-M/Enterprise Manager with PostgreSQL: ≥200
    - ○ Control-M/Enterprise Manager with other databases: Current value + amount required for database + 20
    - ○ Control-M/Server with PostgreSQL: 200 + number of connected Control-M/Agents and Agentless remote hosts + number of connected Control-M/Agents with non-default configuration
    - ○ Control-M/Server with other databases: Current value + amount required for database + 20 + number of connected Control-M/Agents and Agentless remote hosts + number of connected Control-M/Agents with non-default configuration
    - ○ Control-M/Agent: Current value +1 for each instance installed

- SEMMSL (max number of semaphores per semaphore set):
    - ○ Control-M/Enterprise Manager/Server with PostgreSQL: ≥150
    - ○ Control-M/Enterprise Manager/Server with other databases: ≥250

- SEMVMX (max value a semaphore can have): 32767 (system default)
- SEMOPM (max number of semaphore operation can be performed per *semop* system call): ≥100
- SEMMNU (maximum number of processes that can have undo operations pending on any given IPC semaphore): NPROC – 4 (maximum)
- `/proc/sys/fs/file`-max parameter (maximum number of file-handles that the Linux kernel will allocate): 256 for every 4 MB of physical RAM, for example, 2G*1024/4*256= 131072, or set it to ≥65535, as recommended by BMC software
- `/proc/sys/net/ipv4/ip_local_port_range` parameter (the local port range that is used by TCP and UDP traffic): 32768–61000

User limits

Unix/Linux user limits for Control-M/Enterprise Manager and Control-M/Server user accounts need to be set according to BMC recommendations before installation.

- `data` (max data size):
    - ○ AIX, Linux, and Solaris: 2 GB
    - ○ HP-UX: 4GB

- `core` (Core dump size): Same as data size
- `stack` (max stack size): 8MB
- `nofile` (max number of open files): 4096 (do not set the parameter equal value either equal to `/proc/sys/fs/file-max` or unlimited)
- `memlock` (max locked-in-memory address space, memory use): Unlimited
- `fsize` (max file size): Unlimited
- `nproc` (max number of processes): Unlimited

Other requirements

- Initial Shell types for user account:
    - ○ Control-M/Enterprise Manager: csh, tcsh, sh, or ksh
    - ○ Control-M/Server: csh or tcsh
    - ○ Control-M/Agent: csh, tcsh, sh, ksh, or bash

- Language: System locale is set to English before installation
- Other requirements:
    - ○ IPC (Internal Process Communication) subsystem is enabled
    - ○ Dedicated user account is created for each installation
    - ○ Java: JRE (Java Runtime Environment) 1.4.1 or above
    - ○ Preferably >500 MB free space in the `Temp` directory

Storage space related considerations for Control-M

When it comes to allocating disk space for Control-M/Enterprise Manager database, we need to understand that there can be many Control-M/Servers connecting to the same Control-M/Enterprise Manager. All jobs from each connected datacenter are uploaded into Control-M/Enterprise Manager. Therefore, the total number of jobs held by Control-M/Enterprise Manager is the total amount of jobs from each connected Control-M/Server. Even with a single Control-M/Server, the disk space for EM database should still be always bigger than the Control-M/Server database in order to store the additional amount of possible data. For example:

- Control-M/Enterprise Manager has a feature called Archive ViewPoint, which stores the old active environment for users to trace back past active jobs on a later day. The default value is two days, but some user may wants to increase that value to 10 days or even 30 days. Each Archive ViewPoint is a complete dump of the whole active environment of each day. It can take up a significant amount of database space. Imagine 30 days of Archive ViewPoint for five connected datacenters will be become at least 150 archive ViewPoints (plus five active ones) stored in the Control-M/Enterprise Manager database at all times (although it is not recommended to store that many days of Archive ViewPoints).

- The data apart from job definitions are possibly stored in Control-M/Enterprise Manager database, such as alerts, BIM, and Forecast data, global condition data, status of each Control-M component (for example, Control-M/Agent status), different versions of jobs (job version control data), auditing data, and so on.

- The Control-M/Enterprise Manager database should have room or can be increased to accommodate additional datacenters and job definitions in the future.

The same concern applies to Control-M/Server, but not as extreme. Control-M/Server keeps track of each job's status change in its database (for example, from ordered to wait for condition, from wait for resource to start execution, or from executing to ended successfully), this information is called **IOALOG** or **ctmlog** and can take up large amounts of database space, if there are a lot of activities happening in the environment. User can decide how many days of logs are to be kept. Obviously more jobs and more job state changes (cyclic jobs) will generate more logs. It is hard to estimate how big the log is going to be after the environment goes live and how big it's going to grow as the number of job starts to increase. The best we can do is always keep allocating additional space for the database or allow it to automatically grow to fulfill such needs.

Apart from the database size, the disk space allocation for each installation should always be more than the minimal requirement. Here are the reasons:

- Control-M processes produce logs while they are running. The logfiles are stored in the `proclog` directory within the installation folders. Sometimes the logfile can be large, especially when process debug is turned on. A busy environment can produce hundreds of megabytes of debug log within a few minutes. These debug logs may be required by BMC support when the Control-M application is experiencing technical problems and they are critical for troubleshooting. It is important to have enough disk space to store the growth of a normal log as well as additional disk space allowing a debug log to be generated, although in Unix/Linux environments the log directory can be configured to be a link to an NFS disk with much more free space. For Control-M/Agent, they should have a lot more disk space allocated than the 60 MB minimal requirement to store the job output (sysout) generated during their execution, as well as jobs that are executed on Agentless remote hosts which were submitted from this Control-M/Agent (that is, by default, remote execution jobs' sysouts are moved to the Agent machine and stored within the installation home directory). The size of job sysouts can vary, from a few kilobytes to hundreds of megabytes; it really depends on how the actual execution script is written. By saying that, Control-M has a parameter to set how many days of job sysouts are to be kept; anything older than the set value will be removed automatically during Control-M/Server's NDP. Therefore, the estimation of the disk space should be based on the average amount of sysouts generated per day. The number of times and the number of days sysout's record should be maintained. But the additional space for storing sysouts is of less concern if the user decides to redirect each job's sysout directly to a different location, and again in Unix/Linux environments, this folder can be configured to be a link to an NFS disk.

- For Control-M/Agents, it is also necessary to have additional disk space allocated for additional Control Module installation (for disk space requirement of each Control-M Control Module, please refer to the corresponding BMC product release note).

Firewall requirements

It is essential for organizations to configure a firewall in the entire IT infrastructure to prevent unauthorized network access and improve information security. Communications between Control-M components rely on TCP/IP network connections. Certain firewall ports need to be opened between computer systems to ensure such inter-component communication.

Between Control-M/Enterprise Manager Clients and Server Components

In *Chapter 2, Exploring Control-M*, we introduced the four Control-M/Enterprise Manager GUI client components, that is, Control-M/Enterprise Manager Client, Control-M/Desktop, Control-M Configuration Manager, and Reporting facility. These four GUI client components plus EM command-line utilities require communication with a number of Control-M/Enterprise Manager server components. Unless both client and server components are installed on the same machine (in a Windows environment), TCP ports need to be opened between the two machines to allow such communication.

Each of these client components initiates the connection by sending a request to the **Naming Service** residing on the Control-M/Enterprise Manager server. The **Naming Service** will use the same connection session to reply with the details of the desired component's connection. By default, the naming service is listening on **TCP Port 13075**.

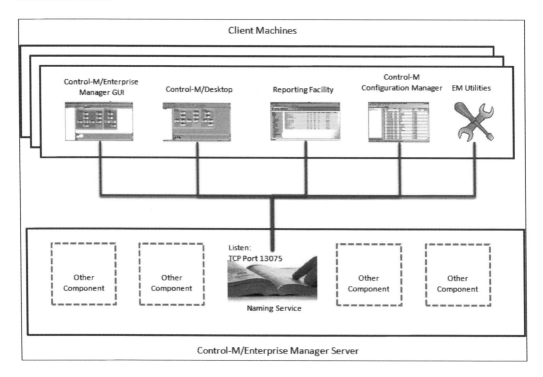

Once the client component receives the connection details from the **Naming Service**, it will connect to the desired server component directly. Such connections can happen between:

- Control-M/Enterprise Manager GUI Client and GUI Server (GSR)
- Control-M/Enterprise Manager GUI Client and BIM/Forecast Server
- Control-M/Desktop and GUI Server (GSR)
- Control-M/Desktop and BIM/Forecast Server
- Control-M Configuration Manager and Configuration Manager Server (CMS)
- Reporting Facility and GUI Server (GSR)
- Reporting Facility's built-in database client and the EM database server
- EM Utility and GUI Server (GSR)

Each server component will act as a CORBA server and listen on a TCP port for connections initiated by client components. Each of these ports is set to random by default, but when there's a firewall between the client components and server components, the listening port of each server component has to be set to a static port or a range of ports, so the corresponding ports can be opened on the firewall for such communication.

The communications between client components and server components can be a two-way communication, that is, when a request is sent from the client component's side, the server component that responds to the request may need to send information back to the requester (for example, displaying jobs, sending GUI action responses). In the recent releases of Control-M (based on CORBA 2.3), bidirectional communication is allowed and has been set by default. In such cases, no additional ports are required to be opened on the client side, and the server component will use the same communication session for return communication.

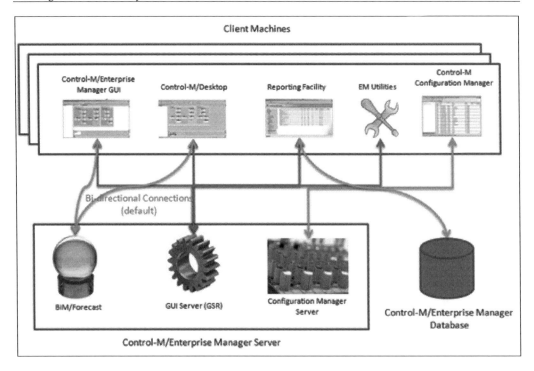

Between Control-M/Enterprise Manager Server Components and Control-M/Server

The communication between Control-M/Enterprise Manager Server Components and Control-M/Server is much simpler. Such a connection can happen between:

- Control-M/Server (CE process) and corresponding EM Gateway
- Control-M/Server **Configuration Agent (CA)** and **Configuration Manager Server (CMS)**

The communication between Control-M/Server CE process and EM Gateway is bi-directional from the perspective of TCP/IP and firewalls. CE process listens on one port (default is 2370).

The communication between Control-M/Server Configuration Agent (CA) and Configuration Manager Server (CMS) uses TCP port 2369 as the default bidirectional communication port.

Between Control-M/Server and Control-M/Agent

When introducing the Control-M/Agent processes in *Chapter 2, Exploring Control-M*, we already touched a topic related to communication between Control-M/Server and Control-M/Agent. The communication between Control-M/Server and Control-M/Agent is as follows:

- Control-M/Agent Listener (AG) process and Control-M/Server (NS process)
- OR, Control-M/Agent Router (AR) process and Control-M/Server (NS process)

In a transient connection mode, Control-M/Agent communicates with Control-M/Server using the Agent-to-Server port (default is 7005). And Control-M/Server communicates with Control-M/Agent using the Server-to-Agent port (default is 7006). Each time the requester will request a new connection for communication, such as Control-M/Server initiates a job submission request or Control-M/Agent communicates with Control-M/Server for job status update.

Persistent connection mode is provided for scenarios where the firewall rule is more restricted and only one-way communication can be enabled. In persistent connection, only a single bidirectional TCP connection is required between Control-M/Server and Control-M/Agent. The initial connection can be initiated by either Control-M/Server or Control-M/Agent and the connection stays on permanently, although for very strict firewall rules it can be restricted so only the Control-M/Server can initiate the persistent connection.

Agentless remote hosts

Control-M/Server submits jobs to the Agentless remote hosts through selected Control-M/Agents. The actual communication happens between the appointed Control-M/Agent and the destination remote host.

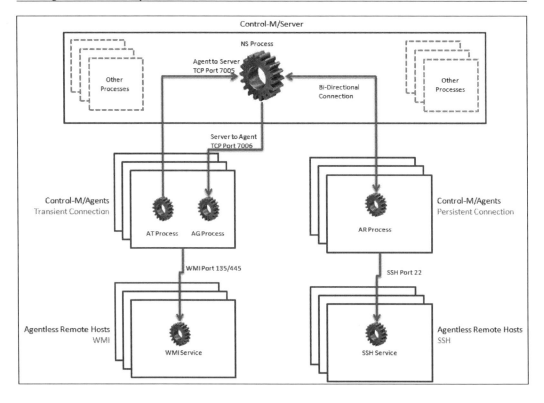

Recall what we have discussed in *Chapter 2, Exploring Control-M*. There are two types of connections between **Control-M/Agents** and **Agentless Remote Hosts**:

- **WMI** (Windows only): Requires TCP port 135 and 445
- **SSH/SFTP** (Unix/Linux or Windows): Requires TCP port 22

Database

In case the Control-M/Enterprise Manager or Control-M/Server is not installed on the same host with its database, the database listening port needs to be open on the firewall for database client access from the Control-M/Enterprise Manager or the Control-M/Server host. The default ports for databases are:

- **PostgreSQL: TCP Port 5432**
- **Oracle: TCP port 1521**
- **Sybase: TCP port 8760 and 8761**
- **MS-SQL: TCP port 1433**

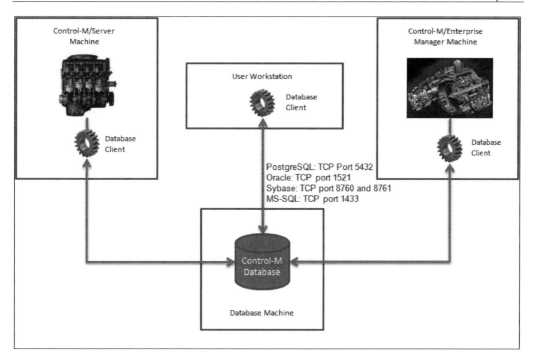

These ports also need to be opened to workstations if the users need access to the Reporting Facility or the administrator wishes to access the database from his or her own computer's database client software (for example, pgAdmin III).

Last things to make sure of before the installation starts

Assume now that we have the machine resources ready and fully configured to meet the Control-M installation requirements. It is worth spending a bit more time to review the following questions:

1. Have we checked the BMC website for operating system compatibility for each Control-M product we are going to install?

2. Have we downloaded the latest `check_req` script from the BMC website? It is a good habit to always double-check for new versions right before each install.

3. If we decided to use a third-party database provided by the organization, has the DBA prepared the database for us according to requirements? Do we have all the required access details for installation? Will someone from the DBA team provide assistance during the installation process?

4. Are the machine's hardware specifications meeting the minimal requirements? More importantly, are they going to be enough to handle future job growth?

5. Is there enough disk space allocated to store not only the application itself, but also other temp files, such as logs, job sysouts, and so on? Can it be quickly expanded if required? Or do I have an alternative location to archive such kind of data?

6. Is the Control-M/Enterprise Manager database going to be large enough to accommodate all the extra information that is going to be stored in its database, as we discussed earlier in the System configuration requirements section, as well as the number of days of archived viewpoint we require?

7. Have the user accounts and home directory (for Unix and Linux systems) been created for each installation? Have they been set to the correct initial shell?

8. Have we double-checked all the kernel parameters (for Unix and Linux systems) and user limits have been set according to requirements?

9. Can machines ping each other using an IP address and hostname? Have these hostnames been inserted into DNS or added into each local host file? Have all the required firewall ports been opened and tested? (Before requesting the firewall port be opened, it is necessary to make sure the default ports or the desired ports are not already being used on the machine.)

10. Have we documented everything about what we have done so far?

If answers for all the 10 questions are yes, it is then time to BEGIN!

Installation

The actual installation of Control-M version 7 is much more straightforward in comparison to the earlier versions. The installation can be performed in both interactive and silent mode. The interactive installation can be a menu or GUI-driven, depending on what component is installing and what type of operating system it is going to be installed on.

In Control-M 7, the three major components, that is, Control-M/Enterprise Manager, Server, and Agent are packaged into the same installation media. Between these three components, there is no rule for the sequence of the installation. We can decide the order based on our own preference. Other components such as Control Modules, BIM, or Forecast are supplied separately and are to be installed after the base components are configured. For example, Control Modules have to be installed after Control-M/Agent is installed, and Agentless remote hosts are to be defined only after Control-M/Server and Agents are both running.

From here, we are going to design a simple batch environment and build it from scratch. Although what we are going to implement is a very small environment compared to what Control-M is capable of, but is enough to demonstrate the idea behind different installation combinations.

Our batch environment includes the following components:

- Number of Microsoft Windows-based workstations with Control-M/Enterprise Manager GUI Client installed
- One Linux machine to hold the Control-M/Enterprise Manager server components and its PostgreSQL database
- A Control-M/Server instance shares the same machine resource and database with the Control-M/Enterprise Manager that it is connecting to
- Another Control-M/Server instance running on its own Microsoft Windows Server using a MSSQL database, connecting to the same Control-M/Enterprise Manager on the Linux machine
- Two standalone Control-M/Agents (one is running on a Microsoft Windows machine and the other one on a Linux machine)
- Two Agentless remote hosts, that is, one is Microsoft Windows-based and the other one is Linux-based
- A number of Control Modules will be installed on top of Control-M/Agents

Here's a list of the machines and components in a table format:

Machine Type	Hostname	Components Installed
Windows	-	Control-M/Enterprise Manager GUI client
Windows	-	Control-M/Enterprise Manager GUI client
Windows	ctm-demo-win-01	Control-M/Server and Agent
		Control-M for Database
		Control-M/Agent
Windows	ctm-demo-win-02	Control Module for AFT and Control-M for Cloud
Windows	ctm-demo-win-03	Agentless Host
Linux	ctm-demo-linux-01	Control-M/Enterprise Manager server components and PostgreSQL database
		Control-M/Server (share the PostgreSQL database with EM) and Agent
		Control Module for AFT

Machine Type	Hostname	Components Installed
		Control-M/Agent
Linux	ctm-demo-linux-02	Control–M Business Process Integration Suite
Linux	ctm-demo-linux-03	Agentless Host

And the logical diagram is shown in the following image:

(From here on, we will switch between Control-M/EM and Control-M/Enterprise Manager, Control Module, and CM.)

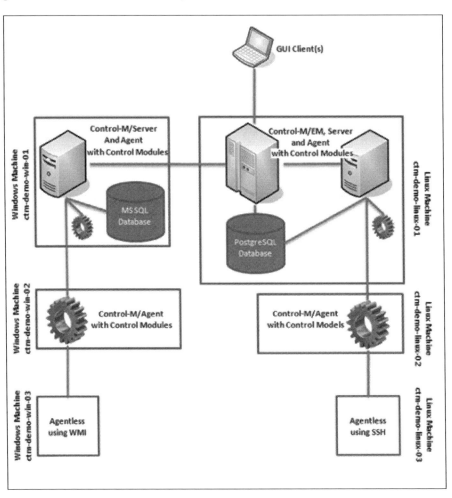

The sequence to our installation is shown in the following image:

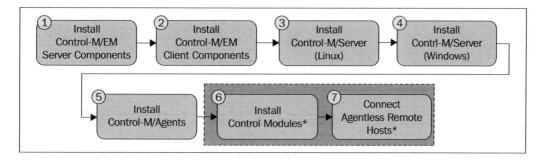

As mentioned earlier, there's no real requirement for the sequence of installation between most of the components. The reasons for us to decide such a sequence are:

- **For Control-M/Enterprise Manager**: During Client installation the installation wizard will ask for the server details and connect to it to verify the connection, although the installation can still continue to the end, even if the Control-M/EM server is not accessible.

- **For Control-M/Servers**: Control-M/Server installation does not ask for the details of Control-M/Enterprise Manager, but if the Control-M/Enterprise Manager Server/Client has already been set up, we can define (or discover) the Control-M/Server in Control-M Configuration Manager straightaway after the Control-M/Server installation is complete.

- **For Control-M/Agents**: Control-M/Agents can be installed before Control-M/Server. However, by doing the installations in our sequence, we can test the Server/Agent connection right after the Agent installation.

- **For Control Modules**: They have to be installed after Control-M/Agent.

- **For Agentless Remote Hosts**: They only can be defined after the Control-M/Server and the parent Control-M/Agent(s) are configured and connected.

In this chapter, we will only demonstrate Control-M installations of the three basic components in a standalone environment. Configuration of Control Modules and Agentless will be covered in *Chapter 5, Administrating the Control-M Infrastructure* and steps for implementing Control-M for high availability will be demonstrated in detail in *Chapter 7, Beyond Everyday Administration*.

Install Control-M/Enterprise manager server components

The general steps for installing Control-M/Enterprise Manager server components in a Linux environment is very similar to installing it in a Unix environment, except the preinstallation configuration items are slightly different.

The installation requires the following steps:

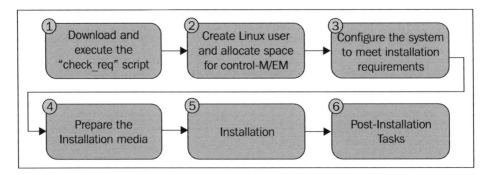

Download and execute the check_req script

The **"check_req" script** (Prerequisites verification) always comes with the installation media, but BMC software may update it from time-to-time to match any new operating system or new kernel release. As we mentioned earlier, it is better to download the latest version from the BMC FTP site every time before the installation.

 The location of the file can change; please refer to the latest version of the Control-M installation guide if the address above is no longer valid.

There should be at least two files within the `ftp` directory, that is, the script (`pre_req.tar.Z`) and a readme file (`README.TXT`). Once we download the latest `pre_req.tar.Z` file, transfer it onto a `Temporary` directory on the machine where the Control-M/Enterprise Manager server components will be installed. We place the `tar` file in the `temp` directory of the target machine **ctm-demo-linux-01**, untar it, and then run it from the root user.

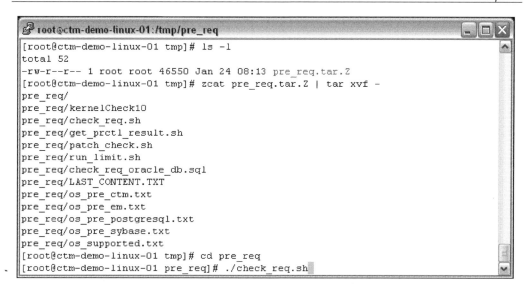

 If using an FTP client to do the transfer, make sure the FTP transfer is set to `binary` mode.

The script will ask us to select the database type that we are going to use for the Control-M installation; in our case, we select **3) PostgreSQL,** that is, a dedicated PostgreSQL Server.

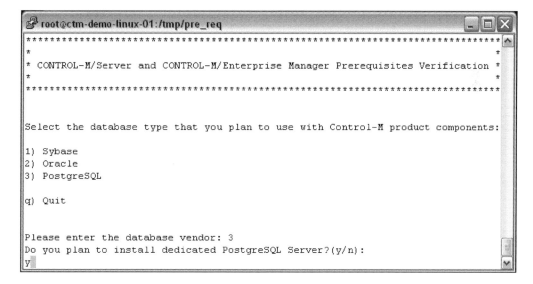

The script only takes a short time to execute and will return the outcome of the checking. In our demo environment, the checking was failed on **ctm-demo-linux-01** due to missing prerequisites. The missing items are:

- **"kernel.shmall" value** should be **higher or equal to 600000000**
- **"kernel.sem (semmni)" value** should be **higher or equal to 500**
- **"ulimit(NOFILES)" value** should be **higher or equal to 1024**
- **"ulimit(FILE)" value** should be **equal to unlimited**

Please note the "ulimits" check was checked against the system's wild user limit setting. We will only need to modify the "ulimits" for the Control-M/EM user, which we are going to create in the next session.

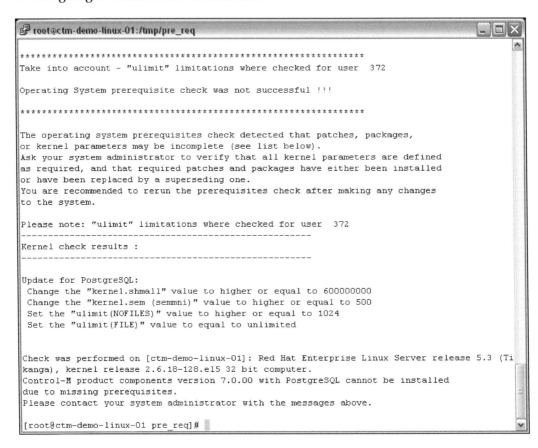

Alternatively, we may get the message - **You can install Control-M Product**. Obviously, it indicates that the system passed the entire checking and it is ready for Control-M installation. However, we still want to check each configuration item against the recommendations to make sure the system is 100 percent optimized for Control-M.

Create a Linux user and allocate space for Control-M/EM

Before creating the Linux user, we want to get an idea about the filesystem structure to know where we should place the Control-M/EM home directory, so it can have enough disk space for installation and the database file. In a production Linux server, we often see multiple filesystems existing on the machine and the root directory always has its own dedicated filesystem which is around 300 MB to 500 MB. In such a case, it is important to place the Control-M/EM home directory under a larger filesystem rather than sharing the root directory, which eventually will be filled up and cause system errors. In our case, because it is a demo environment, there's only one large filesystem mounted on the root directory, so we will go ahead and create the user home directory under the same filesystem.

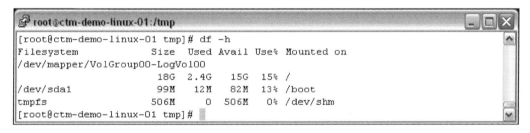

We are going to create the user with a default user ID and group. Alternatively, we can customize the user ID with the **-u** option and group with the **-p** option. We specify the username as **ctmem** with the home directory /opt/ctmem and the default shell /bin/csh. The **-m** option is used so the home directory will be automatically created with the user account.

After executing the command, we should change the default password and log in as the user to make sure the account has been created successfully. Run the **df-h** command to make sure the user is created under the desired filesystem with sufficient space to accommodate the Control-M installation and database.

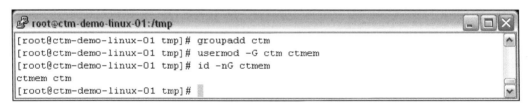

```
root@ctm-demo-linux-01:/tmp
[root@ctm-demo-linux-01 tmp]# useradd -d /opt/ctmem -s /bin/csh -m ctmem
[root@ctm-demo-linux-01 tmp]# passwd ctmem
Changing password for user ctmem.
New UNIX password:
Retype new UNIX password:
passwd: all authentication tokens updated successfully.
[root@ctm-demo-linux-01 tmp]# su - ctmem
[ctmem@ctm-demo-linux-01 ~]$ id
uid=500(ctmem) gid=500(ctmem) groups=500(ctmem) context=root:system_r:unconfined
_t:SystemLow-SystemHigh
[ctmem@ctm-demo-linux-01 ~]$ pwd
/opt/ctmem
[ctmem@ctm-demo-linux-01 ~]$ df -h .
Filesystem            Size  Used Avail Use% Mounted on
/dev/mapper/VolGroup00-LogVol00
                       18G  2.4G   15G  15% /
[ctmem@ctm-demo-linux-01 ~]$
```

Optionally, we can create a dedicated user group for this Control-M/EM account and other Control-M applications that are going to be installed on this machine. At the same time, we can also remove the user **ctmem** from unwanted groups.

```
root@ctm-demo-linux-01:/tmp
[root@ctm-demo-linux-01 tmp]# groupadd ctm
[root@ctm-demo-linux-01 tmp]# usermod -G ctm ctmem
[root@ctm-demo-linux-01 tmp]# id -nG ctmem
ctmem ctm
[root@ctm-demo-linux-01 tmp]#
```

Configuring the system to meet installation requirements

First of all, we will run some simple Linux commands to double-check if the system is meeting the Control-M hardware requirements.

- Command `less /proc/cpuinfo` shows the CPU information
- Command **free -m** shows the free memory and swap size in MB

We know from the output of **"check_req" script** that the **SHMALL** is currently smaller than the required amount, but before we modify the value, we may as well double-check all three shared memory kernel parameters. The current value of these kernel parameters are saved under the /proc/sys/kernel directory. We can **cat** each file and find out the current value of each parameter (for example, cat /proc/sys/kernel/shmall). From the output of the **cat** command, we noticed both **SHMMNI** and **SHMALL** are smaller than the recommended value. We can **echo** the recommended value into these files to make instant changes (for example, echo 600000000 > /proc/sys/kernel/shmall) or use the **sysctl** command to change the value (for example, sysctl -w kernel.shmall=600000000). In our case, we are going to make a permanent change by modifying the /etc/sysctl.conf file (reboot needed).

Please remember to back up the file every time before modifying it.

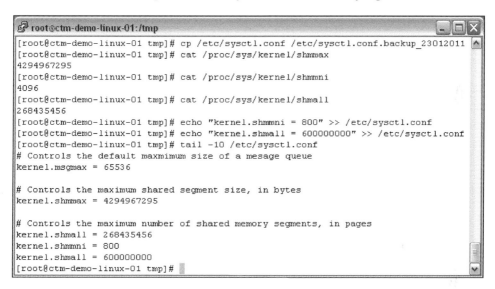

Now let's move onto semaphore parameters. The values of the semaphore parameters SEMMNS, SEMMNI, SEMMSL, and SEMOPM are stored in a single file called sem, again under the /proc/sys/kernel directory. We can **cat** the file to find out the current value and make permanent modifications by echoing the recommended value into the /etc/sysctl.conf file (reboot needed). The sequence of the four values is as follows:

1. SEMMSL
2. SEMMNS

3. SEMOPM

4. SEMMNI

```
root@ctm-demo-linux-01:/tmp
[root@ctm-demo-linux-01 tmp]# cat /proc/sys/kernel/sem
250     32000   32      128
[root@ctm-demo-linux-01 tmp]# echo "kernel.sem = 250 256000 100 1024" >> /etc/sysctl.conf
[root@ctm-demo-linux-01 tmp]# tail -10 /etc/sysctl.conf
kernel.msgmax = 65536

# Controls the maximum shared segment size, in bytes
kernel.shmmax = 4294967295

# Controls the maximum number of shared memory segments, in pages
kernel.shmall = 268435456
kernel.shmmni = 800
kernel.shmall = 600000000
kernel.sem = 250 256000 100 1024
[root@ctm-demo-linux-01 tmp]#
```

The next thing we need to work on is the user limits for the Control-M/EM user. First of all, we can log on as the user **ctmem** and run the command `ulimit -a` to find out the current user limits. After that, we need to log on as root to change the limits by modifying the `/etc/security/limits/conf` file. In this file, we will set both the **soft** and **hard** limit for the user **ctmem** to the recommended values. After the modification is done, we can log on to the user **ctmem** and run the command `ulimit -a` again to verify that the change has taken effect. .

```
root@ctm-demo-linux-01:/tmp
[root@ctm-demo-linux-01 tmp]# vi /etc/security/limits.conf
#         - priority - the priority to run user process with
#         - locks - max number of file locks the user can hold
#         - sigpending - max number of pending signals
#         - msgqueue - max memory used by POSIX message queues (bytes)
#         - nice - max nice priority allowed to raise to
#         - rtprio - max realtime priority
#
#<domain>      <type>   <item>         <value>
#

#*             soft     core           0
#*             hard     rss            10000
#@student      hard     nproc          20
#@faculty      soft     nproc          20
#@faculty      hard     nproc          50
#ftp           hard     nproc          0
#@student      -        maxlogins      4

ctmem         soft     data           2097152
ctmem         soft     core           2097152
ctmem         soft     stack          8192
ctmem         soft     nofile         4096
ctmem         soft     memlock        unlimited
ctmem         soft     fsize          unlimited
ctmem         soft     nproc          unlimited
ctmem         hard     data           2097152
ctmem         hard     core           2097152
ctmem         hard     stack          8192
ctmem         hard     nofile         4096
ctmem         hard     memlock        unlimited
ctmem         hard     fsize          unlimited
ctmem         hard     nproc          unlimited

# End of file
```

Don't forget to check the value of the parameters `/proc/sys/fs/file-max` and `/proc/sys/net/ipv4/ip_local_port_range`. Simply **cat** each file and make sure they are meeting the recommendation.

```
root@ctm-demo-linux-01:/tmp
[root@ctm-demo-linux-01 tmp]# cat /proc/sys/fs/file-max
102279
[root@ctm-demo-linux-01 tmp]# cat /proc/sys/net/ipv4/ip_local_port_range
32768   61000
[root@ctm-demo-linux-01 tmp]#
```

Once everything is done, we need to reboot the system for the configurations we have done earlier to take effect. After the reboot is completed, we can run the **pre_req** script again, just to make sure everything passes the checking.

Preparing the installation media

The installation can be done from a physical installation media or using ISO files downloaded from the BMC EPD site. Physical installation media need to be preordered from BMC software or burned from the ISO file. In most cases, the server is located in a remote location, such as in a datacenter or in the cloud. It is much easier for users to transfer the ISO image file onto the server using FTP or SFTP, rather than physically getting to the server location and loading the CD. As the network speed has been increased in the last few years, more and more people prefer to install from the ISO file.

The Control-M 7 (BMC combined Control-M/Enterprise Manager) and Control-M/Server installation are placed into a single ISO image. The image also contains installation files for the PostgreSQL database. For Linux installations, there are two different images, one for 32 bits and one for 64 bits. For our installation, we will use the 32 bits installation ISO image – `DROST.7.0.00_Linux-i386.iso`.

We can place the ISO file at a temp location such as `/tmp` and mount it to the desired mount point by the root user.

```
root@ctm-demo-linux-01:/media/iso
[root@ctm-demo-linux-01 /]# cd media
[root@ctm-demo-linux-01 media]# mkdir iso
[root@ctm-demo-linux-01 media]# mount -o loop /tmp/DROST.7.0.00_Linux-i386.iso /media/iso
[root@ctm-demo-linux-01 media]# ls -l
total 2
drwxrwxrwx 4 root root 2048 Sep  5 18:24 iso
[root@ctm-demo-linux-01 media]# cd iso
[root@ctm-demo-linux-01 iso]# ls -l
total 17
drwxrwxrwx 2 584 324  2048 Sep  5 17:19 pre_req
drwxrwxrwx 7 584 324  4096 Sep  5 17:19 setup_files
-r-xr-xr-x 1 584 324 10629 Aug  8 21:00 setup.sh
[root@ctm-demo-linux-01 iso]# pwd
/media/iso
[root@ctm-demo-linux-01 iso]#
```

Installation

So far, we have the user created system, configured according to recommendation, and also the installation media is ready to be used. The installation gets carried out by the **setup.sh** script located in the installation source file directory. The user interface of the installation can be graphical or non-graphical. The menu-driven non-graphical mode installation is the traditional way of installing Control-M components on the Unix/Linux environment. We will use the non-graphical mode for this installation, as we will have the chance to experience the graphical interface later on during Windows installation.

For graphical installation, the **$DISPLAY** environment variable needs to be set before starting the installation.

By doing a non-graphical installation, we can record the entire installation process by using **typescript**; simply run the `script` command before executing the **setup.sh** script and run the `exit` command to quit the **typescript** after installation. By doing so, we will have a complete history of the installation process for future reference.

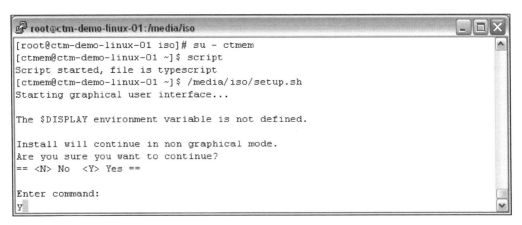

After we agree with the Software License Agreement, we will get to choose what installation we would like to perform. We will select **Control-M specific component | Control-M | Enterprise Manager 7.0.00**. If we go ahead with the default **#1 Control-M 7.0.00** installation option, Control-M/EM, Server and Agent will be installed at once under the same username together with a single PostgreSQL database shared between Control-M/EM and Server.

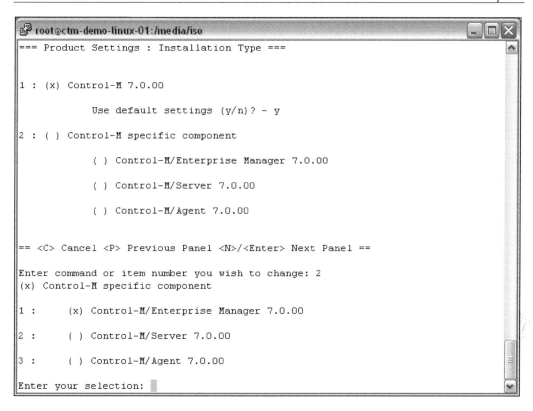

In the **Setup Type** panel, we have an option to customize the installation settings. By choosing this option, we get to see the default value of each item, but this does not necessarily mean we have to change them.

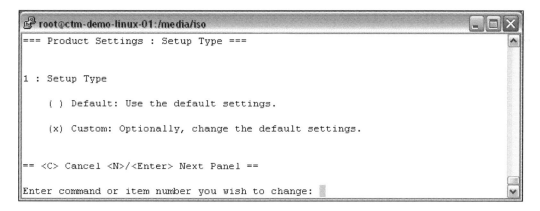

In the **Database Server Type** panel, we leave the default setting to **PostgreSQL** database.

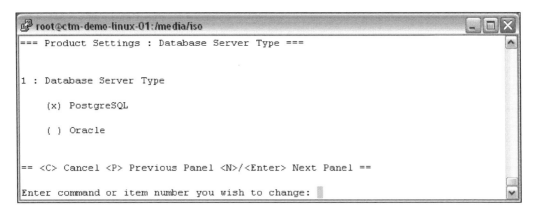

We will install a BMC-supplied PostgreSQL database server dedicated to this Control-M/EM.

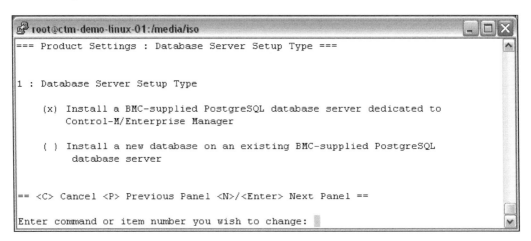

In the **Database Advance Parameters** panel, confirm the **Host interface name** and (PostgreSQL database) **Port number**. It is a good habit to run the Linux command `netstat` from another terminal to make sure the port number is not used by another application (for example, `netstat -na | grep 5432`).

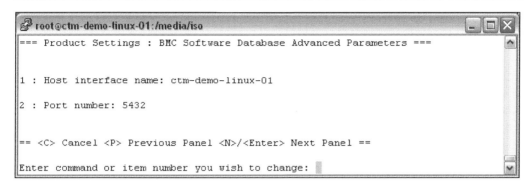

Now, type in the **Database owner password** (DBO) and **Database administrator password** (SA). Make a note of the passwords, because later on we will be using the DBO username and password to log into the GUI client and execute EM utilities. The SA password will be used again during Control-M/Server installation.

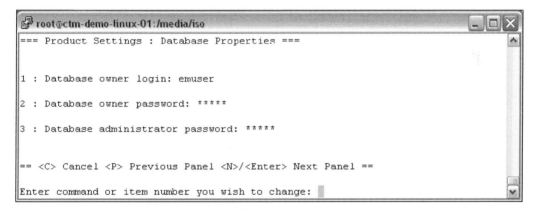

In the **Database Properties** panel, we need to confirm the database name, database size, and the data and system directory full path, as well as the support for CJK (Language support for Chinese, Japanese, and Korean).

The database size should be chosen based on the currently estimated amount of job plus the projection of future job growth even though the PostgreSQL database tablespace is set to **autogrow** by default. This is because Control-M will adjust the internal database parameters according to the selection we made here; if **Small** is selected, most of the performance-related database parameters are set to the amount that is most suitable for small databases (for example, PostgreSQL database server's shared_buffers size). Before selecting the database size, always make sure there is enough disk space on the machine.

Data directory full path is under the Control-M/EM user home directory by default. We can change it if needed, for example, we can place the datafile in a higher performance disk or on an SAN filesystem.

The support for CJK means the database will allow double bytes characters in Chinese, Japanese, and Korean to be stored, such as job descriptions and shout messages. In our case, we will leave it as **no**.

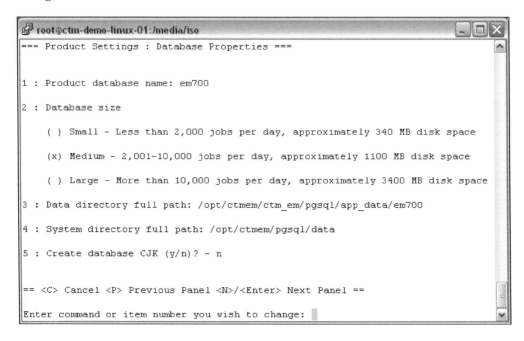

The next panel requires us to specify the CORBA port and the Control-M Web Server port. By default, these ports are **13075** and **18080** respectively. Again, we should run `netstat` from another terminal just to make sure the port numbers are not used by another application.

By now, we have all settings confirmed and ready to start the installation. The installation script provides a configuration summary in the **Summary** panel. We can copy and paste the information down or otherwise retrieve it later from our **typescript**. Once all is confirmed, we can press *I* or *Enter* to start the installation.

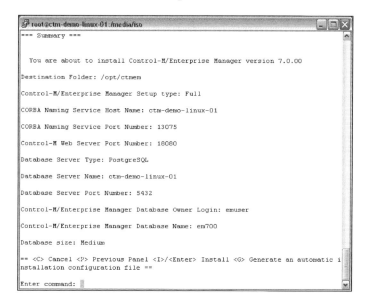

On an average machine, the installation process would take about 5-10 minutes. It populates lines of information on the screen to tell us what is happening in the background. Once completed, we will see a message similar to the following image:

```
root@ctm-demo-linux-01:/media/iso
=== Installation ===

[ Starting to unpack ]
[ Processing package: Control-M/Enterprise Manager Server files ]
[ Processing package: Configure PostgreSQL Server ]
[ Processing package: Configure Control-M/Enterprise Manager ]
[ Processing package: Create User Data directory ]
[ Processing package: Configure Control-M/Enterprise Manager postgreSQL configur
ation ]
[ Processing package: Configure database schema ]
[ Processing package: Creating DB version description file ]
[ Processing package: Configure Control-M Web Server ]
[ Processing package: Configure Control-M/Enterprise Manager ]
[ Processing package: Starting Control-M/Enterprise Manager ]
[ Processing package: Write uninstaller ]
[ Unpacking finished ]

=== Installation Result - Success ===


Installation has completed successfully.

Supplementary information:

To start working with Control-M/Enterprise Manager 7.0.00, you must close
 the current session and open a new one.


[ctmem@ctm-demo-linux-01 ~]$
```

Post-installation tasks

Now we can complete the typescript by typing **exit** and a file called typescript will be created under the Control-M/EM user's home directory.

Once we log out and re-log in as the **ctmem** user, all environment variables added by the installation will become valid. We can check it by using the env command.

Control-M/EM installation starts the following components upon its completion:

- PostgreSQL Database
- CORBA Naming Server
- Control-M/EM Configuration Agent
- Control-M Configuration Server

We can verify the status of these components by running the **check_all** utility as Control-M/EM user. The **check_all** utility will ask for the Control-M/EM DBO username and password that we specified during the installation. We will notice that the **check_all** utility also checks the status of all other EM components, including GCS, GUI_Server, GAS, BIM, and so on. These components are to be started manually through the Control-M Configuration Manager, which will be configured after our Control-M/EM client installation in the next session. At this stage, we should see the **check_all** script output telling us that the CMS, Control-M/EM Configuration Agent, and Naming Service are the only three running components. From the output, we can also see the TCP port number that the Naming Service is currently listening on, which is what we specified during installation (default value – 13075).

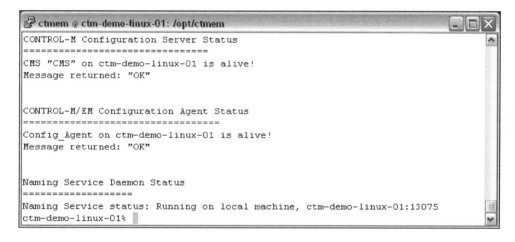

We will keep these processes running as they are and come back to this machine later for the Control-M/Server installation.

Install Control-M/Enterprise manager clients

The Control-M/Enterprise Manager Client we are going to install in this section will be connecting to the Server components that we installed in the previous section. This installation is much simpler; as long as we have the connection details ready, it is just like installing any other Windows-based application (click on the **Next** button).

To keep things simple, at this stage, we would assume there is no firewall between the Control-M/EM server component host and the client host. Each component currently is, by default, listening on a random port for a client connection, apart from the naming service which listens on the fixed port 13075. We will talk about how to define a fixed port/port range for each Control-M/EM server component during *Chapter 5*, *Administrating the Control-M Infrastructure*.

Preparing the installation media

Again with the Control-M/Enterprise Manager client installation, we have the choice to install from a physical media or install using the ISO file downloaded from the BMC EPD site. In our case, we will continue to use the ISO file. The file for the Windows installation is called `DROST.7.0.00_Windows.iso`. It contains the Control-M/EM full installation for Windows (server components and client components), Control-M/Server for Windows, and Control-M/Agent for Windows.

Windows machines do require third-party software to read the ISO file. There are many software packages out on the Internet, such as DAEMON Tools or PowerISO. With these tools, we have the choice to unpack the ISO file into a directory or mount the image onto a virtual CDROM provided by the tool.

Installation

Once we have the ISO unpacked or mounted, we can simply run the `setup.exe` located in the root directory to start the graphical installation.

Because the installation package contains the full Control-M suite, it will start by asking us which product to install. We select **Control-M/Enterprise Manager Client 7.0.00**.

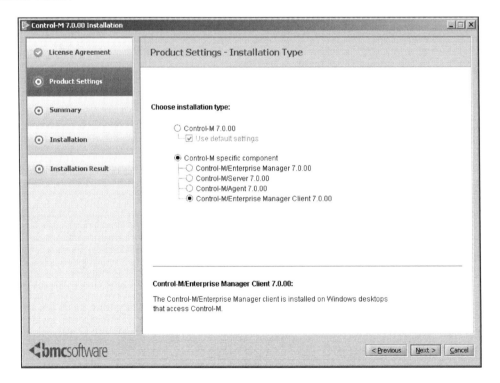

After clicking on the **Next** button, it will ask for the **Installation path, Naming service host name**, and **Naming service port number**. The **Naming service host name** is the server hostname, which we saw during the Control-M/EM server components installation earlier on (where the naming service is currently running) and the port number is the port currently listening by naming service; in our case, it is the default port – **13075**.

Before continuing, we should make sure the naming service host name can be resolved in this machine either by DNS or the local host file. Also, we need to make sure the TCP port **13075** has been opened if there is a firewall in-between the server and client machines. We can click on the **Test** button to verify the connection, but the testing may fail if ping is blocked between the two machines.

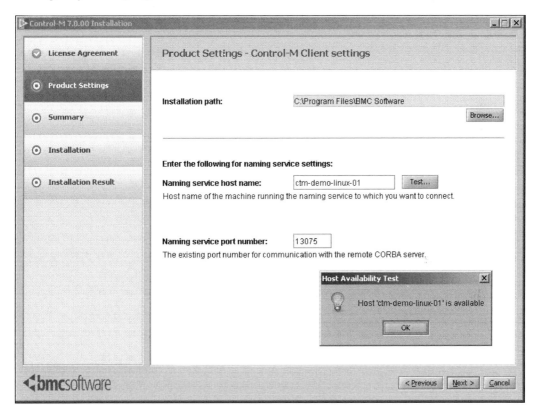

After clicking on the **Next** button, the installation will give us a configuration summary. We will notice there is an entry that says **Control-M/EM instance name: Default**. This means we are installing the first Control-M/EM on this workstation; when more than one installation is installed, each of these additional instances will be known with an instance name, which is to be specified during installation (Control-M installation will only ask for an instance name if the default instance has already been installed). We have the option to generate an **Automate installation file** for silent installs (on other machines in the future). Silent install is another method of installation for Control-M components, which will be covered in *Chapter 6, Advanced Batch Scheduling and Management*. For now, we will click on the **Install** button to start the installation.

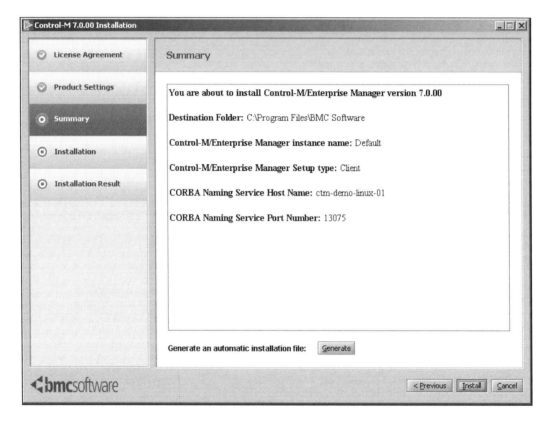

After coming back from a cup of coffee, we should see an **Installation has completed successfully** message and four new icons should be created on the desktop.

Post-installation tasks

If we first click on the **Control-M/Enterprise Manager** (GUI client) icon (the green icon), we will see that the **Server** field in the logon window is empty. This is because the Control-M/EM GUI client tries to talk to the GUI server process located on the Control-M/EM server, which hasn't been defined yet. The GUI server and other components are to be defined through **Control-M Configuration Manager** (we will call it **CCM** from now on). So the first thing to do right after the installation is to start the CCM and define those missing components.

After clicking on the **CCM** icon, we will see that the **server** field is populated with the Control-M/EM server hostname. Because we haven't got any user accounts defined yet, we will use the only valid user account – Control-M/EM DBO's username and password to get into the program. Upon successful authentication, CCM will prompt us with a message asking if we would like to define the GUI server, GCS, and GAS.

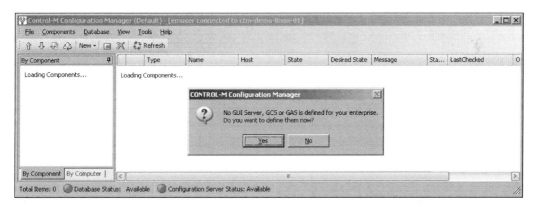

By clicking on the **Yes** button, CCM will create the three components by using the default value and registering them into the Control-M/EM database. Imminently, the three components are shown in the list with **State** as **Down** and **Desired State** as **Up**. Meanwhile, on the Control-M/EM server side, the configuration agent is trying to start each component according to the **Desired State**. Within one-two minutes, we should see each component's **State** become **Up**.

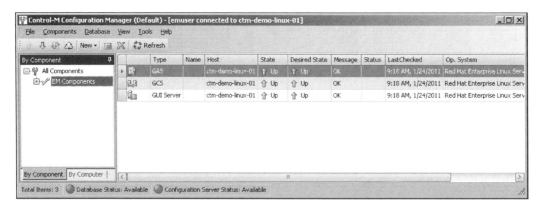

Now if we click on the **Control-M/Enterprise Manager** (GUI client) icon again, we will be able to see the **Server** field populated with the GUI server name. By using the **emuser** account, we are able to log into both Control-M/Enterprise Manager (GUI client) and Control-M/Desktop. Before we get into the details of the GUI features, let's begin the Control-M/Server installation.

Installing Control-M/Server

In this section, we will install two Control-M/Servers, one in the Linux environment (ctm-demo-linux-01) and one in the Windows environment (ctm-demo-win-01). As Control-M/Server version 6.3.01, a Control-M/Agent will also be installed by default as part of each Control-M/Sever installation.

Installation in Linux environment

The steps for installing Control-M/Server in a Linux environment are very similar to the Control-M/Enterprise Manager server components installation we did earlier.

The installation requires the following steps:

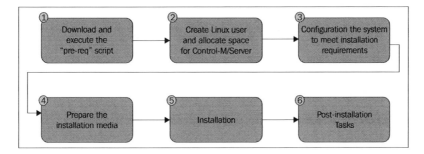

Pre-installation

In Control-M version 7, the prerequisites verification checking applies to both Control-M/Enterprise Manager and Control-M/Server. As this Control-M/Server is going to be installed on the same machine where we installed the Control-M/Enterprise Manager server components earlier, we don't have to rerun the **check_req** checking for this installation unless we are planning to implement the Control-M/Server with a different type of database, such as Oracle or Sybase.

 In such cases, simply rerun the script by root and select the desired database type at the beginning.

Control-M/Server also requires its own user account. After creating the new account, we can let it be part of the dedicated Control-M application group, which we created earlier during the Control-M/EM installation.

```
root@ctm-demo-linux-01:/tmp
[root@ctm-demo-linux-01 tmp]# useradd -d /opt/ctmsrv -s /bin/csh -m ctmsrv
[root@ctm-demo-linux-01 tmp]# passwd ctmsrv
Changing password for user ctmsrv.
New UNIX password:
Retype new UNIX password:
passwd: all authentication tokens updated successfully.
[root@ctm-demo-linux-01 tmp]# su - ctmsrv
[ctmsrv@ctm-demo-linux-01 ~]$ id
uid=501(ctmsrv) gid=502(ctmsrv) groups=502(ctmsrv) context=root:system_r:unconfi
ned_t:SystemLow-SystemHigh
[ctmsrv@ctm-demo-linux-01 ~]$ pwd
/opt/ctmsrv
[ctmsrv@ctm-demo-linux-01 ~]$ df -h .
Filesystem            Size  Used Avail Use% Mounted on
/dev/mapper/VolGroup00-LogVol00
                       18G  2.9G   14G  18% /
[ctmsrv@ctm-demo-linux-01 ~]$ exit
logout
[root@ctm-demo-linux-01 tmp]# usermod -G ctm ctmsrv
[root@ctm-demo-linux-01 tmp]# id -nG ctmsrv
ctmsrv ctm
[root@ctm-demo-linux-01 tmp]#
```

We have already done most of the items related to system configuration during the Control-M/EM installation, but we still need to define the limits for the user **ctmsrv**, as well as review semaphore configurations (if Control-M/Server installation wasn't taken into consideration earlier).

Installation

We run the same **setup.sh** script as we did earlier to start the installation in non-graphical mode. This time, we select "**Control-M/Server 7.0.00**" | **Custom** | **PostgreSQL**. However, in the **Database Server Setup Type** panel, rather than going ahead with installing a dedicated database, we select **Install a new database on an existing BMC-supplied PostgreSQL database server**. By doing so, the installation later on will ask us for the details of the existing database server and create a database within it for our new Control-M/Server.

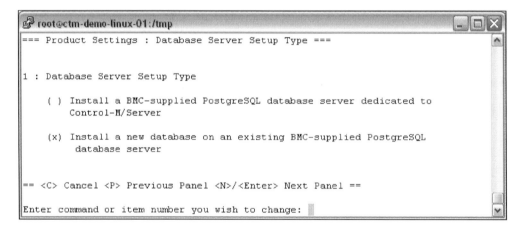

In the **Database Advanced Parameters** panel, the installation needs to identify the database's hostname and listening port number. In our case, the hostname is the local machine hostname and the port number is what we specified for the database during Control-M/EM installation.

In the first **Database Properties** panel, we get to choose the DBO username (default ctmuser) and password for the Control-M/Server database. The DBA password is what we specified earlier during the Control-M/EM (with new database server) installation. Basically, the installation later on will use the connection details and the DBA password to connect the database server in order to create a new database for our Control-M/Server.

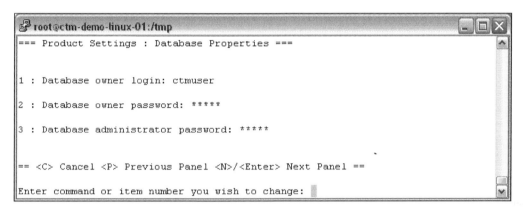

The second **Database Properties** panel will ask us for the database name, data directory path, and whether or not to create the database with CJK support.

The default database name for Control-M/Server version 7 is **ctmrlm700**. We can change it to whatever we want, as long as it is not the same name as the Control-M/EM database or any other existing database within the database server.

Data directory is where the database stores the Control-M/Server database tablespace data file. Before entering the location, we should always make sure that there is sufficient space on the target filesystem to accommodate the initial data size as well as potential growth. Unlike the full database installation, with this one (existing database installation), the installation does not automatically create the directory that holds the datafile. For example, if we want to store the datafile in a directory called `ctrlm700` in the same parent directory where Control-M/EM database tablespace is stored, we have to manually create the directory before continuing with the installation. If we decide to put the datafile under Control-M/Server's home directory or any other directory, we need to make sure Control-M/EM user account has read and write permission to the directory. This is because the datafiles are actually created and accessed by the PostgreSQL server process that is running as a Control-M/EM user.

Generally speaking, what we want to do for this scenario is considered as the best practice – put the Control-M/Server datafiles in the same root path as Control-M/EM datafiles are, but under a dedicated folder.

```
root@ctm-demo-linux-01:/tmp
=== Product Settings : Database Properties ===


1 : Product database name: ctrlm700

2 : Data directory full path: /opt/ctmem/ctm_em/pgsql/app_data/ctrlm700

3 : Create database CJK (y/n)? - n


== <C> Cancel <P> Previous Panel <N>/<Enter> Next Panel ==

Enter command or item number you wish to change:
```

The next panel allows us to specify Control-M/Server-related configurations, including:

- **Local IP host interface name**: This is the hostname that Control-M/Server and the default Control-M/Agent will be known as. It should be what the machine is known as, by itself and by others.

- **Control-M/EM TCP/IP port number**: This is the port number that Control-M/Server is listening on for the Control-M/EM gateway connection. Recall what we have discussed earlier: Control-M/Server actually uses two TCP ports for such communication; the second one is the port number we specified plus one. In our case, we use the default value 2370, which means Control-M will be listening on both 2370 and 2371. It is important to ensure both ports are not already being used on the machine (the installation will also check to make sure both the ports are available).

- **Internal process communication (IPC) port number**: As we discussed in *Chapter 2, Exploring Control-M*, this port is listened by the Control-M/Server RT (Communication Router) process to allow communication between all other Control-M core processes. There will be no connection requests coming from outside the machine to this port.

- **Configuration agent port number**: This is the port that is going to be listened by the Control-M/Server CA (Configuration Agent) process for a connection coming from the Control-M/EM CMS (Configuration Manager Server) process.

- **Agent-to-Server port number**: This is the port number listened by the Control-M/Server NS (Agent Communication) process for communication requests coming from each Control-M/Agent.

- **Server-to-Agent port number**: This port is not listened by Control-M/ Server. This is the default port number that Control-M/ Server will use to communicate with each Control-M/Agent. In special cases, Control-M/ Agents, which would be connecting to this Control-M/Server in the future, should follow (set to listen on) the port number we set here. Otherwise, change it to whatever the majority of Control-M/Agents will be listening on. In addition, the Control-M/Agent that comes with the installation will be listening on the port number we specified here.

```
root@ctm-demo-linux-01:/tmp
=== Product Settings : Control-M/Server Configuration ===


1 : Local IP host interface name: ctm-demo-linux-01

2 : Control-M/EM TCP/IP port number [1025-32767]: 2370

3 : Inter process communication port number [1025-32767]: 6005

4 : Configuration agent port number [1025-32767]: 2369

5 : Agent-to-Server port number [1025-65534]: 7005

6 : Server-to-Agent port number [1025-65534]: 7006


== <C> Cancel <P> Previous Panel <N>/<Enter> Next Panel ==

Enter command or item number you wish to change:
```

The installation will start once we confirm the summary page. From here on, the rest of the installation is automatic; it will print the completion status of each stage on the screen. The entire installation should take less than 15 minutes to complete.

```
root@ctm-demo-linux-01:/tmp
=== Installation ===


[ Starting to unpack ]
[ Processing package: Control-M/Server files ]
[ Processing package: Control-M/Agent files ]
[ Processing package: Configure Control-M/Server ]
[ Processing package: Configure Control-M/Server postgreSQL configuration ]
[ Processing package: Configure database schema ]
[ Processing package: Creating DB version description file ]
[ Processing package: Start Control-M/Server configuration-agent ]
[ Processing package: Configure Control-M/Agent ]
[ Processing package: Write uninstaller ]
[ Unpacking finished ]

=== Installation Result - Success ===


Installation has completed successfully.

Supplementary information:

To start working with Control-M/Server 7.0.00, you must close
 the current session and open a new one.


[ctmsrv@ctm-demo-linux-01 ~]$
```

Post-installation tasks

Same as what we did at the end of the Control-M/EM installation, after the installation is completed, we can exit the typescript, log out, and re-log in the Control-M/Server user to complete the installation.

Only the Control-M/Server CA process is being enabled automatically at the end of the installation, whereas the Control-M/Server core processes are still down at this moment. We can verify the status of Control-M/Processes by running the prf command (*Ctrl + C* to exit). We will see that both the **PROCSTAT** and **PSTAT_REQ** column for each process is marked as **T**. This means the current status and required status for these processes are currently terminated. We can run another command-line utility called show_ca to check the current status of our CA process. If the CA process is running, we will see a response with the process ID and listening port number.

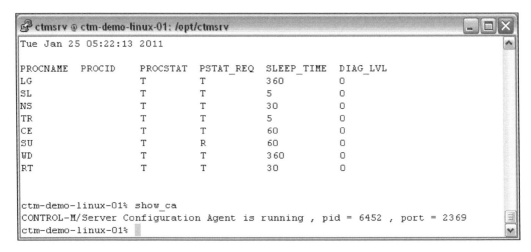

By having the CA process enabled, we can now discover and enable this Control-M/ Server from the Control-M Configuration Manager.

Back to the machine where we installed the Control-M/EM GUI client, we log on to CCM again and go to **Components | New | Control-M/Server and Gateway**, then choose **Discover*** in the pop-up window. The discover process is fairly simple.

First of all, we need to choose a logical **Control-M Name** and **Control-M ID** for the new Control-M/Server. **Control-M Name** later on will become the datacenter name of this Control-M/Server. **Control-M ID** is a three digit code to identify the Control-M/Server. CCM will populate a default ID value, but we can change it to anything we wish, as long as it hasn't been used by other Control-M/Servers. We also need to specify the **Control-M Host** name and the Control-M/Server's CA port number in order for CCM to discover the Control-M/Server. It is essential to make sure the Control-M/EM server component machine can communicate with the Control-M/Server machine by using the hostname we specified (either through DNS or local host file) and is able to access the port (that is, the firewall rule that has been set up for such access).

When we give a new **Control-M Name**, it is the best practice to give a logical name rather than the actual physical name of the Control-M/Server, for example, something such as CTMPROD or CTMSAP that describes what this Control-M/Server is used for, but not something like ctm-demo-linux-01. This is because, one day the ctm may move to a new server and we don't want to have to rename it in Control-M/EM at that time – such a name change will affect many things in Control-M such as job definitions and global condition settings. In our case, we will call it **CTM_LINUX** with three digits, **ID 001**.

The discover feature is based on mechanism between CMS and Control-M/Server CA process. Therefore, it is only available to versions of Control-M/Server which come with the CA process. The Control-M/Server CA process was first introduced in version 6.3.01.

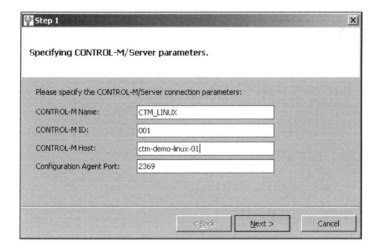

The discover process should be fairly quick; we should see the progress bar reach 100 percent shortly and an output that says **The Control-M/Server parameters were retrieved successfully**. After we click on the **Next** button, it will present us with a summary of our configuration parameters along with **Time zone**, **New day time**, and the **Control-M/EM Port number** values retrieved from the Control-M/Server. We keep the **Active Gateway** option checked by default so the gateway will be enabled and can connect to the Control-M/Server as soon as we click on the **Finish** button.

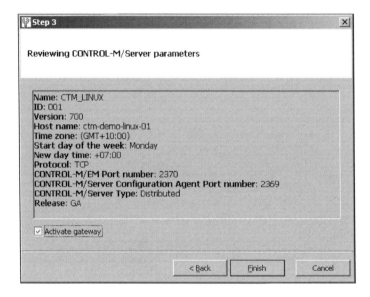

Now we should see two more roles appear in CCM, which are the new Control-M/Server and its gateway. At the beginning, the **Status** of these two items are **Unknown** and **Down** with the **Desired State** as **Up**. After a short time, we should see both statuses become **Up** and suddenly another item, namely, **Control-M/Agent**, appear with **State** as **Unavailable**. This is the default Control-M/Agent that is installed with our Control-M/Server, but it is being enabled.

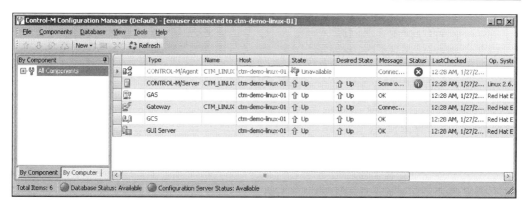

Since we are not at the stage to schedule any jobs yet, we will leave it as it is and move onto the next Control-M/Server installation.

Installation in a Windows environment

Installing Control-M/Server in a Windows environment is purely GUI based, but the steps and information required to fill in during installation are very similar to what we experienced in the Linux installation. Apart from our case, the database parameters are slightly different due to the fact that we are going to configure this Control-M/Server to use the existing MSSQL database.

Pre-installation tasks

The disk image we used for the Control-M/Enterprise Manager client installation (DROST.7.0.00_Windows.iso) also contains the installation of Control-M/Server for Windows. We can once again either unpack or mount the image by using one of the virtual disk tools we mentioned earlier.

As we are going to use the existing MSSQL database, we need to make sure the database is up and ready for use before the installation starts. Control-M version 7 supports MSSQL Server 2005 and 2008. On this machine (**ctm-demo-win-001**), we already have MSSQL 2008 installed and configured. In case the database server is on a different machine, we need to make sure the Control-M/Server host has a compatible version of the MSSQL database client installed and configured to talk to the remote database server. Of course, we need to provide the database port number and SA password during the Control-M/Server installation.

Installation

We execute the `setup.exe` file to start the installation, accept the license agreements, and select Control-M/Server 7.0.00 as the **installation type**. Again, Control-M/Agent is going to be installed with this Control-M/Server instance by default.

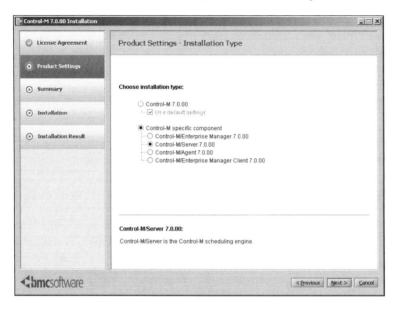

In **Setup Type**, we have to select **Custom**, otherwise the installation will automatically create Control-M/Server with a new PostgreSQL database.

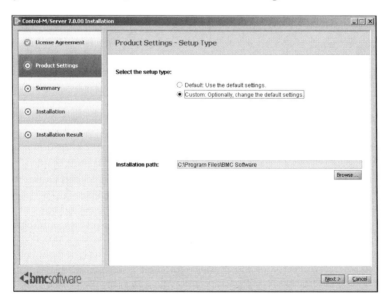

After we select MSSQL as the **Database Server Type**, the installation will ask for the MSSQL server hostname. In our case, it is the local machine.

 Please note the **Test** button only performs a ping to the host, rather than testing the actual connectivity with the MSSQL server.

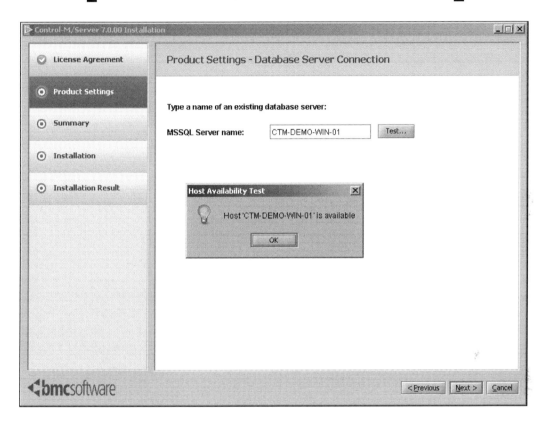

In the **Database Properties** page, we need to specify a DBO username and password for the new Control-M database. Database administrator username and password are also required in order to allow the installation to create the database in the MSSQL server.

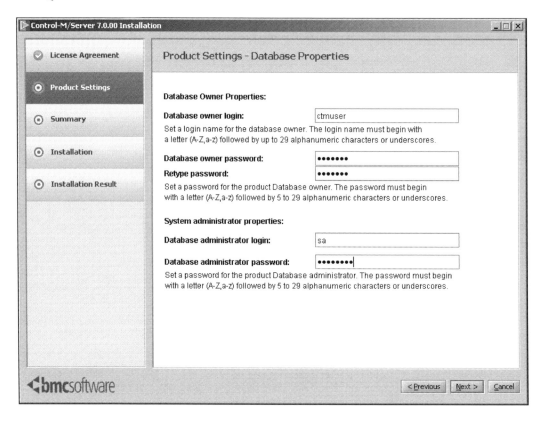

In the second page of **Database Properties**, we have to do the same as we did during the Control-M/EM server components installation – we need to specify the database size according to the estimated number of jobs as well as the database name.

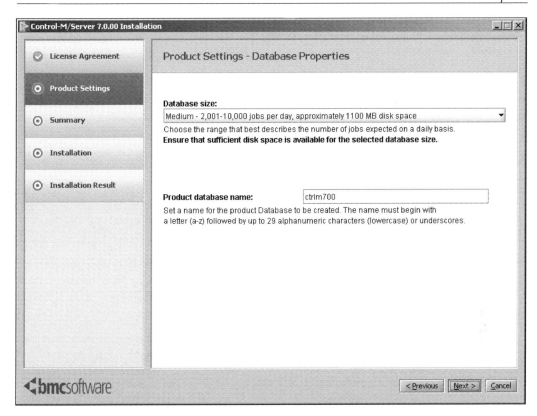

In the third page of **Database Properties**, we are required to provide the data device's and log device's full path, and filename, as well as their size.

For location, it is better to place these files on a disk that provides the best I/O performance. In our case, we are going to put the two files where the MSSQL master and tempdb are located, namely, `C:\Program Files\Microsoft SQL Server\MSSQL10_50.MSSQLSERVER\MSSQL\DATA`.

For filename, we give both of them meaningful names by including the database name within the filename. The actual files will be created later on during installation, according to what we defined here.

For device size, the log device should at least be one-third the size of the data device. Once again, we need to make sure there's sufficient space on the disk to hold these files.

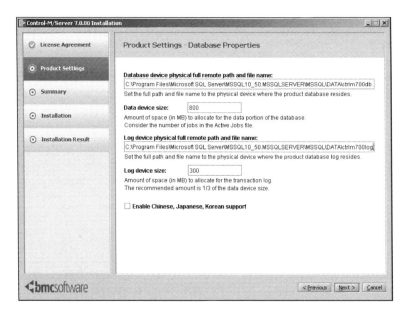

In **Control-M/Server Configuration**, we provide parameters internal to the Control-M/Server. These are exactly the same as what we did in the Control-M/Server for Linux installation earlier on.

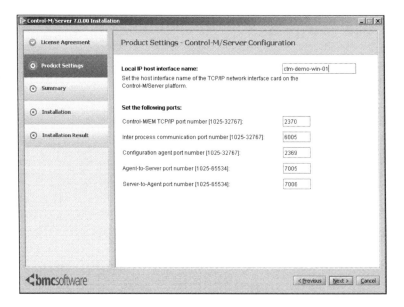

After carefully reviewing and copy/pasting down the installation summary, we click on the **Install** button to let the installation begin.

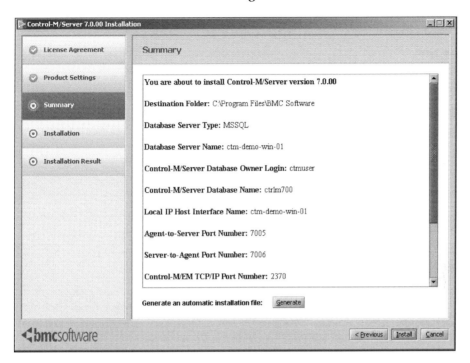

Post-installation tasks

After the installation is completed successfully, we should see that four new Windows services are created. These services are Control-M/Server, Control-M/Server Configuration Agent, Control-M/Agent, and Control-M/Agent FileWatcher. The Control-M Configuration Agent and Control-M/Agent services are started by the installer; the other two are still in the stopped status.

 If installing with a new PostgreSQL database server, we should see that a new PostgreSQL service also got created.

Both `prf` and `show_ca` commands are also available with the Windows version of Control-M/Server and the output of these commands are the same as what we get in the Linux environment. The output of these commands should indicate that all the Control-M/Server core processes are terminated and the CA process is running and listening on port 2369.

Now we can repeat the discover steps we did in CCM earlier to define this new Control-M/Server. After a successful discovery, our Control-M/EM should end up with two Control-M/Servers, two gateways, and two Control-M/Agents showing up in CCM in total.

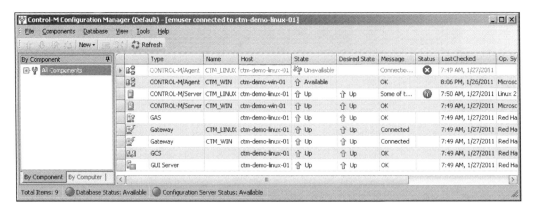

Installing Control-M/Agent

In this section, we will install two Control-M/Agents. One will be installed into a Linux environment (ctm-demo-linux-02) and the other will be installed into a Windows environment (ctm-demo-linux-02).

Installation in Linux environment

Installing Control-M/Agent in a Linux environment is much simpler than installing Control-M/EM or Control-M/Server. It doesn't require us to run the **pre_req** script and we also don't need to worry about any database parameters (it doesn't require one). Once all pre-installation requirements are met, the actual installation should take less than a minute.

Pre-installation tasks

Recall what we discussed in the *System Configuration Requirements* section – each Control-M/Agent installed on the system requires SEMMNS and SEMMNI to be the current value plus 1. This should be done prior to the installation by modifying the / etc/sysctl.conf file, like how we did it earlier during the Control-M/EM installation.

Apart from that, it is just a matter of creating a system user and starting the installation. We will not repeat the process here, as it is the same as what we did for the other two Linux installations. The user we created is called ctmagent, with home directory under /opt/ctmagent, with the default shell /bin/csh and primary group ctm.

One thing we should pay attention to is the available disk space for Control-M/Agent. Although the Control-M/Agent installation itself only requires 50 MB, it is important to reserve additional space to allow additional Control Module installation and storage of job sysouts and other temporary files such as Agent logs and debug dumps. Since the job sysouts by default are stored within the Control-M/Agent installation directory ($HOME/ctm/sysout) and the size can grown dynamically, we would recommend at least 500 MB of space dedicated for Control-M/Agent and preferably not to share the filesystem with the root directory or other applications.

Installation

Control-M/Agent installation needs to be initiated by the root user from the Control-M/Agent home directory. We first log on as root to mount the installation ISO file - DROST.7.0.00_Linux-i386.iso, then we go straightaway to the Control-M/Agent home directory and run the **setup.sh** script as the root user (it has to be executed from the Control-M/Agent home directory).

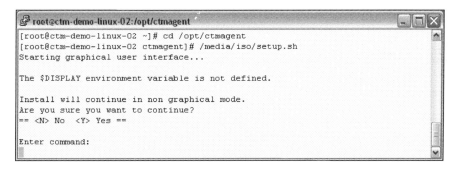

The panel, after we select **Control-M/Agent 7.0.00** installation, will ask us for the primary and authorized Control-M/Server hostname, as well as the **Agent-to-Server** and **Server-to-Agent** port numbers.

As we are going to connect this Control-M/Agent to our Linux Control-M/Server, we will enter the primary Control-M/Server host as **ctm-demo-linux-01**. The **Authorized Control-M/Server hosts** field is designed to allow failover for Control-M/Server to schedule jobs on the Agent in the absence of the primary Control-M/Server. As we are not setting up failover yet, we will leave it blank for now.

The two port numbers we entered here are the same as what we specified during Control-M/Server installation, namely, **7005** and **7006**.

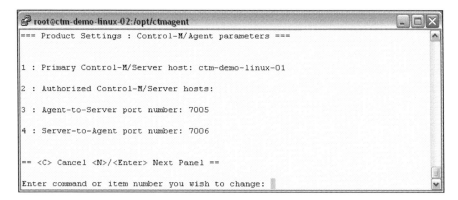

The previous image shows the four parameters we need to specify for our Control-M/Agent installation. The installation should finish within a minute or so and end with a completion status message saying the installation is successful.

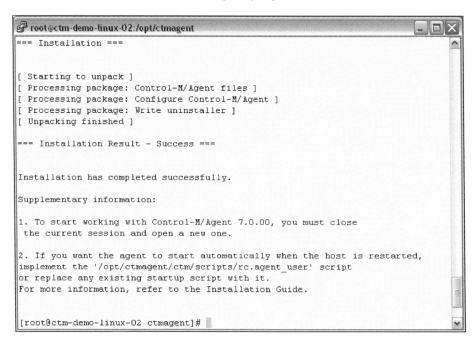

As we may notice, the installation finishes with supplementary information about how to create automatic start-up script so the Agent can start automatically after a server reboot. We will leave this topic to *Chapter 5, Administrating the Control-M Infrastructure*. For now, let's get the Control-M/Agent up and running first.

Post-installation tasks

The installation starts the Control-M/Agent processes upon completion as the root user. We can check the existence of those processes by running the Linux command `ps -ef | grep p_ctm` (that is, all Control-M/Agent processes start with **p_ctm**). We should see two processes are running, namely, AG process (**p_ctmag**) and AT process (**p_ctmat**).

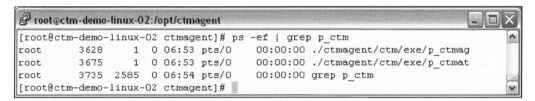

Now we can log on as the Control-M/Agent user and check the communication between the Agent and Control-M/Server by running the utility `ag_diag_comm`. The utility will attempt to connect to the primary Control-M/Server and will provide the outcome along with other communication-related configuration information about the Control-M/Agent. If the test is successful, in the output, we will see **Agent Ping to Control-M/Server: Succeeded**.

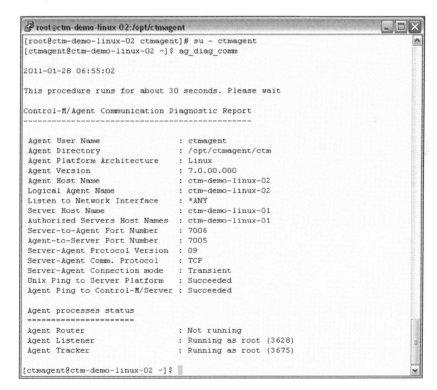

So far, we have our first standalone Control-M/Agent installed. This is not the end yet; before we move onto the Windows Agent installation, we need to connect this Control-M/Agent to the Control-M/Server it belongs to.

There are many methods to discover a Control-M/Agent, and using CCM is one of them. After logon to CCM, we *right-click* on the **Linux Control-M/Server** (CTM_LINUX) and select **New Control-M/Agent** from the drop-down menu. Because the Control-M/Agent is using the default settings, all we need to do is enter in the **Control-M/Agent Host Name** and click on the **OK** button. Optionally, we can click on the **Test** button to perform a communication test to make sure the connection is okay.

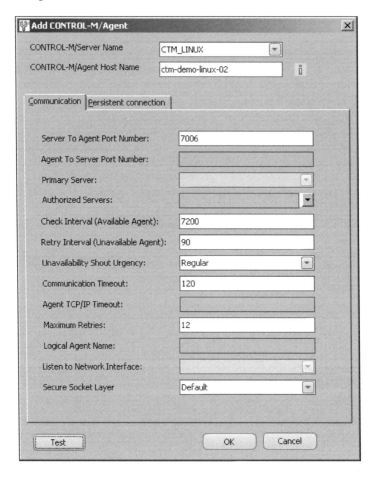

Now we should see an additional Control-M/Agent appear on the list, under (datacenter) the name **CTM_LINUX**.

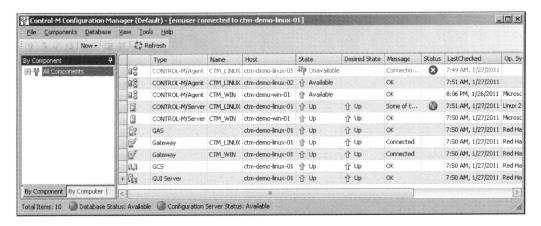

We might wonder why the **ctm-demo-linux-01** default agent is still shown as **Unavailable**. This is because in the Linux environment, the default Agent isn't made active by the installation. We need to log on to the machine and manually start the Agent by running the **start-ag** utility located under `<ctm home dir>/ctm_agent/ctm/scripts` as the root user. The utility will ask for the **Control-M/Agent Unix username** followed by an Agent process which has to be started. Because we are running the utility from the Agent's home directory, the utility will detect the Agent's username automatically. For the process name, we always use the default value – **ALL**.

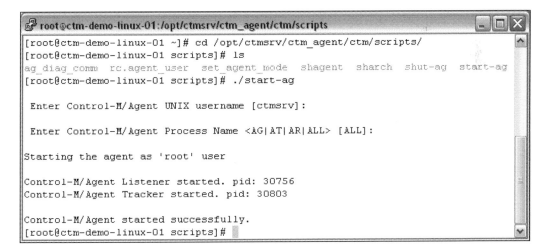

After a short time, we should see the Agent become available in CCM.

Installation in a Windows environment

Installing Control-M/Agent in a Windows environment is very straightforward. It is GUI-driven and the parameters required during installation are very similar to what we have seen during the Linux Agent installation. Rather than repeating each step of the installation, below is a list of things that are different from a Linux Agent installation.

- Control-M/Agent in a Windows environment doesn't necessarily require a dedicated username. By default, the Agent service will log on as the Local System account.

- The first Control-M/Agent installed on the host will be the default instance. The default installation path for the first instance is under `C:\Program Files\BMC Software\Control-M Agent\Default`. This naming is internal to the Control-M/Agent used to identify itself and not by any other application such as Control-M/Server. It is needed so we can install multiple agents on the same Windows server (that is, each gets its own instance name).

- Once the Control-M/Agent is installed, we should see a **Control-M/Agent** service and a **Control-M/Agent FileWatcher** service appear under **Computer Management | Services and Applications | Services**. The Control-M/Agent service has **Startup Type** as automatic, whereas the **FileWatcher** service is disabled by default.

Our installation is going to be performed on **ctm-demo-win-02**. The primary Control-M/Server for this Agent is **ctm-demo-win-01**. After the installation, we can run the **ag_diag_comm** utility from the Windows command line to test the connection with Control-M/Server and then go to CCM to discover this Agent under the datacenter **CTM_WIN**.

Upon successfully adding the Agent, we should be able to see that all the components in CCM are shown as **Available** or **Up**. These components are:

- 2x Control-M/Server
- 2x Gateways (one for each Control-M/Server)
- 4x Control-M/Agents (two for each datacenter)
- 3x Control-M/EM server components, that is, GAS, GCS, and GUI Server

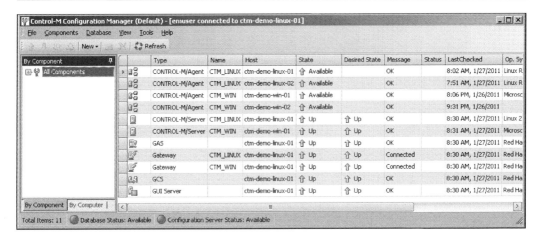

Summary

It has been a long chapter! We started with introducing the concept of the three ages to archive workload automation, and then looked at the different requirements and challenges at each stage. We also talked about sizing and technical considerations that are necessary for building a solid batch infrastructure. Finally, we started to get into the technical details and prepared machines and the environment for the Control-M implementation.

By now, we have a very basic Control-M environment. As we can see, it is not extremely hard to set up an enterprise batch scheduling backbone, as long as we plan everything in advance and follow the guidelines during implementation.

In the coming chapters, we will define and run batch jobs based on the environment we have just built. So, make sure everything is running in your environment before proceeding to the next chapter!

4

Creating and Managing Batch Flows with Control-M GUI

Having a solid batch infrastructure is only the beginning of this journey of workload automation. Just imagine a data warehouse operates 24/7 with no data in it; without batch jobs running, the batch scheduling tool won't present any value to the business. The real ROI of the tool depends on what we schedule in the tool and how we schedule them. In today's business environment, batch processing requirements can get extremely complicated. It is essential for us to master the powerful job scheduling features provided by Control-M and therefore be able to utilize these features to meet the ever-growing batch needs.

In this chapter, we are going to use the Control-M environment we built in *Chapter 3, Building the Control-M Infrastructure*, to define and execute batch flows. We will begin with a detailed explanation of the important concepts within Control-M that are related to job scheduling. Based on it, we will explore basic features of Control-M GUI by defining and running some simple jobs. Once we feel a bit more comfortable, we will create a batch processing scenario and define a more complicated batch flow to meet the processing needs.

By the end of this chapter, you will:

- Be able to understand and explain important batch scheduling-related concepts within Control-M
- Have the ability to define batch jobs by using Control-M/Desktop

- Be familiar with Control-M job features to meet complex scheduling requirements
- Be able to use Control-M/Enterprise Manager GUI Client to monitor and manage active jobs

The Control-M way – continued

Earlier in *Chapter 2, Exploring Control-M*, we briefly introduced some basic Control-M terminologies such as, what is a "job", the purpose of "job condition" and "resource", and the meaning of "post-processing", as well as how Control-M handles job submission.

In this chapter, before we start to define and schedule jobs in Control-M, let's spend some extra time to continue expanding our mind with the "Control-M way of thinking" by looking into more details of the following key concept:

- Contents of a job definition
- Lifecycle of a job
- New Day Procedure (NDP)
- User Daily

Contents of a job definition

"Job" is the smallest element in a Control-M batch environment. Each job has its own set of definitions. By interrupting the definition, the Control-M/Server would know which machine to submit the job to, when to submit, what to trigger, and what other actions to take after the job is completed. These job definitions are stored in the Control-M's database for Control-M itself to access, but they have also been made human readable via the Control-M/EM GUI and command-line utilities:

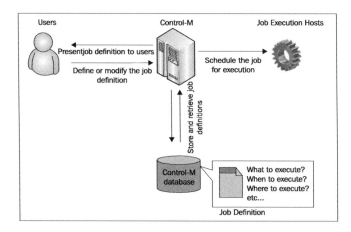

"What" #1: job type

In order to schedule a job to be triggered, first of all Control-M needs to know what exactly we want to execute. This first comes down to the question of "Job Type".

Control-M has a variety of job types to meet different scheduling needs. The most common job type is "OS". "OS" job type refers to tasks that are submitted to the destination machine's operating system for execution (for example, a Unix script or a command). For this job type, Control-M/Agent interacts with the operating system directly from the job's start to finish. "WINDOWS" job type is similar to "OS" job type, and apart from that it allows the user to enter some additional MS Windows-specific job parameters and of course, it only can be used for MS Windows jobs. Other job types are application-specific job types, such as SAP jobs, Informatica jobs, web services jobs, and so on.

The support for each job type depends on the system environment and Control-M/Agent configuration. In other words, except the standard "OS" job type which is supported by all Control-M/Agents, the rest of them are only to be used under special system configurations or required to be handled by additional Control Modules.

Every now and then, we will see one or more new job types become available when an additional Control-M feature is introduced or when a new Control Module is released. Here's a complete list of job types available in Control-M version 7 at the time of writing this book:

Job type	Requirement
OS	No requirement for Standard Control-M/Agent or Agentless
AFT	Control Module for Advance File Transfer
Control-M BIM	Batch Impact Manager
Control-M Report	Windows Machine Installed With Control-M/EM GUI client
Database	Control-M for database
File Watcher	Standard Agent and Control Module for Advance File Transfer
JAVA	Control-M Business Process Integration
MSG (Messaging)	
WS (Web Services)	
OEBS (Oracle E-Business Suite)	Control Module for Oracle E-Business Suite
Peoplesoft	Control Module for Peoplesoft

Job type	Requirement
SAP Business Warehouse (Info Package and Process Chain)	Control Module for SAP
SAP Data Archiving	
SAP R3	
WINDWOS	Standard Control-M/Agent in a Windows environment
Informatica	Control-M for Informatica
EC2, VMware, and Bladelogic	Control-M for Cloud

For the rest of the chapter, we will assume everything we talk about is with regard to OS job type, unless specially specified. We will discuss external application job types in detail during the advanced scheduling topics in *Chapter 6, Advanced Batch Scheduling and Management*.

"What" #2: task type

After selected the job type, we also need to identify the type of task that Control-M is going to trigger. There are five different task types available to choose from. These task types are **Job**, **Detached**, **Command**, **Dummy**, and **External**.

- Job is the most common task type. In Microsoft Windows and Unix/Linux environments, it refers to the triggering of an executable file. For example, a Unix shell script or a Perl program.

- Detached in Control-M for Distributed Environments is similar to the task type Job, but it is only to be used for triggering .exe executable files on a MS Windows platform.

- Command is used if we want to run an operating system command as a job, as if we are running it from the command line. For example, `useradd -d /home/jason -s /bin/ksh -m jason` or `ls -lrt JAN* > /tmp/output.txt`.

- Dummy job doesn't actually trigger anything on the job execution host. As soon as it starts, it goes directly to perform post-processing (if defined) and then goes into a complete state. Dummy job can be used as a "controller" (also known as, "place holder") to trigger other jobs or job flows. For example, we can use dummy job as a starting point to kick-off a batch flow or a number of batch flows.

- Task type: External refers to jobs that are not submitted by Control-M, but require Control-M to monitor the jobs' running and therefore can perform post-processing tasks according to its execution status. For example, SAP R/3 jobs with job mode set to External*.

*Control Module for SAP offers external job mode so that Control-M can detect and monitor SAP jobs that are initiated by SAP itself.

"Who" #1 – owner of the job

There are two aspects around the topic of "who". First, we need to specify the owner for each job so that Control-M can execute the jobs on behalf of the desired user. "Owner of the job" refers to the operating system's user that the job will be running as. For each job submission, Control-M/Agent uses the owner information specified in the job definition to execute the job. It is essential to specify the appropriate user for each job, so while executing the job process it can have the required permission and environment settings to complete its work.

On Unix and Linux operating systems, Control-M/Agent processes are set to run as "root" by default. When an OS type job is submitted to the job execution machine, the Control-M/Agent will spawn the job process under the desired user account according to the "owner of the job" value specified in the definition. As Control-M version 7, Control-M/Agent can be set to run as a non-root user and still able to spawn new job processes according to the owner value specified in the job definition.

On MS Windows operating systems, Control-M/Agent service is set to "Log on as" "Local System account" by default. Under such settings, Control-M/Agent will run each "OS" or "WINDOWS" job under the Local System account without checking the "owner of the job" value in job definitions. Control-M/Agent for Windows can also be set to "log on as user" mode to enable job submission according to "owner of the job" value.

We will discuss these different logon modes in detail when we talk about Control-M security in *Chapter 5, Administrating the Control-M Infrastructure*.

"Who" #2 – author of the job

For Control-M itself, it keeps track of Control-M/EM users who create or modify each job. "Author of the job" has no direct relation to "owner of the job". It refers to the person who creates or updates the job. It is the Control-M/EM GUI user ID (if enforced from settings) of the person who is editing the job definition. Control-M keeps track of such information for security and auditing purposes. The information is stored as part of the job definition in the Control-M database, and it doesn't get sent to the Control-M/Agent during job execution.

Again we will discuss about it in more depth in the chapter on security. For now we only need to know that this is compulsory for each job definition.

"Where" #1 – job's execution host

In a centralized batch environment, the batch jobs are likely to be submitted for execution on a variety of hosts rather than only the local machine where Control-M/Server is running. Control-M/Server maintains a list of the machines that are eligible for job submission. Upon each job submission, Control-M/Server will read the job execution host information from the job definition and send the job to that destination for execution.

The "destination" can be a standalone Control-M/Agent hostname, which is also called a node ID, or a nodegroup name. If it is a nodegroup name, Control-M/Server will use its internal round-robin-based load balancing algorism to decide which Control-M/Agent within the node group is going to be the actual job execution host; or, the job can be set to run on all available nodes within the node group (that is, in active environment, a job instance will be created for each node within the node group).

"Where" #2 – storing job definitions

Jobs definitions are physically stored in the Control-M database. In order to be user-friendly, Control-M presented these jobs to the user in two types of logical hierarchies.

Datacenter/Table/Job

Just like how we sort files into different folders on a computer, in Control-M jobs are logically stored into different "scheduling tables" and each table belongs to a particular datacenter. When creating jobs we normally would place inter-related jobs into the same scheduling table for convenience. There are two types of job tables, one is the traditional scheduling table (simple table) and the other one is the SMART table.

In *Chapter 2*, we mentioned "From job point of view, a **Datacenter** represents the scheduling engine where the jobs are stored and triggered from". In general terms, a datacenter refers to a Control-M/Server defined in Control-M/EM and everything belongs to it, such as job definitions and connected Control-M/Agents, as well as jobs instances, resources, and conditions in the active environment.

Traditional table doesn't offer anything apart from a single-layer logical container of jobs. The reason we call it traditional table is because it has been around since the very first version of Control-M. It is still the most common method that people are using today.

SMART tables is newly introduced in Control-M version 7; it is the enhancement of the earlier version's **Group Scheduling Table**. SMART table is not only a logical container of jobs; it also has certain behaviors similar to a job, such as, it allow users to define table level scheduling criteria, in/out conditions, post-processing definitions, and so on. We can imagine SMART table as a "big dummy job" but with child jobs "stored" in itself. During batch running, SMART table will need to meet its prerequisite conditions first in order for its child jobs to start. SMART table has different states which are similar to a job. It can be in waiting, executing, ended OK, and ended not OK states. Once the contained child job(s) starts running, the SMART table's state will simultaneously change to executing and it will only end when all child jobs within are completed. SMART table also allow sub-tables to be created within it. Child jobs and sub-tables can inherent some of their parent SMART table's scheduling criteria:

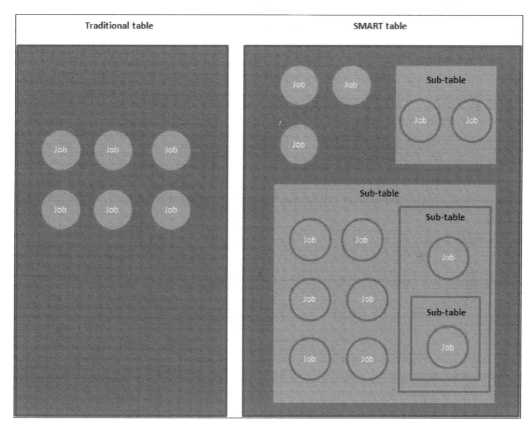

Application/Group/Job

In the real world, jobs belong to different applications within the organization, and each application can have different groups of jobs to serve different purposes. Control-M provided the Application/Group/Job logical view to reflex the real origin of jobs at the business level regardless of which Control-M scheduling table they reside in.

For example:

- Application 1: DW (Datawarehouse)
    ◦ Group 1: ETL
    ◦ Group 2: DBA
    ◦ Group 3: Cube_Build

- Application 2: Finance
    ◦ Group 1: Journal
    ◦ Group 2: Invoicing

This logical hierarchy makes job management and monitoring much easier. For example, by using this hierarchy operation people can quickly identify which application and group a problematic job belongs to.

The Application/Group/Job logical view has no conflict with the Datacenter/Table/Job hierarchy. Jobs that belong to the same application group can be logically stored into different tables; also jobs in the same table can be logically grouped into different applications and groups.

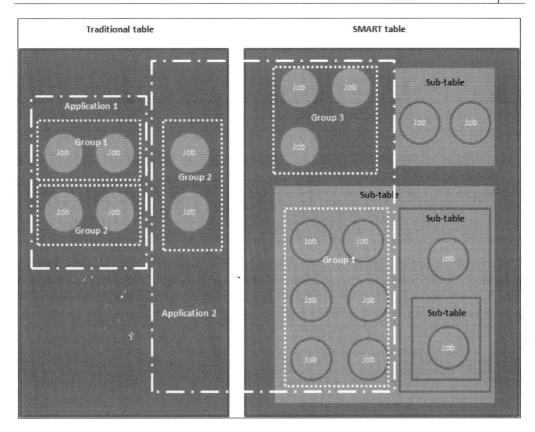

"When" #1 – job's scheduling date

Within each job definition, we define the desired date for a job to be scheduled. Some jobs are required to be executed daily; some are required to be executed weekly or monthly. We provide such information as part the job definition to allow Control-M to automatically activate the job on those desired days.

Defining a job's scheduling date

For each individual job, we can define its scheduling dates by specifying: which days of a month (Month Days) or which days of a week (Week Days) in conjunction with which months the job is to be activated. The relationship between Month Days and Week Days can be an AND or OR in order to meet special schedule requirements, such as activate the job on the 20th of each month AND it has to be a Friday, or activate the job on the 21st of each month OR on a Sunday (regardless of the date).

Based on the defined schedule dates, we can optionally set the following active period for each job:

- **Active from**: Control-M will schedule the job according to the job's scheduling dates from the date specified

- **Active to**: Control-M will stop scheduling the job when the date specified is reached

- **Active from ~ to**: Control-M will schedule the job according to its scheduling dates in-between the period specified ("from" date must equal or smaller than "to" date)

- **Active until ~ and from**: Control-M will schedule the job according to its scheduling dates outside the period specified ("until" date must be equal to or smaller than "and from" date)

Active From/Until is a useful feature that can be used to control when jobs will be put into the production system without having to also do all the creation work on the same day. For example, we can define all the jobs today and schedule their production from 12/2012. Control-M also provides us the option to set once-off individual scheduling dates for jobs.

Calendars

Imagine a situation when hundreds of jobs from different applications are all required to run on each public holiday. It is inefficient for us to repeatedly define the same schedule for large amounts of jobs that require similar scheduling dates. Instead, in Control-M we can define the common scheduling dates in a calendar and assign it to those jobs. Calendars are fully customizable; users can define any schedule days according to jobs' common scheduling requirement. Most commonly seen calendars are working days, weekends, and public holidays.

Within job definition, we can apply rules in conjunction with the associated calendar to meet even more complicated schedule requirements, such as, scheduling the job on the second to last day of each month.

There are two types of calendars— Relative/Regular and Periodic. We will explain the Relative/Regular calendar type in detail later on in this chapter by using scheduling samples and explain Periodic calendar in *Chapter 6*.

Rule-Based Calendar (RBC)

Rule-Based Calendar* (RBC) is a different concept to the calendars we just introduced. Remember earlier on we discussed that jobs within a SMART table can inherent the parent SMART table's scheduling criteria; each RBC is a set of scheduling criteria (just like a job) defined within a SMART table which is to be used by itself and can be inherited by its child jobs and sub-tables, as well as child jobs within the sub-tables.

For each SMART table, we can define multiple RBCs for different scheduling requirements. Each job can choose to inherent zero to all RBCs from its parent SMART table and the relationship between the selected SMART tables can be defined as AND or OR.

*Prior to Control-M version 7, they were called **Scheduling Tags**.

Retro job

Retro is a scheduling option that can be selected for jobs and SMART tables. By enabling the option, Control-M will schedule the job retroactively if the job's original schedule date is missed due to Control-M outage on that day. For example, Control-M/server has been down since the 5th of Jan due to hardware failure. When Control-M/Server is eventually recovered on the 7th, Control-M/Server will order jobs that are defined to be scheduled on the 7th as per normal, together with jobs that are defined to be scheduled on the 5th and the 6th with "retro" option selected. Control-M will ignore jobs that are to be scheduled on the 5th and the 6th but without the "retro" option selected, simply because their schedule date has already passed.

"Retro" option is useful for jobs that are not date-sensitive but cannot be missed, such as a log cleaning job or a low priority backup job.

"When" #2 – time frame for job submission

In Control-M we can limit the job's execution into a pre-set time frame. The time frame rule consists of From and Until two time values. Both the time values are specified in hh:mm format. Seconds are ignored. Depending on the scheduling requirement, we can use these two time values standalone or combined. The scenarios are as follow:

- When both From and Until time are specified: Control-M will only trigger the job if all other prerequisites are met in-between the "From" and "Until" time. While outside the time frame, even if all other prerequisites are met the job will not run.

- When only `From` time is specified: Control-M will automatically set the blank "Until" time with the next New Day time and trigger the job in-between the time frame given that all other prerequests are met before the next New Day starts.

- When only `Until` time is specified: Control-M will automatically set the blank "From" time with the previous New Day time and trigger the job in-between the time frame given that all other prerequisites are met before the "Until" time arrives.

Without specifying this rule, the active job will run as soon as all other prerequisites are met.

"When" #3 – cyclic jobs

By default, each active job instance only gets submitted once. If we want the job to be triggered again, we need to create another active instance or wait for the job's next schedule. However, there are chances we might need to trigger the same job to run multiple times throughout a day. For example, a process runs every two hours to consolidate purchase orders generated in the last hour, or a housekeeping script runs every 15 minutes to recycle logs. With the cyclic option, we can let Control-M rerun the same active job instance at a set interval or at a list of specific times. It saves the effort of redefining the same job with different "from" times just for the purpose of running it at different time points.

In cyclic definitions, we can set the job to rerun at fixed intervals (for example, every 15 minutes or a specifically specified interval (for example, 1st rerun after 60 minutes, 2nd rerun after 1 hour, and 3rd rerun after 2 days). The intervals can be start counting from the end time or start time of the job's previous execution. For example, if we set the job's rerun interval to 10 minutes and the job's previous execution took 15 minutes; by counting from the job's start time, the next execution will start as soon as the previous execution finishes, whereas by counting from the end time the next execution will start 10 minutes after. In addition, we can set the job's rerun at fixed time points, such as 2:00 p.m., 5:00 p.m., and 7:35 p.m., and so on.

Control-M trades each rerun of the cyclic job as a new execution. When the job's rerun time comes, Control-M will re-assist all prerequisites of the job before submitting it for execution. We can define a cyclic job to run only within a desired time frame by applying the "from" and/or "to" time value to it. The total number of job's rerun can also be limited by specifying a job parameter called **Maximum reruns**.

"When" #4 – manual confirmation jobs

In some cases whether a job should be triggered or not needs to be justified by a human. Control-M allows us to define the job as a "Wait for confirmation", that is the job will not run until confirmed by a user. If all prerequisites of the job are met before the manual confirmation, Control-M will submit the job as soon as it is confirmed. If the job is confirmed by the user but still hasn't got all prerequisites, Control-M will submit the job only when all prerequisites are met. Manual confirmation action can be done using both Control-M/EM GUI and Control-M/Server command-line utility.

"When" #5 – job condition

Job condition is an important Control-M concept because it is the driver behind cross-platform scheduling. Within Control-M, job conditions link interrelated jobs together into a logical job flow regardless of their execution host. It defines a group of job's execution sequence and can potentially affect each job's submission time.

In order to build the dependency between two jobs, we need to define "Out-condition" in the job (definition) that is supposed to run first and define the matching "In-condition" in the job (definition) which is going to run after. We call the first job as the second job's predecessor and call the second job as the first job's dependent. Of course, a job can have multiple predecessors and dependents in one or multiple levels of depth.

Each condition is nothing more than a text with a date value stored in the Control-M database. At a job's completion, if the job has "Out-condition(s)" defined, Control-M will store the condition(s) text with its defined date into the database. Later on when Control-M is analyzing a job for submission, it will look into the database for the matching condition's name as well as the condition's date. If both are matching, the dependent job's "In-condition" is considered as satisfied. If the "Out-condition" produced by the predecessor job has a date different to the dependent job's "In-condition" date, the dependent job's "In-condition" is not considered as satisfied. A small range of date options can be selected to meet different scheduling needs; the options are:

- ODAT: Used to inherit the job's original scheduling date
  - ○ Example: If the job was scheduled on 12/01, the condition's date will be 12/01
- PREV: Used to calculate to the job's previous scheduling date
  - ○ Example: If the job was scheduled on 12/01, the condition's date will be 11/30

- NEXT: Used to calculate to the job's next scheduling date
    - Example: If the job was scheduled on 12/01, the condition's date will be 12/02
- $$$$−: Used to ignore the date, only examines the condition name
    - Example: If a job has an "In-condition" with date set to ****, it will be satisfied by any job's "Out-condition" that has the same name regardless of the date
    - ****: Same as above
- STAT: Used when the condition doesn't have a date-dependent
    - Example: "Out-condition" defined with STAT will satisfy any job that has the same "In-condition" name and date value set to STAT (useful for jobs that are logically related but not date-dependent)

Each job can have multiple "In-conditions". The relationship between these conditions can be AND, OR, or customized. With AND relationship, all "In-conditions" have to be available in order for the job to be triggered (given all other prerequisites are met). Whereas with the OR condition the job will be triggered as long as one of the specified conditions is available (given all other prerequisites are met). Customized relationship allows us to define the individual relationship between every two conditions (when more than two "In-conditions" are defined). For example, in order for job F to run, we require either job A finished OR job B AND C both finished:

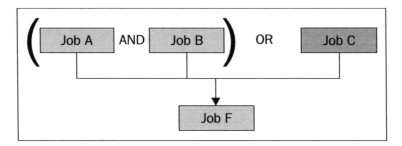

"When" #6 – resource and job priority

The term **Resource** in Control-M is the logical representation of actual resources associated with the job's execution in the real world. Such resources can be the amount of available memory, number of allowed open sessions to a database, or an exclusive access to a file. Control-M has two types of logical resources; one is called Quantitative resource, and the other is called Control resource. Resource is an optional job parameter designed to improve the overall control of batch execution.

Quantitative resource

Quantitative resource in Control-M is used to represent physical resources that are able to be measured by number (for example, percentage of memory, number of tape drives). For each quantitative resource, we first define the total available quantity in Control-M's resource pool and then define the quantity required by each individual job in the job's definition. The name of the quantities resource is up to the user. Jobs that require the same type of physical resource should be defined with the same quantitative resource name in their job definition. The quantity required by each job is estimated and defined by the user.

In the active environment, by the time a job's other prerequisites are met (such as time and condition), Control-M/Server will check the quantitative resource pool to find out if there's enough amount of resource available for the job to run. If so, Control-M/Server will subtract the required amount of resource needed by the job from the resource pool (also known as, allocate resource to the job) and submit the job for execution. The subtracted resource will get added back into the resource pool (also known as, releasing resource) by Control-M/Server after the job is completed. If there's not enough resource available in the pool for a job to run, the job will stay in the `waiting for resource` state until the required amount of resource is available. The outstanding resource could be released by completed jobs that also used the same resource or manually added by someone via the GUI or command-line utility.

Job priority is used in conjunction with quantitative resource. In a situation where there are many jobs waiting for the same quantitative resource, we can give priority value to each job therefore allowing the more important job to be submitted first when the resource becomes available.

However, in some cases a job may not be generated to get submitted first even when it has the highest priority. Imagine a situation when a large amount of lower priority jobs commonly require less amount of quantitative resource than the high priority job. Before the high priority meets its other prerequisites, its required quantitative resource may have already been taken by a number of lower priority jobs. When some of the lower priority jobs are ended and the resource is released, the total amount of available resource may still not be enough for the high priority job to run. In this situation, Control-M/Server will imminently submit other (lower priority) waiting jobs that require less or equal amount of available quantitative resource. In order to avoid this issue, we can define the job as "critical". For a critical job, Control-M will reserve the required quantitative resource each time when it gets released by other jobs, and hold them until it has accumulated enough for the critical job to be submitted.

Control resource

Just like how operating systems or databases use locks, Control-M uses control resource to manage resources that are to be commonly used by a number of jobs (for example, a file or database table). There are two types of accesses to a control resource, either shared or exclusive.

Shared access is for those jobs that are allowed to access the resource at the same time. For example jobs that are running "select" query to a database or performing a read operation to a file. **Exclusive access** is for those jobs that required solo access to the resource, for example a job that is performing a truncate operation to a database table or doing rotation to a logfile.

Control resource also can be used for controlling the batch execution on a larger scale. For example, we can define all jobs that belong to the same job execution host with the same shared control resource. When the job execution host is required to be taken offline for maintenance, instead of figuring out which jobs are to be paused, we can submit a dummy job or manually occupy the resource as exclusive, therefore preventing all jobs that have the same resource from submitting.

"When" #7 – time zone

Jobs belonging to the same Control-M/Server may not be present at the same location. Those jobs at different locations may require to be triggered according to their local time zone. In order to archive this, we can specify time zone information in each job definition. Jobs without the time zone information (by default) will be scheduled according to the Control-M/Server's time zone.

What happens right after the job's execution is completed?

So far we have been talking about job definitions that can affect the job's submission and running. With Control-M we can also define post-processing rules in each job definition to let Control-M automatically perform a number of predefined actions after the job execution is completed. These rules can be performed in general or as reactions to the job's certain execution outcomes.

PostProc

PostProc refers to the post-processing tasks to be performed by Control-M after the job is completed. We specify possible events for Control-M to detect and accordingly what action is to be performed. The events include the job's completion or failure. The action is a notification (SHOUT) sent by Control-M to a predefined destination (SHOUT destination) such as, Control-M Alert Window or e-mail addresses. By using this feature, we can manage the batch running by exception instead of staying in front of the screen to watch every single job's execution around the clock:

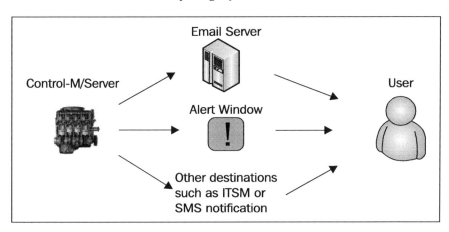

The other small optional feature provided as part of PostProc is the job output handling (Sysout handling). By default, after each job's execution, the job sysout is kept by Control-M/Agent (stored under Control-M/Agent's home directory). We use this feature when we would like to do something more about these sysouts, such as copy or move them to a different location, print them out or simply delete them right after the job execution.

Step

Step is a powerful feature which allows Control-M to perform post job execution actions according to the job's execution result, in other words Control-M will analyze the job's sysout and perform predefined actions that are matching the detected keywords. This feature takes "managing by exception" to the next level by automating "reaction" tasks which were traditionally performed by humans. For example, a file copy job can fail with a message **cannot find target file**. Instead of receiving an alert from Control-M and manually rerunning the job, we can define **Step Codes** in the job definition to let Control-M perform the rerun actions when such a message is detected in the job's output.

Within each Step Code, we are required to define the searching keywords and the action(s) to be performed. Multiple statements can be defined within each job to handle different scenarios and the action to be performed for each scenario can be one to many:

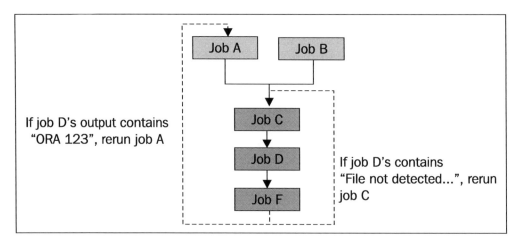

Autoedit facility

In computer programming, people use variables so that the program can execute with information only available at runtime. Control-M provides similar functionality called **Autoedit facility** to allow more flexible job execution.

Autoedit variables

There is a chance that the job's parameters are not known until runtime, such as:

- The job's script does invoice look-up that requires the current date as an input argument
- A file transfer job requires the latest generated file's filename to perform the transfer
- A file processing job (after the file transfer job) needs to know which file was transferred so it can process the right file (share the variable with the file transfer job above it)

Instead of hard-coding all job parameters and then modifying them manually at runtime, in Control-M we can define `Autoedit` variables as part of the job definitions and use them in many places, such as, to input arguments for a job's script or command, as parameters for application-specific jobs, or even include them as part of the job's post-processing parameters (for example, content of an e-mail notification). The value of `Autoedit` variables are to be dynamically assigned at the job's runtime and it can also be shared among different jobs.

There are different types of `Autoedit` variables with different scopes to be used for different purposes. We will introduce some of the most commonly used variables later while we define our sample job flow.

Autoedit expressions and functions

`Autoedit` expressions and functions allow us to manipulate the value of `Autoedit` variables at the Control-M level, such as assign the value of one `Autoedit` variable to another, perform add or subtract between two `Autoedit` variables where both have numeric value, join two `Autoedit` variables where both have string value, or extract part of a string and then assign it to a new `Autoedit` variable.

We will also demonstrate how to use `Autoedit` expressions and functions in our samples.

Lifecycle of a job

Lifecycle of a job is one of the most important concepts in Control-M. It is referring to a series of state changes of a job from being defined to getting scheduled as an active job, then from waiting for execution to be submitted, then from execution to completion and finally the active job instance gets removed by Control-M. Fully understanding this concept will make batch flow design and job management much easier and error free.

Write/Load, Upload/Download, Order/Force, and Hold

Jobs we created in Control-M Desktop are called **Job Draft**. We need to perform a **Write** action to save those job definitions into Control-M/EM database's job definition table set. Jobs stored in this database then become accessible by other Control-M Desktop users (by doing **Load** on the same jobs from their Control-M Desktop). But this still doesn't mean we are able to schedule the jobs for execution because Control-M/Server still doesn't know anything about them yet.

In order for Control-M/Server to schedule the jobs, we need to make a duplication of the job definition onto the Control-M/Server by performing an **Upload** action. By doing so, Control-M/EM will send the job definitions to Control-M/Server behind the scene and Control-M/Server will then save them into its own job definition table set. Jobs stored in Control-M/Server can be transferred back into Control-M/EM database by performing a **Download** action.

Once the jobs are stored in Control-M/Server database, we can perform an **Order** action to let Control-M/Server examine the job's scheduling criteria (that is, whether or not the job is eligible to be scheduled on that day). If the criteria are met, Control-M/Server will make the job become active by placing it into another set of tables (active job file). For jobs in the active job file (AJF), Control-M/Server will constantly review each job's prerequisites (for example, time, condition, resource, and so on) and trigger them when all prerequisites are met.

In case we want to let Control-M trigger a job which is not to be scheduled on that day, we can do a **Force** action instead of Order. When Force action is performed, Control-M/Server adds the job into its active job file without reviewing the job's scheduling criteria.

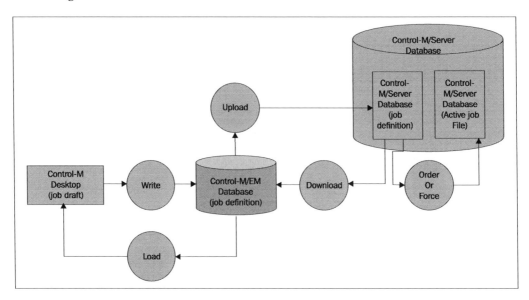

Active job's job definition can also be partially modified on-the-fly. This is extremely useful when we need to alter the job only for a particular day's run without affecting the original job definition. For example, a job has "from time" defined as 9:00 p.m. but today due to scheduled maintenance we cannot run the job until after 10:30 p.m. Instead of modifying the job's definition and then restoring it after the event, we can simply change the "from time" of the active job instance. In order to modify an active job, we need to place the job on Hold first. When a job is on Hold, Control-M/Server will not trigger the job even if all prerequisites are met. This stops the job from being submitted while we are modifying it. There are a number of items that cannot be modified, including:

- Task type
- Job owner and author
- Job's running host (node ID or node group)
- Changing a job from a normal job to cyclic job or vice versa

State of a job

Job definitions are static and stateless. But once they become active, they can have the following possible states:

- **Waiting for user confirmation**
- **Waiting for submission**
    - ○ Waiting for "from time" (or passed its "to time")
    - ○ Waiting for In-condition
    - ○ Waiting for the next rerun (cyclic jobs)
    - ○ Job is on hold
- **Waiting for resource**
    - ○ Waiting for quantitative resource or control resource
    - ○ Waiting for Control-M/Agent to become available for job submission
- **Executing**
- **Ended OK**
- **Ended NOTOK**
    - ○ Job failed with OS return code other than 0 (by default)
    - ○ Control-M/Server failed to submit the job
- **Disappeared** (Agent status is unknown)

From the user point of view, different states of the job are presented in different colors in Control-M/EM GUI Client. Control-M/Server in the backend stores each job's execution state in a database table. We can define post-processing rules within jobs to let Control-M/Server react to job states, such as:

- If the job has been in execution for X amount of time, send alert e-mail to person Y
- If the job has been executing for more than X amount of time, send alert to Control-M Alert Window or trigger a third-party script which sends SMS to person Y

Control-M also gives us the option to artificially control an active job, so that it changes from its current state to another instantly. Such as:

- Force a job into OK state (before it gets submitted or after it failed)
- Manually rerun a completed job (the job's state is ended either OK or NOTOK)
- Bypass a job's prerequisite(s) (for example, In-condition, time limit, resource)
- Manually add the job's missing In-condition(s)
- Skip the job or run the job as a dummy job
- Bypass job's post-processing

New Day Procedure (NDP)

New Day Procedure (NDP) is a Control-M proprietary concept in terms of automated housekeeping of the batch environment. We can understand NDP as a "refresh" of the datacenter that happens daily at a particular time. During NDP, Control-M/Server performs a series of tasks to make the batch environment ready for the next day.

We can define when we want the NDP to happen for each Control-M/Server. It is important to choose the right time because during NDP the Control-M/Server is in suspended mode and therefore no job can be triggered during the period. The NDP time should be set at a time when there will be minimal impact to the batch environment. The default time is 7 a.m.

Two of the NDP tasks we are going to talk about in this chapter are: active job ordering and cleaning.

Active job ordering

In the earlier section, we discussed how we can turn a job definition active by manually ordering it. For jobs that are to be scheduled regularly, we can let NDP's built-in functionality handle the ordering process automatically.

NDP orders jobs on a table by table basis. For a range of pre-selected job tables (and SMART tables) NDP will review each job within the table and decide whether or not it should be ordered on the day by analyzing its scheduling criteria. If the job's scheduling criteria are met, NDP will create an active job instance of the job in AJF— very similar to what happens when we manually order a job. Once the entire NDP processing is completed, Control-M/Server will start analyzing each of the active jobs for submission.

Active job cleaning

Active jobs do not stay in the AJF forever; otherwise the Control-M/Server database size will grow infinitely. Therefore, each time before the active job ordering starts, NDP needs to perform a cleaning action to remove any jobs that are ordered previously. The cleaning is based on the active job's state at the time. The possibilities are:

- For jobs that are ended OK, NDP will remove them
- For jobs that are ended NOTOK, NDP will keep them for one more day
- For jobs that are still executing, NDP will keep them (each day's NDP will re-visit them and perform action on them until they become ended OK or NOTOK)
- For jobs that are in disappeared state, NDP will keep them
- For jobs that are still waiting for submission (including cyclic jobs), NDP will clean them

Sometimes we might want to keep those jobs that are yet to be submitted in the AJF for a little longer than one day. The reason for this can vary but the most common one is in case the job's prerequisites are only going to be met at a later day. In order to do so, we can specify a maxwait parameter in the job definition. So each day NDP will decide whether or not to remove the job by comparing the actual date with the date the job's was ordered and its maxwait value.

Control-M Date and Odate

Control-M/Server keeps track of the current date and the value gets refreshed each time during NDP. We call it the Control-M dates because the value can be different from the actual calendar date if we don't set the NDP to run at midnight. For example, if we set NDP to run at 12:00 pm, the Control-M date will only get updated to the current calendar date after midday.

By default the Control-M date is assigned to each job when they get ordered. It is called the **Original Scheduling date (Odate)**. By using the Odate we can distinguish job instances with the same name that are ordered on different days or the same name job conditions that are generated on different days (when the condition's date is set to ODAT in job definition). When manually ordering jobs, we have the option to customize the job's Odate. Odate can also be applied to SMART tables.

Having an Odate in each active job instance can be very handy when it comes to running date-specific jobs in parallel. For example, we schedule a job to process a file which gets generated daily but sometimes it can be delayed. If the file is delayed, it can get generated on the next day together with the file which is meant to be generated on that day. In such a case, for the same job we can have two instances, one with yesterday's Odate and one with today's Odate, to process the two files accordingly.

User Daily

Ordering a job during NDP is not the only automatic method of creating job instances in the active environment. In fact, each job table (and SMART table) has a definition field called **User Daily** which is to be defined by users. In order to let the table be ordered by NDP, we need to specify its User Daily name as SYSTEM. Apart from that, any other value specified will be ignored during NDP.

The ordering outside of NDP is done by a Control-M/Server utility called ctmudly. This utility can be triggered manually from command line or scheduled by Control-M. In the command line all we need to do is to specify the User Daily name and the desired Odate for the jobs. ctmudly will look for tables (or SMART tables) stored in Control-M/Server that have the matching User Daily name. For the matching tables, Control-M will review each job within and order those jobs whose scheduling criteria are met for that day. The same User Daily name can be used by multiple tables, which means these tables will be ordered together when the ctmudly utility for this User Daily is executed:

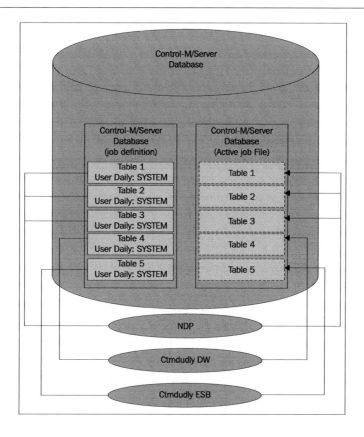

This feature allows shortening the NDP duration; it also provides a cleaner view if jobs are ordered closer to the time they need to run, and improves overall performance of Control-M. We will re-visit this topic in detail during *Chapter 7, Beyond Everyday Administration.*

Working with Control-M Desktop and EM GUI Client

By now we should have a good understanding of the important concepts within Control-M. So let's get practical and apply the knowledge we learned so far in this chapter by logging into Control-M/EM GUI Interfaces to define and run some real jobs.

The two Control-M/EM GUI Interfaces we are going to use soon are the Control-M Desktop for creating job definitions and Control-M/EM GUI Client for monitoring and controlling active job instances.

Control-M Desktop – the Workspace

When we double-click on the **Control-M Desktop 7.0.00 (Default)** orange color desktop shortcut icon, a pop-up window will appear and ask us for login username and password*. Because we haven't defined any new Control-M/EM users yet, we have to use the only account available, which was created during Control-M/EM server components installation – the **emuser** account. We can also skip the login by choosing the **Connect Later** option. By choosing this option, Control-M/Desktop will load up and allow us to use it in offline mode until we need to perform actions that require connection to Control-M/EM server, such as uploading and downloading jobs.

*We should see our Control-M/EM server hostname populated into the "Server" filed automatically. That means the Control-M Desktop has successfully located the GUI server.

Once we get into Control-M/Desktop, a Local Workspace will open by default. A workspace is where we normally define and modify jobs. Local Workspace means that jobs defined in there are not applied to Control-M/EM database unless we perform a Write action. We can also open an Online Workspace by selecting **New | File | Online Workspace**. With this mode, jobs are directly written into the Control-M/EM database as we are working on them. Of course, the Online Workspace requires connection with Control-M/EM server. If we have previously selected **Connect Later** during the initial login, the login window would pop up again by now and ask for Control-M/EM username and password.

Apart from the standard drop-down menus and toolbars on the top, Control-M Desktop GUI is dominated by the opened workspace and it is divided into three areas by the default viewing settings. On the left is the **Tree View** of jobs. Just like what we see in Windows Explorer, in here jobs are grouped either by Application/Group/Job or Datacenter/Table/Job. On the upper-right is the area for displaying individual jobs as well as the primary area we use when creating or modifying jobs. Jobs are displayed in `Flowdiagram` mode by default and can be grouped into Application/Group/Job or Datacenter/Table/Job types of hierarchies. The lower-right is the **Network Overview**. When the primary display area is not enough to display all jobs, we can see an over all picture of the job connection map from here. By holding the left mouse button within Network Overview, we are able to choose the portion of the job network to be displayed in the primary display area.

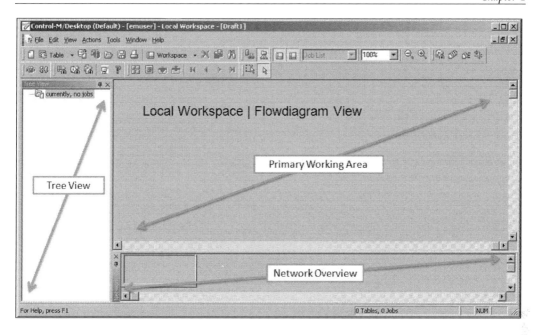

We can also display the jobs in `Job List` mode, by selecting **View | Job List**. In list mode, jobs are displayed in table form and we can sort the job according to column names. When `Job List` mode is selected, the Network Overview will disappear automatically.

For safety reasons, normally the user would define and modify jobs in offline mode first and perform the write action when everything is checked and confirmed. In order not to let users confuse between the two workspaces, the background color of online workspace's primary area and network overview area are in yellow, whereas in local workspace they are blue. Since Control-M/EM version 6.4.01, we are allowed to have multiple workspaces open; irrespective of whether Local or Online.

Control-M/EM GUI client – Active ViewPoint

There are two ways to get into the Control-M/EM GUI client. One way is to click on the **Control-M Enterprise Manager 7.0.00 (Default)** green icon on the desktop, the other way is to click on the same icon located in Control-M Desktop toolbar. Getting into Control-M/EM GUI client also requires login, but we can avoid logging in twice if it is initiated from a Control-M Desktop that has already been logged on.

Once the Control-M/EM GUI client is opened, we should see a majority of blank area other than the drop-down menus and toolbars. The blank area is for showing `ViewPoints`. In Control-M/EM, **Active ViewPoint** is used for displaying current active jobs and for us to perform manual actions on these jobs.

We can open an Active ViewPoint by choosing **File | Open ViewPoint**. We should see a pop-up window with a list of available ViewPoints. These are the predefined ViewPoints that fit different viewing needs. The name of each ViewPoint is pretty much self-explainatory and we can even define customized ViewPoints to meet our own viewing needs. For now, we will choose **All Jobs** to start with.

Once we have the All Jobs ViewPoint opened, we should see a layout which is very similar to what we saw in Control-M Desktop. The primary display area should have a writing that says **Empty ViewPoint**. This is because so far we haven't got any job ordered yet. With the Control-M/EM GUI client, we can also have the jobs displayed in a list format by clicking on **View | Job List**.

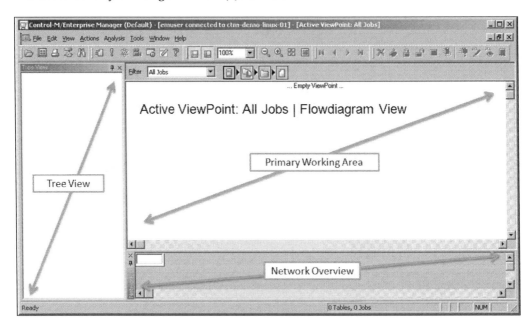

Defining and running jobs

Navigating around Control-M Desktop and EM GUI Client is fairly simple and straightforward. The most frequently used features are all shown as icons in the Toolbars area by default. Soon we will get to know these icons during the process of creating and managing jobs. We will start with a simple command-line job and gradually get into a bit more complicated job scheduling scenario.

Creating the first job – Hello World!

Almost all programming books start with teaching how to use the programming language to print "Hello World!". We will follow this tradition by creating our first job to print "Hello World!" in the job's output.

First, let's go back to Control-M Desktop and click on the first icon in the Toolbar – **New Job** (alliteratively choose **Edit | New | Job** or *Ctrl + J*). Now we should see a new job editing window popup in front of us.

Because we have two datacenters defined in our environment (CTM_LINUX and CTM_WIN), first of all we need to decide which datacenter the job will be belong to. Once the datacenter is chosen, the job's choice of execution hosts are limited to Control-M/Agents that are defined within that datacenter.

We first begin with the **General** tab. Within the **General** tab, we are required to specify what-, who-, and where-related job definitions. Our job definitions are as follows:

Item	Value
Job Name	**HelloWorld**
Task Type	**Command**
File Name	**HelloWorld**
Command	**echo 'Hello World!'**
Parent Table	**SimpleJobs**
Application	**Demo**
Group	**FirstDemo**
Owner	**ctmsrv**
Author	**emuser**
Description	**This is our first job to print "Hello World!" in the job's output**

- **Job Name**: **Job Name** is a free text field (allow 1- 64 characters) used for recognizing jobs in Control-M. The job name should at least make sense and reflect the purpose of the job. (In the real world, table, application, group, and job names normally follow a standard; for example, start with two characters pre-fix to indicate the application they belong to. In this case it is easy for job filtering and reporting).

- **Task Type**: We chose **Task Type** as **Command** because we are going to let the job directly trigger Unix/Linux command line `echo Hello World!`.

- **File Name**: File Name refers to the actual script file we are going to run when the **Task Type** is Job (allow 1- 64 characters). Because we are running a command here, the **Task Type** field is not mandatory. But in order to keep our jobs consistent across the board, we will give it a value the same as our **Job Name**. **File Name** is also called **Mem Name** in Control-M.

- **Command**: We enter the command-line argument here just like how we would execute it from the terminal (1 - 512 characters). If the command is more than 512 characters, we should consider storing the command line into an executable file and execute it as "Task Type – job".

- **Parent Table**: We haven't created any tables yet but we can just give it a name **SimpleJobs** (allows 1- 20 characters). By doing so, a traditional job table called **SimpleJobs** will get created automatically as the job is created.

- **Application and Group**: Application and Group names are also purely up to us to decide (allow 1- 64 characters). Later on if we use the same application and group names when we define other jobs, these jobs will be automatically grouped together.

- **Owner**: Because we are planning to execute the job on the Linux Control-M/Server's host, we have to define an existing operating system user as the job owner (allow 1- 30 characters). We wanted to run the job as the Control-M/Server user, therefore we define it as **ctmsrv**.

- **Author**: We don't have security settings to restrict the author value as yet; therefore theoretically we can enter any value to this field (allow 1- 64 characters). We enter **emuser** as the value because we are currently logged on as **emuser**.

- **Description**: This is a free text short description of the job (allow 1- 4,000 characters).

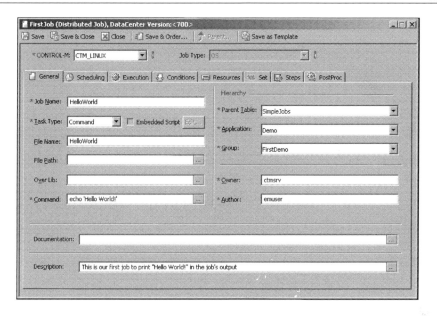

Now we move onto the Scheduling tab. In the Scheduling tab we can define When—which dates the job is to be scheduled on. For now let's define that this job is to be scheduled on every day of the month and every month of the year. After we click the **All** button in **Month Days** and the **All** button in **Months**, we can see every single day of the month and every month is now highlighted in blue color. This means as long as the job's table is reviewed for scheduling by NDP or User Daily each day, this job will be scheduled everyday of the year and forever.

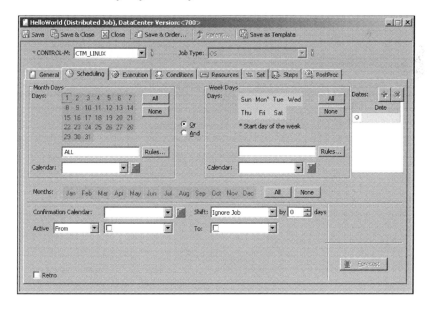

We continue on to the **Execution** tab. In the Execution tab, we can define the job's execution host – another Where. This information is to be defined in the **Node ID/Group** field. Because we are going to run the job on the Linux Control-M/Server host, we can leave this one blank. By leaving it blank Control-M/Server will submit the job onto its default local Control-M/Agent. So, nothing needs to be changed in this tab for the moment.

Now we can click on the **Save and Close** button located on the top of the job window to save what we have defined so far into the workspace.

After saving the job, we should see a new item show up in the Primary Working Area that has our Application Name written. By double-clicking the item twice, we should see our job "HelloWorld" appear within the Application and Group we defined. We can also expand the view by using the **Expand All** icon located in the toolbar. If we only want to work at the group or job level without worrying about the level(s) above, we can use the **Step into/out from the current level** toolbar icons to zoom-into and zoom-out from different levels.

We can view the same job in the **Table** hierarchy by clicking on the **View Hierarchy Datacetner/Table/Job** icon located in the toolbar. The **Expand All** and **Step into/out from the current level** icons are also applied to the **Table** hierarchy view.

Write, Upload, and Order the job

The job we have created so far is only saved as a job definition within our current Control-M Desktop Local Workspace. As we mentioned earlier in this chapter, we need to perform Write, Upload, and Order actions in order to run the job.

Write

The Write action refers to save all jobs definitions that are currently defined within the Local Workspace. We can perform the Write action by clicking on the **Write Jobs to Control-M/EM** icon located in toolbar. After clicking on the icon, a pop-up window will show up and list all tables that have been defined in the Local Workspace. We will highlight the only table on the list, **SimpleJobs**, and click on the **Write** button:

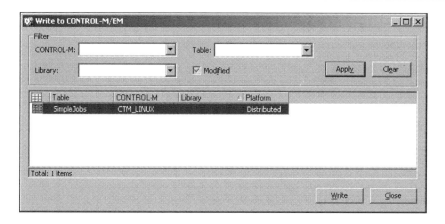

Shortly another pop-up window will appear with the result of the Write action –
Table SimpleJobs was successfully written to Control-M/EM database. By now, the
job definition has been saved into Control-M/EM database.

Upload

Now we need to Upload the job from the Control-M/EM database into the
Control-M/Server database, so that the job can be ordered later.

We click on the icon located in toolbar called **Table Manager** or go to the drop-down
menu **Tools | Table Manager**. In the **Table Manager** we first select the datacenter
where our job belongs to, **CTM_LINUX**, and click on the **Apply** button. Now the table
we just defined will show up on the list. We highlight the table and click on the **Upload**
button located on the top of the table manager window. After confirming it, we will see
an **Action report window** show up with a message that says the upload is successful.

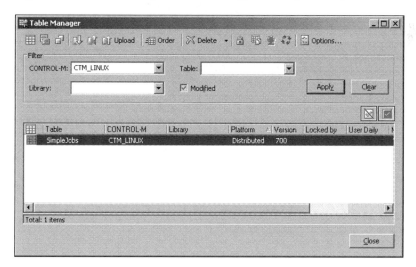

In **Table Manager**, we are also able to view the job by double-clicking on the table name, followed by clicking on the job name in the **Table Content** pop-up window. In here we can modify the job and save the changes. But please note the change we saved here will directly apply to Control-M/EM database but not affect the job we just defined in Local Workspace. In order to see an updated version of the job in Workspace, we need to perform a Load action by clicking on the Toolbar icon **Load from Control-M/EM** and selecting the desired datacenter, table, and job.

Order

This is the last step to let the job become active. So far, both Control-M/EM and Control-M/Server have a copy of the job we just defined. The order action will allow Control-M/Server to review the job's scheduling criteria and create its active job instance in the Active Job File for execution.

While we are still in the Table Manager, we make sure our table is highlighted and then click on the **Order** button located on the right side of the **Upload** button. A pop-up window called **Order/Force Parameters** will ask us how we would like the job to be ordered. By default, the job will be ordered with the current Control-M day – ODAT and we do have the option to order the job on a different day. **Upload table before ordering** option is ticked by default, but because we have just uploaded the table we can tick this option off. Once we click on the **Order** button, the **Action report** window will show up again with a message that says the ordering is successful.

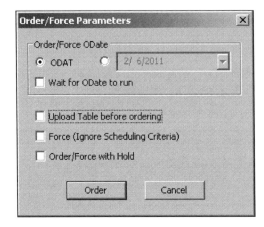

 We also noticed there's an `orderno` given for our job in the **Action report** window. For each active job instance, Control-M will give a unique order number to the job. It is a base 36 number counting from 1. It is useful for tracking active jobs.

Monitor and Control the Job

Now, if we go to the Control-M/EM GUI client, we should see an item appear within the primary working area with **CTM_LINUX** written – our datacenter name. By double-clicking multiple times or clicking on the **Expand All** toolbar icon we should see the **HelloWorld** job appear within **CTM_LINUX/Demo/FirstDemo**. More likely the job will be in Green color, which means the job has completed by the time we switch over from Control-M Desktop (that is, only a command-line job, therefore it should complete very quickly).

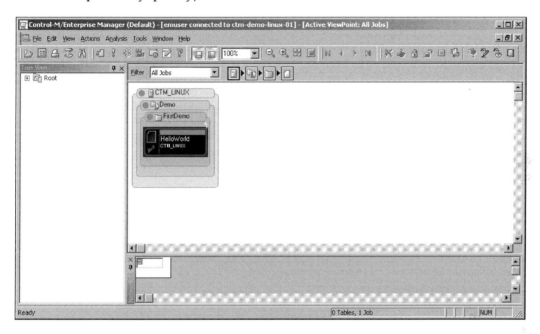

If we double-click on the job (or select the job and click on the toolbar icon **Job Action: Properties**, a window will pop up which is very similar to the job definition window in the Control-M Desktop. But soon we will notice most of the fields are grayed out. We also see the "Scheduling tab" in the job definition tab is replaced with **Active** tab. This is because the job's scheduling dates-related criteria are irrelevant for each active job instance. Instead, the active window shows the active job's Order ID (orderno), Job ID, Current Status, Order date, and Rerun counter, as well as additional information indicating the job's start/end time and average runtime. If we move to the next tab, we will see the default job execution hostname is populated into the **Node ID** field. We also see value **AA** has been populated into the **Priority** field*.

Order ID gets generated each time the job is ordered, whereas Job ID gets generated each time the job is submitted for execution. If we rerun the same job instance many times, we will see the Job ID gets updated each time when the rerun starts.

*Priority "AA" is the lowest job priority in Control-M. It is the default priority for jobs unless specified during job creation.

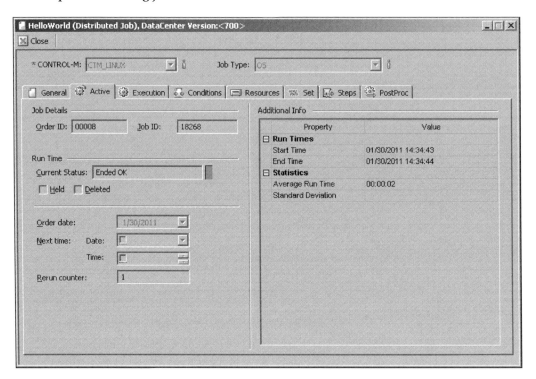

Job Sysout

Now let's have a look at the job's output – job Sysout. We right-click on the job and select the **Sysout...** option in the menu or click the toolbar icon **Job Action: Sysout...**. Now we should see two pop-up windows appear; one provides a list of sysouts available for viewing and it also provides each job execution's starting and ending time, ending status (Operating System return code), sysout size, and state. The other window shows the actual job output*. There are many very handy features provided with the sysout window, such as Find keywords, Show line number, Toggle bookmark, and so on.

*Since Control-M version 7, if the job has only executed once, the Control-M/EM GUI client will open the only sysout by default.

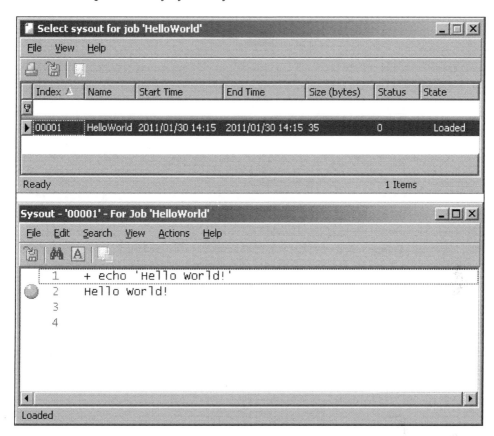

Rerun a Job

If we really want to see what the job is like when it's executing, we can manually rerun the job by right-clicking on the job and selecting **Rerun** or clicking on the toolbar icon **Job Action: Rerun**. A pop-up window will ask if we really want to rerun the job; once we click on **Yes** we will see the job imminently turns yellow and back to green again. Yellow means the job is in an executing state.

Job Log

We can get to know the job's execution history details by looking at the job log. When we right-click on **Log**, a pop-up window will appear with all history related to this job instance. Each history has a timestamp, a code and a description (message). From here, we can identify when the job was ordered, when it was submitted, and start and end execution time, as well as a run count for each execution. The job log window also provides some basic features including Find keyword and font change.

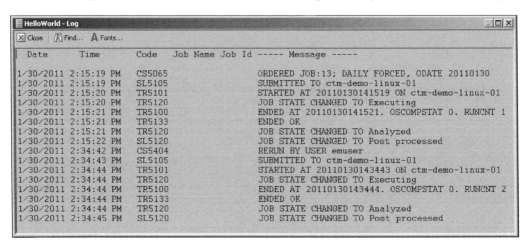

Job Statistics

We can check the job execution statistics by right-clicking on the job and selecting **Statistics**. In this window, we can see each job execution's starting and ending time, elapsed time, and CPU time. Job statistics also provides the average job elapsed time and CPU time. In the job **Statistics** window, we also can perform "Find keyword" and change the display font.

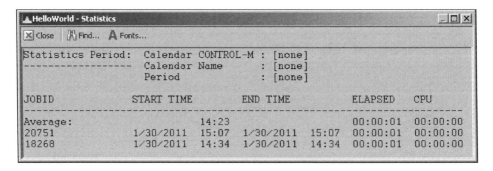

Modifying and rerunning the job

There are two ways to modify a job but the outcomes are rather different. One is to modify the static job definition from Control-M Desktop; the other way is to modify the active job instance. By modifying the static job definition, the change will be applied to the job permanently. Whereas if we modify the active job instance, the change will only apply to the instance itself rather than affecting how the job will be ordered and run in the future.

Modifying the static job definition

Static job definition modification is done via Control-M Desktop. If we have already closed the Control-M Desktop window, we can use the shortcut in the Control-M/ EM GUI Client's toolbar – **Start Control-M Desktop** icon.

After we open the Control-M Desktop, we should see a brand new Local Workspace open in front of us. First we need to Load the job we defined earlier back into this workspace. By clicking on the **Load from Control-M/EM** icon, a **Load Job (Local)** window will appear. From there, we can select the table we would like to load and it also allows us to apply filters to limit the displayed jobs. Once the desired table is selected (all jobs under that table will be selected), we can click on **Load** to let the job appear in our workspace:

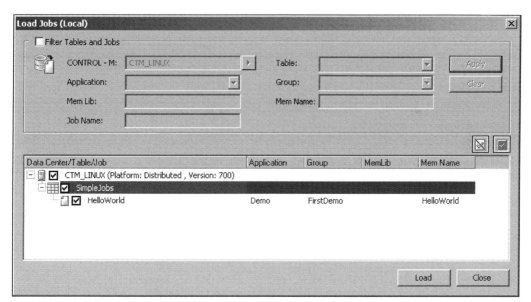

We expand the job and double-click on the job to open the definition window. This time we will modify the job's **Task Type** from **Command** to **Job**. We notice that the **Command** field has grayed out and the **File Path** field has become editable. The **File Path** field is for us to specify where the actual executable script is stored on the job execution host. Before we enter any value into it, let's go to the job execution host to create the script.

Commonly, batch scripts are executed by a dedicated user defined in the operating system (we can call it a "batch user"), and the scripts are stored under the batch user's home directory or somewhere the batch user has the permission to access. We will use this method later on for the more complicated job flow. For now we will just put the script under /tmp directory.

We connect to ctm-demo-linux-01, log in as user ctmsrv (Control-M/Server user), go to /tmp directory and use vi text editor to create a file called HelloWorld. sh. Within the file, we define the following code:

```
!#/bin/sh
echo 'Hello World!'
```

Once saved and exited, make sure to change the permission of the file to owner executable and also verify that the owner of the file is ctmsrv:

```
ctm-demo-linux-01% pwd
/tmp
ctm-demo-linux-01% ls -la Hello*
-rw-r----- 1 ctmsrv ctmsrv 31 Jan 30 17:18 HelloWorld.sh
ctm-demo-linux-01% cat HelloWorld.sh
#!/bin/sh

echo 'Hello World!'
ctm-demo-linux-01% chmod 750 HelloWorld.sh
ctm-demo-linux-01% ls -la Hello*
-rwxr-x--- 1 ctmsrv ctmsrv 31 Jan 30 17:18 HelloWorld.sh
ctm-demo-linux-01%
```

Now we come back to Control-M Desktop, enter **/tmp** into the **File Path** field and change the value of **File Name** filed into **HelloWorld.sh**. By doing so, during job execution Control-M will "join" the two fields together to trigger the actual job script:

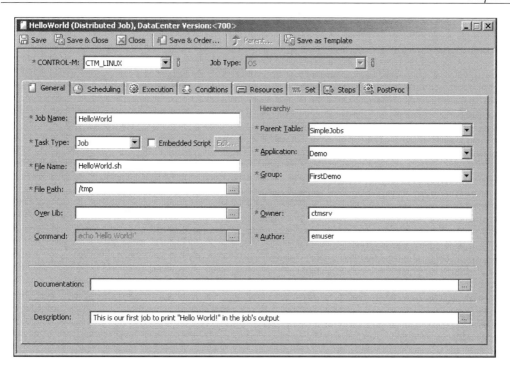

This time instead of going through the **Save | Write | Upload | Order** process, we will directly order the job by clicking on the **Save & Order** option located on top of the job editing form.

After we click on the button, the same **Order/Force Parameters** window will pop up. This time we have to tick the **Upload Table before ordering** option because we haven't uploaded the updated job definition to Control-M/Server yet:

After clicking on the **Order** button, we can see there are two messages showing up in the **Action Report** window, which are a combination of what we see during Write, Upload, and Order:

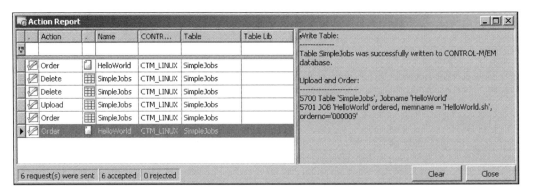

Now if we go back to Control-M/EM GUI client, we should see a second **HelloWorld** job appear under application **demo** and group **FirstDemo**. We also noticed the text displayed in the job is **HelloWord.sh** instead of **HelloWorld**. This is because Control-M/EM GUI client display job's **Filename (MEMNAME)**, by default.

For script jobs (**Task Type**: **Job**), we can view and modify the script from Control-M/EM GUI client directly without logging in to the actual job execution machine. This is done by clicking on the **View/Edit JCL** option*. We can find this feature from the Toolbar or the job's menu (right-click on the job). If we modify the script here, the change will be applied to the actual script stored on the server.

*The name **View/Edit JCL** was originally inherited from Control-M for Mainframe.

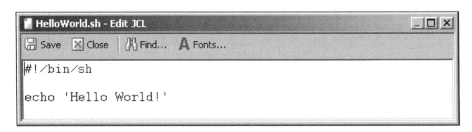

As we mentioned earlier, the changes we made to the job definition are permanent. If we order the job again, we will see that the new job instance also has the same value in **Task Type**, **File Name**, and **File Path**.

Modifying the active job instance

Let's use the job we just ordered to have a look at how to modify an active job instance on-the-fly. We right-click on the new **HelloWorld** job and select the **Hold** option from the menu. By doing this, the job is in modifiable state and it will not run even if all prerequisites are met. In a few seconds, we should see a yellow color lock appear at the lower-right corner of the job. Now if we double-click on the job. we should see the job window open with modifiable fields:

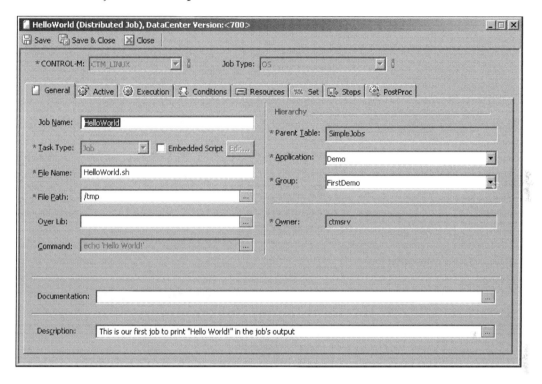

What we are going to modify is, instead of running the script located on the job execution host, we will store the script within the job definition by using the "Embedded Script" feature.

First of all, select the **Embedded Script** tick box. Once we have done that the * at the **File Path** will disappear and the **Edit** button next to the **Embedded Script** text will become available. We simply click on the button and paste the content of the script into the pop-up window. There's a **Load from File…** option is designed if we want to load the script from the workstation we are using:

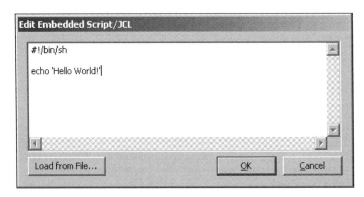

After clicking on the **OK** button the script is stored in the job and we can feel free to remove the value in **File Path** field because the job will no longer go to that directory to locate the script. Now we can click on the **Save & Close** button located on the top of the job editing window and then right-click on the job and select **Free**. Once the yellow lock icon is gone, we can right-click the job again and select **Rerun** to re-submit the job for execution.

One more thing to mention is the **File Name** field. If the job is going to be submitted to a Unix/Linux environment, we can have any name we want. But if it is a Windows job, the **File Name** still has to have an executable file extension (for example, .bat or .exe). This is because during job submission, Control-M/Agent will create a temporary script with the name we specified on the job execution host to store the content of the script and then execute it. In Windows environments, if the file hasn't got an executable file extension; the operating system simply rejects it and causes the job to fail. We will get the following error message in Control-M joblog:

```
Field "File Name" in Job Editing Form must include
an extension for running an Embedded Script job on
Windows, for example ".CMD".
```

A more complicated job flow

Based on what we have learned so far, let's look at a more complicated scenario. In this section, we will create a job flow that does some batch processing on incoming files and then sends the output file to a number of destinations for further processing. The story is as follow (the scenario we are presenting may not be realistic and there might be better ways to achieve the outcome, but the purpose here is to demonstrate features of Control-M):

There is a type of datafile constantly getting generated and accumulating in a source directory. Each datafile contains records of "staff name, title, department, location, staff ID, staff password" in .csv format. Once in every 30 minutes, we are going to copy these files into a staging area, clear the source directory, and process these source files in batch mode by combining them into a single file. Then we will sort the records, removing duplications, and splitting the records into different files according to each record's "department" column and store each of these files into each "department's" own directory accordingly. There are six different kinds of departments in total and the destination directories are located on two different machines (three on each machine). Once all department output files are created, we will combine the contents of these department files into a history file with a timestamp (one history file on each machine), and then clean the staging area for the next batch of source files to be processed. This processing happens on each working day (except weekends and Australian public holidays) from 9:00 p.m. to 06:00 a.m. next day. Sample of the datafile:

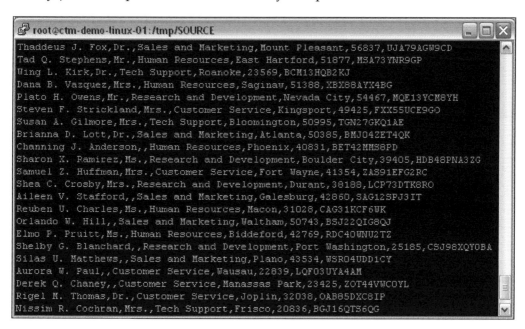

Based on the requirement in the previous exercise, we came up with the following jobs:

- Job MOVE_SourceFiles runs on ctm-demo-linux-02 to move all files called SOURCE_CSV_<ID>.csv from the source directory into our staging area for processing every 30 minutes (from its start).

- Job JOIN_SourceFiles runs right after each execution of MOVE_SourceFiles on ctm-demo-linux-02 to join the delivered source files at the staging area in a large file called SOURCE_CSV_JOINED.csv.

- Job SORT_JoinedFile runs on ctm-demo-linux-02 to sort the entries in SOURCE_CSV_JOINED.csv by the staff's Firstname into alphabetic order and produce an output file called SOURCE_CSV_SORTED.csv.

- Job REMOVE-DUPLICATE_SortedFile runs on ctm-demo-linux-02 to remove any duplicate entries in file SOURCE_CSV_SORTED.csv and produce a file called SOURCE_CSV_NO-DUPLICATE.csv.

- Job COPY_ProcessedFile_department*:
  - COPY_ProcessedFile_department-01/2/3 three jobs run parallel on ctm-demo-linux-02 to move file SOURCE_CSV_NO-DUPLICATE.csv into three separate directories located on ctm-demo-linux-02.
  - COPY_ProcessedFile_department-04/5/6 three jobs run parallel on ctm-demo-win-01 to move file SOURCE_CSV_NO-DUPLICATE.csv into two separate directories on ctm-demo-win-01.

- Job FILTER_Record_department*:
  - FILTER_Record_department-01/2/3 run on ctm-demo-linux-02 and ctm-demo-win-01 parallelly to filter records from the file according to each destination's requirement.
  - FILTER_Record_department-04/5/6 run on ctm-demo-win-01 parallel to filter records from the file according to each destination's requirement.

- Job JOIN_Records_department*:
  - Jobs JOIN_Records_department-01/2/3 run on ctm-demo-linux-02 to feed the filtered data with a timestamp into a common history file located on ctm-demo-linux-02 – HISTORY_LINUX.txt.
  - Jobs JOIN_Records_department-04/5/6 run on ctm-demo-win-01 to feed the filtered data with a timestamp into a common history file located on ctm-demo-linux-02 – HISTORY_WIN.txt.

- Job `CLEAR_Staging` runs on `ctm-demo-linux-02` to clear any files created in the staging directory during the processing; therefore, the job flow can start over again from `MOVE_SourceFiles` job for the next iteration.

Special requirements:

- The transfer only happens each day between 9:00 p.m. and 06:00 a.m. next day.

- Job `MOVE_SourceFiles` can only pick up the next batch of source files (rerun) if all down flow jobs are completed. In other words, if the down flow jobs are running for more than 30 minutes, `MOVE_SourceFiles` needs to wait for the last job of the flow to complete before picking up new files.

- If `MOVE_SourceFiles` did not move any files during iteration (that is, no source files were generated since the last time the directory was cleaned), then instead of triggering rest of the flow, it will wait for the next rerun and trigger the down flow jobs if there are files being moved.

- The history file is to be written by only one job at a time.

- The job flow doesn't run on weekends and Australian public holidays.

- If any of the jobs fail, an alert should be raised to Control-M Alert window.

Here's a diagram of the job logic:

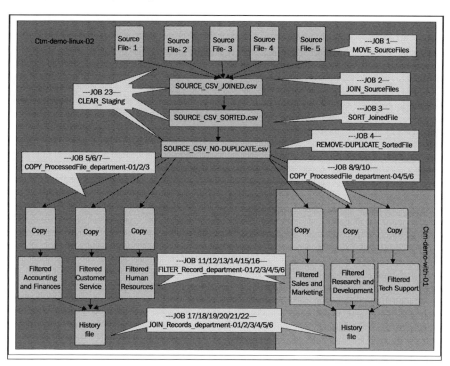

Defining SMART table, application, and group

We decided to use the SMART table for this job flow. First of all, we will create the SMART table in Control-M Desktop and define the application and group name for it.

We open Control-M Desktop with a new Local Workspace, click on the black arrow next to the "Table" Toolbar icon and select "SMART Table" (or we can just click on the "Table" icon and make sure the pop-up table editing form says "Distributed SMART Table" on the top, otherwise click on the "SMART Table" tick box located in the upper-middle area of the table editing form). Once the table editing form is opened, we enter the following value into the SMART Table editing form:

Tab	Field	Value
	Control-M	**CTM_LINUX**
General	**Table**	**FP-FixedTime**
General	**UserDaily**	**SYSTEM (We let Control-M NDP order the job each day)**
General	**Application**	**Demo**
General	**Group**	**SecondDemo**
General	**Author**	**emuser**
General	**Description**	**Container of the file processing jobs on CTM_LINUX**
Scheduling	**RBC Name**	**ALL**

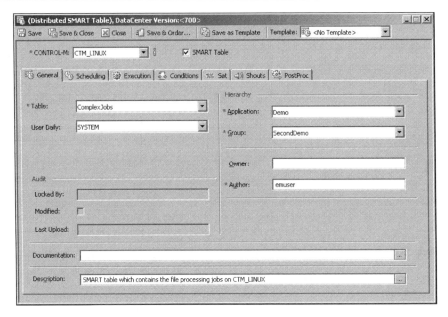

In order to save the job we have to specify at least one **RBC Name** under the **Scheduling** tab, but we will leave the actual scheduling information empty for now.

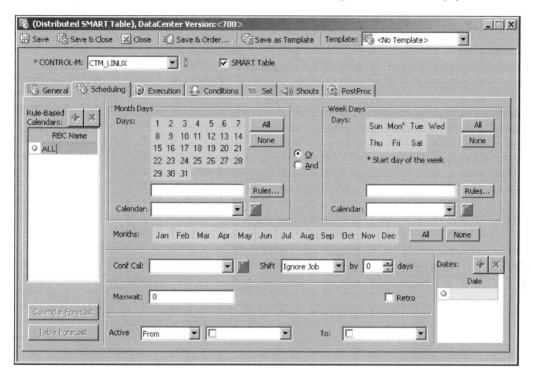

SMART tables are specific to datacenter. Because we have jobs running under the Windows agent that are connected to the Windows Control-M/Server, we need to define a second SMART table for datacenter CTM_WIN to contain those jobs. Instead of creating another SMART table from scratch, we can right-click on the SMART table we just created in Control-M Desktop and select **Copy and Edit...**. In the table editing form, simply change the **Control-M** name from **CTM_LINUX** to **CTM_WIN** and click on **Save & Close**.

By now, we have two SMART tables in the workspace under the same application and group.

Building cyclic jobs

The first job we are going to build is `MOVE_SourceFiles`, which requires to be submitted every 10 minutes (counting starts from the end of last execution) between the time frame of 09:00 p.m. to 06:00 a.m. It will be a cyclic job with a fixed rerun interval.

We create the job by right-clicking on the SMART table for **CTM_LINUX** and clicking on **Add Job**. We will notice in the new job editing form there are number of fields common to the SMART table which are automatically populated with the value we specified earlier. The rest of the parameters we specified in the job editing form are as follows:

Tab	Field	Value
General	Job Name	MOVE_SourceFiles
General	Task Type	Job
General	Embedded Script	Yes
General	Embedded Script Content	#!/bin/sh mv /home/file_tran/source/SOURCE_CSV_*.csv /home/file_tran/staging/.
General	Filename	MOVE_SourceFiles.sh
General	Owner	file_tran (A user called "file_tran" has been defined on the job execution machine)
General	Description	Move the datafiles from source directory into staging directory
Scheduling	Rule-Based Calendars	ALL (By clicking on the **Select** button and selecting RBC as **ALL**)
Execution	Node ID/Group	ctm-demo-linux-02
Execution	Submit between	2100 to 0600
Execution	Cyclic Job	Yes
Execution	Cyclic Job Run Times	Rerun every 30 minutes from job's "Start"

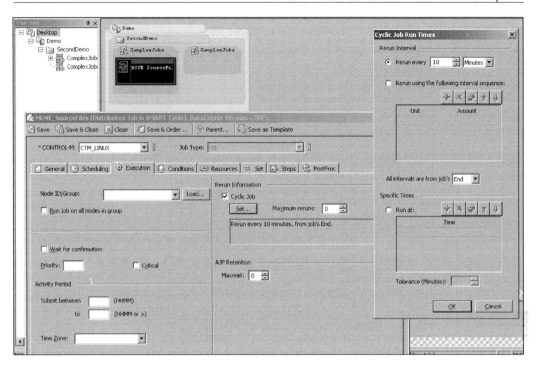

Once we save the job editing form, we will notice a job appear under the SMART table. It has a special icon which represents that it is a cyclic job.

Based on this job, we can simply do **Copy and Edit** to create the next job JOIN_SourceFiles. Two things to keep in mind are:

- This job still needs to be cyclic but we don't have to specify a rerun internal. This is because the rerun of the job is limited by the predecessor job's completion (once we have job conditions defined between them). That is, all down flow jobs have to wait for the predecessor job to complete and send out the required "Out-condition" for them to start and they are all controlled by the first job in the flow which only runs every 30 minutes.

- This job doesn't require "from" and "to" time. If the next execution of MOVE_SourceFiles is out of the time frame, MOVE_SourceFiles will not run and therefore, will not produce the condition to fulfill the "In-condition" of JOIN_SourceFiles.

After we defined JOIN_SourceFiles, we can do a **Copy and Edit** on this job to create all the other jobs.

Please note, when we define those Windows jobs by **Copy and Edit** (that is, jobs that are going to be running on `ctm-demo-win-01`), we need to change each job's **Control-M** value from **CTM_LINUX** to **CTM_WIN** and the value of **Node ID/Group** should be **ctm-demo-win-01**.

Here's a summary of each job that we are going to create:

Tab	Field	Value
General	Job Name	JOIN_SourceFiles
General	Task Type	Job
General	Embedded Script	Yes
General	Embedded Script Content	#!/bin/sh cat /home/file_tran/staging/SOURCE_CSV_*.csv > /home/file_tran/staging/SOURCE_CSV_JOINED.csv
General	Filename	JOIN_SourceFiles.sh
General	Owner	file_tran
General	Description	Join all source files into a single file
Scheduling	Rule-Based Calendars	ALL (By clicking on the **Select** button and select RBC as **ALL**)
Execution	Node ID/Group	ctm-demo-linux-02
Execution	Cyclic Job	Yes
Execution	Cyclic Job Run Times	Rerun every 0 minutes from job's "Start"
General	Job Name	SORT_JoinedFile
General	Task Type	Job
General	Embedded Script	Yes
General	Embedded Script Content	#!/bin/sh sort /home/file_tran/staging/SOURCE_CSV_JOINED.csv > /home/file_tran/staging/SOURCE_CSV_SORTED.csv
General	Filename	SORT_JoinedFile.sh
General	Owner	file_tran
General	Description	Sort records by staff first name according to alphabetical order
Scheduling	Rule-Based Calendars	ALL (By clicking on the **Select** button and select RBC as **ALL**)
Execution	Node ID/Group	ctm-demo-linux-02

Tab	Field	Value
Execution	Cyclic Job	Yes
Execution	Cyclic Job Run Times	Rerun every 0 minutes from job's "Start"
General	Job Name	REMOVE-DUPLICATE_SortedFile
General	Task Type	Job
General	Embedded Script	Yes
General	Embedded Script Content	#!/bin/sh
		cat /home/file_tran/staging/SOURCE_CSV_ SORTED.csv | uniq -u > /home/file_tran/staging/ SOURCE_CSV_NO-DUPLICATE.csv
General	Filename	REMOVE-DUPLICATE_SortedFile.sh
General	Owner	file_tran
General	Description	Remove duplicate records from the file
Scheduling	Rule-Based Calendars	ALL (By clicking on the **Select** button and select RBC as **ALL**)
Execution	Node ID/Group	ctm-demo-linux-02
Execution	Cyclic Job	Yes
Execution	Cyclic Job Run Times	Rerun every 0 minutes from job's "Start"
General	Job Name	COPY_ProcessedFile_department-01 COPY_ ProcessedFile_department-02
		COPY_ProcessedFile_department-03
General	Task Type	Job
General	Embedded Script	Yes
General	Embedded Script Content	##!/bin/sh
		cp /home/file_tran/staging/SOURCE_CSV_NO- DUPLICATE.csv /home/file_tran/dest/$1
General	Filename	COPY_ProcessedFile_department-01.sh COPY_ ProcessedFile_department-02.sh
		COPY_ProcessedFile_department-03.sh
General	Owner	file_tran
General	Description	Copy the sorted file into destination directory
Scheduling	Rule-Based Calendars	ALL (By clicking on the Select button and select RBC as **ALL**)
Execution	Node ID/Group	ctm-demo-linux-02

Tab	Field	Value
Execution	Cyclic Job	Yes
Execution	Cyclic Job Run Times	Rerun every 0 minutes from job's "Start"
General	Job Name	COPY_ProcessedFile_department-04 COPY_ProcessedFile_department-05
		COPY_ProcessedFile_department-06
General	Task Type	Job
General	Embedded Script	Yes
General	Embedded Script Content	echo "y" | pscp -pw pa88w0rd file_tran@ctm-demo-linux-02:/home/file_tran/staging/SOURCE_CSV_NO-DUPLICATE.csv c:\file_tran\dest\%1\SOURCE_CSV_NO-DUPLICATE.csv
General	Filename	COPY_ProcessedFile_department-04.bat COPY_ProcessedFile_department-05.bat
		COPY_ProcessedFile_department-06.bat
General	Owner	SYSTEM (value ignored)
General	Description	Copy the sorted file into destination directory
Scheduling	Rule-Based Calendars	ALL (By clicking on the **Select** button and select RBC as **ALL**)
Execution	Node ID/Group	ctm-demo-win-01
Execution	Cyclic Job	Yes
Execution	Cyclic Job Run Times	Rerun every 0 minutes from job's "Start"
General	Job Name	FILTER_Record_department-01
		FILTER_Record_department-02
		FILTER_Record_department-03
General	Task Type	Job
General	Embedded Script	Yes
General	Embedded Script Content	#!/bin/sh
		cat /home/file_tran/dest/$1/SOURCE_CSV_NO-DUPLICATE.csv | grep "$2" >> /home/file_tran/dest/$1/$1.csv
		rm /home/file_tran/dest/$1/SOURCE_CSV_NO-DUPLICATE.csv

Tab	Field	Value
General	Filename	FILTER_Record_department-01.sh
		FILTER_Record_department-02.sh
		FILTER_Record_department-03.sh
General	Owner	file_tran
General	Description	Filter the file according to department name
Scheduling	Rule-Based Calendars	ALL (By clicking on the **Select** button and select RBC as **ALL**)
Execution	Node ID/Group	ctm-demo-linux-02
Execution	Cyclic Job	Yes
Execution	Cyclic Job Run Times	Rerun every 0 minutes from job's "Start"
General	Job Name	FILTER_Record_department-04
		FILTER_Record_department-05
		FILTER_Record_department-06
General	Task Type	Job
General	Embedded Script	Yes
General	Embedded Script Content	find %2 c:\file_tran\dest\%1\SOURCE_CSV_NO-DUPLICATE.csv >> c:\file_tran\dest\%1\%1.csv
		ech 'y' | del c:\file_tran\dest\%1\SOURCE_CSV_NO-DUPLICATE.csv
General	Filename	FILTER_Record_department-04.sh
		FILTER_Record_department-05.sh
		FILTER_Record_department-06.sh
General	Owner	SYSTEM (value ignored)
General	Description	Move the sorted file into remote destination directory
Scheduling	Rule-Based Calendars	ALL (By clicking on **Select** button and select RBC as **ALL**)
Execution	Node ID/Group	ctm-demo-win-01
Execution	Cyclic Job	Yes
Execution	Cyclic Job Run Times	Rerun every 0 minutes from job's "Start"

Tab	Field	Value
General	Job Name	JOIN_Records_department-01
		JOIN_Records_department-02
		JOIN_Records_department-03
General	Task Type	Command
General	Embedded Script	Yes
General	Embedded Script Content	echo %%TIMESTAMP >> /home/file_tran/dest/ HISTORY_LINUX.txt ; cat /home/file_tran/ dest/%%DIRNAME/%%FILENAME >> /home/ file_tran/dest/HISTORY_LINUX.txt
General	Owner	file_tran
General	Description	Join records into a history file
Scheduling	Rule-Based Calendars	ALL (By clicking on the **Select** button and select RBC as **ALL**)
Execution	Node ID/Group	ctm-demo-linux-02
Execution	Cyclic Job	Yes
Execution	Cyclic Job Run Times	Rerun every 0 minutes from job's "Start"
General	Job Name	JOIN_Records_department-04
		JOIN_Records_department-05
		JOIN_Records_department-06
General	Task Type	Command
General	Embedded Script	Yes
General	Embedded Script Content	echo %%TIMESTAMP >> C:\file_tran\dest\ HISTORY_WIN.txt & more C:\file_tran\ dest\"%%DIRNAME"\"%%FILENAME" >> C:\ file_tran\dest\HISTORY_WIN.txt
General	Filename	JOIN_Records_department-04.bat
		JOIN_Records_department-05.bat
		JOIN_Records_department-06.bat
General	Owner	SYSTEM (value ignored)
General	Description	Join records into a history file
Scheduling	Rule-Based Calendars	ALL (By clicking on the **Select** button and select RBC as **ALL**)
Execution	Node ID/Group	ctm-demo-win-01
Execution	Cyclic Job	Yes
Execution	Cyclic Job Run Times	Rerun every 0 minutes from job's "Start"

Tab	Field	Value
General	Job Name	CLEAR_Staging
General	Task Type	Job
General	Embedded Script	Yes
General	Embedded Script Content	#!/bin/sh rm /home/file_tran/staging/*.csv
General	Filename	CLEAR_Staging.sh
General	Owner	file_tran
General	Description	Clean the staging area for the next transfer
Scheduling	Rule-Based Calendars	ALL (By clicking on the **Select** button and select RBC as **ALL**)
Execution	Node ID/Group	ctm-demo-linux-02
Execution	Cyclic Job	Yes
Execution	Cyclic Job Run Times	Rerun every 0 minutes from job's "Start"

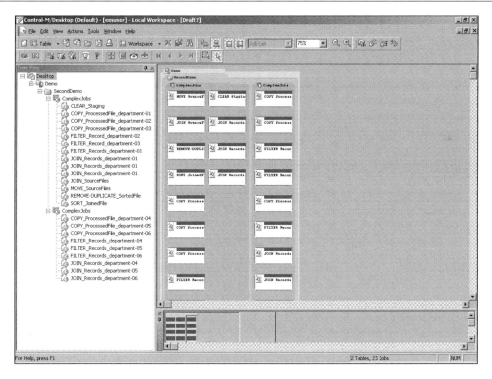

We should end up with two SMART tables and 23 jobs.

Utilizing the Autoedit facility

We utilize the Autoedit facility to reduce the complicity of our batch flow and make it become much more flexible. We can define Autoedit variables from the **Set** tab within the job editing form. For each Autoedit variable, we are required to enter the variable name and value. There are four types of Autoedit variables in total, which are **Job Submission Variables**, **System Variables**, **User-defined Variables**, and **Variable list**. We introduced the first three types in our job definitions.

Job submission variables

Those $1 and %1 that appeared in our job scripts are the arguments to be assigned at each job's runtime. As such we can use generic script for jobs that perform the same task rather than hard-code job-specific information into each individual definition. For each job we define "Autoedit variables" to hold the job-specific value and let it get passed to the script by Control-M during job submission.

The variables PARMn we used in the sample jobs are Job Submission type variables. Whatever value we assigned to these variables will be passed to the job script as arguments; the number n is the sequence number of the argument (from 1 to 32). For example, PARM1 refers to the first argument of the script; the value of PARM1 will be assigned to the corresponding variable in the script— $1 in Unix/Linux and %1 in Windows. Therefore, executing echo 123 in a Unix/Linux shell script is equivalent to executing echo $1 in the script and assigning PARM1 = 123 in the job definition:

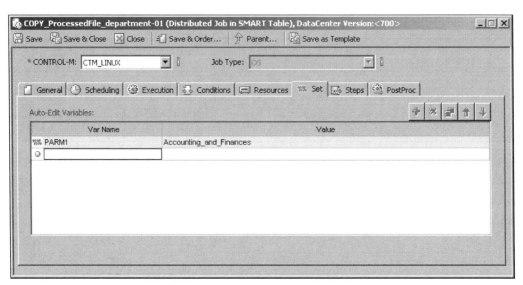

Here's a summary of all Job Submission types of Autoedit variables that we assigned to the jobs:

Job Name	PARM1	PARM2
COPY_ProcessedFile_ department-01	Accounting_and_ Finances	
COPY_ProcessedFile_ department-02	Customer_Service	
COPY_ProcessedFile_ department-03	Human_Resources	
COPY_ProcessedFile_ department-04	Sales_and_Marketing	
COPY_ProcessedFile_ department-05	Research_and_ Development	
COPY_ProcessedFile_ department-06	Tech_Support	
FILTER_Records_ department-01	Accounting_and_ Finances	Accounting and Finances
FILTER_Records_ department-02	Customer_Service	Customer Service
FILTER_Records_ department-03	Human_Resources	Human Resources
FILTER_Records_ department-04	Sales_and_Marketing	"Sales and Marketing"
FILTER_Records_ department-05	Research_and_ Development	"Research and Development"
FILTER_Records_ department-06	Tech_Support	"Tech Support"

(There are other types of job submission variables available for different types of operating systems. PARMn is one of the most commonly used job submission variables in the Windows and Unix/Linux environment).

User-defined Variables

With User-defined Variables, we get to choose the variable name and decide where they will be used. The variable can be used at many places within the job. It can be embedded into a job's command line (**Task Type** has to be **Command**), or included it as part of the SHOUT message. Within the job definition, the variable is to be invoked by the %% pre-fix followed by the variable name (case sensitive). The scope of User-defined Variable is at the job level, but with special syntax they can also be used at the SMART table and Datacenter (Global variable) level*.

*In this example, we only introduce job level User-defined Variables. SMART table-level variable will be discussed in *Chapter 8, Road to Workload Automation*.

We have used three User-defined Variables in the task type command job—JOIN_Records_department-0x. These variables are: %%TIMESTAMP, %%DIRNAME, and %%FILENAME. Just as we did for the Job Submission Variables, User-defined Variables are also to be specified in the **Set** tab.

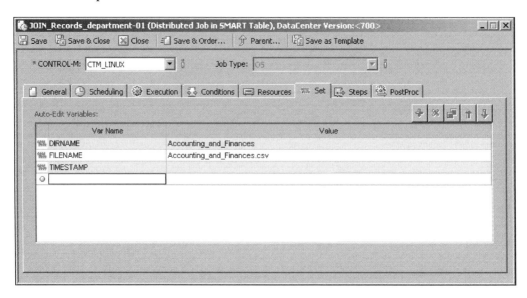

Variable DIRNAME represents the department output file directory and FILENAME represents the name of the department file. During job's runtime, Control-M will insert the value of the variables into the command line to execute. For example, based on the variable values in the screenshot, during the job's runtime command-line argument more C:\file_tran\dest\"%%DIRNAME"\"%%FILENAME" will become more C:\file_tran\dest\"Accounting_and_Finances"\"Accounting_and_Finances.csv.

Variable TIMESTAMP is a little bit special; we will enter the name but leave the value blank for the next section – *System Variables*. Apart from that, here is a summary of all Job Submission type of Autoedit variables we assigned to jobs (excluding %%TIMESTAMP):

Job Name	DIRNAME	FILENAME
JOIN_Records_ department-01	Accounting_and_ Finances	Accounting_and_ Finances.csv
JOIN_Records_ department-02	Customer_Service	Customer_Service.csv

Job Name	DIRNAME	FILENAME
`JOIN_Records_` `department-03`	`Human_Resources`	`Human_Resources.csv`
`JOIN_Records_` `department-04`	`Sales_and_Marketing`	`Sales_and_Marketing.` `csv`
`JOIN_Records_` `department-05`	`Research_and_` `Development`	`Research_and_` `Development.csv`
`JOIN_Records_` `department-06`	`Tech_Support`	`Tech_Support.csv`

System Variables

System Variables are a group of Autoedit Variables that are reserved by Control-M to hold commonly used system information. The variable can be datacenter-wide or limited to each individual job. These variables are such as system date, year, job name, datacenter name, Control-M date, and so on. The values of these variables are updated automatically when they change or only available at individual job's runtime (before or after job's execution— such as job's return code or job's average runtime).

The system variables we used in our example are `%%DATE` and `%%TIME`. In our `JOIN_Records_department-0x` jobs, we print the combined value of these two variables as a timestamp into the history file before each time the records are dumped. Instead of directly invoking the two variables in the script, we assigned the value of these two variables into a single User-defined Variable `%%TIMESTAMP` by using Autoedit Expression – "." (String concatenating):

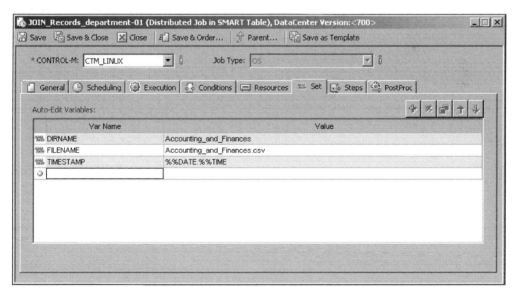

During the job's runtime, the value of `%%DATE` will be resolved into `yymmdd` and `%%TIME` will be resolved into `hhmmss`. Therefore, `%%TIMESTAMP` will be resolved into `yymmddhhmmss`. For example, `%%DATE` is `20110211` and `%%TIME` is `201700`, similarly, `%%TIMESTAMP` will be `20110211201700`.

Linking jobs with job conditions

Creating job conditions to link related jobs together in Control-M Desktop is fairly straightforward. The simplest way is to left-click on a job and drag the mouse to its down flow job. Upon releasing the mouse button, we will see a line appear between the two jobs with two arrows one on each side of the line—one pointing out from the job we clicked on, and the other pointing at the dependent job. By doing this, Control-M Desktop will automatically create an Out-condition entry in the job we initially selected and an In-condition entry in the dependent job. By default, the name of the condition is `<job name>-ENDED`.

After the two jobs are linked, we can open each job editing form and go to the **Conditions** tab to look at the actual condition entry. The Out-condition should have a **Name**, **Date**, and **Effect**, whereas the In-condition should only have a **Name** and **Date**. The **Name** of the In and Out conditions in the two related jobs has to be the same in order for them to be linked together. The **Date** values are **ODAT** by default, which means during runtime the condition date will be the same as the job's odate. The **Effect** of the Out-condition should be a + sign, which means the condition will be generated upon the job's successful completion.

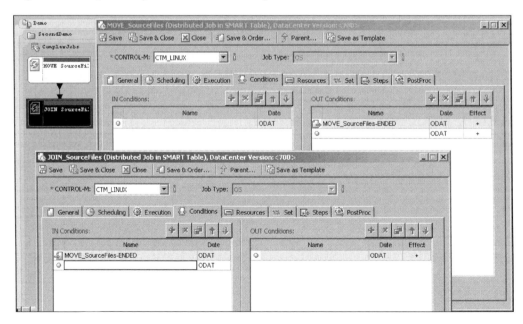

Alternatively, we can manually define conditions by directly creating entries in the **Conditions** tab. All we need to make sure of is that the condition **Name** and **Date** are the same between the inter-dependent jobs and that the Out-condition **Effect** sign is set to **+** .

We repeat the process by following the sequence of the job execution. We should end up with the following job logic (we are not there yet to define the condition between the two datacenters):

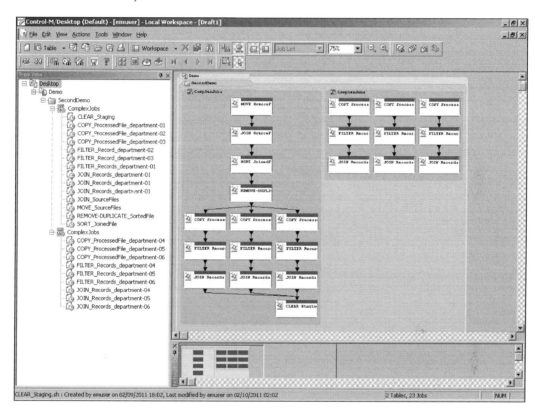

If we define Out-condition with a - **Effect**, it means that upon the job's successful completion, the specified condition will be deleted rather than added (given the condition already exists). We normally define a job's In-condition(s) also as its Out-condition(s) but with a - sign; by doing so the condition(s) will be deleted after the job uses it (them) – assume there are no other jobs that require the same condition as their In-condition.

From a general housekeeping point of view, deleting In-condition with each job will reduce the number of "used" conditions stored in the Control-M database. But in some cases, this is required for meeting special scheduling requirements. For example in our case, each job is defined as cyclic but the rerun only has to be happened at the job flow level. That is, jobs are only allowed to perform rerun when the entire batch flow's previous execution completes successfully and reaches the next rerun time to process the next batch of source files. In this case, for each job we have to delete the In-condition as soon as the job is completed and let it wait for its predecessor to re-send the In-condition. Otherwise, each job will get re-submitted imminently after execution and cause the whole job flow to go out of sync.

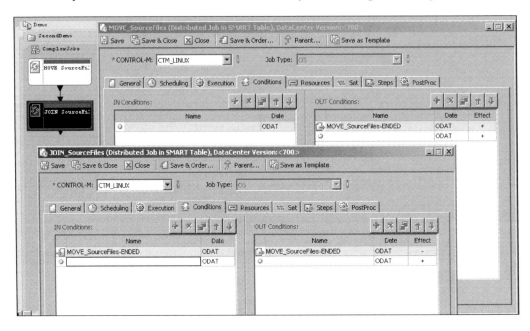

In our example, the conditions in-between REMOVE-DUPLICATE_SortedFile and its dependent jobs (COPY_ProcessedFile_department-01/2/3) are a bit tricky with the deletion. At the moment the Out-condition generated by REMOVE-DUPLICATE_SortedFile triggers all three COPY_ProcessedFile_department-01/2/3 (one-to-many). If we define the deletion within one of the three jobs, there is a chance the condition will get deleted before one or both of the other two jobs "use" it. The quick and easy way to fix this issue is to let REMOVE-DUPLICATE_StoredFile generate a dedicated condition for each dependent job (3x one-to-one conditions) and let each dependent job delete its own In-condition.

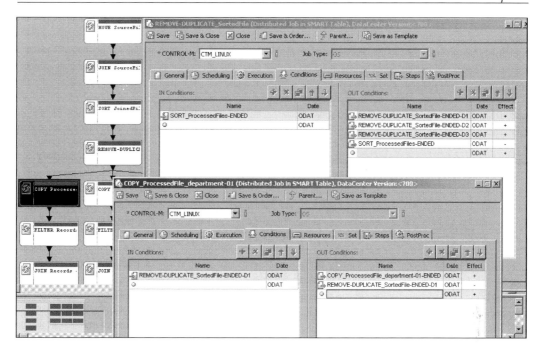

Summary of the related conditions:

Job name	Out-condition name
REMOVE-DUPLICATE_SortedFile	REMOVE-DUPLICATE_SortedFile-ENDED-D1 (+)
	REMOVE-DUPLICATE_SortedFile-ENDED-D2 (+)
	REMOVE-DUPLICATE_SortedFile-ENDED-D3 (+)
COPY_ProcessedFile_department-01	REMOVE-DUPLICATE_SortedFile-ENDED-D1
COPY_ProcessedFile_department-02	REMOVE-DUPLICATE_SortedFile-ENDED-D2
COPY_ProcessedFile_department-03	REMOVE-DUPLICATE_SortedFile-ENDED-D3

The other thing to mention is the **CLEAR_Staging** job. This job requires all three predecessor jobs to complete and produce the Out-conditions in order for it to run (many-to-one). Therefore, we need to make sure the **In-condition relationship** is set to **AND between all conditions** (by default the relationship is set to **AND**, but it is a good habit to always check it).

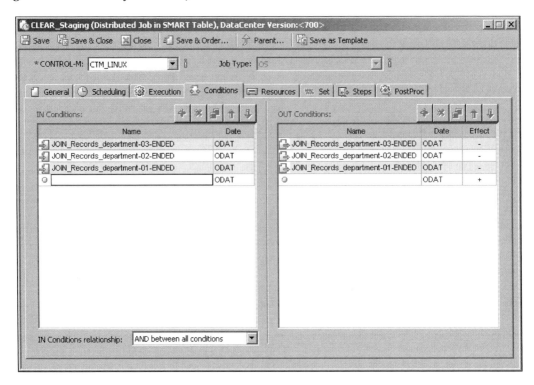

Summary of the related conditions:

Job name	Out-condition name
JOIN_Records_department-01	FILTER_Records_department-01-ENDED (+)
JOIN_Records_department-02	FILTER_Records_department-02-ENDED (+)
JOIN_Records_department-03	FILTER_Records_department-03-ENDED (+)
CLEAR_Staging	FILTER_Records_department-01-ENDED
	FILTER_Records_department-02-ENDED
	FILTER_Records_department-03-ENDED

Defining Global Conditions

If we use the same method we did for creating normal conditions to link jobs between two datacenters, we will see a line appear between the jobs but that doesn't mean the conditions will work during runtime (that is, during runtime conditions generated within each Control-M/Server are only known by that Control-M/Server). In order for cross-datacenter jobs' In-condition to be satisfied, we have to define them as "Global Conditions".

The way global condition works it that the Control-M/EM's GCS (Global Condition Server) needs to be "notified" for conditions that are global. In order for GCS to be notified, we need to choose a pre-fix for the cross-datacenter condition and register it as a **Global Condition Pre-Fix** in Control-M/EM.

Deciding the Global Condition pre-fix

We need to choose a unique pre-fix for global conditions to avoid normal condition names starting with the same characters also getting processed by GCS. For example we can add the Out-condition's datacenter name into the beginning of the condition name, or use some special keywords. Such as, in our case we add `LINUX_` in front of the normal condition names to indicate the conditions are coming from the Linux datacenter—`LINUX_<job name>-ENDED` and use `WIN_` in front of the conditions that are coming from Windows datacenter—`WIN_<job name>-ENDED`:

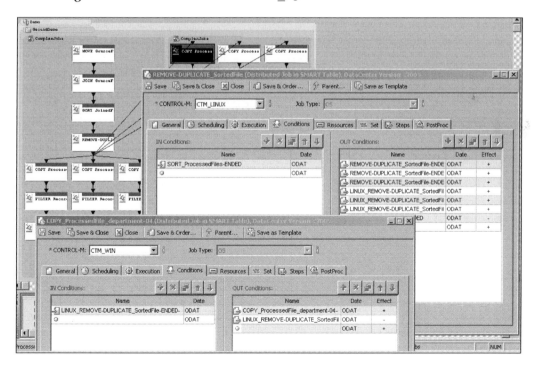

In our example, jobs involved with Global Conditions are as follow:

- Job `REMOVE-DUPLICATE_SortedFile` in the `LINUX_CTM` datacenter triggers jobs `COPY_ProcessedFile_department-04/5/6` in the `WIN_CTM` datacenter.
- Job `CLEAR_Staging` depends on the completion of `JOIN_Records*` jobs in the `LINUX_CTM` datacenter as well as the `JOIN_Records*` jobs in the `WIN_CTM` datacenter.

Summary of the related conditions:

Job name	Out-condition name
`REMOVE-DUPLICATE_SortedFile`	`LINUX_REMOVE-DUPLICATE_SortedFile-ENDED-D4 (+)`
	`LINUX_REMOVE-DUPLICATE_SortedFile-ENDED-D5 (+)`
	`LINUX_REMOVE-DUPLICATE_SortedFile-ENDED-D6 (+)`
`COPY_ProcessedFile_department-04`	`LINUX_REMOVE-DUPLICATE_SortedFile-ENDED-D4`
`COPY_ProcessedFile_department-05`	`LINUX_REMOVE-DUPLICATE_SortedFile-ENDED-D5`
`COPY_ProcessedFile_department-06`	`LINUX_REMOVE-DUPLICATE_SortedFile-ENDED-D6`
`JOIN_Records_department-04`	`WIN_JOIN_Records_department-04-ENDED (+)`
`JOIN_Records_department-05`	`WIN_JOIN_Records_department-05-ENDED (+)`
`JOIN_Records_department-06`	`WIN_JOIN_Records_department-06-ENDED (+)`
`CLEAR_Staging`	`WIN_JOIN_Records_department-04-ENDED`
	`WIN_JOIN_Records_department-05-ENDED`
	`WIN_JOIN_Records_department-06-ENDED`

By now, we should have the following job relationship showing in Control-M Desktop workspace:

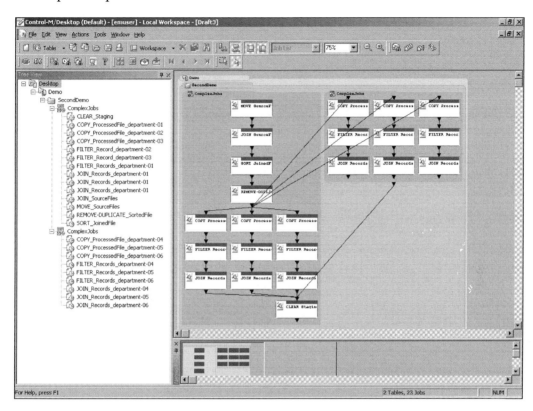

Registering the Global Condition pre-fix

Once we decide the global condition pre-fix and defined them into jobs, we need to let Control-M "know" the details of the pre-fix. This can be done in both the Control-M Desktop and Control-M/EM GUI client.

In Control-M Desktop, we go to the drop-down menu **Tools** and choose **Global Conditions** (or press *Ctrl + Shift + G*). A **Global Conditions Prefixes list** window along with a **Refresh Filter** window will pop up. We can leave everything in the filter as *(as we haven't defined anything as yet) and then click on **OK**. In the **Global Conditions Prefixes** window, we can click on the **Add (Insert)** toolbar icon or **Action | Add** to start adding pre-fix. In the new pop-up window, we need to enter the pre-fix name and the direction of the condition—Distributed From/To.

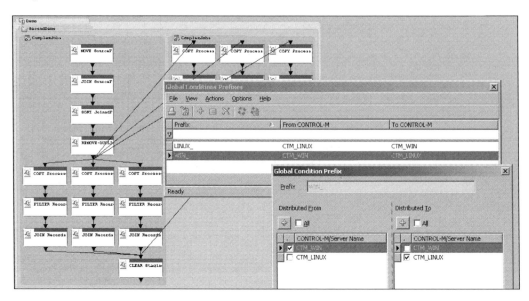

Our first pre-fix LINUX_ is to be coming from CTM_LINUX and going to CTM_WIN as well as the opposite direction. After you have entered the value and clicked on **OK**, we should see the pre-fix appears in the pre-fix list window. Then we can repeat the same process to add pre-fix **WIN_**. We need to add pre-fix in the opposite direction so that when a global condition is removed from the destination DC, that 'remove' action gets passed back to the source DC.

Creating calendars

Now we need to define calendar definitions so that our jobs can be automatically scheduled on the required dates. Recall the scheduling requirements—"This processing happens on each working day (except weekends and Australian public holidays)". In order to achieve this, we need to define a calendar—"non-Public Holidays (Australian)".

Calendars can be created from **Calendar Manager** located in Control-M Desktop's drop-down menu **Tools | Calendar manager** or toolbar icon **Calendar Manager**. In **Calendar Manager**, we click on the **New** icon to create a new calendar. We begin with selecting the calendar's **Control-M** name (Datacenter), the name of the calendar, and its type. Fist we will build the **NonAustPubHoliday** calendar in **CTM_LINUX** as a **Relative/Regular** type.

In the calendar definition, we first need to confirm the year of the calendar and then select the dates to be included. We can select each date individually or use the **Advanced** option to choose by month or week days. For this calendar, we will we select **Mon** to **Sun** in the **Advanced** option; followed by un-marking each holiday date from the calendar by left-clicking on each date. After entering a brief description, we can click on **Apply** and **Close** to finish the calendar definition:

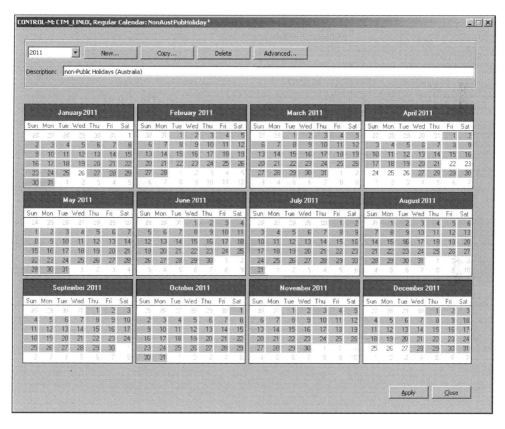

Now we can perform "Copy" on the calendar to create the same calendars for datacenter **CTM_WIN**. This is done by highlighting the calendar name in **Calendar Manager** and clicking on the **Copy** icon, then selecting **CTM_WIN** as the datacenter name for the new calendar.

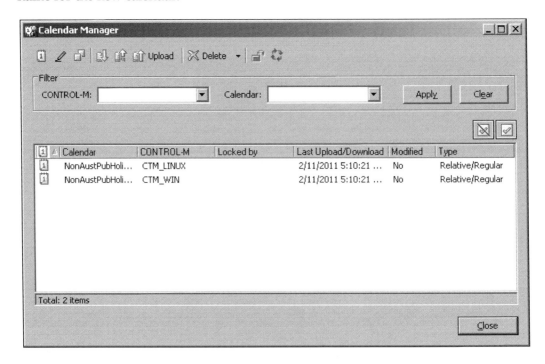

Before we close the Calendar Manager, we need to perform an Upload action (by highlighting the two calendars and clicking on the **Upload** icon) to let the two Control-M/Servers to receive the calendar definitions.

Last thing we need to do is to assign the calendars to jobs. Because, we are using the SMART table, once the calendar is applied at the table level all child jobs will inherit the same scheduling dates (because we have already pre-selected the RBC in each job definition). We right-click on the each of the two SMART tables in Control-M Desktop workspace and select **Edit**. In the SMART table editing form, we go to the **Scheduling** tab, make sure our RBC **ALL** is highlighted then select **NonAustPubHoliday** in the calendar drop-down list located in the **Month Days** section and select **Mon**, **Tue**, **Wed**, **Thu**, and **Fri** in the **Week Days** section. We need to make sure the relationship between the two is **And** to allow Control-M schedule the jobs when the given day is selected in both. Before clicking on **Save & Close**, we need to make sure every month in the **Months** section is also selected.

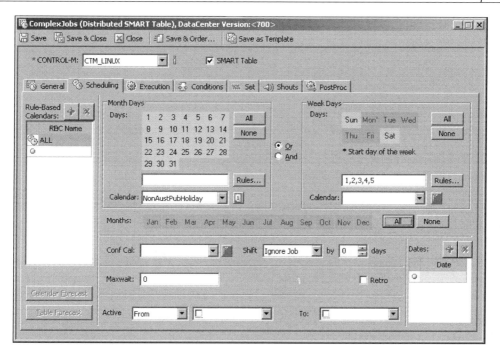

In fact there is a lot more to "play with" around the calendar topic. The details can pretty much take up a whole chapter. So instead, we will leave it to the reader to discover.

Adding job post-processing and job steps

We are going to add some simple job post-processing definitions and job steps to achieve "managing by exception" and allow the job to recover itself during a common failure.

Post-processing

At this stage, we don't have e-mail or SMS Shout destinations set up. So we will create some very simple post-processing rules for job failure notification. The rule we are going to create is to allow an alert to be sent to Control-M Alerts Window when the job fails.

Instead of creating the rule for each job one-by-one, we can perform a mess update on all jobs. By clicking on the **Find and Update** icon located in the toolbar or going to **Edit | Find and Update**, we will have the utility window open. In this window, we first need to define the "find" rules and define what update actions need to be performed. In our case, we want to apply the update to all jobs so we keep **Find Control-M like *** in the **Find** section and set the update criteria in the section below it.

We need to define the following Post-processing criteria:

- **When: NOTOK**
- **To: EM**
- **Urgency: Regular**
- **Message: %%JOBNAME failed**

This Post-processing rule means Control-M will send an alert to **Control-M/EM Global Alert Server (GAS)** when the job has ended NOTOK, and the alert message will include the failed job's job name (using Autoedit variable).

Now we can click on the **Update** button in the **Find and Update** window to apply the change to all the jobs:

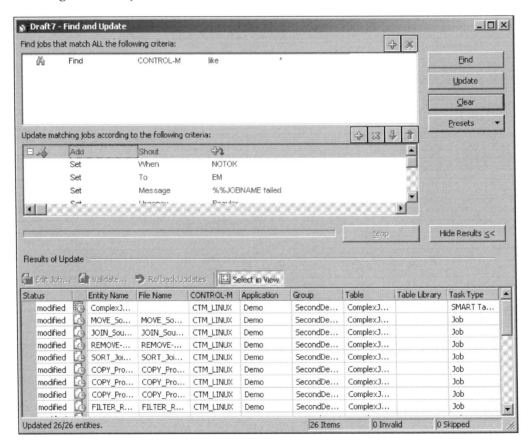

Now, if we open any jobs in the workspace, we should see the following entry appear in the **PostPorc** tab:

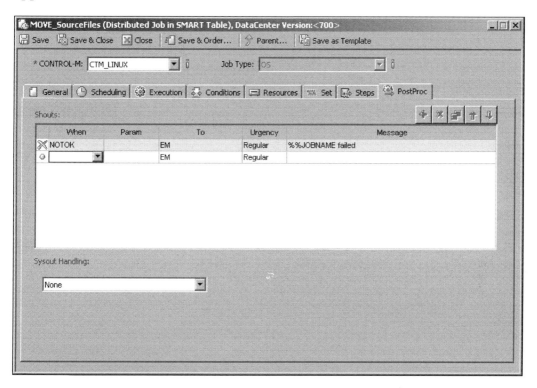

Job steps

Our job flow is pretty much ready to go, but there's still a small problem with the job rerun. Recall what we did with the job conditions. Within each job we defined additional Out-conditions to be identical to the job's In-condition with a - sign to avoid job rerun right after a successful execution. However, Control-M will only remove the condition if the job completed sucessfully. What if the job failed?

Well, at the moment if the job failed, the In-condition will not be removed which will cause Control-M to re-submit the job if all other prerequisites of the job are met. And because we have the Post-Processing setup, the job will keep rerunning and keep failing, therefore producing the alert message each time when it fails. We don't want to get mad by the repeating alerts; therefore, we need to come up a way to stop the job from getting re-submitted automatically if it fails. This is done by defining a **Step Code** in each job definition.

We need to add the following entries into the **Steps** tab within each job definition except our first job – MOVE_SourceFiles:

- **On Statement**
  - ○ **Statement = ***
  - ○ **Code = COMPSTAT!0 (job's OS return code is not equal to 0)**

- **DO: Condition**
  - ○ **Name = <the In-condition name that triggers the job execution>**
  - ○ **Date = ODAT**
  - ○ **Sign = "-" (without the "")**

(If the job has multiple In-conditions, the **Do: Condition** part needs to be repeated for each In-Condition.)

The statement we just defined means that during job Post-Processing, if the job's OS return code is not equal to 0 (which means the job ended NOTOK), Control-M will delete the condition that has the job's ODAT (the job's In-condition).

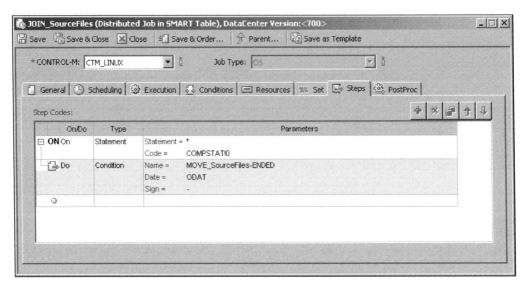

The reason we do not include MOVE_SourceFiles is because we do want it to automatically rerun if the job fails because no files are to be picked up at the time or if the Move action fails. The rerun will happen 10 minutes after the job fails because we have rerun the interval defined for this job.

Working with Resources

Control-M Resource is going to be used in our example to manage jobs that can be run in parallel. There are three execution points within the process flow that have such a possibility. These jobs are:

- Copying the processed file to department folders:
    - ° `COPY_ProcessedFile_department-01/2/3` on ctm-demo-linux-02
    - ° `COPY_ProcessedFile_department-04/5/6` on ctm-demo-win-01

- Applying department filter to produce department-specific output file:
    - ° `FILTER_Records_department-01/2/3` on ctm-demo-linux-02
    - ° `FILTER_Records_department-04/5/6` on ctm-demo-win-01

- Joining the department output file into history file:
    - ° `JOIN_Records_department-01/2/3` on ctm-demo-linux-02
    - ° `JOIN_Records_department-04/5/6` on ctm-demo-win-01

Quantitative Resource

For the first two execution points listed previously, we do allow them to be executed in parallel. However, as those jobs are going to perform operation on files, we should limit the number of concurrent running jobs to ensure maximum disk performance. We can apply such a limit by using the **Quantitative Resource** job parameter.

We open one of those jobs' editing form (for example,`COPY_ProcessedFile_ department-01`) and go to the **Resource** tab. In the **Resource** tab, we create a logical resource called **DISK_IO** with **Required Usage** equal to **1** and then **Save & Close** the job:

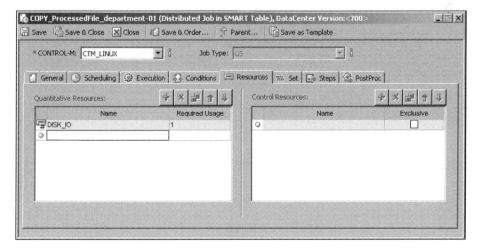

We can manually repeat the process for the rest of the jobs. Or we can use **Mass Update** with the following rules:

- Filter: "Find Job/Sub-table Name like COPY_ProcessedFile*"
    - ○ Criteria: Add "Quantitative Resource", set Name: DISK_IO, set Quantity: 1

- Filter: "Job/Sub-table Name like FILTER_Records*"
    - ○ Criteria: Add "Quantitative Resource", set Name: DISK_IO, set Quantity: 1

Once done, we have to define the total quantity of the resource for each Datacenter. This has to be done in Control-M/EM GUI client, by selecting **Quantitative Resource** in the **Tools** drop-down menu. Within the **Quantitative Resource** window, once we click on the **Add (insert)** button, we need to enter the resource name in the **New Resource** pop-up window, and then select the Control-M (Datacenter) name and the maximum quantity. We only want two jobs to be submitted concurrently in each Datacenter; therefore, we enter **2** as the maximum value. After repeating the same process for the other Datacenter, we can click on the **Refresh** icon to see the update. Now the **Quantitative Resources** window should have the following two entries:

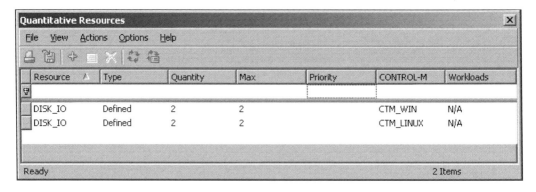

During job execution, we will see that the quantity gets substituted from the executing job. And once the job finished the execution, the resource will be added back.

Control Resources

For the FILTER_Records_department* jobs, we only allow one job to run at a time on each job execution host, simply because the job does write to the history file and we don't want the history file to get messed up because two or more jobs are accessing it at the same time. Using **Exclusive Control Resource** is like applying a virtual lock to the file, so that only one job can write to it at any given time.

Defining Control Resource is fairly simple. All we need to do is go to the job edition form's **Resource** tab and add a new **Control Resource** entry. Because we only want one job to run at a time, we have to mark the resource as **Exclusive**. This means other jobs that have the same control resource defined need to wait for the currently running job to complete. In this case, we can guarantee that the file will not be modified by two or more jobs at the same time.

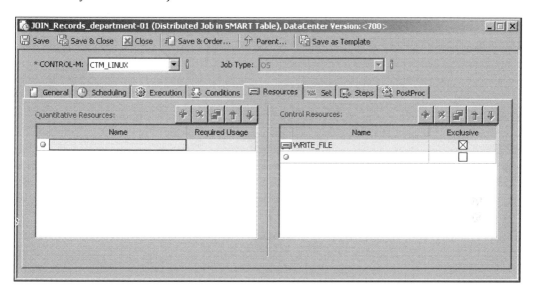

Having a "Start" job

Before we save the job for scheduling, let's check if something is missing. Let's take a look at the whole picture and think about how the job flow will behave. We can see that the first job MOVE_SourceFiles will run every 30 minutes and upon successful movement of the source files into "staging", it will post out an Out-condition to trigger the next job JOIN_SourceFile. And once JOIN_SourceFile is completed successfully, it will trigger the next one SORT_JoinedFile and so on. Because we have the "PostProc" statement defined, if any job fails, the job flow will stop there and the job will send a SHOT to the Control-M/EM Alert window.

We keep looking until the end of the job flow and finally we begin wondering that since we set MOVE_SourceFile to rerun every 30 minutes, what is going to happen if the entire flow cannot finish within 30 minutes? Well, if this is the case, MOVE_SourceFile will start regardless and therefore cause problems further down the flow because part of the job flow is still processing files from the last batch and the staging area hasn't got cleaned by the last job – CLEAR_Staging.

In order to fix this problem, we can let CLEAR_Staging to be the prerequisite of MOVE_SourceFile. How do we do it? Well, one option is to add an Out-condition in CLEAR_Staging and add the same name and date In-condition in MOVE_SourceFile. By doing this, MOVE_SourceFile will not start unless CLEAR_Staging completed.

This method so far resolved the original problem but also created two new problems:

- How can we start MOVE_SourceFile at the very beginning to process the first batch of files?

- We noticed that by adding the condition, MOVE_SourceFile is no longer displayed at the beginning of the job flow. It is okay but not very user-friendly because we want the job flow to reflect the job execution's logical order.

With the first problem, we can create a Start job to kick-start the job flow for the first time. The start job is a dummy job, it does nothing more than posting an Out-condition for job MOVE_SourceFile to start the first execution of the day. Within MOVE_SourceFile, now we would have two In-conditions. We need to set OR relationship between the two, which means the job will get submitted if any one of the two conditions is met (given all other prerequisites are also met). And of course we need to define the same Out-conditions with - sign. In this case, the very first execution of the MOVE_SourceFile will be triggered by Start job, and all other re-runs will depend on the 10 minute limit as well as the finish of the previous run of the entire job flow.

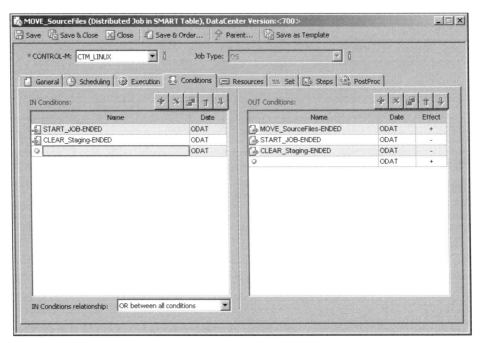

We can easily fix the job layout problem by using a **Do Condition** within the **Set** tab of job **CLEAR_Staging** instead of directly defining the condition in the job editing form's **Condition** tab. We define the statement as follow:

- **On Statement**
    - ○ **Statement = ***
    - ○ **Code = COMPSTAT=0 (job's OS return code is equal to 0)**
- **DO: Condition**
    - ○ **Name = CLEAR_Staging-ENDED**
    - ○ **Date = ODAT**
    - ○ **Sign = "+" (without the "")**

This is opposite to what we did earlier—deleting condition using "Step" if the job failed. The Step Code we defined will produce the same effect as we define an Out-condition in the **Conditions** tab. The only difference is that Control-M GUI will not display the condition line by default*.

*We can let Control-M GUI display a doted line for each "Do (add) Condition". We will discuss how to configure this setting in the coming chapter.

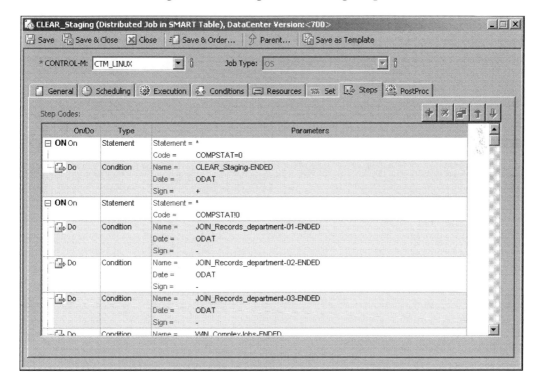

By now, our batch flow is 100% ready to go. It should look like the following in Control-M Desktop:

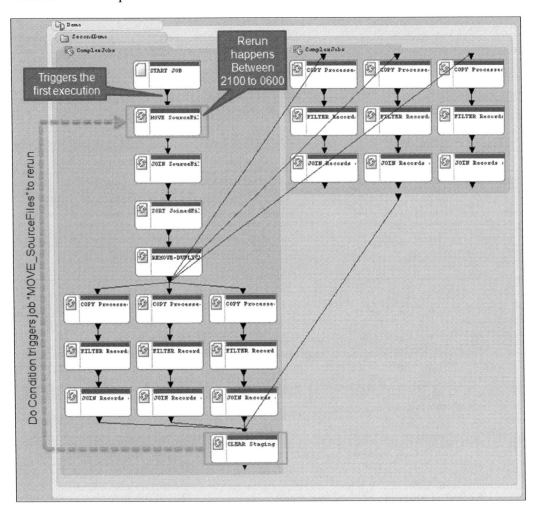

The last thing to do is to perform a Write and Upload so that the job definitions will be saved into Control-M/EM and Control-M/Server database. Because we have defined calendar and user daily "SYSTEM" for these jobs, Control-M/Server will automatically order the jobs during the next NDP, if it is not a weekend or Australian public holidays (for examples in this book). Now you can do something else or go to bed if it is late, and check the active job tomorrow morning after NDP.

Summary

Excellent! Now we have completed this chapter. At the beginning of this chapter, we looked at the important job scheduling concepts of Control-M in depth and applied them by defining some simple jobs in Control-M Desktop and managed them using Control-M/EM GUI client. Then we took it one step further by defining a complete batch flow to meet a scheduling requirement.

From now on we have a little job flow scheduled daily in our Control-M environment. Will the batch flow processes the files as expected? It is yet to be discovered. But one thing we know for sure is that the jobs will be scheduled each day in Control-M for execution.

As we now have real jobs running in Control-M, in the next chapter we will take a look at the necessary admin tasks that need to be performed in Control-M.

5
Administrating the Control-M Infrastructure

By now, we not only have our own Control-M batch infrastructure configured, we also have jobs running in it. Isn't it cool? We definitely have a good start on the journey towards the Golden Age – Workload automation! However, before we get too excited, we need to keep in mind that in order to get the most out of Control-M, we need to discover and utilize its add-on features, try our best to expand the batch environment, and maintain every component in its best shape by keeping them up-to-date with the latest patches and fixes.

In this chapter, we will be looking at general administration tasks involved with running Control-M. We will start with installing additional Control-M components and applying fix packs. Then we will identify the components that are required to be installed regularly and discuss the best way to perform these installations to meet the expansion of the batch environment, followed by topics on some frequent administration tasks, such as stop/start Control-M components and define GUI users, as well as touch points on the topic of customizing Control-M GUI.

By the end of this chapter, you will be able to:

- Perform common installation tasks, such as fix pack and add-on components installation.
- Deal with installation of components that can happen on a regular basis.
- Master frequent administration tasks, such as stop/start components and manage GUI users.
- Know where to configure and customize Control-M GUI.

Additional component installations

The Control-M components that we installed during *Chapter 3, Building the Control-M Infrastructure* were the most essential ones to get us started, but they definitely aren't the whole lot. Recall what we have discussed during *Chapter 2, Exploring Control-M* – there are two types of add-on components. One type provides general feature enhancements to Control-M, such as Batch Impact Manager, Forecast, and Batch Discovery. Others are control modules, which are to be installed on top of Control-M/Agents to expand Control-M's scheduling capability. Some of these add-on components are part of the base Control-M license, but the majority of them may require an additional cost to acquire.

These additional components may not be installed during the initial Control-M implementation, but are likely to be required down the track; the installations will become general administration tasks.

During this section, we will implement the following components onto our existing Control-M environment:

- Features enhancement:
    - Batch Impact Manager
    - Control-M/Forecast

- Additional scheduling capability (control modules):
    - Control-M for database
    - Control Module for advanced file transfer
    - Control-M Business Process Integration Suite

We will not cover Control-M for cloud installation as the procedure is very similar to other CM installations.

Installation of BIM and Forecast

BIM and Forecast are often discussed together in the business service management context, but technically they are two separate Control-M/EM add-on components that do not depend on each other. They are to be implemented on top of a fully working Control-M/EM (server components) installation. Upon successful installations, we will see the corresponding features in Control-M/EM GUI client become available.

Installation

Similar to the base components installation, BIM and Forecast installation can be done from a physical installation media shipped by BMC software or, alternatively, by using compressed binary or ISO files downloaded from the BMC EPD site. The compressed files are separately made for Windows and Unix/Linux (.zip for Windows and .tar.z for Unix/Linux), whereas the .iso file contains the installation for both environments.

We chose to use the .tar.z files for our installation because they are much smaller than the iso image files to transfer (that is, the .tar.z file is Unix/Linux specific, whereas the iso image file also includes installation for Windows). We download the BIM and Forecast, two Linux installation files, from the BMC EPD site and ftp them into a temp directory (For example, /tmp) of our Linux server ctm-demo-linux-01, where the Control-M/EM server components are installed. The two files are DRCBM.7.0.00.REDHAT.tar.z (BIM) and DRFOR.7.0.00.REDHAT.tar.z (Forecast).

Now, we log on the machine as user **ctmem**, navigate to the /tmp directory, and create two separate directories (one called bim and the other called forecast) to store the unpacked files. We execute the following two commands within each directory to untar the installation files: zcat /tmp/DRCBM.7.0.00.REDHAT.tar.z | tar xvf - and zcat /tmp/DRFOR.7.0.00.REDHAT.tar.z | tar xvf -.

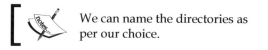 We can name the directories as per our choice.

Before the installation starts, we need to make sure at least the Control-M/EM database server is running. We can check the database status by running the check_ server command. If the script returns **OK**, we can then go ahead with the installation.

The installation process is very straightforward; all we need to do is execute the setup.sh scripts located in each of the two temp directories one after another. During each installation, the script will automatically detect the Control-M/EM home directory and ask us to confirm (in our case, the home directory is /opt/ctmem/). After pressing *I*, the installation will start and it will only take a few seconds to complete.

```
ctmem @ ctm-demo-linux-01: /tmp/bim
=== Summary ===


   You are about to install BMC Batch Impact Manager version 7.0.00

Destination Folder: /opt/ctmem/

== <C> Cancel <P> Previous Panel <I>/<Enter> Install <G> Generate an automatic i
nstallation configuration file ==

Enter command: i

=== Installation ===


[ Starting to unpack ]
[ Processing package: BMC Batch Impact Manager files ]
[ Processing package: Configure BMC Batch Impact Manager ]
[ Processing package: Write uninstaller ]
[ Unpacking finished ]

=== Installation Result - Success ===


Installation has completed successfully.

ctm-demo-linux-01%
```

Post-installation tasks

After the installation, we should see two new components appear in CCM – BIM and Forecast Server. The **Desired State** of the two components is set to **Up** by default and their **Actual State** should be **Up** already, or should be about to turn into **Up** shortly.

In our environment, the BIM and Forecast servers are created automatically in CCM because we already got the GUI server defined and running in Control-M/EM during our BIM and Forecast installation. In case BIM and Forecast are installed right after Control-M/EM installation (that is, before a GUI server is defined), we need to manually define the components through **New | Control-M/EM Component** in CCM.

Once both of the two components' actual states are **Up**, we will see the following processes running on the Control-M/EM server host (that is, by issuing `ps -ef |` `grep <CTM/EM OS username>` command in a Unix/Linux environment):

- `emforecastsrv`
- `embimsrv`

Last but not the least, BIM estimates the service completion time based on the current and historical job statistics. Therefore, in order for BIM to provide accurate calculations, we need to make sure the machine clock of Control-M/EM server host (where BIM is running), and all Control-M/Server hosts, are set to the correct time zone and are synced at all times. For example, for Redhat servers, we can synchronize the system clock to **Network Time Protocol (NTP)** by running the `ntpd` service or running `ntpdate` command regularly (that is, schedule it as a Control-M cyclic job).

 BIM can handle the time difference calculation for machines that are located in different time zones.

Configuring BIM web interface

Forecast server is pretty much Plug and Play, whereas BIM has an optional web GUI feature, which requires minor after-installation configuration. The engine behind the web GUI feature is the BIM Web Application, which relies on either Control-M/EM built-in web application server (preconfigured by default), or a third-party web application server.

As we are going to use the built-in Control-M/EM web server, the configuration is as simple as starting the web server by running the `start_web_server.sh` script as the Control-M/EM OS user account. The output of the script should indicate the web server is running, and lists the hostname and port number (default port is **18080**).

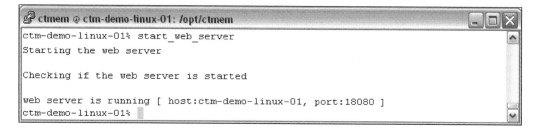

In the later Fix Pack of version 7 Control-M/EM, the web server startup is part of the based components start up, together with Naming server, CMS, and so on.

Now we can use our GUI user account to log in to the BIM web GUI page from a browser by typing the following address: `http://<ctmemHost>:18080/bim` (in our case, it is `http://ctm-demo-linux-01:18080/bim`). We need to make sure the **Host** drop-down list is populated with the correct server host value before clicking on the **Login** button (`ctm-dem0linux-01` in our case). Of course, after login we can't see any services listed yet, but we will define BIM services and re-visit this web GUI during the next chapter, *Chapter 6, Advanced Batch Scheduling and Management*.

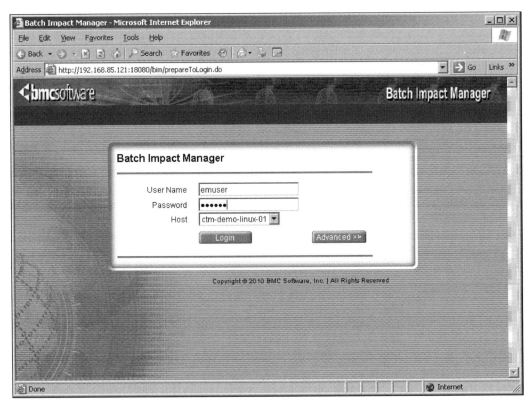

Alternatively, we can use our own **JSP (Java Server Pages)** supported web server to host the BIM web application. The third-party web server can be running on the same machine as Control-M/EM or on a different machine. In order to configure BIM application server with such a kind of web server, we need to get the BIM web application deployment files and deploy them to the web server. These files are called `bim.ear` and `bim.war` located under `~/ctm_em/etc/bim/webapp` directory in a Unix/Linux environment.

```
ctmem @ ctm-demo-linux-01: /opt/ctmem/ctm_em/etc/bim/webapp
ctm-demo-linux-01% cd /opt/ctmem/ctm_em/etc/bim/webapp
ctm-demo-linux-01% ls -l
total 48752
-rw-r--r-- 1 ctmem ctmem 8297339 Jan 24 08:50 bim.ear
-rw-r--r-- 1 ctmem ctmem 8297389 Jan 24 08:50 bim_ssl.ear
-rw-r--r-- 1 ctmem ctmem 8306129 Jan 24 08:50 bim_ssl.war
-rwxr-xr-x 1 ctmem ctmem 8297288 Jul  2  2010 bim_template.ear
-rwxr-xr-x 1 ctmem ctmem 8306050 Jul  2  2010 bim_template.war
-rw-r--r-- 1 ctmem ctmem 8306082 Jan 24 08:50 bim.war
drwxr-xr-x 3 ctmem ctmem    4096 Jan 24 08:49 config
ctm-demo-linux-01%
```

We can access the BIM web GUI page through `http://<ctmemHost>:<port number>/bim` or `http://<ctmemHost>/bim` if the default port 80 is used.

Installation of Control Modules

In this section, we will perform Control Module installations onto our existing Control-M/Agents to expand their scheduling capability. We are planning to install the following Control Modules on the specific target hosts:

Hostname	Control Module
ctm-demo-win-01	Control-M for database
ctm-demo-win-02	Control Module for Advanced File Transfer (AFT)
ctm-demo-linux-01	Control Module for Advanced File Transfer (AFT)
ctm-demo-linux-02	Control-M Business Process Integration (BPI) Suite

The installation steps for these control modules are straightforward and very similar. Each installation can be performed either in interactive or silent mode. We will demonstrate the interactive installation of Control-M for database and CM for AFT installation on the two Windows servers, followed by silent installation of CM for AFT on the first Linux server. Then, we will finish up with interactive installation of Control-M BPI Suite on the second Linux server. The goal is for us to have a general idea of the installation so we can perform any control module installations in both environments in the future.

Pre-installation considerations

The following is the pre-installation checklist for each Control Module. Before we install a Control Module, we should always check the corresponding product release notes to make sure every item on the list meets these requirements:

- System and environment requirement:
    - Minimum RAM
    - Required disk space in the installation home directory's filesystem
    - Free space in /tmp directory (for Unix/Linux environments)
    - CPU type and architecture (for example, x86, x86_86, ia64)
    - Operating system version and service pack level

- Control-M component compatibility:
    - Control-M/EM version and fix pack level
    - Control-M/Server version and fix pack level
    - Control-M/Agent version and fix pack level

- Other Requirements:
    - Control-M for database: Database type and version, configure firewall ports (if existing) for the CM to access databases on remote servers
    - CM for AFT: Configure the required firewall ports (if existing) for file transfers (for example, port 21 for FTP and port 22 for SFTP)
    - Control-M for BPI: Sun Java JRE version, application server type and version (for example, JBOSS, BEA Weblogic, and WebSphere MQ), and compatible technologies (for example, WSDL, UDDI, and EJB)

We have no choice but to install the 6.4.01 version of Control-M for database and CM for AFT, and also the 6.3.02 version of Control-M for BPI, because they were the latest versions at the time this book was written. Lower version Control Modules are normally compatible with equal or higher version Control-M/Agents; saying that we should still check the product release notes for such compatibility information before the installation.

For Windows environments, Control-M for Database 6.4.1 can only be installed on 32-bit versions, but that doesn't mean we cannot use the CM to trigger jobs in databases that are running on 64-bit Windows operating systems. Control-M for databases comes with its built-in database connectivity functionality to connect with the supported databases running on remote hosts, regardless of the system architecture.

Installation – Control-M for database

Control-M for database installation is provided in `.iso` format for Unix/Linux and `.zip` format for Windows on the BMC EPD site. The Windows installation `.zip` file we are going to download is called `DRMQL.6.4.01_WIN.zip`.

The installation needs to be performed by users with administrator privileges on the Windows computer. We also need to make sure there are no jobs running on this Control-M/Agent before and during the installation (for example, in Control-M/EM GUI, place a hold on waiting to execute jobs belonging to this Control-M/Agent and wait for all running jobs that belong to this Control-M/Agent to complete, then place a hold on them if they are cyclic jobs to prevent reruns). This should be kept in mind when planning for a production installation because it can potentially cause an outage.

Once all the prerequisites are met, we can go ahead and unzip the installation package and execute the `<temp dir>\setup.bat` executable file. During Control-M for Database installation, we will be asked to select the Control-M/Agent on which it is to be installed in our environment; **Default** is the only option for selection in the drop-down menu because we only have one Control-M/Agent installed on `ctm-demo-win-01` (the Control-M/Agent instance name: **Default**). Confirm it and continue to the next screen. We will see that the installation has already automatically picked up the destination folder. After pressing the **Install** button, the entire installation process should only take less than a minute and finish with the **Installation has completed successfully** message.

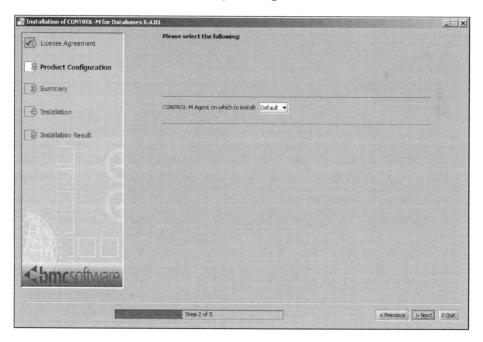

Installation – Control Module for Advanced File Transfer

CM for AFT installation is only provided in `.tar.z` (for Unix/Linux) and `.zip` (for Windows) formats on the EPD site. We will be downloading both OS types, but will make sure that the files we are going to download and use are matching our system architect (for example, x86, x86_64, or ia64, and so on).

Interactive installation

The CM for AFT interactive installation process in Windows machine is very similar to the Control-M for Database installation, apart from the `setup.bat` executable being located under `<temp dir>\windows\`.

The only configuration requirement during the installation is to select the Control-M/Agent instance name. Same as what we did during the previous installation, we will select **Default** because we have only one Control-M/Agent installed on the host `ctm-demo-win-02`. On the **Summary** page, before we click on the **Install** button, we will choose to generate an **automatic installation script** so we can use it later for the silent installation. By clicking on the **Generate an automatic installation script** button, we will be asked to enter a filename for saving the script (in xml format).

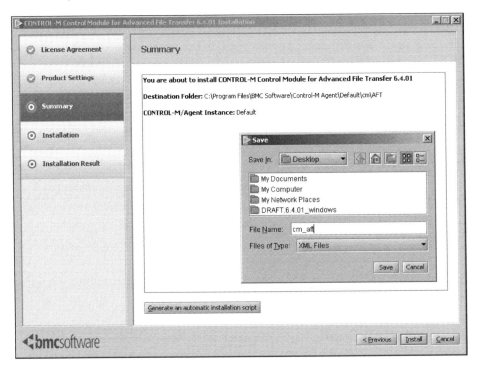

Again, the installation process will take less than a minute and we should end up getting a **Completed Successfully** message.

Silent installation

On host `ctm-demo-linux-01`, because we are installing the CM for AFT onto the Control-M/Agent installed together with Control-M/Server, we have to log on as the Control-M/Server OS user to perform the installation (normally it is the Control-M/Agent OS user account; in our case, the Control-M/Agent on `ctm-dem-linux-01` was installed as part of the Control-M/Server by default). There are two requirements that need to be met before the normal (that is, interactive) installation starts:

- We have to make sure there are no jobs running on the Control-M/Agent and then shut it down by issuing the `<Agent Home>/ctm/shut-ag` command as the root user

- We have to set the **DISPLAY** environment variable for the Control-M/Agent user on the installation machine and have the xServer running on our workstation to display the installation GUI

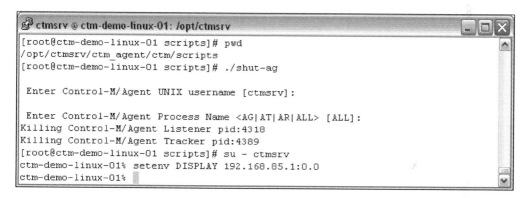

With the `shut-ag` command, if we run it from the Control-M/Agent home directory, the **Enter Control-M/Agent Unix username** field will be populated with the correct username automatically. If we run it from any other directory, the utility will populate **root** into that field and in such case, we have to manually change it to the correct value – the Control-M/Agent (identified by its OS user account) that we are going to shut down.

Because we are going to perform the installation in silent mode, we can ignore the second requirement and just make sure the agent processes are down during the installation. When we are ready to perform the installation, we will have to switch to the Control-M/Agent user (the Control-M/Server user in our case) in order to execute the installation script. Silent installation is to be started by running the following command: `<temp file location>/Linux-i386/setup.sh -silent /tmp/cm_aft.xml`.

```
ctmsrv @ ctm-demo-linux-01: /opt/ctmsrv
ctm-demo-linux-01% /tmp/aft/Linux-i386/setup.sh -silent /tmp/cm_aft.xml
Created tracer log file at '/opt/ctmsrv/log/BMC_cmaft_Install_2011.02.18.02.01.2
8.log'
[ Starting automated installation ]
[ Starting to unpack ]
[ Processing package: Checking whether agent is running ]
[ Processing package: CONTROL-M Control Module for Advanced File Transfer files
]
[ Processing package: Configure CONTROL-M CM for AFT ]
[ Processing package: Write uninstaller ]
[ Unpacking finished ]
[ Automated installation ended SUCCESSFULLY ]
ctm-demo-linux-01%
```

After we receive the **Automated installation ended SUCCESSFULLY** message, we can switch back to the **root** user and start the Control-M/Agent by issuing the `<Agent Home>/ctm/start-ag` command.

Installation – Control-M Business Process Integration Suite

Control-M BPI Suite's Windows and Unix/Linux installations are combined into a single `.iso` file. Once we download the file called `DRCOB.6.3.02` from the BMC EPD site and transfer it to the Linux server `ctm-demo-linux-02`, we need to perform the following tasks before the installation:

- Mount the `.iso` image as root (for example, mount onto /media/iso)
- Define the Java binary directory in the Control-M/Agent's PATH variable and make sure it is the Sun (Oracle) Java, not GNU Java
- Confirm there are no jobs running on the agent and shut down Control-M/Agent by running the `shut-ag` command as the root user

 Sun (Oracle) Java can be downloaded from the following website: `http://www.java.com/en/download/manual.jsp`.

Once all three prerequisites are met, we can go ahead and start the installation by running the `<iso mount point>/Unix/setup.sh` script.

During the installation, we need to choose the components we would like to install. The two components are: **Control-M Control Module for Business Process Integration** and **Control-M Business Process Integration Interface**. CM for BPI contains the three sub-components for Java, Web Service, and Message Queue. These three components allow Control-M to trigger business processes as jobs, whereas Control-M BPI Interface is designed to allow external business processes to invoke Control-M (for example, trigger a job execution in Control-M). We will install both the components for this installation.

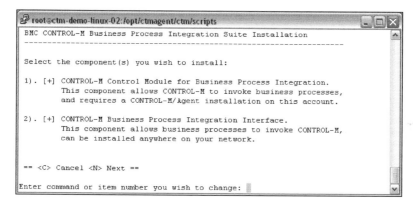

Once we confirm the installation details on the **Summary** screen, we can start the installation. Upon a successful installation, we will see a message that says, **Web Services and Messaging server for BPI Interface started successfully**. We need to log out and re-log in as the Control-M/Agent user to finish the installation and then start the Control-M/Agent by running the `start-ag` command as root.

Now, if we run a `ps -ef | grep <CTM/Agent OS user>` command, we should see there are two new Java processes running under the Control-M/Agent user account.

```
[ctmagent@ctm-demo-linux-02 ~]$ ps -ef | grep ctmagent
ctmagent   5953    1  0 15:54 pts/0    00:00:00 java -cp lib/ctm.bpi.ifc.jar:axi
s/lib/jaxrpc.jar:jetty/lib/org.mortbay.jetty.jar:jetty/lib/commons-logging.jar:j
etty/lib/javax.servlet.jar:axis/lib/saaj.jar:axis/lib/axis.jar:axis/lib/commons-
discovery-0.2.jar:axis/lib/wsdl4j-1.5.1.jar:axis/lib/log4j-1.2.8.jar:jaxm/lib/ja
xm-api.jar -Djava.security.auth.login.config=conf/jaas.config com.bmc.ctm.bpi.if
c.ws.server.WsApiManagerServer
ctmagent   6003    1  0 15:55 pts/0    00:00:00 java -cp lib/ctm.bpi.ifc.jar:axi
s/lib/jaxrpc.jar:jetty/lib/org.mortbay.jetty.jar:jetty/lib/commons-logging.jar:j
etty/lib/javax.servlet.jar:axis/lib/saaj.jar:axis/lib/axis.jar:axis/lib/commons-
discovery-0.2.jar:axis/lib/wsdl4j-1.5.1.jar:axis/lib/log4j-1.2.8.jar:jaxm/lib/ja
xm-api.jar com.bmc.ctm.bpi.ifc.msg.accounts_manager.AccountFileListener
root       6254 2588  0 15:57 pts/0    00:00:00 su - ctmagent
ctmagent   6255 6254  0 15:57 pts/0    00:00:00 -csh
ctmagent   6282 6255  0 15:58 pts/0    00:00:00 ps -ef
[ctmagent@ctm-demo-linux-02 ~]$
```

Post-installation tasks

Generally speaking, after each CM installation, we need to import each CM-specific job editing form into the Control-M Desktop and install each CM utility add-on into the CCM and Control-M/EM server.

 Installing add-ons into the CCM and Control-M/EM servers is not required for some CMs.

Importing CM-specific job editing forms

For each CM, there is a dedicated job editing form for us to specify the application-specific job parameters during the job creation. In the job editing window, once we select the desired **Job Type** from the drop-down menu, we will see that an additional tab will appear down below.

These job editing forms are provided with the CM installation package as xml files for us to import into the Control-M Desktop (the .xml files are normally stored under the Forms directory within the installation package). The import is done from each individual Control-M Desktop by selecting **Tools | Import Application Forms**. However, for Control-M 7, job editing forms are preincluded for most of the CMs, except Control-M for Informatica and CM for Cloud because they were released after Control-M/EM version 7 base release.

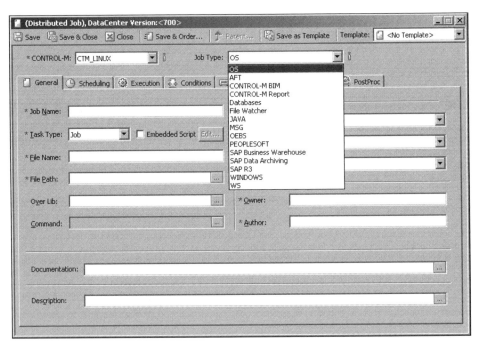

We can still open CM jobs on a Control-M Desktop that hasn't gotten the job editing form imported. In this case, we can only see common job details, but not the CM-specific definition.

Installing CM utility add-ons into the CCM and Control-M/ EM server

CCM can display installed CM(s) under each Control-M/Agent and allow us to perform a series of configuration tasks on them through the CCM GUI. In order to have the configuration feature enabled, we need to install CCM add-ons that came with each CM, but before we talk about how to install the add-ons, we need to make sure the CMs we installed are showing up in CCM.

In CCM, we may or may not see those newly installed CMs under each Control-M/ Agent imminently. In case we don't see them, we can log on to each Control-M/ Server machine and issue the `ctmgetcm` command to force a discovery. In Unix/ Linux systems, we have to log on as the Control-M/Server user to issue the command, whereas for Windows machines, we can just open a CMD window and run the command as long as the Control-M/Server home directory is in the PATH environment variable (by default). For the utility, we are going to specify the following:

- NodeId: The Control-M/Agent name that we want to perform the discovery on

- ApplType: All CM application types that are installed on the Control-M/ Agent ("*" by default)

- Action: Display the available application types and retrieve the records to CCM (type `Get`)

For example:

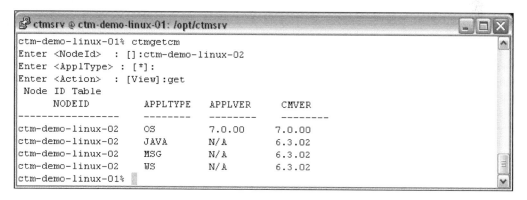

Once we have done this for all the Control-M/Agents in both the Control-M/Servers, we can come back to CCM and click on the **Refresh** button to allow the previously installed CMs to show up. Then, if we *right-click* on any of the CM entries, we will see that a menu will come up with options, such as **Account Management...** or **Configuration Management...** (CM for AFT).

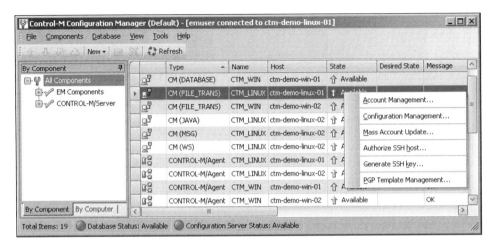

These options are the CM utilities we were talking about. Again, because we are running the Control-M version 7, most of the CM utilities are already included in the Control-M/EM GUI client base installation. Otherwise, we can install these utilities by running the executable normally located under the CCM directory within the installation package. Some CMs only require utility installation on the CCM (EM client) side, and some require both CCM and Control-M/EM Server side.

- For the CCM side, all we need to do is log on to each Control-M/EM GUI client workstation to execute the .CMD executable under `<installation CD or package directory>\CCM\EM_Client`.

- For the Control-M/EM server side, we need to see the following:

  ○ If Control-M/EM server is running on Windows, we need to execute the .CMD executable under `<installation CD or package directory>\CCM\EM_Server\Windows` and then restart the **Control-M Configuration Manager server** service through **Computer Management | Services and Applications | Services**.

  ○ In our case, we are running the Control-M/EM Server on the Unix/Linux environment. We need to execute the .sh script under **<installation CD or package directory>/CCM/EM_Server/Unix** and then restart the **Control-M Configuration Manager server** process by issuing the `stop_cms` and `start_cms` commands.

In order to schedule CM jobs, we need to use each CM's account utility to define the accounts (connection profiles). We will leave this part for the next chapter once we have better ideas about what kind of jobs will be defined.

Expanding and updating the batch environment

In real environments, the implementation of BIM and Forecast is more or less a once-off type event, but implementing Control-M/Agents and Control Modules on new job execution machines could happen at any time, based on demand. On top of everything, we also need to keep each component up-to-date by applying fix packs and patches on an ongoing basis.

Ongoing installation of Control-M/Agents and Control Modules

As the batch environment starts to grow, Control/Agent and Control Module requests can be generated whenever a batch requirement is identified on particular host(s) and sometimes these requests can come very suddenly and may only allow a very tight time frame for setting up the Control-M/Agent and Control Modules. Within the short time frame, as a Control-M administrator, we need to perform a number of tasks to get everything going. These tasks in general are:

- Check and make sure the machine meets the installation requirements (for example, hardware, disk space, OS type, and version)
- Request access to the target machine and gain appropriate privilege to perform the installation
- Request the Control-M/Agent user and batch user (optional) to be created by the system administrator
- Request firewall ports to be opened (for example, for Server/Agent communication)
- Installation and configuration customization
- Discover Control-M/Agent from the Control-M/Server and test Agent/Server communication
- Define and test Control Module accounts (if any CMs are installed)
- Create automatic start-up scripts for the Control-M/Agent

We will explain automatic start-up scripts and demonstrate how to create them during the later part of this chapter.

It is important to come up with a quick and convenient way for such kind of implementations so that the requests can always get completed on time and trouble free.

Organizations with a more matured Control-M batch environment may choose to include the Control-M/Agent installation as part of the standard server build for new machines (that is, include Control-M/Agent in the OS build image). In such cases, we can go ahead and discover the Control-M/Agent in Control-M and start to schedule jobs at the point of time when the server is ready. For existing machines that haven't gotten Control-M/Agent installed, larger organizations may have the datacenter automation tool (for example, BMC Bladelogic or Redhat Satellite server) to automatically deploy preconfigured Control-M/Agent installation packages onto these target hosts. Other organizations without such tools may still want to build script-based silent installations to save themselves from labor-intensive manual installation and configuration, as well as reduce the chances of human mistakes.

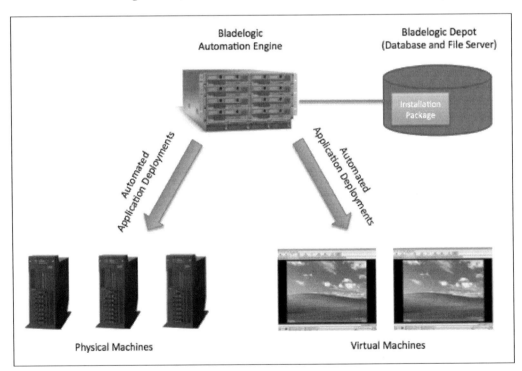

The bottom line is, no matter what installation method is used, we should have a standard installation procedure and configuration template to ensure consistent deployment across the entire organization. The recommendations are:

- Control-M/Agent should be installed in the same home directory, for example:
  - Unix/Linux: `/opt/ctmagent`
  - Windows: `D:\Program Files\BMC Software\Control-M Agent`
- If a dedicated filesystem is allocated to Control-M/Agent, keep the file system size consistent
- Always define the same OS user account and group, for example:
  - Unix/Linux: username **ctmagent**, group **ctm**
  - Windows: username **ctmagent**, as part of the **Administrators** group (applicable only if the Control-M/Agent is set to **logon as this account**)
- Use the same **Server-to-Agent** port for all Control-M/Agents that are connecting to the same Control-M/Server, unless the port has been taken by other applications on the Agent machine
- Have standard batch users for submitting jobs, and having the same location to store job scripts (for example, `/opt/batch_user1/scripts`)

Installing multiple Control-M/Agents on the same host

So far, we have only installed one Control-M/Agent on each job execution host, but in some cases, we may want to install multiple Control-M/Agents on the same host to meet special scheduling requirements. Such a scheduling requirement can be, for example, having two Control-M/Servers submitting jobs onto one machine. In this case, we have to implement one Control-M/Agent to handle each Control-M/Server's job submission requests (having two Control-M/Servers submit jobs onto one single Control-M/Agent at the same time is not allowed).

On Unix/Linux machines, the installation of multiple Control-M/Agents is just a matter of creating a new OS user account for each Control-M/Agent instance and running the installation for each user. On Windows machines, after the first (default) Control-M/Agent installation, we need to specify a Control-M/Agent instance name for each additional one we are going to install.

For each Control-M/Agent, during installation, we need to specify the corresponding Control-M/Server hostname as its **Primary Control-M/Server Host** and as the only **Authorized Control-M/Server Host**. We also need to make sure the **Server-to-Agent** TCP port number is unique for each Control-M/Agent on the same host, so each Control-M/Sever can communicate with the correct Control-M/Agent instance.

 We can have the same Control-M/Server connect to two or more Control-M/Agents residing on the same machine. In this case, each Control-M/Agent still has to listen on different Server-to-Agent TCP ports, and on the Control-M/Server side, we need to configure the Server-to-Agent port specifically for each of these Control-M/Agents.

In our environment, we will install a second Control-M/Agent on hosts `ctm-demo-linux-02` and `ctm-demo-win-02`. The second Control-M/Agent on `ctm-demo-linux-02` will be talking to the Windows Control-M/Server and the one on `ctm-demo-win-02` will be talking to the Unix Control-M/Server.

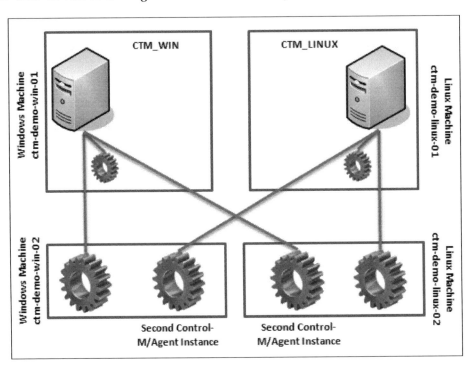

For the second Control-M/Agent on `ctm-demo-linux-02`, we will create a new OS user called **ctmagent2**, define `ctm-demo-win-01` as **Primary Control-M/Server Host**, and use **17006** as **Server To Agent Port**.

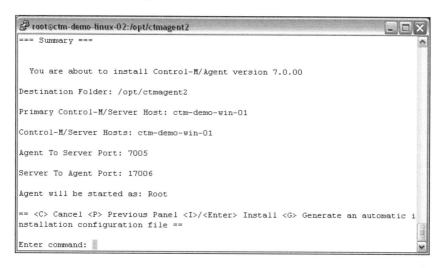

For the second Control-M/Agent on `ctm-demo-win-02`, we don't need to create a Window OS user, but do need to specify the Control-M/Agent instance name. We will specify **ctmagent2** as the instance name, for **Primary Control-M/Server Host**, we will define **ctm-demo-linux-01** and **17006** as **Server To Agent Port**.

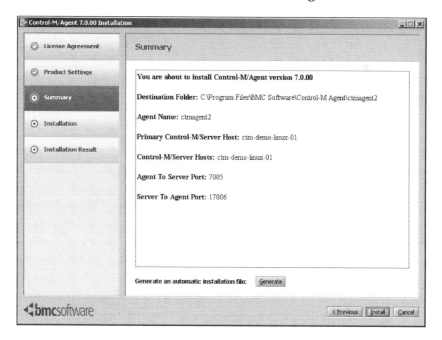

After the installations, we can go ahead and define each Control-M/Agent from the CCM. In the **Add Control-M/Agent** window, we need to make sure the combination of **Control-M/Server Name** and **Control-M/Agent Host Name** is correct and change the **Server To Agent Port** number value from default **7006** to **17006**. Upon successful discoveries, we should see two additional Control-M/Agents appearing on the list.

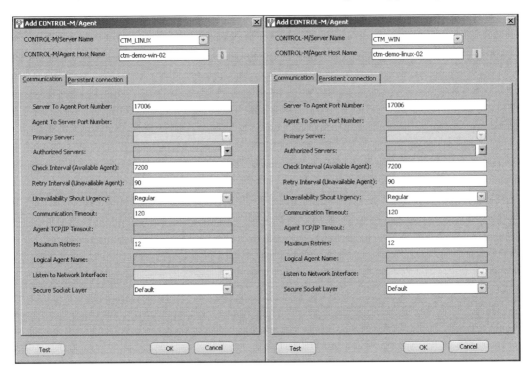

Defining Agentless remote hosts

Instead of installing Control-M/Agents for every single request, we can use Agentless technology to schedule jobs on remote hosts. We have discussed the Pros and Cons of using Agentless earlier. In this section, we will look at how to define Agentless remote hosts in Control-M for both Linux and Windows environments.

Remote host job execution will be defined for the following job execution machines:

- `ctm-demo-linux-03` through `ctm-demo-linux-01` by using SSH
- `ctm-demo-win-03` through `ctm-demo-win-01` by using WMI

We can define multiple Control-M/Agents connected to the same remote host. In this case, when one of the Control-M/Agents is failing, the Control-M/Server can still submit jobs to the remote host through other available Control-M/Agents. To reduce confusion, we will use the local Control-M/Agent for each remote host for now and look at how to add the second one later on in this chapter.

> Since the release Control-M/Server 6.3.01, each Control-M/ Server installation will install a Control-M/Agent by default. The primary reason for this is that we can use the default Control-M/Agent for Agentless remote job executions.

Unix/Linux remote host (using SSH)

As the Agentless Technology process is going on, Control-M uses SSH to communicate with remote Unix/Linux hosts for job submission. We need to follow three steps in order to set up a remote host:

- Choose the Control-M/Agent that will be used for the remote host job submission

- Choose the connection parameters to the remote host, including:
    - ° SSH server Port (default Port 22)
    - ° Encryption algorithm – BLOWFISH (default), AES, DES, and 3DES

- Choose a predefined owner or define a new owner and choose one of the following authentication methods:
    - ° Password authentication
    - ° Key authentication

> SSH can also be used for Windows machines, but the user needs to get a third-party SSH software for Windows remote hosts (for example, OpenSSH).

We can predefine the owner information and select the appropriate one for each connection profile. Normally, we define a common batch user across multiple machines or define the application-specific user that exists on many machines, such as an Oracle user. In our case, we will define two users, one called **app1** that uses password authentication and the other called **app2** that uses key authentication.

New remote hosts can be added in CCM through **New | Remote Host**. For user **app1** with password authentication, it is just a matter of entering the required information during each step, as follows:

1. Select the correct Control-M/Server Name - **Name, CTM_LINUX**, and the desired Control-M/Agent name to be used for connection local: `ctm-demo-linux-01` (Execution Agent).

2. Choose **SSH** and leave **SSH server Port** and **Encryption Algorithm** with their default values.

3. Choose **I want to define a new owner for this host** and enter the username - **app1** and its password.

Once the request is submitted, we should receive a **Save completed successfully** message and see a new entry created in the CCM called **Remote Host** with the hostname `ctm-demo-linx-03`, state **Available**, and message **Connected via ctm-demo-linux-01**. By this time, Control-M has already done a **SSh** connection-level validation in the background.

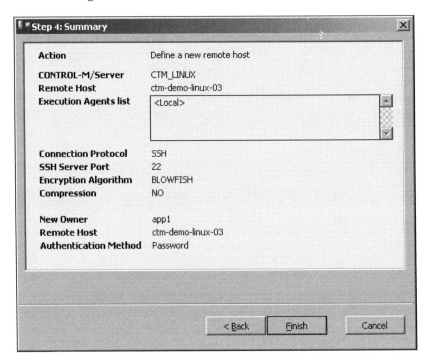

The process for defining the key authentication user **app2** is a bit more complicated. We need to generate a SSH key pair (a public key and a private key) from Control-M, and distribute the public key to the remote hosts so the **Control-M/Agent** who holds the private key can access them through **SSH Tunnel** over the normal TCP/IP network.

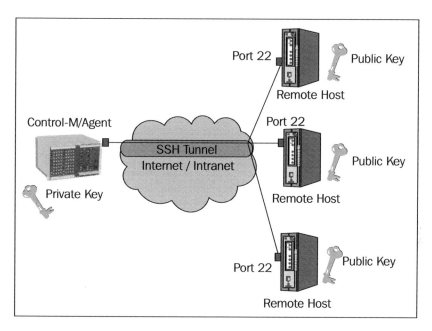

First of all, we need to generate a SSH key. This can be done from CCM through **Tools | Security | Manage Agentless SSH Keys**.

In the **Manage Agentless SSH Keys** window, press the + sign to create a new key. We need to give a name to the key, enter a **Key Passphrase**, and select the **Key generation parameters**.

The key name is up to us to decide. We enter "ctm_agentless" so it can be easily distinguished from non-Control-M SSH keys. The passphrase is a second-level security for the key and it will be asked each time we want to open or delete the key. For **Key generation parameters** we just leave everything as the default values.

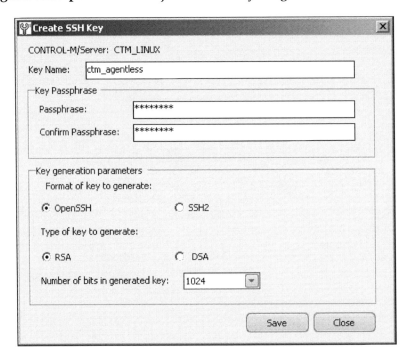

Once we click on the **Save** button, a pop-up window will tell us that the key has been created successfully and ask us if we would like to save the public key on the system we are using.

It is handy to save the key because we will need to distribute it to the remote host later on.

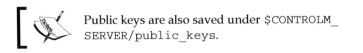

Public keys are also saved under $CONTROLM_ SERVER/public_keys.

A public key is to be distributed to all the remote hosts that are to be connected. In our case, the machine will be ctm-demo-linux-03 and the user is **app2**. On the remote host, we need to enter the content of the public key into the user's authorized_keys file. The file is located under ~/.ssh/authorized_keys. If the file doesn't exist, we can manually create it, but make sure the permission is set to owner read- and write-only (chomd 600). Right after this, we can copy and paste the content of the public key from our workstation to the remote host.

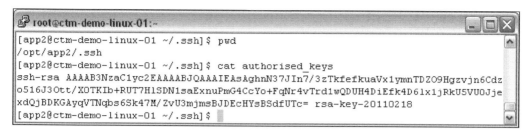

```
root@ctm-demo-linux-01:~
[app2@ctm-demo-linux-01 ~/.ssh]$ pwd
/opt/app2/.ssh
[app2@ctm-demo-linux-01 ~/.ssh]$ cat authorised_keys
ssh-rsa AAAAB3NzaC1yc2EAAAABJQAAAIEAsAghnN37JIn7/3zTkfefkuaVx1ymnTDZO9Hgzvjn6Cdz
o516J3Ott/XOTKIb+RUT7HlSDN1saExnuPmG4CcYo+FqNr4vTrd1wQDUH4DiEfk4D6lx1jRkU5VUOJje
xdQjBDKGAyqVTNqbs6Sk47M/ZvU3mjmsBJDEcHYsBSdfUTc= rsa-key-20110218
[app2@ctm-demo-linux-01 ~/.ssh]$
```

The last step is to define the owner and its associated hostname in **Owner Authentication Settings**. In CCM, we go to **Tools | Security | Owner Authentication Settings**. In the pop-up window, we press the **+** icon to add a new account. We enter **app2** as the owner and `ctm-demo-linux-03` as the host name, and then select the **Use Key Authentication (SSH Only)** option. In the drop-down list of **Key Name**, we select the newly created key, **ctm_agentless**, and enter the **Passphrase**. Before clicking on **OK**, we can press the **Test...** button to test authentication. By doing so, Control-M in the background will use its private key to connect with the remote host. If the SSH connection is okay and the private key matches the remote host's public key, the test should return with the message **Owner credentials are: Valid**.

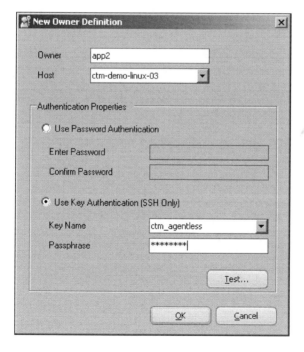

Windows remote host (using WMI)

On Windows machines, WMI technology is more commonly used for running Agentless job submissions, mainly because this technology comes with the Windows OS (XP, Windows Server 2003, or later). Here are a number of steps required for setting up WMI-based Windows remote hosts:

1. The Control-M/Agent used for Agentless remote host job submission must run under **This Account** logon option and the account has to be a domain user with the administrator privilege.

2. At least one owner is defined for remote job submission and the owner has to be a member of the administrator group on the job execution host.

3. Create a shared directory on the remote host for storing temporary sysout files and make sure both the Control-M/Agent domain user and the job owner(s) have the read and write permission to the directory.

4. Ensure that the WMI service is running on the remote host and the firewall has been configured accordingly.

On Windows computers, the Control-M/Agent service runs as **Local System account** by default. In order to use the Control-M/Agent for remote job submission, we need to switch the service to run as **This account**. We first have to decide which Windows user account we want the Control-M/Agent to run as. We need to make sure the user we are going to use is a domain user and a member of the administrator's group. Control-M/Agent service's logon option can be modified through **Computer Management | Services and Applications | Services** (restarting the service is required). In our case, we have a domain called `ctm-demo.ctmexpers.com`, and a domain user called **ctmagent** that has administrator privileges.

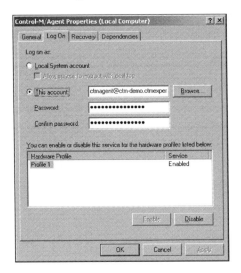

On the remote job execution hosts, we need to decide each job execution owner and make sure they are members of the administrator group too. In our case, we defined the following two users:

- `app1@ctm-demo.ctmexperts.com`: a domain user with administrator privilege
- `ctm-demo-win-03\app2`: a local user of `ctm-demo-win-03` with local administrator privilege

We need to define each user account in **Owners Authentication Settings**. In the **Owners Authentication Settings | New Owner Definition** window, we need to specify the owner name in <location>\<username> format (for example, **ctm-demo-win-03\app2**). The location can be a domain name (for domain account) or a machine name (for local account). The owner definition can be used across many hosts if a domain user is defined.

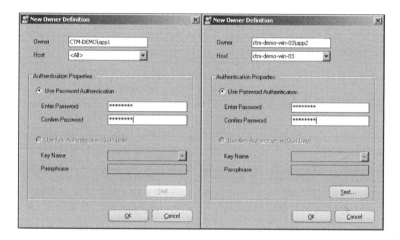

Control-M requires a place on the remote computer to store the job's sysout (and the temporary job execution script). Upon each job submission, two files will be created under the directory: a `.cmd` file that stores the job script and a `.dat` file that stores the job sysout. Once the job is completed, the `.cmd` file will be removed and the `.dat` file gets copied back to the Control-M/Agent who initiated the job to allow steps processing and sysout viewing from the GUI.

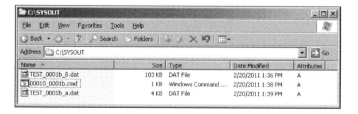

All job owners on the remote host must have the read and write permission to the directory and it also needs to be shared with the read and write permission for the Control-M/Agent domain user.

Finally, during addition of the new remote host, we need to make sure the following steps are followed:

1. Select the correct **Control-M/Server** name (**CTM_WIN**) and the desired Control-M/Agent name to be used for connection (Local: ctm-demo-win-03).

2. Choose **WMI** and specify the SYSOUT directory path (C:\SYSOUT).

3. Because we have already defined the job owner, we can skip the step by choosing **I already have owners defined for this host**.

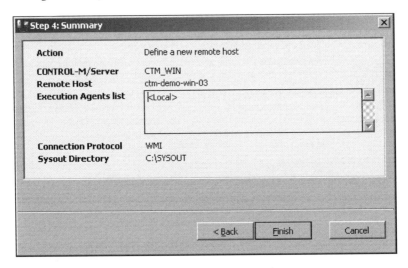

Once committed, we should see the new remote host appear in CCM with the state **Available** and message **Connected via ctm-demo-win-01**.

Applying Control-M fix packs and patches

Well, the answer is: only install the fix pack or patch when needed.

For each Control-M product, BMC software releases fix packs every few months for bug fixes and general product improvement. Each fix pack's release notes would normally include:

- What's New: New features introduced with the fix pack
- Enhancements: Product improvement wishes generated in the past that have been implemented in this fix pack (normally associated with a CAR ID)

- Corrected problems: Product defects and bugs identified in the past that have been fixed in this fix pack (normally associated with a CAR ID)

- Open issues and known problems - Product defects and bugs that were identified in the past, but haven't been fixed in this fix pack (normally associated with a CAR ID)

Fix pack covers a range of enhancements and fixes, whereas each **patch** is only released specifically for one or few critical bugs that are to be fixed urgently. These bugs are normally or potentially affecting a large number of users, therefore it is not advisable to wait to release them until the next fix pack's release. Each patch is released with a technical bulletin.

It is important to maintain the Control-M environment up-to-date, but on the other hand, as Control-M administrators, we need to decide the most appropriate time and method to apply these fix packs.

It can be hard to find the best time window to apply a fix pack or a patch on the production environment because the installation of most of the fix packs and patches requires a system outage. It is especially difficult for the Control-M/Server and Control-M/EM Server as the impact will be large scale. We need to find the time frame that brings minimal impact to the business, but as the batch environment grows, this task becomes even more challenging – just imagine a Control-M environment that handles real-time batch 24/7 with GUI users across multiple time zones.

In the coming chapters, we will demonstrate how to use Control-M Forecast to identify maintenance windows that only bring the minimal impact to batch running.

Deciding the method of installing fix packs and patches is also important, especially for GUI clients, Control-M/Agents, and Control Modules. Again, this is related to the size of our batch environment. It is easy enough to apply fix packs and patches on a handful of GUI clients and Control-M/Agents, but what about organizations with hundreds of GUI clients and thousands of Control-M/Agents? Maybe by the time they finish applying fix pack 1 on all machines, fix pack 2 is already released.

When to apply fix packs and patches

We can justify the value of the fix pack by looking through its release notes and thinking about questions such as, "Do I need these improvements right now?", or "Have I ever experienced these bugs?", or "Is there a chance I will experience these bugs in the near future?". Control-M fix packs are accumulative; in other words, if we skip fix pack 1 and install fix pack 3 later on, then fix pack 3 will cover all improvements and fixes made in fix pack 1. Based on this fact, if all answers to those questions are no, then we can simply skip the fix pack and wait for the next one or even the one after to be released.

The same logic applies to patches. Bugs fixed in the patches may or may not relate to our environment. It is good to keep an eye on the release, but not necessarily apply them. For example, if we are using PostgreSQL database, there's no reason to apply a patch to fix a problem that only occurs if Control-M is running with Oracle.

Fix packs and patches are normally first tested on testing environments for a period of time before they get pushed out to development, followed by production, in case there are fresh issues introduced with the new release. Upon pushing the releases to production, the request normally needs to be submitted through change control, with the explanation of the risk and a list of impacted items or potentially affected jobs. The change is only to be applied when it is approved by all the related parties (such as application owners). In case Control-M is already down due to a known bug, we may choose to implement the corresponding fix pack or patch on the spot through an emergency change request.

> In organizations, the Control-M administrators normally request a regular outage change window that occurs fortnightly or monthly for applying fix packs or other regular maintenance tasks for Control-M. In this case, they save time on opening a new change request and seeking for approval before each fix pack installation.

Because our environment is freshly built and still small, it is better to apply this fix pack now, rather than wait until it gets busier and more complex.

How to apply fix packs and patches

In terms of installation methods, we can perform the installation manually or use a third-party datacenter automation tool to deploy the package.

For Control-M/EM server components and Control-M/Servers, organizations normally use the manual installation method to apply fix packs and patches. This is because the installation procedures for these components are relatively complicated and the number of machines required for the installation is not huge.

For Control-M/Agent and GUI clients, the workload depends on the number of target installation hosts. Same as installing Control-M/Agents, larger organizations with huge number of Control-M/Agents have to utilize their datacenter automation tool (for example, BMC Bladelogic Application Release Automation) for the Control-M/Agent fix pack installation and use the desktop automation tool (for example, BMC Bladelogic Client Automation) to push GUI client's fix packs on to each staff's workstation.

Organizations that are not yet at a high level of automation may apply Control-M/Agent fix pack on a group-by-group basis; that is, they divide the Control-M/Agent into groups according to a guideline, such as geographic location, type of platform, or application, then apply fix pack to each group, and are therefore able to manage the risk and handle impact. For GUI clients, as a common sense, we can let the user install the fix packs themselves or rely on the organization's desktop support team, formerly known as BMC Marimba.

Fix pack and patch installations in our environment

In this section, we will be looking at the technical aspects of fix pack and patch installations for our existing Control-M environment. Because the installations are fairly easy and kind of similar to other installations we have done earlier, we will be focusing more on the procedures rather than the actual installation.

First of all, we go to the BMC support website and select the product name and version from the A-Z Supported Product List to find out the most recent fix pack and paths that meet our environment. We identified that:

- Control-M/EM version 7 has:
  - ○ Fix pack 1 released on 30 December 2010
  - ○ Patch 001, 002, and 102 released in-between 21 October 2010 and 06 February 2011

- Control-M/Server version 7 has fix pack 1 released on 7 February 2011
- Control-M BPI Suite 6.4.02 has fix pack 1 released on 7 March 2010
- CM for AFT 6.4.01 has patch 002 released on 14 June 2010
- Control-M for Database 6.4.01 has fix pack 1 released on 2 September 2010

These were the facts at the time when the book was written.

According to the release notes and technical bulletins, we realized that we do not need to install any of the Control-M/EM patches because:

- Patch 001 and 002 have been covered in Fix Pack 1
- Patch 102 is related to Migration Toolkit; we are not migrating from an older version of Control-M, therefore, we are not affected by the bug described

The installation file for each fix pack and patch can be downloaded from the BMC ftp site. We can find the link within each release notes or the technical bulletin. These files can also be found from the EPD site or obtained from the BMC sales representatives (in CD/DVD format).

In each fix pack's filename, BMC software uses a five character code to describe the product name, followed by version, fix pack, or patch version, and then the OS type. Fix pack versions are given in <fix pack version>00 format (patch versions are given in <fix pack version><patch version (two digits)> format). For example, PANFT.7.0.00.100_windows.exe means it is the 32-bit windows installation of Control-M/EM fix pack 100.

Before the fix pack or patch installation, we need to look at the compatibility section of the release notes to make sure the environment and other related Control-M components are meeting the requirements. We also need to read through the installation section of the release notes to understand the installation steps and to understand what components need to be brought down during installation. For example, for the Control-M/Server fix pack 1 installation, we need to stop the Control-M/Server Configuration Agent and Control-M/Server.

Here's a summary of our installation:

Component	Fix Pack/Patch Version	Outage Items	Impacts
Control-M/ EM Server Component	PANFT.7.0.00.100	Gateway processes, GUI Server, GAS, GCS, BIM, Forecast, Configuration Agent, CMS, CORBA naming service, and EM Web Server	This impacts all GUI users, global conditions, all job alerts, and BIM web GUI
Control-M/EM GUI Client	PANFT.7.0.00.100	Local EM GUI, Desktop, CCM, and Reporting Facility	This impacts the local users
Control-M/ Server	PACTV.7.0.00.100	Control-M/Server CA and Control-M/Server	This impacts running of all active jobs , and the users who are not able to upload and download job tables*
Control-M BPI Suite	PACOB.6.3.02.100	Control-M/Agent	This impacts all jobs on the Control-M/ Agent, BPI Interface
CM for AFT	PAAFT.6.4.01.002	Control-M/Agent	This impacts all jobs on the Control-M/ Agent
Control-M for Database	PAMQL.6.4.01.100	Control-M/Agent	This impacts all jobs on the Control-M/ Agent

The actual installation is not rocket science; it is just a matter of executing the installation script under the correct user. Most common fix pack installation failures are caused by components not shutting down correctly; we will be looking at the best way to stop and start components in the *Frequent Administration Tasks* section shortly.

In addition, some CM fix pack installations require re-importing of job editing forms, as well as re-installation of CM utility add-ons into the CCM and Control-M/EM server.

Installing additional Control-M GUI clients

Before we move onto the next topic, we still need to have a look at the most "painful" regular installation task - installing additional Control-M GUI Clients.

The installation process itself isn't that painful; it is only a matter of loading the CD/DVD and just pressing the **Next** button as required. The troublesome part is that users may be located in different geographic locations and sometimes, we cannot rely on users to do the installation on their own and expect them to apply the fix packs on time. On the other hand, as the Control-M administrator, we do not want to become a passionate desktop support either.

Well, apart from initiating the installation by a desktop automation tool, there are two alternative solutions, which can also free us from doing the hard work on a machine-by-machine basis. One is the classic method – use Citrix. The other is a bit more modern – use Control-M/EM Web Launch. In this section, we will only focus on how to create and deploy Control-M/EM Web Launch, rather than getting into the details of how to play around Citrix application launch, as there is no difference with setting up either of the applications.

Control-M/EM Web Launch was originally introduced with Control-M/EM 6.3.01 FP3. It is not a web GUI of Control-M/EM, as many people first thought when it was released. Instead, it allows a packaged GUI client installation to be deployed and automatically configured on many computers through a web page; therefore, we no longer need to manually install, configure, and patch GUI installations on individual client computers. The down side of Web Launch is that the reporting Facility is not distributed as part of the package.

We decided to use Web Launch for our Control-M environment to make our life easier. We need to build the Web Launch package from an existing Control-M/EM GUI client installation (master GUI client installation). The steps are as follows:

1. Log on to the Control-M/EM server machine (`ctm-demo-linux-01`) to stop the Control-M/EM web server by running the `stop_web_server` utility as the Control-M/EM Linux user (for example, emuser). If the Control-M/EM server components are running on a Windows environment, we need to shut down the web server through **Computer Management | Services and Applications | Services | Control-M Web Server**.

2. Make sure port 18080 and 8005 (default web server ports) are not taken on Control-M/EM server machine and can be accessed from client computers.

3. Log on to a workstation with Control-M/EM GUI client installed:

    ◦ Make sure the workstation can access the `www.w3.org` website

    ◦ Log on to CCM and go to **Tools | Control-M/EM Web Launch Prepare Package**

4. In the **Prepare Package** window, enter:

    ◦ hostname of the web server: `ctm-demo-linux-01` (Control-M/EM server component machine)

    ◦ Port number: 18080 (default value)

    ◦ Instance name: `ctm_demo` (at our own choice)

5. Because we are creating the Web Launch from a GUI client, we need to manually transfer the packaged files onto the web server, whereas, for Control-M/EM server components and client installation (on Windows only), the transfer is automatic. Following are the steps for transferring the packaged files:

    ◦ On the workstation, get the `.tar` file generated under `<Control-M/EM Home Dir>\emweb\deploy` (for example, `C:\Program Files\BMC Software\Control-M EM 7.0.00\Default\emweb\deploy`)

    ◦ Transfer the file onto our Control-M/EM server machine, log on as EM user and untar the file under `$HOME/ctm_em/etc/emweb/tomcat/webapps`

6. Start the web server by running **start_web_server** as the EM server Linux user, or start the **Control-M Web Server** services if it is a Windows environment.

 During this time, the BIM Web GUI will become unavailable if it is using the default web application server.

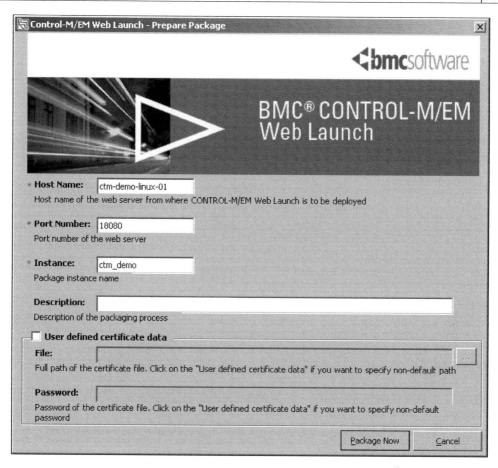

Now, we log on to the workstations where Control-M/EM GUI clients are to be installed, open a browser, and go to `http://<Web Server Host>:<Web Server Port>/web-launch/`. On the web page, we can click on any application icon to start the installation. No matter which icon we click on, the web launch will install the entire package onto the workstation. Upon completion, the component login window will pop up according to the icon we clicked (for example, if we clicked the CCM icon, the installation will finish with prompting us the login window for CCM). For users who do not have administrator privileges on their own local machines, the deployment can still be performed by the user if the **DisableMSI** parameter is enabled in the Windows registry. The parameter can be enabled by locating or creating the registry key `HKEY_LOCAL_MACHINE\Software\Policies\Microsoft\Windows\Installer` and creating a new DWORD value with Value Name **DisableMSI** and Value Data **0**.

We can push out new Web Launch packages each time we update the master GUI client installation, such as after installing a new fix pack, or once a new job form is imported. We need to make sure each time we specify the same instance name, port number, and hostname, otherwise **Web Launch** will build it into a new instance rather than overwriting the existing one. On the user side, during each time when the GUI client starts, it will automatically communicate with the web server in order to check for package updates and refresh itself if there's a new version. If the web server is down at that time, the checking will be skipped to ensure that the GUI user can still log in.

Frequent administration tasks

Installing Control-M components and fix packs is not the whole story of administrating Control-M. Once everything has been built and pushed into production, then, as Control-M administrators, it is our responsibility to maintain the environment. Having said that, Control-M is not a high-maintenance software application, If everything was set up properly at the beginning, all we now need to perform are just very general administration tasks, such as stop/start components, define new GUI users, and configuring Control-M to fit our needs and so on.

Control-M provided user-friendly GUI features and command-line utilities for us to perform the everyday administration tasks. In this section, we will review these common tasks and introduce the related Control-M built-in administration features and tools.

Stop/start components

How to stop/start a Control-M component is a must-learn skill for every Control-M administrator. This is required not only before and after a fix pack or component installation, but also during troubleshooting.

We have already touched base on how to start and stop Control-M components during the installation sections. In fact, there are many different ways to stop/start a component to suit different situations. It is important for us to know the differences between them, therefore we can choose the right tool for the right situation.

Manually stop/start components

We have used CCM to stop/start Control-M/EM server components and Control-M/Server in *Chapter 3*, *Building the Control-M Infrastructure*. Control-M also provided command-line utilities for us to manually stop, start, and check each component. These utilities are handy to use while we are on the server machine or when the CCM is not available.

Control-M/EM server components

In Unix/Linux environments, Control-M/EM utilities are stored under the `<Control-M/EM Home Dir>/ctm_em/bin/em` directory, with symbolic links stored under the `<Control-M/EM Home Dir>/ctm_em/bin` directory. We can execute these commands from anywhere as long as we log in as the Control-M/EM user, because the `<Control-M/EM Home Dir>/ctm_em/bin` directory has been set into the user's PATH environment variable by default.

All utilities related to stop and start components are listed in the following table (for Unix/Linux environments):

Component Name	Utilities for stop and start		
Database	**start_server*, stop_server***	**start_all,**	
Naming Server	**start_ns_daemon, stop_ns_daemon**	**stop_all**	
	orbadmin ns start, orbadmin ns stop		
CMS	**start_cms, stop_cms**	**root_ menu (option 1)**	**em ctl (stop only)**
Configuration Agent	**start_config_agent, stop_config_ agent**		
GCS	through CCM GUI	**em ccmcli**	
GUI Server			
GAS			
BIM			
Forecast Server			
Gateway			
EM Web Server	**start_web_server, stop_web_server**		

*If Control-M/EM owns the database

Normally, we would first issue the **start_all** command to start the four core components (since the release of Control-M/EM Fix Pack 2, EM Web Server also gets started when issuing the **start_all** command), and then, all other components will be automatically managed by the Configuration Agent according to their desired states in CCM. Individual command-line utilities are provided to allow us to start the core components one-by-one. The usage of these utilities is very straightforward – just a matter of logging in with an EM user account and executing them. We would use them if there's a problem with the startup and we need to find out which component is failing. These utilities are also useful if we only need to restart certain components after a fix pack or patch installation. The starting sequence for these components is as follows (the sequence for stopping the components goes the other way around):

Database | Naming Server | CMS and Configuration Agent | Everything else (by changing the desired state through CCM).

Most of the utilities listed above are not available if the Control-M/EM server is running in the Windows environment, except the **orbadmin**, **em ccmcli**, *and* **em ctl** *utilities. Instead, we can stop/start each core component and EM Web Server from* **Computer Management | Services and Applications | Services**.

 Core components are as in the PostgreSQL Database (owned by Control-M/EM), Naming Server, CMS, and Configuration Agent.

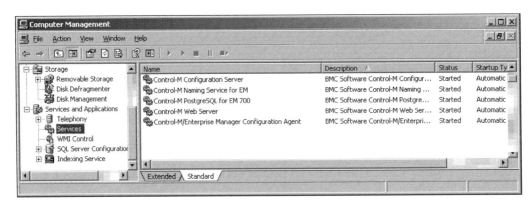

The em `ccmcli` utility allows us to perform CCM actions from the command-line interface. For example, setting a component's desired state or recycling a component. If we log on the Control-M/EM server host as EM user account and execute the command, we will see the full usage details of the utility. The basic syntax of the command related to stop/start components is:

```
em ccmcli [-u <user> [-p <password>] | -pf <password file>] [-s <CMS
name>] [-t <component type>] [-n <component name>] [-h <component
host>] [ [-cmd <command>]
```

With this command, we need to specify:

- User login details in either of the two formats:
    - **-u <user> - p <password>**: EM GUI client username and password.
    - **-pf <password file>**: The full path of a password file contains the user name and password (in case we schedule the command as a job and don't want to show the password in the command line). The password file needs to be in the following format:
        - `user=<user>`
        - `password=<password>`
- **-s < Configuration Server Name>**: The name of the CMS; normally it is the hostname of the Control-M/EM server component machine's hostname (for example, `ctm-demo-linux-01`).
- **-t <component type>**: The name of the EM component (Gateway, GUI_Server, GCS, GAS, BIM, Forecast_Server, and so on).
- **-n <component name>**: Logical name given to the component.
- **-h <component host>**: The hostname of the machine where the component is running (that is, sometimes a GUI server can be running on another machine other than where the CMS is running).
- **-cmd <command>**: The command we want to execute for the component, similar to what we can do from CCM GUI (start, stop, ignore, recycle, and so on).

For example, we executed the stop command for GCS on `ctm-demo-linux-01`, which is equivalent to setting the desired state of GCS to **Down** in CCM.

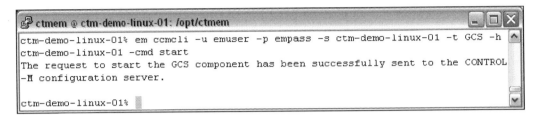

The `em ctl` utility has greater power compared to the `em ccmcli` utility. The `em ctl` utility can operate on any Control-M/EM server component except the database. It can be used for stopping a component, debugging a component, and refreshing a component's settings, but it cannot be used for starting a component. It only accepts the Control-M/EM database owner's username/password and interacts with the processes directly rather than relying on CMS.

The basic syntax of the command varies for different components. We can run the `em ctl` command without specifying any argument to see the full usage information. As an example, we execute a `shutdown` command for the Configuration Agent; basically, the command shuts down the Configuration Agent, as well as everything managed under it (without changing each component's desire state).

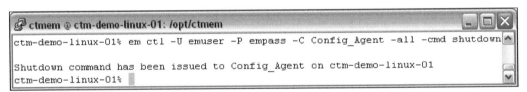

If we use `em ctl` to shut down components under the management of the Configuration Agent (BIM, GCS, GAS, Forecast, Gateway, and GUI Server), the components will be restarted imminently by the Configuration Agent (given that the Configuration Agent is running). This is because, by issuing this command, we only stopped the current running process without changing the component's desired state. By the time the component is stopped, the Configuration Agent will detect it and restart a new process within a short period of time. This command can be scheduled as a job in order to automatically recycle a component.

Before the release of Control-M/EM version 7, the command on Unix/Linux environment was ecs ctl. Version 7 still accepts ecs ctl in case users have jobs that have migrated from the old environment that runs this command, similarly em ccmcli was known as ecs ccmcli. If the Control-M/EM server is installed on a windows environment, these commands are ctl and ccmcli.

Each time, before we issue stop commands to a Control-M/EM server component, it is necessary to make sure all other dependent components have been already stopped in CCM. It is also a good habit to double-check and make sure the component is running after we started it.

There are a number of ways to check the state of the component (most of them are Unix/Linux environments only):

Component Name	Utilities for status checking			
Database	check_server*		check_all	
Naming Server	orbadmin ns status*			em ctl
CMS	check_cms			(-cmd life_check)
Configuration Agent	check_config_agent		root_menu (option 1)	
GCS	through CCM GUI	em ccmcli		
GUI Server				
GAS		(-cmd details)		
BIM				
Forecast Server				
Web Server	emweb_status			

*If Control-M/EM owns the database

 orbadmin, ccmcli, and ctl are the only utilities available in the Windows environment.

For example:

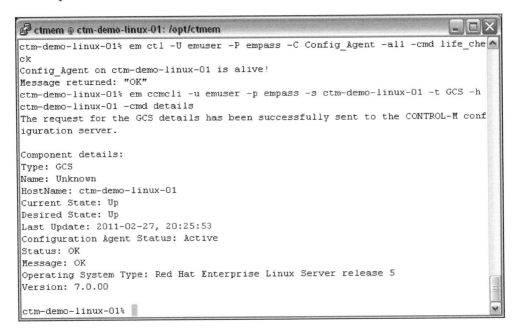

```
ctm-demo-linux-01% em ctl -U emuser -P empass -C Config_Agent -all -cmd life_che
ck
Config_Agent on ctm-demo-linux-01 is alive!
Message returned: "OK"
ctm-demo-linux-01% em ccmcli -u emuser -p empass -s ctm-demo-linux-01 -t GCS -h
ctm-demo-linux-01 -cmd details
The request for the GCS details has been successfully sent to the CONTROL-M conf
iguration server.

Component details:
Type: GCS
Name: Unknown
HostName: ctm-demo-linux-01
Current State: Up
Desired State: Up
Last Update: 2011-02-27, 20:25:53
Configuration Agent Status: Active
Status: OK
Message: OK
Operating System Type: Red Hat Enterprise Linux Server release 5
Version: 7.0.00

ctm-demo-linux-01%
```

Control-M/Server components

The start/stop for Control-M/Server is much simpler than Control-M/EM, simply because there are not as many components.

Control-M/Server utilities are stored under the `<Control-M/Server Home Dir>/ ctm_server/scripts` directory. We can execute these commands from anywhere as long as we log on as the Control-M/Server user, because the `<Control-M/Server Home Dir>/ctm_server/scripts` directory has been set into the user's PATH environment variable by default.

These commands are (for both Windows and Unix/Linux environments):

Component Name	Utilities for stop and start			
Database	**startdb*, shutdb***			**ctm_menu (option 1)**
Control-M/Server CA Process	**start_ca, shut_ca**	through CCM GUI	**em ccmcli**	
Control-M/Server	**start_ctm, shut_ctm**			

*If Control-M/Server owns the database

In Windows environments, the start and stop of these components can also be done through **Computer Management | Services and Applications | Services**. The three services are:

- Control-M PostgreSQL
- Control-M/Server service
- Control-M/Server Configuration Agent service

The starting sequence for these components is as follows:

Database | Control-M/Server CA Process (Optional) | Control-M/Server

For stopping Control-M/Server and its components, normally we would first change the **Desire State** of Control-M/Server in CCM to **Down**. After its real state is changed to **Down**, we can go ahead and shut down the Control-M/Server CA process, followed by its database.

Control-M/Server can be functional as normal without having the CA process running. By not having the CA process we simply lose the control and visibility of the Control-M/Server (and its Agents) in CCM (and through **em ccmcli** utility). On the other hand, if we are going to start or shut down Control-M/Server by start_ctm/ shut_ctm utility or through ctm_menu, we need to make sure the CA process is down or the desired state of the Control-M/Server in CCM has been set to ignore, otherwise as soon as Control-M/Server is started or stopped by utility, the CA process will change the state of the Control-M/Server to the desire state set in CCM. The stopping sequence for Control-M/Server components through command-line utility is as follows:

Control-M/Server CA Process (if running) **| Control-M/Server | Database**

The utilities for checking Control-M/Server and its components are (most of them are for both Windows and Unix/Linux environments):

Component Name	Utilities for status checking			
Database	**shserver***			
Control-M/Server CA Process	**show_ca**	through CCM	**em ccmcli**	**ctm_menu (option 1)**
Control-M/Server	**Shctm**	GUI		

*If Control-M/Server owns the database

For **shserver**, **show_ca**, and **shctm**, if there's no output; that means the component is not running. Utility **shserver** is only available for the Control-M/Server running in a Unix or Linux environment.

Control-M/Agent components

Control-M/Agent is also very easy to stop and start, because all we need to worry about are the Control-M/Agent Listener process, Tracker process, and in addition, the Router process, if we are running a persistent connection.

In Unix and Linux environments, we need to execute the **start-ag** and **shut-ag** script under the <Control-M/Agent Home Dir>/ctm/scripts directory to control all Control-M/Agent components, which we have already used many times during CM installations previously. In Windows environments, the start and stop of Control-M/Agent is done through **Computer Management | Services and Applications | Services | Control-M/Agent Service**.

 For the earlier versions of Control-M/Agent in the Windows environment, the AG, AT, and RT processes were three separate services. They were combined into a single service since Control-M/Agent version 6.4.01, but in the backend, they are still individual processes rather than three types of threads within a single process.

In CCM, or through the **em ccmcli** utility, we are only allowed to perform recycling on the Control-M/Agents. The **-cmd** option for recycling the Control-M/Agent in the **em ccmcli** utility is **recycle**.

In terms of getting to know the status of a Control-M/Agent, we can check it through CCM for all Control-M/Agents. For a Unix/Linux environment, we can execute the **shagent** command with the Control-M/Agent user account. If the Control-M/Agent is running, the command will reply with the running processes, otherwise it will return nothing.

Most of the Control Modules stop and start as the Control-M/Agent stops and starts, but some of them do require a manual start-up or shutdown, such as CM for the Peoplesoft's **psftcm shut** utility and Control-M for the BPI Web Services Interface's **stop_ctmwsapi** and **start_ctmwsapi** utilities. For detailed information, please see the corresponding Control Module product user guide.

Configuring automatic startup script

In real environments, we would like to set the Control-M components to be able to start-up automatically. As such, during a machine reboot, we don't need to manually start the affected components one after another. It saves us a lot of additional administration work and at the same time, it ensures the Control-M components can come back online at the earliest after the machine is up and running, therefore minimizing the impact on batch processing.

In Windows environments, each Control-M service's **Start up Type** is set to **Automatic** by default, so we don't need to worry about it. For Unix and Linux environments, Control-M has also made it simple by providing us scripts to set up automatic start-ups for Control-M/Server and Agent. All we need to do is execute the scripts under the correct user. It is recommended to be done right after each installation.

For Control-M/Server:

1. Log on the Control-M/Server machine as the root user.

2. Copy the `rc.<Control-M/Server OS User>` file under `<Control-M/Server Home dir>/ctm/scripts` into the `/etc/rc.d` directory, and rename it to `<Control-M/Server OS User>`.

3. Create a symbolic link of the file just created under `/etc/rc.d/rc2.d` (run level 2) and call it `S89<Control-M/Server OS User>`.

For Control-M/Agent:

1. Log on the Control-M/Agent machine as the root user.

2. Copy the `rc.agent_user` file under `<Control-M/Agent Home dir>/ctm/scripts` into the `/etc/rc.d` directory, and rename it to `<Control-M/Agent OS User>`.

3. Create a symbolic link of the file just created under /etc/rc.d/rc5.d (run level 5) and call it S89<Control-M/Agent OS User>.

```
root@ctm-demo-linux-02:/
[root@ctm-demo-linux-02 ]# cp /opt/ctmagent/ctm/scripts/rc.agent_user /etc/rc.d/ctmagent
[root@ctm-demo-linux-02 ]# ln -s /etc/rc.d/ctmagent /etc/rc.d/rc5.d/S98ctmagent
[root@ctm-demo-linux-02 ]# ls -l /etc/rc.d/rc5.d/S98ctmagent
lrwxrwxrwx 1 root root 18 Feb 16 19:51 /etc/rc.d/rc5.d/S98ctmagent -> /etc/rc.d/ctmagent
[root@ctm-demo-linux-02 ]#
```

Defining additional GUI users and groups

Once Control-M/EM GUI clients are installed onto new workstations, we also need to create access for the users so that they can access Control-M, but only with the appropriate privileges. The privileges are normally based on the user's job role so they only have access to things (for example, certain Control-M jobs and tables) that are relevant to them and can only perform actions that they are allowed to (for example, okay to hold/free jobs, but not allowed to rerun jobs).

Creating users and defining their privileges is done through the **Authorizations** window located under either Control-M/EM GUI or Control-M Desktop's **Tools** drop-down menu. From there, we can define each user with a unique username and password, along with the user's privileges. For users that are to have the same or similar privileges, we can define the common privileges at a group level and associate these users with that group (that is, define the user as a member of the group). Users can be included in more than one group to inherit multiple group-level privileges.

 Re-login is required each time for the new privilege to be applied to the user. Without a re-login, the user account will maintain its old privileges.

Authorization of configuration items

In a freshly installed Control-M/EM, there is always one admin user – emuser, and three default groups – AdminGroup, BrowseGroup, and UpdateGroup. In the authorizations window, if we double-click on either the user or one of the groups, we will see many different tabs with some preconfigured values. At this stage, we will introduce each tab except LDAP group, Workloads, and Services.

Active tab

In the **Active** tab, we can select the jobs and tables to be shown to the user (or users within the group) by applying **Job Filter**, followed by defining the allowed actions to be performed on the filtered jobs.

For example, if we apply **Include in Jobs and Tables Filter** with **Field** as **CTM Name**, **Value** as **CTM_LINUX**, and select **All Browse actions**, the user (or users belonging to the group) will be able to see all the jobs belongs to the datacenter **CTM_LINUX** and view their logs, but will be unable to perform any other action on the jobs or update them.

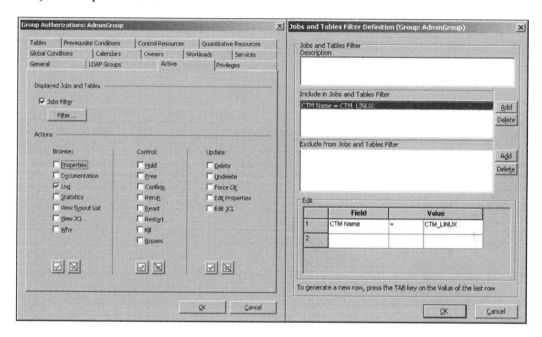

Tables and calendars

For each user (or group), we can define their access level to tables and calendars stored in Control-M (through two separate tabs). We need to select the Datacenter name, Table/Calendar name, and the access level. Wildcard * can be used in the Datacenter name and Table/Calendar name field. The **Access Level** choices are:

- **Browse**: The user can only view the specified calendars/jobs in the specified table

- **Update**: The user can add new tables/calendars and modify the specified (existing) table/calendars. In the **Tables** tab, the update access level also allows the user to order and force jobs within the specified table

- **Full**: On top of the update access level, the user can also delete tables/calendars

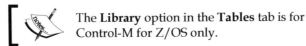

The **Library** option in the **Tables** tab is for Control-M for Z/OS only.

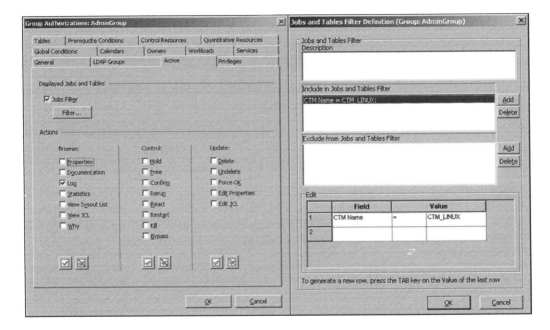

Prerequisite conditions and global conditions

In the **Prerequisite Conditions** tab, we specify the Control-M name, Condition name, and the user's access level. Again, wildcard * can be used for the Control-M name and Condition name, and the **Access Level** options are (operating from the **Prerequisite Conditions** window under Control-M/EM GUI client's **Tools** drop-down menu):

- **Browse**: The user can see the condition.
- **Update**: The user can add new conditions (modify the existing conditions is not allowed).
- **Full**: The user can add and delete conditions (modify the existing conditions is not allowed).

Global Conditions are very similar to prerequisite conditions, except that for each user or group, we only need to define the global condition's prefix and the user's access level. For each global condition, the prefix cannot be modified once it is defined. Only the users with update and full access levels are allowed to modify the Condition's Distributed From/To definitions. The **Global Conditions** window is available under both the Control-M/EM GUI client and Control-M Desktop.

If no prerequisite/global condition is defined, the options in the **Tools** drop-down menu will be grayed out for that user.

Quantitative and control resources

For the **Quantitative Resources** and **Control Resources** tabs, we also specify the Control-M name, resource name, and access level, for each resource type and the user's access level (Under **Tools | Quantitative Resources** window):

- **Quantitative Resources**
    - ○ **Update**: The user can add new **Quantitative Resources** and modify the existing resource's Max Quantity
    - ○ **Full**: The user can add new **Quantitative Resources** and update or delete existing Quantitative Resources

- **Control Resources**
    - ○ **Update**: The user can add new Control Resources (modify existing resource's type is not allowed)
    - ○ **Full**: The user can add new Control Resources and update or delete existing Control Resources (modify existing resource's type is not allowed)

Owners

We can see this privilege where we map the relationship between the Control-M/ EM GUI user and the actual job owner. The mapping is defined by specifying the combination of the Control-M name, the actual job owner, and the Node ID/Group the job will be executed on. By having this privilege defined, the GUI user/group will only have the rights to write job definitions to EM when the specified execution host and OS user are defined in the jobs. For example, if we define CONTROL-M as **CTM_LINUX**, Owner as **sap**, and Node ID/Group as **sap_app-01**, the job defined with the Owner root for the same CONTROL-M and Node ID/Group by the GUI user/group will be rejected during writing to EM.

Wild card * can be used for all three fields. The `<local>` selection in Node ID/ Group's drop-down menu refers to the local Control-M/Agent – for job definitions that have the Node ID/Group field left empty.

Privileges

The **Privileges** tab is where we give the user (or group) access to Control-M's monitoring, configuration, and administration-related facilities. There are 18 such items grouped into four categories. Access levels can be selected for each item (for example, full access or browse only).

For individual user definitions, there's an additional access-level option called **Default**. By selecting this option, the user will inherit the group-level definition (or the highest group-level definition if the user is a member of multiple groups). Otherwise, the user's access level will override the group definition.

Member of

The **Member Of** tab is only available to individual user definition windows. It is the place for us to define groups that the user belongs to.

Once a user account is a member of one or many groups, it will inherit the highest privilege regardless of its definition within the user or group authorization.

Customizing Control-M GUI

Once we become more familiar with Control-M, we can tweak its behavior a little bit to suit ourselves. We can change the settings of Control-M/EM GUI and Control-M/Desktop through **Options** located under each application's **Tools** drop-down menu.

Each item in the **Options** window is pretty much self-explanatory. We will make some changes to the Control-M GUI in our environment to get the general idea, rather than going through every single configuration item.

After the reconfiguration is done, we can re-pack and re-deploy the Web Launch Package, in order for everyone to have the same settings.

Control-M/EM GUI

First of all, in **Environment | General**, we would like to select **Auto open viewpoint** and **Last viewpoint**. This option saves us from selecting the viewpoint every time we start Control-M/EM GUI.

Secondly, in **Flowdiagram | Nodes**, we would like to change the "**Title**" from "**MEMNAME**" into **JOBNAME** and change the first field from **Control-M Name** to **NODE_ID**. In this case, by looking at the flow diagram, we will know which job belongs to which job execution host.

Control-M Desktop

In order to match up with Control-M/EM GUI, we also change the title display of each job in Control-M Desktop in (**Flowdiagram | Nodes**):

- NodeTitle: JobName/MemName
- First Field: Node ID/Group
- Second Field: Owner

Apart from the above, in **Flowdiagram | Links**, we will select **Add Out Condition with minus sign when creating job dependency**. Remember, in *Chapter 4* we had to duplicate the jobs' in-conditions into the out-condition fields with the minus sign, so the conditions will get deleted automatically imminently after job execution. By selecting this option, each time we click and drag the mouse to create a condition, the out condition will also get created, which means it will save the manual work.

Summary

Now we should feel much more confident with our Control-M skills, not only on the implementation and scheduling side, but also on the administration side.

In this chapter, we started with installing the additional Control-M components – BIM and Forecast, followed by discussing tasks involved in expanding and updating the Control-M environment. We talked about different methods of performing regular installation tasks, such as applying fix packs and installing Control-M/EM GUI clients, as well as demonstrated how to define Agentless remote hosts in both Linux and Windows environments by using the two connection methods. Towards the end, we also got to perform some everyday administration tasks, including stop/start Control-M components, defining Control-M/EM user authorizations and customizing the GUI.

Those new components we installed during the beginning of this chapter were not only for good looks but also for additional functionality. In the coming chapters, we will be working on how to utilize these new components so we can get the most out of Control-M.

6
Advanced Batch Scheduling and Management

Greedy people always try to do everything at once and expect an instant result, as an outcome, they either end up making a huge mistake or lose their drive due to the extreme stress they cause themselves. On the contrary, as successful people always say, in order to get to the ultimate goal, it is important to walk slowly by taking one step at a time and gradually bringing up the speed rather than trying to run from the beginning. We have been following the successful people's guideline by taking baby steps on the road to workload automation. However, today I am glad to tell you that we are at the stage where we can speed up a little bit! We now have a solid batch infrastructure with jobs running, as well as the necessary knowledge and skill to manage it, that is, it is the time to come out of the Stone Age and enter into the Bronze Age!

In this chapter, we will first migrate some existing batch processing tasks into Control-M, and then make improvements to our file processing job flow by utilizing Control-M's more advanced job scheduling features and Control Modules to meet the additional functionality requirements. We will also be looking at how to use BIM and Forecast to take our batch monitoring and management to the next level. Last but not the least, we will analyze our batch running by using various types of reports generated from the Control-M Reporting Facility.

By the end of this chapter, you will:

- Be able to use the right Control-M feature to migrate existing batch processing tasks and meet complex scheduling requirements.
- Be familiar with more advanced Control-M/Enterprise Manager GUI features and add-on functionalities (BIM and Forecast) to monitor and manage larger amounts of batch processing with less effort.
- Have the skill to identify hidden or potential issues with batch processing from reports generated by Control-M's Reporting Facility.

Importing existing batch processing tasks

The official ending of the Stone Age for an organization is when we no longer can find any batch processing that is still running outside of Control-M over the entire IT environment. This is harder to achieve than it sounds. Even with matured Control-M sites, we could occasionally see that there is batch processing done in CRON, Windows scheduled tasks, or other schedulers. Our objective is to find the simplest way with the least amount of risk involved in bringing those tasks into Control-M.

Importing CRON jobs into our environment

CRON jobs are the easiest-to-identify batch processing to be migrated into Control-M. Once they are migrated, we can make instant improvements simply by replacing time match scheduling with condition-based scheduling to shorten the total processing time, as well as letting each job automatically generate a status notification for quicker failure response.

Manually re-defining CRON jobs in Control-M has become history. Since Control-M/EM version 6.4.01 fix pack 1, we are able to directly import CRON tab files into Control-M through the GUI. This importing facility is a feature of Control-M Desktop. It reads crontab files and coverts each line into a command type Control-M job and can automatically populate the job's executable filename, path, owner, and schedule days.

During this section, we will be using this feature to import the following CRON jobs from ctm-demo-linux-01 and ctm-demo-linux-02 into Control-M:

Script name	Owner	Start time	Schedule days
ARCHIVE_App1Log.sh	app1	02:00am	Everyday
ROTATE_App1Log.sh	app1	03:00am	Everyday
ARCHIVE_App2Log.sh	app2	02:00am	Everyday
ROTATE_App2Log.sh	app2	03:00am	Everyday
MOUNT_RemoteFS.sh	hkeeper	04:00am	Everyday
REMOVE_OldBackup.sh	hkeeper	04:15am	Everyday
CHECK_LocalSpace.sh	hkeeper	05:00am	Everyday
CHECK_RemoteSpace.sh	hkeeper	05:15am	Everyday
BACKUP_MainFS.sh	hkeeper	05:30am	Everyday

The crontab file is stored under each Linux user. We need to extract the contents into a `.crontab` text file and then transfer to the computer of our Control-M/EM GUI client for importing. Since these jobs are totally the same on both the machines, we only need to perform the export/import for one machine and then copy and mass update those jobs for the second machine.

For Host ctm-demo-linux-01

The export can be done by logging on as each job owner on `ctm-demo-linux-01` and executing `crontab -l > <owner>.crontab`. We use the owner's name as the name of the file because Control-M populates the filename into each job's **owner** field.

Once we have the file ready on the workstation, we open a new Workspace in Control-M Desktop, go to **File | Open**, and select **File of type** as *.crontab to open the crontab text file (only one file is allowed to be opened in each Workspace).

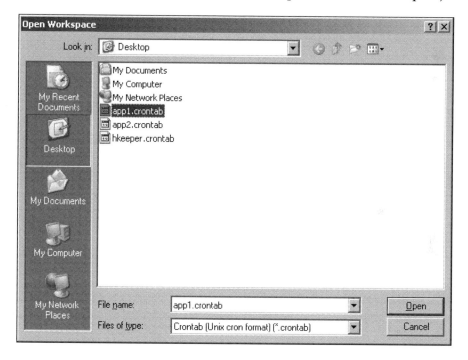

Once the file is opened, we should see the CRON jobs appear in the Workspace. Each job has been set to the task type as Command with the **Command** field, **owner**, and **scheduling dates** populated. We still need to make a number of changes in order for these jobs to run correctly in Control-M, including:

- Mass update (common fields among all jobs):
    - Datacenter name: CTM_LINUX
    - Author: emuser (our GUI login user)
    - Execution node ID: ctm-demo-linux-01
    - Table name: DAILY_MAINT-LINUX-01 (jobs are imported into the traditional job table by default)
    - Application: APP1, APP2, and HKEEPER
    - Group: DAILY_MAINT-LINUX-01

- For individual jobs:
    - Job name: The job's script name plus the job execution host's unique name, that is, LINUX-01 (so later on we can distinguish between the same job running on different machines)
    - File name: The job script name
    - Others: Description and any additional definitions such as Steps and PostProc: As required

 For fields listed above, except for datacenter and job execution hostname, the values defined are purely up to the user.

Since we planned to save all these jobs into the same job table, each time after editing the imported job, we should write it into the EM database and reload it back after the next crontab is loaded into a new workspace.

Once all jobs are imported and edited, we go back to each crontab file to find out the logic between these jobs and covert the time-based scheduling into logic-based scheduling by linking them with conditions.

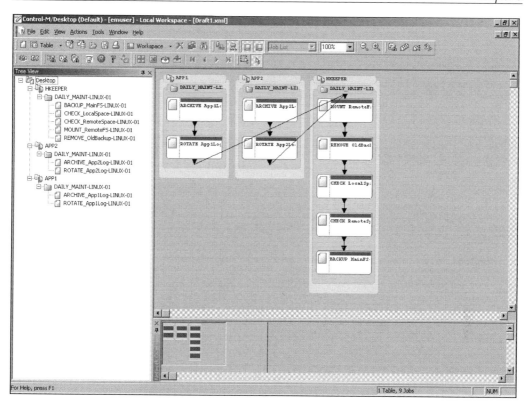

Because the jobs which will be submitted follow a logical sequence, we only need to define a start time for the very first job, that is, **ARCHIVE_App1Log-LINUX-01** and **ARCHIVE_App2Log-LINUX-01**. There are many ways to achieve this. For example, we can define the start time 2:00am in both of these two jobs, or convert them into a SMART table and define the start time at the SMART table level. In our case, once the job flow is duplicated for `ctm-demo-linux-02`, we will create a SMART table that starts at 2:00am to contain all jobs, that is, converting the two traditional tables as the SMART table's sub-table.

For Host ctm-demo-linux-02

Once the completed job flow for `ctm-demo-linux-01` has been written into the EM database, we can perform a Mass Update on these jobs to modify their execution Node ID into `ctm-demo-linux-02`, and the table and group name into `DAILY_MAINT-LINUX-02`. The hostname (that is, `-LINUX-01` post-fix) included as a part of each job name and each condition name cannot be easily modified by Mass Update, that is, we only want to update the prefix part of the job/condition name. But rather than doing a job-by-job manual update, we can export them into a `.xml` file (**File | Save as**, select **File of type** as `.xml`) and do a find and replace in text editor.

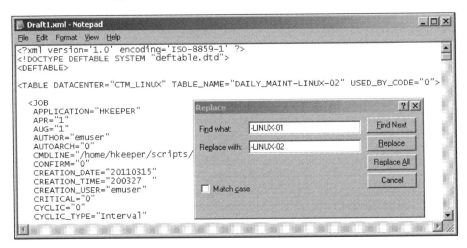

After the modification is done, we open a new workspace and load the jobs back in through **File | Open Workspace**, select **files of type** as `.xml`, followed by a loading table `DAILY_MAINT-LINUX-01` into the same workspace.

All we need to do in order to convert them into a sub-table is:

- Create a SMART table called `DAILY_MAINT` with Application ALL, Group `DAILY_MAINT-LINUX`, and RBC ALL (select `all Month days` in `all month`).

- Create two sub-tables under the SMART table. The name can be the same as the two traditional tables (that is, `DAILY_MAINT-LINUX-01` and `DAILY_MAINT-LINUX-02`).

- Expand the Tree View and drag each traditional table into the corresponding sub-table.

Now we should see that the two traditional tables have disappeared and all jobs are transferred into the two sub-tables. Before we write and upload these jobs, we need to define a start time for the SMART table, that is, Submit: from 2:00am, as well as enter **SYSTEM** into the **User Daily** field so the jobs will get ordered during NDP.

Our job flow now looks like the following screenshot:

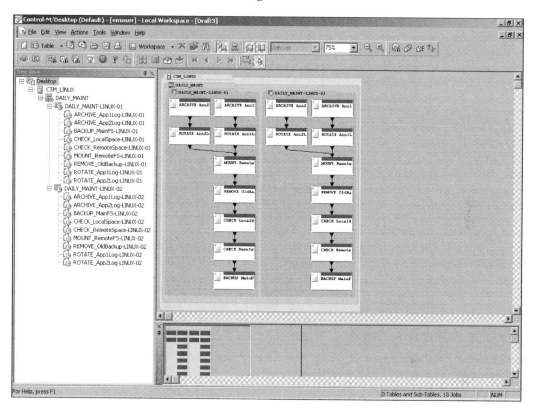

While we are uploading the table in table manager, we can delete those temporary tables created during importing or leave them for further reference (they are not defined in any userdaily, and therefore will not be ordered).

Over time, users around the world have developed their own way of performing conversion against other scheduling environments (that is, TWS and Dollar Universe). The Control-M community websites are good places to find such information or for seeking expert help.

Enhance the file processing batch flow

Now let's recall the file processing scenario from *Chapter 4, Create and Manage Batch Flows with Control-M GUI*. Back then, we defined a job flow to pick up a set of files in every 30 minutes on `ctm-demo-linux-02` and process them in batch mode, that is, by joining and sorting records and removing duplicates. The processed file will be filtered for three record types and get archived into a history file. At the same time, the processed file will also be duplicated into `ctm-demo-win-01` for filtering another three record types and archiving. The next set of source files will get picked up only if the current processing is finished and the 30 minutes interval is reached.

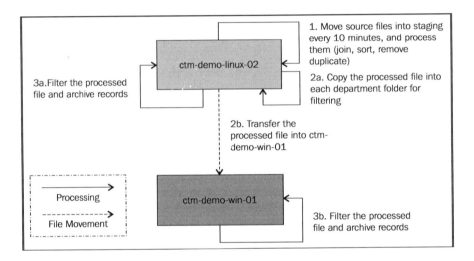

Now the requirement has changed a little bit. The application owner requires us to process the source files as they are produced rather than in batches every 30 minutes. That is, as soon as there's a set of source files generated (many files are contained in one set) the processing job flow will get triggered to process those files. The application owners will provide a flag file each time when a set of source files is created. The flag file is named with the source file's common prefix and set ID. For example:

- Flag file `SOURCE_CSV_01` indicates that a set of source files (set #01) with the prefix `SOURCE_CSV_` is generated successfully, including:
  - `SOURCE_CSV_01aa.csv`
  - `SOURCE_CSV_01ab.csv`
  - `SOURCE_CSV_01ac.csv`, and so on

- Flag file SOURCE _CSV_15 indicates that a set of source files (set #15) with the prefix SOURCE_CSV_ is generated successfully, including:
    - ◦ SOURCE_CSV_15aa.csv
    - ◦ SOURCE_CSV_15ab.csv
    - ◦ SOURCE_CSV_15ac.csv and so on

Additionally, the application owner believes that the current flat file archiving method (dumping into a history file) is not easy to maintain. They would like to have the records history (on the Windows machine only) to be archived into a database table.

By using the advanced Control-M features installed in the last chapter, we are not only able to fulfil these needs, but also making some enhancements to the file transfer of the processing. The new job flow will become:

- Replace the 30 minutes iteration (file pick up) with **event triggering,** that is, by using Control-M Filewatch facility to monitor the source file's creation. As soon as the flag file appears, Control-M Filewatch will trigger the rest of the job flow to process the corresponding set of source files.

- On ctm-demo-win-01, once the filtering jobs are finished, we will use Control-M for the Database to trigger a database query that loads the history file into an MS SQL database table.

- In addition, we are going to replace the script-based file transfer by CM for AFT job. Host ctm-demo-linux-01 that has the CM installed will be in charge off running the AFT job to transfer files from ctm-demo-linux-02 to ctm-demo-win-01.

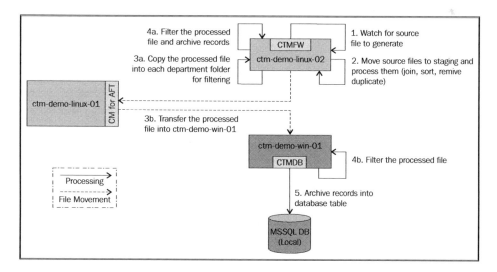

By making these modifications, the performance of the overall processing is improved because the next batch of processing can start as soon as the new files arrive instead of waiting for the next fixed-time cyclic iteration. Whereas with our original file processing job flow, in a worst case scenario, the previous processing may finish within five minutes and even new files arrive immediately. Moreover, our file processing job flow will not rerun to process the new files until 25 minutes pass (that is, 30 minutes from the job's previous start time). On the other hand, we can also get a processing delay if the new source files are generated after the job flow's next iteration start time (for example, job flow starts rerun at 2:30am, the source files are generated at 2:31am). In this case, the MOVE_SourceFiles job will have an empty run and the source files will only get processed 29 minutes later during the next rerun. This will not only cause a delay of the current batch, but also increase the amount of data to be processed by the next rerun if more source files are generated within the 29 minute waiting period.

From an administration point of view, we are not only meeting the application owner's new requirement, but we are also making the file processing job flow easier to maintain and more secure by replacing script-based file transfer with AFT.

Control-M filewatch

As the filewatch job is going to be added into the beginning of batch flow, let's first have a look at the Control-M Filewatch technology to figure out how we can define the job to meet this event-triggering requirement.

Technical background

Control-M Filewatch is a feature that comes with Control-M/Agent, which is able to detect a specific file's creation or deletion. It requires knowing the name and path of the file to be watched, followed by a set of watching rules. We can define the actions to be triggered in Control-M based on the outcome of the file detection, such as:

- For a specific file's **creation**, let filewatch detect such an event and trigger the corresponding job flow to process the file.

- Some applications may generate a temp file during processing and remove it after the processing is finished. Use filewatch to detect deletion of the file to initiate downflow jobs within the business process, as well as trigger notifications to users by e-mail or SMS.

- Filewatch can also detect when a file's size increment is stopped (that is, becomes static). This feature can be used to make sure the watched file is complete before Control-M continues on the next step. For example, when the target file is being transferred from a different machine or dumped from a database table, filewatch will make sure the down flow processing only starts when the file transfer or data dumping is complete.

Before we start to define the filewatch job, let's first look at the methods to invoke the technology and how to define filewatch rules.

Invoking methods

Control-M's Filewatch facility can be invoked as a utility or run constantly as a background service (Windows only).

When running Filewatch as a utility (command: **ctmfw**), we need to specify detection rules as arguments in the command line. We can also pre-store all rules in a configuration file and specify the file path as the only argument. When rules are directly defined as arguments, only a single file can be monitored during each execution. Whereas by using the configuration file, we can define multiple rules to let **ctmfw** monitor many files at once. We can trigger the utility from command line (both Unix/ Linux and Windows) or submit it as a Control-M job. The basic syntax for the utility is:

- When specifying rules as arguments: **ctmfw <file to be watched> {rules}**
- When a configuration file is used: **ctmfw –input <rule file>**

When running filewatch from Control-M, we can either run it as a command job or use the job type **FileWatch**. Control-M provides us with a dedicated job editing form for the job type **FileWatch**, which allows us to specify filewatch rules in a GUI interface.

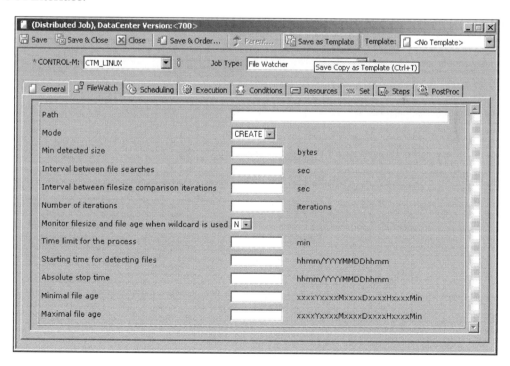

The **FileWatch** utility will exit if:

- All rules are met for the file that was being watched (return code: 0)

- Specified rules contain an error (return code: 1)

- At timeout, not all rules are met for the file that was being watched (return code: 7)

When we schedule the Filewatch utility as a Control-M job, we can set the job post-processing action(s) to be triggered for each return code. If the rule file is used, post-filewatch actions can be defined within the file.

When running Filewatch as a service on Windows machines, we need to start the Windows service called **Control-M/Agent FileWatcher** from **Computer Management | Services and Applications | Services**. We can also set it to automatic startup so that the service gets started each time the machine is rebooted.

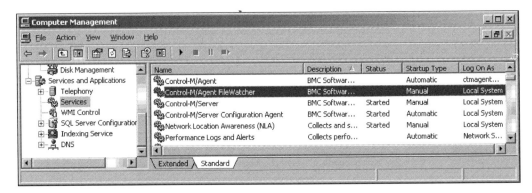

The Filewatch service, the watch rules are to be defined in a rule file – `<CTM/Agent home>\DATA\rull.dat`.

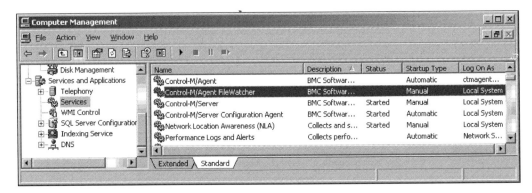

This rule file location is not hardcoded. filewatch service gets to know the location of it by reading its configuration file `CTM/Agent home>\DATA\ctmfw.cfg`, which also means we can make our own rule file and modify the default filename and path in `ctmfw.cfg`.

Filewatch rules

Control-M Filewatch at least needs to know the file to be watched and its full path (214 characters max). Other rules will follow their default value, unless we specify otherwise. Within the filename, we can use the wildcard ? to replace one character or * to replace many characters. For example, we have a file that is to be watched that has the following format: `prefix_no<sequence id>_<day of the week>.csv`

- Watch for file called `source_no1_friday.csv`:
    - `ctmfw /home/file_tran/source/source_no1_friday.csv`
- Watch for a similar file with any single digit sequence number:
    - `ctmfw /home/file_tran/source_no?_friday.csv`
- Watch for a similar file with any sequence number on any day of the week:
    - `ctmfw /home/file_tran/source_no?_*.csv`

Additional watch rules can get a little bit complicated, but at the same time, they provide the ability for filewatch to meet a wider range of file detection requirements. For watching individual files, these rules are:

- **Mode**: Tells filewatch either it needs to detect a file's creation (CREATE) or deletion (DELETE). Default: CREATE.
    - **CREATE**: If wildcard is used in the filename, filewatch will choose which file to watch based on the alphabetical order of the filenames (0-9 followed by a-z)
    - **DELETE**: If the file to be watched doesn't exist at the time filewatch is started, filewatch will first wait for the file's creation and then continue to watch for its deletion. If the wildcard is used in the filename, filewatch will exit only if all matching name files are deleted
- **Interval between file searches**: While filewatch is running, how often (in seconds) it should check for the file's creation or deletion. Default: 60.
- **Min detected size**: Filewatch will return successful only if the watched file's size is equal or larger than xB/K/M/G (B: Bytes, K: Kilobytes, M: Megabytes, G: Gigabytes). Default: 0 (will return successful as long as the file exists, regardless of its size).

- **Monitor file size and file age when wildcard is used**: When a wildcard is used, by default, filewatch will exit successfully as soon as the matching name file is created without checking the file size against the minimal detected size. By setting this parameter to **Y**, filewatch will monitor the detected file's size when a wildcard is used.

- **File size comparison (to detect if the file size stays static)**
  - ○ **Interval between file size comparison iterations**: After the file's creation is detected (and it is greater than or equal to the minimum detected size), this rule determines how often (in seconds) filewatch should check the file size to recognize it as unchanged. Default: 10
  - ○ **Number of iterations while the file size is static (for file size comparison)**: After the file's creation is detected and its size is determined to be greater than or equal to the minimum detected size, how many times filewatch should check the file size to recognize it as unchanged. The iteration counter gets reset if the file size changed between the checks. Default: 3

- **Filewatch's Start/Stop Time**
  - ○ **Time limit for the watching**: Time length (in minutes) for detecting the creation or deletion of the file. If the file did not get created or deleted upon timeout, filewatch will exit with return code 7. Default: 0 (no time limit)
  - ○ **Starting time for detecting files**: A set time (in YYYYMMDDHHMM or HHMM for current date) to tell filewatch when to actually start watching the file (that is, before the set time arrives, the filewatch process remains active, but doesn't actually do anything). Default: NOW
  - ○ **Absolute stop time**: A set time (in YYYYMMDDHHMM or HHMM for current date) to tell filewatch when to stop watching the file and exit. Upon timeout, filewatch will exit with return code 7. Default: +0000 (watch forever)

- **File Age**
  - ○ **Maximal age of file**: How old (?Y?M?D?H?Min) the file has to be at most, to become eligible for filewatch to watch it (according to the file's time stamp). Default: NO_MIN_AGE (no limit).
  - ○ **Minimal age of file**: How old (?Y?M?D?H?Min) the file has to be at least, to become eligible for filewatch to watch it (according to file's time stamp). Default: NO_MAX_AGE (no limit).

During filewatch utility's execution, it will resolve each parameter in the following order:

1. Mode
2. Min detected size
3. Interval between file searches
4. Interval between file size comparison iterations
5. Number of iterations while the file size is static
6. Time limit for the watching
7. Monitor file size and file age when wildcard is used
8. Starting time for detecting files
9. Absolute stop time
10. Maximal age of file
11. Minimal age of file

We specify each value of the parameter by directly entering its value without using a parameter flag. The filewatch utility will read the parameters according to the previously listed sequence. As such, we have to define the value of each parameter; even the default value is used. For example:

```
ctmfw /tmp/output*.txt CREATE 15B 5 10 3 0 Y S NOW +0000 1Y2M3D1H5Min
1H20Min
```

The preceding command line will be resolved into:

- File: `/top/output*.txt`
- Mode: CREATE
- Min detected size: 15 Bytes
- Interval between file searches: 5 sec
- Interval between file size comparison iterations: 10 sec (default)
- Number of iterations while the file size is static: 3 iterations (default)
- Time limit for the watching: 0 - no time limit (default)
- Monitor file size and file age when wildcard is used: Y
- Starting time for detecting files: NOW (default)
- Absolute stop time: +0000 - no stop time (default)
- Maximal age of file: 1Y2M3D1H5Min – no older than 1 year 2 month 3 day 2 hours and 5 minutes
- Minimal age of file: 1H20Min – created at least 1 hour and 20 minutes ago

As we mentioned earlier, we can let the filewatch utility detect multiple files creation or deletion when rule file is used. By using global rules, we save our time on repeatedly defining the same rule for individual watches within the same rule file. As these global rules are similar to their corresponding individual rules, we summarized them into a comparison table:

Global Rule	Corresponding Individual Rule	Comments
INTERVAL	"Interval between file searches" and "Interval between file size comparison iterations"	In seconds. Default: 10.
MIN_SIZE	"Min detected size"	In Bytes. Default: 0 (as long as the file is created, regardless of its size).
MON_SIZE_ WILDCARD	"Monitor file size and file age when wildcard is used"	Default: N.
Filewatch's Start/Stop Time		
WAIT_TIME	"Time limit for the watching"	In minutes. Default 0 (no time limit).
FROM_TIME	"Starting time for detecting files"	HHMM. Default: 0000 (Now).
STOP_TIME	"Absolute stop time"	YYYYMMDDHHMM or HHMM for current date. Default: 0 (no stop time).
File Age		
MAX_AGE	"Maximal age of file"	?y?d?h or ?H?Min. Default 0 (no limit).
MIN_AGE	"Minimal age of file"	?y?d?h or ?H?Min.
		Default 0 (no limit).

There is an additional global rule called **CYCLIC_INTERVAL**. It allows the filewatch utility or service to perform the same detection multiple times within one execution (that is, without restarting the filewatch process or service). This means that after the filewatch performs many iterations based on its **INTERVAL** and reaches the **WAIT_TIME**, instead of exiting, it will start over again to re-detect the file according to the same rules. **CYCLIC_INTERVAL** defines this interval (In minutes). Filewatch will continue to restart its detection upon the end of a cyclic interval indefinitely or when STOP_TIME is reached. The interval's value has to be larger than **WAIT _TIME**. Default 0 (will only attempt to detect the file once).

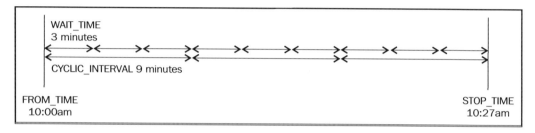

Following the global rules, we also need to specify individual rules for each file to be watched. The individual rule needs to include the file to be watched, its mode (that is, CREATE or DELETE), additional rules (optional), and post Filewatch actions (optional). The statements' syntax is:

```
ON_FILEWATCH <file to be watched> {rules}

THEN

<actions>

ELSE

<actions>

END_ON
```

Actions are required to be taken only once per line. If the `ON_FILEWATCH` statement completes successfully, filewatch will perform actions under the `THEN` statement, otherwise actions (if any) under `ELSE` will be performed. The action can be:

- Run a command: `DO_CMD <command>`
- Add or delete a condition: `DO_COND <condition name> <condition date> <+|->`

- Exit Filewatch: `DO_EXIT [exit code]`
- Terminate the "ON_FILEWATCH" statement with status NOTOK: `DO_NOTOK [exit code]`
- Terminate the ON_FILEWATCH statement with status OK: `DO_OK`

When a wildcard is used in the ON_FILEWATCH statement, filewatch will store the detected filename into a variable called `%FILENAME%`.

 When executing filewatch with rules specified directly on the command line or using the filewatch job editing form, we can still define the actions above, that is, define them as **On-do Statements** in the Control-M job's **Steps** tab.

Defining filewatch job

In our case, we will use filewatch to detect a 0 bytes flag file with the prefix "SOURCE_CSV_" and "remember" the full file name (prefix+set#). Then add an in-condition to trigger dependent jobs to process the corresponding set of source files (that is, with the same prefix+set#).

In order to achieve this, we need to:

- Define a Control-M job to trigger the Filewatch and add the job into the existing file processing job flow at the appropriate position.
- Use a wildcard in the filewatch to detect the flag file with any set#.
- Set an appropriate value for the Interval between file searches to ensure that the file will get picked up with minimal delay.
- Define `DO_CMD` to assign the detected flag file's filename (from `%FILENAME%`) into an Autoedit Variable for other jobs to access.
- Define `DO_COND` to trigger the down flow jobs.

Adding the job

Before we add a new job into the flow, let's make a copy of the original job table, that is, `FP-FixedTime` by renaming the SMART table name into `FP-EventDriven` and group name into ThirdDemo. After the jobs are loaded into a new Control-M Desktop workspace, we can perform modification through find and replace or simply edit the SMART table. By editing these key fields at the SMART table level, the change will be reflected to all jobs under it.

Because we need to get the filename from `%FILENAME%`, we will be defining the filewatch rules in a rule file and schedule the **ctmfw –input <rule file>** as a command job in Control-M. The command job is to be added in between `START_JOB` and `MOVE_SourceFiles`. This job will be a cyclic job with an interval of 0 minutes. It takes over all in-conditions from `MOVE_SourceFiles`, which means it will be triggered if `START_JOB` ended (first iteration) or `CLEAR_Staging` finished (previous cycle completed). For `MOVE_SourceFiles`, the only in-condition will be the completion of the filewatch job.

We also need to decide where we want to store the filewatch rule file. It really depends on the site's standards, as long as the ctmagent OS user account is able to access the location and has sufficient permissions to read the file. In our case, we define an `OURSTUFF` folder under Control-M/Agent's home directory and create a sub-directory `fw_cfg` under it to store the rule file. Our rule file will be called `DETECT_FlagFile-ThirdDemo.cfg` (<job name>-<group name>.cfg).

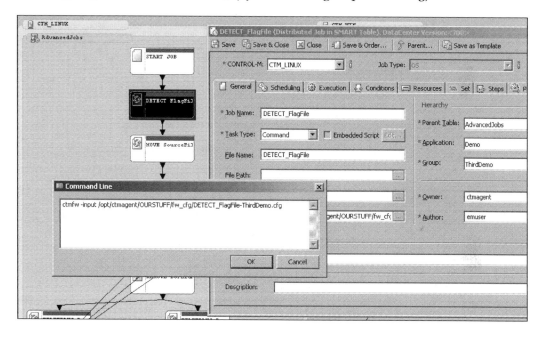

Defining filewatch rules

In our rule file, we defined the filewatch's detecting interval, file to be watched, watch mode, and DO_CMD actions. The values of these parameters are as follows:

- Global rule INTERVAL with value 3
- Filewatch will perform the scan every 3 seconds
- File to be watched: /home/file_tran/source/SOURCE_CSV_??
  - We use two ? single character wildcards to represent the set# (the last two characters of the filename is the set#). We cannot use the * wildcard here because that will allow filewatch to pick up normal source files such as SOURCE_CSV_01aa.csv.
- Mode: CREATE
  - We are watching the file's creation. If there are multiple flag files already existing at the time when filewatch was started, the file with the smallest set# will be picked up.
- DO_CMD ctmvar (...)
  - We need to run the ctmvar utility to assign the watched file's filename to a SMART table level Autoedit variable so the down flow jobs can access it
- DO_CMD rm %FILENAME%
  - We remove the watched file, so the next time the file watch will not pickup the same flag file again

We are not too worried about generating the out-condition for the down flow job here because the out-condition is generated by the Control-M job upon successful execution of the filewatch.

The rule file will look similar to the following screenshot:

```
root@ctm-demo-linux-02:~
#*****************************************************************************
# Global Parameters
INTERVAL 3

# ON_FILEWATCH statements
ON_FILEWATCH /home/file_tran/source/SOURCE_CSV_?? CREATE
THEN
DO_CMD ctmvar -ACTION SET -VAR "%%\AdvancedJobs\SOURCEFILE_PREFIX" -varexpr %FILENAME%
DO_CMD rm %FILENAME%
END_ON
#*****************************************************************************
```

SMART table level autoedit variable

Autoedit variables we used in *Chapter 4, Create and Manage Batch Flows with Control-M GUI* are the job level variables, that is, the variable is defined within the job and can only be accessed by that job. Control-M also offers Autoedit variables at the global (datacenter) level and SMART table level. With these variables, any job within the same scope (datacenter or SMART table) is able to reach the variable. When assigning variable values, `%%\<variable name>` indicates it is a global variable and `%%\<SMART table name>\<variable name>` indicates it is a SMART table variable.

In the current job flow, we need to let the down flow job be able to access the filename picked up by filewatch. As such, we need to use SMART table level variables so the value assigned by filewatch can be accessed by any jobs within the SMART table.

We use Control-M/Server Autoedit variable utility ctmvar to assign the variable value. The basic usage for ctmvar is:

```
ctmvar -ACTION < SET | DELETE | LIST >

[ -VAR "<Variable>" ]

[ -VAREXPR "<Variable Expression>" ]

OR:

ctmvar -ACTION LOAD -FILENAME <Filename Contains the list of
variables>

OR:

ctmvar -input_file <Filename contains parameters for the utility>
```

We are using the SET action here to assign the filename inside `%FILENAME%` (variable expression -VAREXPR) into the SMART table variable `%%\FP-EventDriven\SOURCEFILE_PREFIX` (variable name -VAR). With the SET action, it will create the variable if it doesn't exist or update the value if it does exist. With the -VAR parameter, we can specify all three types of variables – global, SMART table, or job. The syntax is:

- Global: `-var "%%\<variable name>"`
- SMART table: `-var "%%\<SMART table name>\<variable name>"`
- Job: `-var "%%\<SMART table name>\<job name>\<variable name>"`

Originally, we hardcoded the prefix of the source file (SOURCE_CSV_*.csv) into the job script of MOVE_SourceFiles for it to move the files from source into staging. Now we need to replace it by the dynamic prefix, which is to be fed by the filewatch. As we have got the prefix stored in the SMART table variable, it is just the matter of how to let MOVE_SourceFiles access it.

We will create a parameter variable in MOVE_SourceFiles (**PARM1**) and assign the value of SMART table variable with an ending string *.csv to it. In this case, **PARM1** will be resolved to:

- When the flag file is SOURCE_CSV_01, **PARM1** value is SOURCE_CSV_01*.csv

- When the flag file is SOURCE_CSV_15, **PARM1** value is SOURCE_CSV_15*.csv

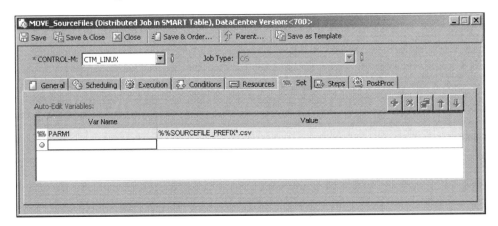

Thus during runtime, the mv $1 /home/file_tran/staging command line will be resolved into (for the examples above):

- move SOURCE_CSV_01*.csv /home/file_tran/staging

- move SOURCE_CSV_15*.csv /home/file_tran/staging

 In case there's a same name variable at the lower-level scope, Control-M will determine which variable to use in the following order: Local Job, SMART table, Datacenter. In other words, if there's a variable name defined in both job level and SMART table level with different value, while the job is running Control-M will access the job level variable value. If a job tries to use a variable that does not exist at the job or SMART table level, Control-M will check at the global level. However, if there's no such variable defined even at the global level, Control-M will assign the reserved word **CTMERR** to the variable.

There is a lot more to the topic of Autoedit variable. We will discuss them in the later examples as we use them.

Advanced file transfer

The next job we need to define is the AFT job to replace the script-based file transfer from `ctm-demo-linux-02` to `ctm-demo-win-01`. We have already discussed the benefits of using AFT verses transfer scripts in *Chapter 2, Exploring Control-M*. In this section, we will be looking at the technical aspect of AFT and defining AFT jobs.

Technical background

Control Module for AFT allows us to perform file transfer between hosts by using the standard FTP/SFTP protocols. It is in fact an FTP/SFTP client. It relies on FTP/SFTP services running on the source and destination machine to perform the transfer. Transfer can happen between different types of operating systems, such as from Linux to Windows or from Windows to Unix. The module itself isn't required to be installed on all hosts (source and destination) for the transfer. Possible transfer scenarios are:

- **Host 1** (with AFT installed) transfer to **Host 2** (without AFT installed)
- **Host 2** (without AFT installed) transfer to **Host 1** (with AFT installed)
- **Host 3** (without AFT installed) transfer to/from **Host 2** (with AFT installed) via **Host 1** (with AFT installed)

FTP/SFTP service is not required for the machine with AFT installed (also known as Local CM). For other hosts, either a source or destination FTP/SFTP service has to be up and running to accept file transfer requests.

AFT needs to have user accounts on both source and destination hosts to perform the transfer. For FTP transfers, we need to specify the port number (TCP port# 21, by default), as well as the source and destination username/password in each transfer account. For SFTP transfers (TCP port # 22 by default), we have the option to select between password authentication and key authentication.

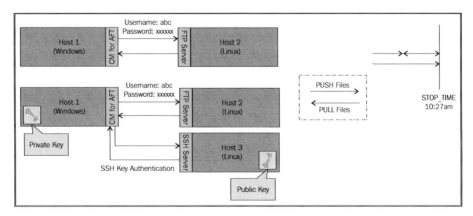

Each AFT account can be used by many AFT jobs for different transfers. On the other hand, each AFT job can only be associated to one AFT account, and it is able to handle a maximum of five transfers at the same time between the two hosts defined in the account. Within each AFT job, the file movement direction of individual transfers are up to us; that's why we did not require to specify a source and destination in the account definition. During runtime, progress and statistics of the transfers are visually presented in the active job instance.

Besides normal file transfer, CM for AFT also provides some additional features, including:

- Verify destination file size after transfer
- Verify checksum
- Restart from the point of failure
- Encryption and compression
- Pre and post commands
- Filewatch

Verifying destination file size after transfer

Verify destination file size is to be set at the account level. With this option turned on, AFT will compare the destination file size to the source file after each transfer. The transfer will be marked as failed if the file sizes are different.

This feature is set to **on** by default for each account definition.

Verifying checksum

Verify checksum takes the destination file integrity check to the next level. It relies on the FTP Server to execute checksum commands (XMD5 or SITE CHECKSUM) to perform verification of the file at the end of each transfer.

This feature is also to be set at the account level and it is set to **off** by default. It is normally used by organizations having regulations that require file integrity check.

Restarting from the point of failure

In case failure occurs during the transfer, AFT has the option to allow transfers to be restarted from the failure point, rather than started from scratch. It is in fact using the REST FTP command on the FTP server to archive the feature.

This is an account level setting, and it is set to **off** by default. **Restart from point of failure** is useful when the files to be transferred are large and have to be completed within a timeframe. It can save a lot of time, especially when the failure happens towards the end of the transfer.

Encryption and compression

When an SFTP method is used for the transfer, encryption is also used for the transfer, and we also have the option to enable compression. The available encryption options are: Blowfish (default), AES, ARCFOUR, DES, and 3DES.

We can override the account level setting for each transfer at the job level.

Pre and post (transfer) actions

At the job level, we are allowed to set pre and post (transfer) actions for each transfer. These actions are:

- General post action
    - After the completion of a successful transfer, keep (default), delete, rename, or move the source file
    - If a file with the same name exists on the destination location, the file transfer will overwrite (default), append, abort, or skip the file
    - After the completion of a successful transfer, the destination file will be left as it is (default), renamed, or moved
    - After the completion of a successful transfer, create an empty file
- Pre and post FTP commands
    - Change file permission (chmod)
    - Create a directory (mkdir)
    - Rename a file (rename)
    - Remove a file (rm)
    - Remove a directory (rmdir)

Filewatcher

AFT also has some basic filewatch abilities. The term basic is in comparison to the Control-M Filewatch utility. In a file transfer scenario rather than try to time when the file will become available to decide when the AFT should start, we can define filewatch rules so the AFT job can start regardless of whether the file is available or not and let the transfer begin only when the desired file becomes available.

For each transfer, we can set the following filewatch rules (for file creation only):

- Minimum file size (in Bytes): The filewatch will complete successfully only if the minimum file size is met.

- Time limit:
  - ○ Maximum time to wait (in minutes): Time length (in minutes) for detecting the creation of the file. If the file did not get created or deleted upon timeout, filewatch will exit with return code 7.
  - ○ Wait until (HHMM): A set time to tell filewatch when to stop watching the file and exit. Upon timeout, filewatch will exit with return code 7.

We can use a wildcard with the filename to be watched. For the detected file, we can assign the filename to an Autoedit variable. We also have the option to let AFT transfer all files that match the wildcard.

AFT's filewatch feature can be useful when we want to watch for a file creation on a remote machine that does not have Control-M/Agent installed (as long as that server has FTP/SFTP services). With the ctmfw utility, we must have a Control-M/Agent installed on the host where the files are to be watched.

Implementing AFT jobs

There are three steps for us to replace the file transfer script with an AFT job. Firstly we need to analyze the requirement or the existing file transfer script to identify the source and destination host. If there's no Control-M/Agent on either host, we need to have a third party machine that has AFT installed to perform the transfer. Secondly, we need to decide what type of transfer protocol will be used for the transfer. Based on this, we can go ahead and define the accounts in AFT and make sure the FTP/SFTP ports between the source and the AFT host and AFT and the destination host are open on the firewall. The last thing to do is to define the AFT job and specify the file, destination file path, and transfer requirements (for example, binary/ASCII transfer, restart from point of failure, pre/post commands, and so on).

Creating an AFT account

Control-M offers both a GUI and command-line menu interface for us to define AFT accounts. If we have the CCM add-on that came with the CM package installed, we are able to directly define the account for any AFT installation through CCM. Alternatively, for CM for AFT installed on Unix/Linux machines, we can access the command-line account configuration menu by running the ctmaftacc utility as the Control-M/Agent user account on the individual Agent machine. If we have the DISPLAY environment defined, the utility will bring us a GUI window on the x-window terminal session. For CM for AFT installed on Windows machines, we can access the same GUI-based account configuration tool by going to **Start | All Programs | BMC Control-M | Control-M/Agent 7.0.00 (Default) | Configure Application | File Transfer CM tab**.

For our job flow, we will define one account through CCM and the another one by using the command-line menu on ctm-demo-linux-01.

First we will define the transfer account between ctm-demo-linux-02 and ctm-demo-win-01. For this transfer, we will be using key authentication between ctm-demo-linux-02 and ctm-demo-linux-01 and use password authentication between ctm-demo-linux-01 and ctm-demo-win-01.

By *right-clicking* on the file transfer module (CM FILE_TRANS) of ctm-demo-linux-01 listed in CCM, we will see a drop-down menu appear with account management-related options.

Setting up key authentication for AFT is similar to what we have done with setting up Agentless accounts with SSH. We need to generate a SSH key pair first and distribute the public key to ctm-demo-linux-02. In the drop-down menu's **Generate SSH key** option, we need to specify the **Key Name**, **Key Passphrase**, and select key generation parameters. Once it is saved, we will be told that the key has been created successfully and will be asked if we want to save the public key onto our workstation. In case we don't want to save the public key, it can still be retrieved at <Agent home directory>/ctm/cm/AFT/data/Keys. Now we need to distribute the key to the account that AFT needs to connect with on host ctm-demo-linux-02. Same as what we did for Agentless, the key needs to be saved under ~/.ssh/authorized_keys* and make sure that the file's permission is set to owner read and write only (chomd 600).

Coming back to CCM, now we need to create the actual account in **Account Management** in the drop-down menu. After clicking on the + sign (add new account), we will be asked to enter:

1. **Account Name** and (authorized) **Control-M/EM Users** are asked in step 1. The EM user we specify here will have the rights to select the account when creating jobs. In our case, we will name the account **ProcessedFile_LIN02toWIN01** and select **emuser** as the only authorized user.

2. In these two panels, we will be asked to define account details for **Host 1** and **Host 2**. It doesn't really matter which host goes first, because in an AFT job definition, we can define a transfer to go either way (that is, both can be the source or destination). In our case, we put down ctm-demo-linuix-02 as **Host 1** and ctm-demo-win-01 as **Host 2**. For **Host 1**, we first need to enter the hostname and un-tick the **Local CM** option, enter the username (leave the password blank) and select the communication protocol as **SFTP(SSH)**. In the **Private Key Name** drop-down list, we will see the key that was just defined. We need to choose this key and enter the **Key Passphrase** (if one was previously defined during key generation). For **Host 2**, we just need to enter the hostname, username, and password for the FTP connection.

3. We will keep the default option, **Verify destination file size**, ticked and continue to the final step.

4. In this panel, we can run an account validation and click the **Finish** button to save the account definition.

 We have to have an FTP server configured and running on `ctm-demo-win-01`.

Now we should see a new entry appear in the account management window, and if we click on it, we will see something similar to the following screenshot:

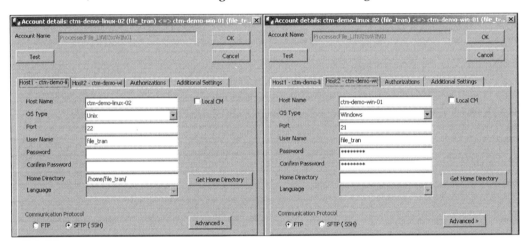

To standardize file transfer across the board and make the transfer progress become visualized, we decide to use AFT to replace the local file copy jobs `COPY_ ProcessedFile_department-xx` that are running on `ctm-demo-linux-02`. By doing so, we also reduce 3 jobs down to 1, that is, performing all three file copy actions within the same AFT job.

We will be defining this job using the `ctmaftacc` command-line menu. Because AFT is installed on `ctm-demo-linux-01`, we need to log on the machine and switch to the Control-M/Agent user to run the utility. The utility can be executed from any directory as long as we log on as the Control-M/Agent user (has been set to PATH by default during installation), otherwise we can find it under the `<Control-M/ Agent home>/ctm/cm/AFT/exe/` directory.

Once we get into the utility, we can press the **a** option to add a new account. The required parameters are the same as what needed to define in CCM. If we do an **e** edit account, we will see that the account we defined earlier is on the list. For this transfer, we will have both **Host1** and **Host2** defined as `ctm-demo-linux-02` and using SFTP key authentication.

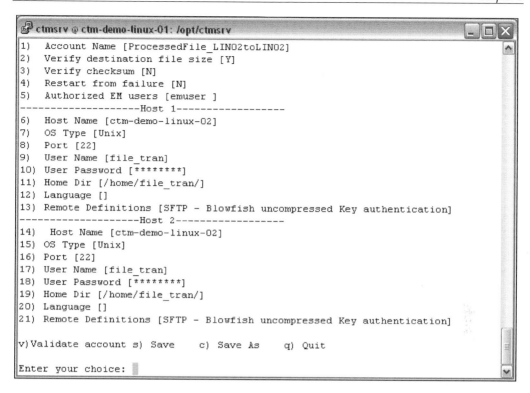

```
ctmsrv @ ctm-demo-linux-01: /opt/ctmsrv

1)   Account Name [ProcessedFile_LIN02toLIN02]
2)   Verify destination file size [Y]
3)   Verify checksum [N]
4)   Restart from failure [N]
5)   Authorized EM users [emuser ]
-------------------Host 1-------------------
6)   Host Name [ctm-demo-linux-02]
7)   OS Type [Unix]
8)   Port [22]
9)   User Name [file_tran]
10)  User Password [********]
11)  Home Dir [/home/file_tran/]
12)  Language []
13)  Remote Definitions [SFTP - Blowfish uncompressed Key authentication]
-------------------Host 2-------------------
14)   Host Name [ctm-demo-linux-02]
15)  OS Type [Unix]
16)  Port [22]
17)  User Name [file_tran]
18)  User Password [********]
19)  Home Dir [/home/file_tran/]
20)  Language []
21)  Remote Definitions [SFTP - Blowfish uncompressed Key authentication]

v)Validate account s) Save    c) Save As    q) Quit

Enter your choice:
```

We can press **v** to validate the account and make sure to save it before quitting the utility.

Defining the AFT job

Back in Control-M Desktop, we will be making the following changes to the job flow:

- Replace COPY_ProcessedFile_department-04/5/6 in CTM_WIN with the AFT job FILETRANS_ProcessedFile_LIN02toWIN01 in CTM_LINUX.

- Replace COPY_ProcessedFile_department-01/2/3 in CTM_LINUX with the AFT job FILETRANS_ProcessedFile_LIN02toLIN02 in CTM_LINUX.

We have to run the FILETRANS_ProcessedFile_LIN02toWIN01 job in datacenter CTM_LINUX because the Control-M/Agent for executing the job is defined under CTM_LINUX, but it really make no difference to the file transfer.

When creating the job, we have to select the job type **AFT** and make sure the correct **Node ID/Group** is selected to allow the AFT account to be loaded from the Agent machine. In the **AFT** tab, we can choose to load or enter the account name, as well as select or enter the path for each transfer. In the transfer definitions, the yellow arrow indicates the direction of the transfer. If we click on it, we can change the direction or select the **watch and transfer** option (can also happen for both directions). As we know, the files are already there by the time the transfer takes place, and we don't need to use the watch option. For a source file, we need to enter the full path and filename. For a destination file, we only need to enter the directory so that the filename will remain. We will keep the **Binary** transfer mode without worrying about any advanced features.

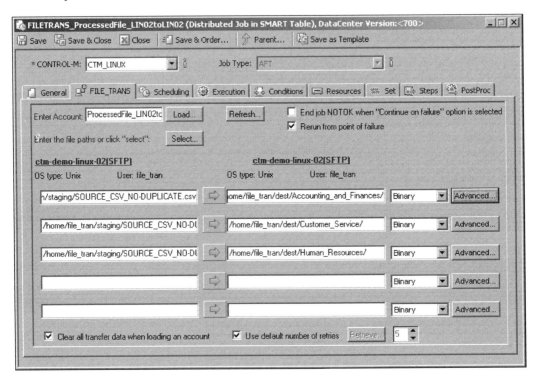

On the condition side, instead of having each individual `COPY_ProcessedFile_`
`department-xx` job post a condition to its own down flow `JOIN_Records_`
`department-xx` job, we let the AFT job post all three conditions to each job.

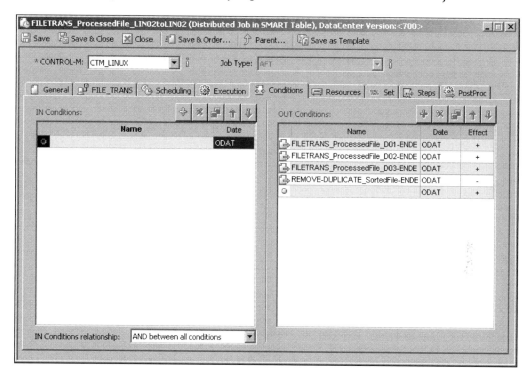

Same thing goes for `FILETRANS_ProcessedFile_LIN02toWIN01`; the only difference
is the out conditions is required to have a `LINUX_` `global` prefix.

In normal situations, we don't need to define individual conditions for each down
flow job. We need it in our job flow because all jobs are cyclic with interval 0
minutes. Therefore, each job needs to delete its in-condition right after execution to
prevent immediate rerun; that is, they are only eligible for rerun at the next iteration
of the whole job flow. If all three down flow jobs are sharing the same in-condition,
there is a chance the condition will get deleted by the job that ran and finished first,
even before others started.

The last thing that needs to be done is to link the two AFT jobs with their predecessor job REMOVE-DUPLICATE_SortedFile. Again, REMOVE-DUPLICATE_SortedFile should post a dedicated in-condition for each AFT job.

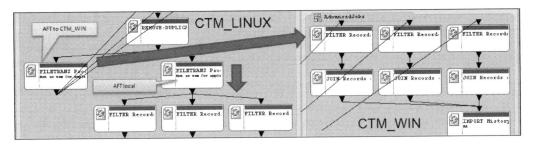

Control-M for database

The last job to be added into the flow is the database job to load the history file into a database table. We already have a database table called HISTORY_WIN defined in the database demo on the MS SQL server running on ctm-demo-win-01. The database table has the following columns:

Column Name	Data Type	Allow Nulls
staff_name	varchar(30)	N
title	varchar(5)	Y
department	varchar(30)	N
location	varchar(30)	N
employeeid*	varchar(10)	N
password	varchar(15)	N

*Primary Key

In this section, we will define a Control-M Database job on ctm-demo-win-01 to perform this task.

Technical background

Control-M for database is one of the newer released Control Modules that allows us to define and schedule database jobs directly from Control-M. It saves us the effort of writing and maintaining database scripts, at the same time, centralizing the database account management (through CCM).

Currently, Control-M for database supports Oracle (9i, 10/11g), MS SQL (2000/5/8), and DB2 9 databases, with the ability to trigger SQL queries, SQL scripts, store procedures, and SSIS (SQL Server Integration Services) packages. The database server doesn't have to be running on the same machine as where the Control-M database is running for jobs to be triggered, in other words, as long as the database servers are reachable on the network, the Control-M database is able to submit jobs to them.

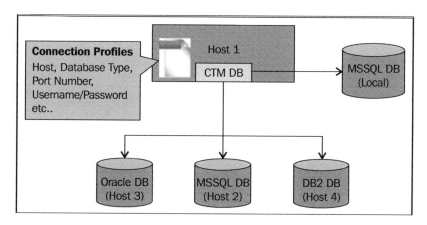

Similar to the AFT jobs, we need to create an account in Control-M for each database connection profile. Control-M for database operates on its own built-in database connection facility. Therefore, database clients are not required. The only prerequisite for scheduling a database job is to have the appropriate firewall ports open between the Control-M database machine and the database machines.

Implementing Database CM jobs

Creating Database CM jobs is much simpler than our previous experience with the AFT job. As long as we know the type of database, machine name, connection port number, account, what to execute, and when to schedule it, we can go ahead with defining the job.

Creating a database connection account

Database connection profiles are to be defined from CCM. In CCM, we right-click on the Database module (CM DATABAE) of `ctm-demo-win-01` and select **Account Management** and press the **+** sign in the pop-up window to define a new account.

In the **Add Account** window, we are required to define:

- **General**
    - ○ **Account Name**
    - ○ **Database Type and Database Version: We can select them from the available database types and versions. The choice we made here will affect the rest of the definition items in the coming panels. In our case, we will select MS SQL and version 2008.**

- **Database Type Specific (Based on MS SQL database)**
    - ○ **Host Name and Port Number: The host that the database is running and the port it is listening. In our case, the MS SQL database server is installed on the local machine. Therefore, we can enter localhost.**
    - ○ **Database Name: Name of the database. In our case, it is called demo.**
    - ○ **Authentication: Depends on the setting on the database server. We are using SQL Server Authentication.**
    - ○ **User Name and Password: The user who has the rights to perform the task.**
    - ○ **Advanced Connection Configuration: Includes the setting for Maximum concurrent connections, Number of connection retries, Connection retry timeout, and Connection idle time. It is suggested to seek recommendation from a DBA.**
    - ○ **SSIS Package Passwords: Only required if we are going to schedule SSIS packages.**

We can test the account in the last panel of the account definition window, before testing the connection we need to make sure the database is running and the port has been opened on the firewall (if any). Once we save the connection profile, we should see a new entry appeared in the account management window. We can double click on it to view and modify the account.

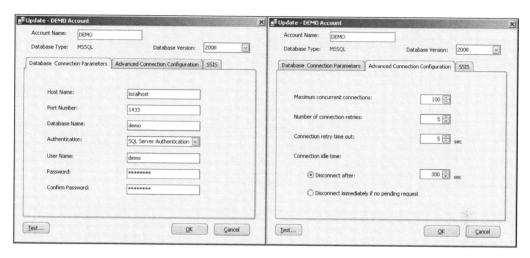

Defining Database CM Job

Again, back into our job flow in Control-M Desktop, we will be replacing `JOIN_ Records_department-04/5/6` jobs with `IMPORT_Records_department-04/5/6` database CM jobs right after each of the three "`JOIN_Records_department-xx`" jobs accordingly in `CTM_WIN`.

Control-M for Database also has its own job type, that is, **Database**. Just like AFT jobs, when creating the job, we need to make sure the correct **Node ID/Group** is selected so we are able to load the account that we defined earlier. Once the account is selected in the **DATABASE** tab, the **Database Type** will be populated automatically and the options in **Execution Type** will be changed accordingly.

For our job, we will select **Execution Type** as **Open Query** and type the query into the **Query Text** field. Our query will perform a bulk load to import the data from each department's filtered csv file into the database. We also let the job append log and query output to job SYSOUT as text by selecting the options in **Sysout Handling**.

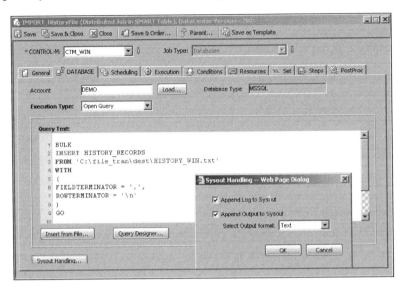

As we saw, the query is loading input data from an Autoedit variable %%**IMPORT_ FILE**. In this case, all three Database CM jobs will have the same query text. The import file name is constructed in the job's **Set** tab – `C:\file_tran\ dest\%%DIRNAME.\%%FILENAME`

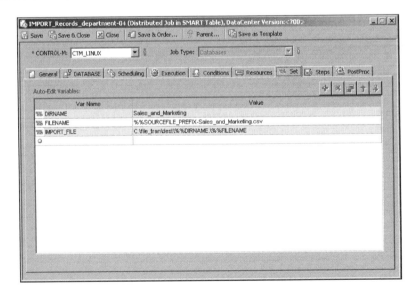

In terms of conditions, each of these three jobs will have an In-condition coming from the corresponding **FILTER_Record_department-04/5/6** job and post out Out-condition with the WIN_ global condition prefix to the CLEAR_Staging job on the CTM_LINUX side.

Once we have all jobs and conditions defined, we need to remove the User Daily SYSTEM from the table definitions of FP-FixedTime SMART tables and put them into the two newly created FP-EventDriven tables. By doing this, the FP-FixedTime group will no longer be ordered during NDP and FP-EventDriven will be ordered instead. One last thing we have to do is to perform write and upload for all four tables so the changes will be saved into Control-M/EM and Control-M/Server database.

The completed job flow will be look as shown in the following screenshot:

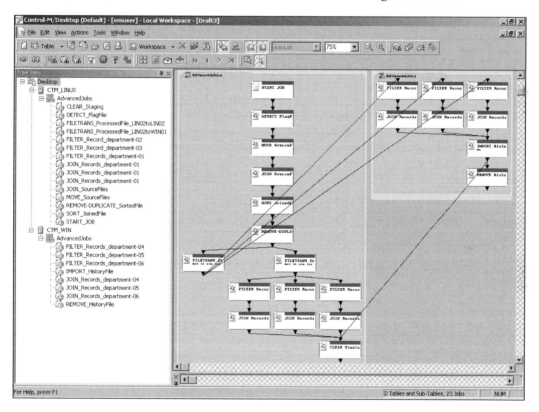

Advanced batch management

So far we have been defining all kinds of jobs, but haven't really had a closer look at how to manage these jobs running in Control-M/EM. We know some of the basics from working on the Hello World jobs, but those were not enough to manage complex batch flows in a larger scale environment.

Over the years, Control-M has made significant improvements in the area of batch management. Features offered in Control-M version 7 have overtaken the standard definition of cross-platform batch monitoring. By mastering the advanced batch management features of Control-M/EM, we will be able to manage jobs in real environments efficiently and effectively.

ViewPoints

ViewPoint is the centre of the universe for viewing and managing jobs across the entire environment. Essentially it is a collection of jobs filtered by a certain criteria and displayed in a certain hierarchy. The Collection, the Filter, and the Hierarchy can be configured by the Control-M administrator. Multiple ViewPoints can be defined and multiple ViewPoints can be opened within one GUI Client at any given time. But the purpose of a ViewPoint is far more than just providing us with a real-time graphical representation of what jobs are doing on each of the job execution machines. It gives us basic control over them. As the number of jobs keeps growing in Control-M and the job flows become more complicated, it is necessary for us to discover and fully utilize the features provided by ViewPoint.

Viewing jobs in Active ViewPoint

Active ViewPoint shows job instances that are currently in AJF with different colors to reflect their status. With the right privileges, GUI users are allowed to interact with these jobs, as in, they can view job details and perform actions on them. In active ViewPoint, status change of any active job always gets updated in real time, and actions performed on a job also gets processed imminently.

If we log on to our Control-M/EM GUI client and open an active ViewPoint, we would see the FP-EventDriven job flow we defined earlier and the maintenance job we imported earlier in this chapter are currently showing. This is because they get ordered daily through the user daily SYSTEM.

Comparing the current job flows with the display of the Hello World! job instance in *Chapter 4*, the main differences are listed as follows:

- These jobs are linked together by job conditions.
- Connected jobs do not necessarily belong to the same machine.

With the conditions going everywhere on the screen, we can easily see that the jobs are becoming more complicated. Just imagine more than 25,000 jobs displayed in the same window in front of us; how can we manage them?

Fortunately, the potential sizing-related difficulties GUI users will be facing have been taken into consideration, simply because Control-M is positioned as an enterprise-level batch scheduling platform. Control-M offers different ways for us to quickly locate one or many desired jobs.

Find feature

It is easy to get around in the Control-M/EM GUI client while the total number of jobs is small. However, as the Control-M environment starts to grow, it can be a little bit challenging sometimes for us to locate a particular job. Control-M offers the Find feature for us to instantly locate jobs based on search criteria. It is available in both ViewPoint and Control-M Desktop Workspace through **Edit | Find Jobs** (*Ctrl+F*) or the **Find jobs** shortcut icon.

The Find criteria is not the same for the EM GUI client and Control-M Desktop, but the idea is similar. Most of the fields allow us to use a wildcard, such as Control-M, table, job name, and so on. Control-M will highlight jobs that are meeting the search criteria in the current ViewPoint or Workspace. Entered search criteria can be saved as Presets for frequent use. In ViewPoint, we also have the option to use **View | View Selection** to open those highlighted jobs in a **Selection View**.

Dynamic filter

Active job instances' status can change at any time. We can use the Find feature to locate all current executing jobs, but the selected job may not still be executing in the next minute or second. Sometimes if we need to meet monitoring criteria which are not offered by any available ViewPoints, we can define these filter rules in a Dynamic Filter.

Dynamic Filter rules can be defined through **View | Dynamic Filter** or the shortcut at the top of the ViewPoint. Once we apply a Dynamic Filter, jobs meeting the filter rules will appear in the ViewPoint, and jobs showing ViewPoint that no longer meet the rules will imminently disappear. Again, we can define frequently used filter rules in Presets. For example, if we want to monitor all the currently executing jobs in the CTM_LINUX datacenter, we would define a dynamic filter with the Control-M name CTM_LINUX and select **Executing** in **Status**. By doing so, jobs that are in executing status will be displayed and disappear once they are completed.

In a real world environment, ViewPoints are normally defined by Control-M administrators and can be used by all users, whereas Dynamic Filters are defined by a user and only affect that user's view.

Print

The print feature allows us to print the currently opened ViewPoint. Users normally install a virtual PDF printer so that they can export the job diagram to a PDF file. Commonly used virtual PDF programs are CutePDF and BullZip.

Performing job actions in Active ViewPoint

One of the major benefits of using an enterprise-wide cross-platform batch scheduling tool is that we can perform actions on different jobs with the same approach without specific knowledge of the system or application, that is, whether it is a Windows, Unix, PeopleSoft, SAP or ETL job.

We have already used some of the job-related actions in *Chapter 4, Create and Manage Batch Flows with Control-M GUI* on the Hello World! active job instances, such as hold/free job, rerun, confirm, view sysout/log, view statistics, view/edit JCL. In this section, we will look at the other available actions that we haven't came across.

Delete/Undelete

The delete action is to be performed on jobs that are being held and not in executing state. Deleting a job does not really remove the job from AJF on the spot. Instead, Control-M puts a deleted mark on the job to indicate the job is no longer active. From the user side, if the **All Jobs** ViewPoint is selected, the deleted jobs will be displayed with a red cross symbol on it; if **All Active Jobs** ViewPoint are selected, a job will disappear as soon as the deleting action is performed. The job will only get physically deleted from AJF in the next NDP.

Control-M allows us to undo a job's deletion as long as the job hasn't been removed from AJF. In order to do so, we have to open the **All Jobs** viewpoint and select **Undelete** on the desired job. Once the job is undeleted, it will be back to a normal active job and treated by NDP as all other normal jobs, that is, NDP removes the job according to the value of its maxwait parameter.

Deleting job is useful when we need to order a new instance of a job flow to replace the existing instance in AJF. For example, when re-ordering our file processing job flows, we will see the new jobs are linked together with existing jobs because their in/out condition names are matching. It can be very confusing and easy to cause human mistakes (for example, free/confirmed the wrong job for execution). By deleting the old instance and viewing jobs from an **All Active Jobs** viewpoint, the old instance job flow will be filtered out.

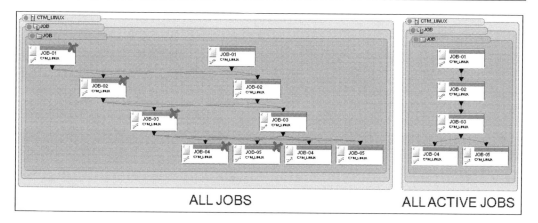

ALL JOBS | ALL ACTIVE JOBS

Kill

The kill action can be applied to any executing jobs. It is equivalent to terminating a process on the operating system, such as running a `kill -9 <process id>` command on Unix/Linux machines. Once a job is killed, it will go into the **Ended NOTOK** state in Control-M.

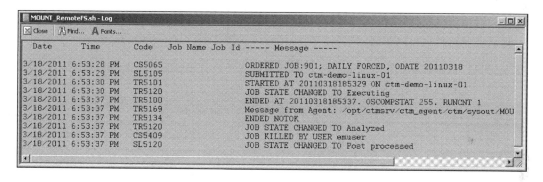

The kill action is normally used when we know a job is not doing what we expect it to do. We terminate the job instantly instead of waiting for it to complete. For example, our file watch job is in the running status to detect incoming files, but we know for a fact that no more files will be coming, so we kill the job so that it can be removed in the next NDP.

Force OK/Force OK with no post processing

Force OK action is to be applied to end **NOTOK** jobs. Once **Force OK** is performed, Control-M will treat the job as if it was completed OK. Therefore, continue to run all post processing actions (for example, post out-conditions, perform when – OK shouts). Since Control-M version 7, we have been allowed to perform **Force OK** without letting the job run post processing – **Force OK** with no post processing.

Force OK is useful in situations where the failed job has been manually rerun successfully in the backend (that is, form command line). Therefore, we can continue with the rest of the batch flow. For example, our COPY_ProcessedFile_ department-01 job failed because someone changed the permission of the destination directory. After we log on to the machine and reset the permission, we can either come back to Control-M to rerun the job or manually transfer the file, and then force the **job OK** in Control-M.

Why/Enhanced Why

For jobs that are in the waiting for schedule state, we can perform why on the job to find out why the job is waiting and not running (for example, missing in-conditions, resources, or requires manual confirmation). For jobs located in traditional tables, why will be performed at the job level only. If the job is located in a SMART table or a sub-table, the checking will be performed on the SMART table, sub-table, and the job itself.

If the job cannot be submitted due to missing in-conditions, why will provide a list of the missing conditions (condition name and date). We have the option to manually add the conditions in the Why window to trigger the job. By doing so, the condition with the specified date will get generated in Control-M/Server, which means any other jobs requiring the same in-condition will also get triggered.

Sometimes, we cannot just force the missing in-condition to trigger a job, regardless of what is happening with the indirectly-related jobs above. With the Enhanced Why feature, we are able to find all predecessor jobs of the selected job that haven't ended (or ended as not ok). We can let the Enhanced Why feature find jobs **With path** or **Without path**.

- **With path**: All unfinished (or not finished successfully) predecessor jobs will be highlighted.

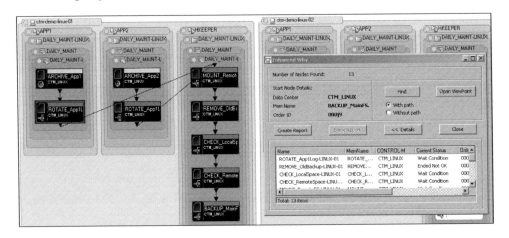

- **Without path**: The top-most unfinished (or not finished successfully) predecessor job will be highlighted.

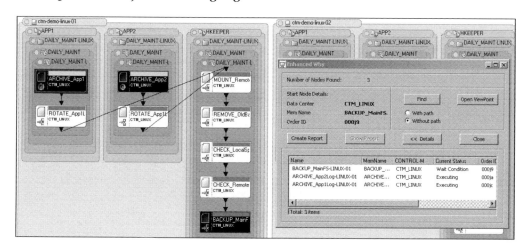

We are able to view the highlighted jobs in a new ViewPoint by clicking on the **Open ViewPoint** button.

Bypass

Bypass is a new feature introduced in Control-M version 7. It allows the user to select which pre-requisites or post-processing steps of the job can be skipped, or even choose to skip the entire execution of the job. Most of the options are relevant to jobs that are in waiting for the execution state. Bypassing post-processing also applies to jobs that are in the execution state. The options are:

- **Pre-Submission (Run Now)**: Ignore any pre-requisites so that the job can start imminently

- **Skip Job**: Submit the job to run as a dummy job as soon as its in-conditions are arrived, ignore other pre-requisites, including Time Limits, Quantitative Resources, Control Resources, and so on.

- **Individual By-pass Options**
    - ° **Pre-submission**: Ignore individual job submission pre-requisites, including "Time Limits", "Quantitative Resources", "Control Resources", and so on
    - ° **Run as Dummy Job**: Execute the job as a dummy job, and use in conjunction with "pre-submission" options
    - ° **Post Processing**: Let the job skip post processing upon completion (for example, On-Do statements, Shouts). This option can be assigned to jobs in the "waiting for submission" or "executing" states.

Bypass gives us a lot more flexibility to control the execution of job flows. Before this feature was introduced, each time the user would have to hold the job and open the job definition window to manually remove the pre-requisites or post-processing steps that were to be skipped. For cyclic jobs (for example, our file processing job flow), in order to allow the job to rerun as per normal, all removed items have to be re-added before the job's next execution. With the bypass option, we can achieve what we wanted without modifying the job definition.

Branch Menus and Neighborhood

The Branch Menus feature allows us to navigate to the selected job's predecessor or successor. If there is more than one predecessor or successor, we have the option to select which job we would like to navigate to. The selected predecessors or successors will be the only highlighted job in ViewPoint.

The Neighborhood feature is similar to Branch Menus, but with more advanced functionalities. There are four direction options available:

- **Predecessor**: Jobs in the same flow that are above the selected job and require to be completed before the current job can start.
- **Dependent**: Jobs in the same flow that are below the selected job and require the selected job to be completed before they can start.
- **Direct Relationship**: A combination of predecessor and dependent.
- **Radial**: Jobs in the same job flow that are located in all directions of the selected job.

For each direction option we selected, we are also able to specify Radius. It allows us to select the level of dependencies (range: 1-99999) that should be highlighted in the ViewPoint. After clicking on the **Find** button, the related jobs will be displayed in the **Network Neighborhood** window and we can click on the **open ViewPoint** button to display the highlighted jobs in a new ViewPoint.

The Neighborhood feature enables us to quickly identify related jobs in a complex job flow. For example, if a job fails or is running longer than normal, we can use the Neighborhood to look up the job's dependent to figure out what other jobs will be consequently delayed. On the other hand, if an important job is to be started at around 2pm but hasn't started at 3pm, we can check its neighborhood-predecessor to find out if any job above it has failed or has been running too long.

Critical Path

Critical Path is a must-have feature in batch scheduling tools. It allows us to find the shortest execution path between two indirectly dependent jobs.

In Control-M, the **Critical Path** feature will highlight jobs belong to the critical path between the two selected jobs and also can calculate the total runtime for the path based on each job's average runtime or last runtime. The two selected jobs must be indirectly connected.

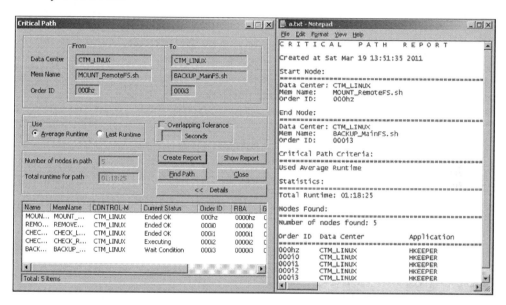

For total runtime calculations based on the last runtime, the recorded last runtime of each job may not come from the same iteration. For example, some jobs on the critical patch have finished and some are still executing or waiting for execution. In this case, the last runtime of the finished jobs will be from the current execution, whereas the last runtime of the "executing" or "waiting for execution" jobs will be from the execution from the last iteration (for example, another day). As a result, there can be an overlap between a given job's start time and its predecessor's end time. Control-M allows us to specify an **Overlapping Tolerance** value (in seconds) for the total runtime calculation to take into consideration.

The Time Machine – Archived ViewPoint

What we already know is that the ViewPoint was designed for us to monitor and manage active jobs, but what we don't know yet is that Control-EM also archives past ViewPoints for certain days to allow us to view them at a later time.

Archived ViewPoint is useful when we need to trace back to the past. For example, on Monday, we find out a job flow was delayed by 3 hours, but its predecessor jobs were executed on Saturday and have been removed from AJF by the previous NDP. With Archived ViewPoint, we can easily open that day's ViewPoint and locate the jobs to check their status and ending times.

We can open an Archived ViewPoint through **File | Open Archived ViewPint**. We have to first select jobs under which Control-M/Server we would like to see, because Archived jobs are displayed only at a per Control-M/Server basis. Then we select from the available Nets. Each Net is an Archived ViewPoint of a given day with a start and an end time. Once the Net is selected, we get to choose the ViewPoint, that is, the same as what we do with active ViewPoints.

A new ViewPoint is created after each NDP run. During NDP, a new set of active jobs gets populated into each Control-M/Server's AJF and once NDP is completed, Control-M/EM will download them as the current Net. At the same time, the previous ViewPoint will become an Archived ViewPoint. Normally, the start time of a ViewPoint is the time when that day's NDP is completed and the end time is right before the next NDP starts. There are special cases where a new ViewPoint will get built if a force download happens. We will talk about force download in the coming chapters.

Archived ViewPoint has a pink background. What we see is the status of each job at the end of the time frame. We can use **Tools | Playback** to view the job status changes during the entire time period. The playback speed can be x events per step or x seconds per step. Alternatively, we can manually enter a particular time to view.

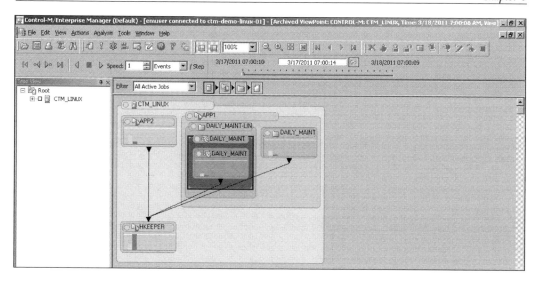

In our case, since earlier we had changed the user daily settings on the file processing job tables, the `FP-FixedTime` table is no longer being ordered. If we want to re-check how those jobs used to run, we can open the archived ViewPoint of that particular day and do a playback. However, no matter how powerful Control-M is, we only can view the past, but cannot change what has already happened.

Creating ViewPoint

Apart from the handful of ViewPoints available to select from, we can create our own display of job hierarchy and/or job collection to meet special operation needs in a complex batch environment.

Hierarchy

We can create new ViewPoints from **File | New ViewPoint** in the Control-M/EM GUI client. After giving a name and description to the new ViewPoint, we will be asked to select an existing hierarchy or create a new hierarchy. We are required to provide a name for the new hierarchy and allowed to define up to four levels of grouping.

For example, our life would become easier if we can monitor maintenance jobs in a per node ID view. We create a **New Hierarchy** called **Maintenance Jobs Only** and select the four layers as **Node ID, Application, Group, SMART table**.

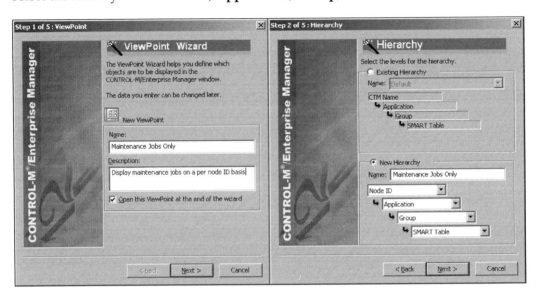

The hierarchy options also include application-specific selections, such as defining AFT, Database, or SAP job fields as hierarchy layers. These options are to be worked together with the job collection definition, so only relevant jobs will be displayed in the ViewPoint.

Collection and default filter

Followed by the hierarchy rules, we can define up to four collection definitions and four filter definitions to limit what will be displayed in the ViewPoint.

In our case, we will set the collection to limit the jobs by **Group LIKE" DAILY_ MAINT*** so only the group name that starts with **DAILY_MAINT** will be displayed. For the default filter, we will select **Delete = False**. Therefore, only active jobs are displayed by default.

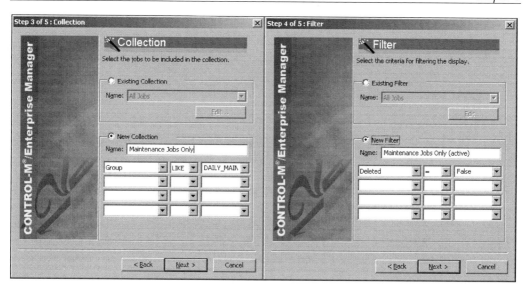

The reason we call it the default filter is because once we select the ViewPoint in the Control-M/EM GUI client, the filter we defined will be applied, but we still able to change to other filters through the **Filter** drop-down menu located at the top of the ViewPoint.

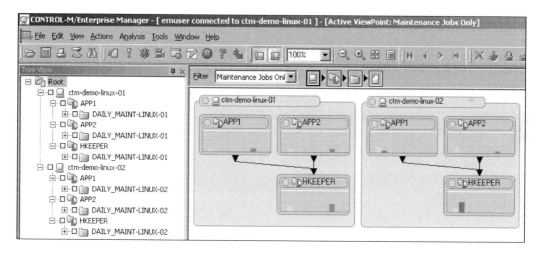

For performance reasons it is much better to always use a collection of all jobs and use the filter to limit what jobs appear in the ViewPoint. In this case, the system only has one collection defined and used by all ViewPoints. Therefore, it improves the performance of EM GUI Server, as it only needs to load jobs into its memory once.

Forecasting

We have already discussed the purpose of Control-M Forecast in *Chapter 2, Exploring Control-M*, and configured the component in our Control-M environment in *Chapter 5, Administrating the Control-M Infrastructure*.

Functionality-wise, when defining or modifying jobs, Control-M Forecast allows us to view individual or multiple jobs' projected scheduling dates. For existing jobs that have been running for a while, we can select a particular day in the future and let Forecast calculate each job's start and completion time and apply speculated events to estimate the impact.

Job scheduling plan forecasting

Earlier, when we defined job's scheduling date criteria, all we could do was enter what we believed was correct into the job definition and expected them to be correct. There have been many cases where a job normally runs ok and suddenly does not get ordered on a particular day, due to the job author not considering special days when creating the job. This kind of mistake doesn't occur every day, but can cause a lot of trouble, such as delaying its dependent jobs or even directly impacting the business.

Once Forecast is installed and running, the "Forecast button", located in the scheduling tab of each job and SMART table editing form, will become available. This feature calculates the job or SMART table's scheduling plan, based on what we defined. It allows us to see exactly which day the job will be scheduled for, thus helping us detect any scheduling errors. For example, with our FP-EventDriven SMART table, the forecasted schedule plan will be displayed in a calendar form with "to be scheduled" days marked in blue.

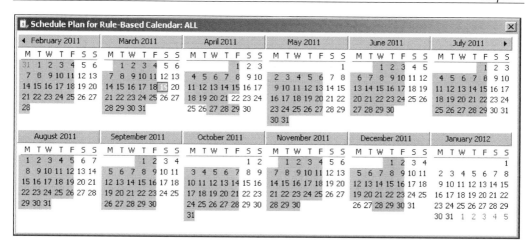

We can also compare multiple job scheduling plans by highlighting the desired SMART tables and/or jobs and selecting **Forecast** in the right-click menu. The result can be exported as a yearly or daily job order report into a flat file.

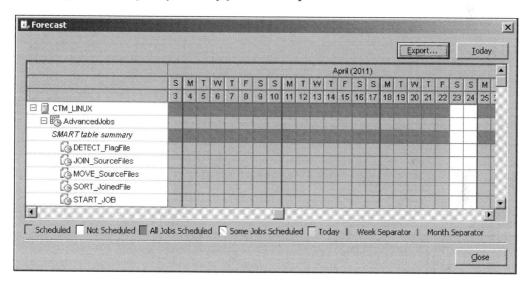

Forecast ViewPoint

Forecast ViewPoint is one of Control-M's most powerful GUI features (add-on feature). It uses job statistic data to calculate each individual job's start and end time for a given day in the future and allows us to apply What-if Scenarios that can potentially affect some or all jobs' execution times. The simulation is displayed by Forecast ViewPoint within the Control-M Desktop.

Forecast ViewPoint is very straightforward to use. Once we click on **File | Load Forecast**, we will first be asked to select an order date and define the view filter to limit the jobs to be displayed. After committing it, we will see that the jobs meeting the filter definition are displayed in the GUI with estimated start and end times.

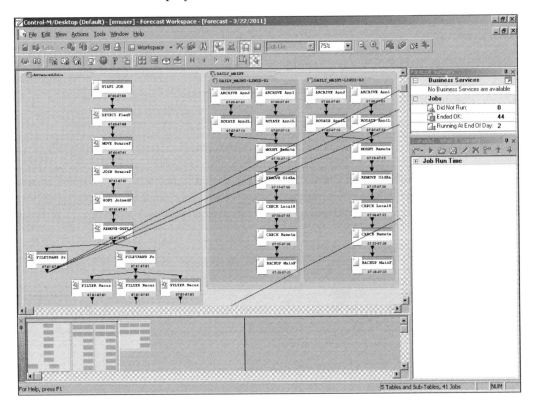

We can apply What-if scenarios by right-clicking on the job and selecting the option from Add What-if. For example, our daily maintenance job flow running on ctm-demo-linux-01 normally begins at 07:00am and finishes at 07:35am. Job ARCHIVE_ App2Log-LINUX-01 at the beginning of the job flow was estimated to start at 07:00am and finish at 07:05am. Now, if we apply What-if: set the job runtime to 10 minutes, all dependent jobs will start late by 10 minutes and finish late by 10 minutes. As a result, the entire job flow's end time will have a 10-minute delay.

Once we have multiple What-if scenarios defined, we can switch between them or try different combinations. The **Forecast Summary** window on the upper-right corner will tell us how many jobs did not run, ended ok, and are running at the end of the day based on the original forecast and selected What-if scenarios.

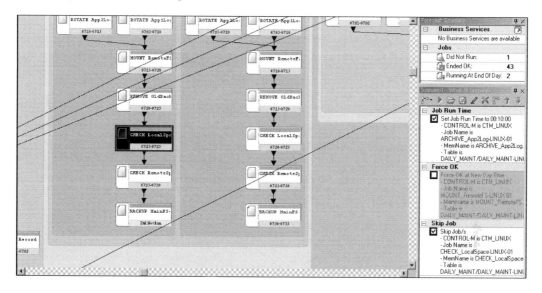

Some normal job actions we introduced earlier during the ViewPoint section are also available in the job's right-click menu, such as Neighborhood, Branch menus, and Why.

Managing batch flows as services

With critical jobs, no matter if they run daily, fortnightly or monthly, generally speaking, each of them would have a finish deadline to meet the SLA. It would be easy to monitor them if it was a single job that starts at time x and finishes at time y, but normally this is not the case in a cross-platform and cross-application scheduling environment. In complex job flows, a critical job can have many predecessor jobs running on different hosts or even owned by other applications. Each of the predecessor jobs are more than likely linked to other jobs, which may or may not be relevant to our critical jobs. Thus in the event of a job failure on the critical path, it is a pretty challenging task for us to figure out which problematic job would have a real impact on the completion time of our critical job.

Managing batch flows as services begins with identifying critical jobs and understanding their business priority. Once we define the critical job as a service, BIM will use its internal algorism to detect all predecessors of the critical job and perform ongoing monitoring on them. BIM also has the ability to detect and act upon different kinds of events, such as, when job(s) on the critical path failed, service is potentially late, and job(s) on the critical path is running too long/short. By having these facilities, we are able to focus on the failed jobs that are directly impacting the completion of critical jobs.

Defining services

Defining services in Control-M is very straightforward. All we need to do is create a BIM job (task type: BIM) and then use a condition to link it behind the critical job. Once the job flow becomes active, BIM server will automatically detect all predecessors of the BIM job and monitor the running status of each of them. At the same time, the service will be displayed in the service monitor and BIM web interface. Within the same job flow, we can define multiple services to monitor different critical jobs. Each of the critical jobs can have common predecessors, and they also can be predecessors or dependent on each other.

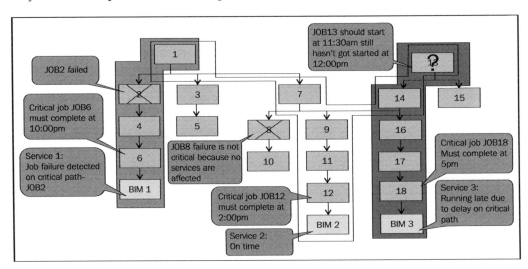

In this section, we are going to create a BIM job for each of our daily maintenance job flows running on `ctm-demo-linux-01` and `ctm-demo-linux-02`. First, we add a new job into the SMART table/sub table, that is, `DAILY_MAINT/DAILY_MAINT-LINUX-01`. We call the job `BIM-DAILY_MAINT-LINUX-01` and specify its job type as Dummy. Once we change the job type to Control-M BIM, we will see an additional job tab called BIM appearing in the editing form. For each item in the form:

- **Service Name**: The name we specify here will be displayed in the service monitor and BIM web interface. It should be something that can be understood by the application owners at a business level.

  Our value: Daily Maintenance for applications on LINUX-01

- **Priority**: Business priority of the service.

  Our value: 3 (default)

- **Service Must Complete At (HH:MM)/After Order Time (HH:MM)**: The acceptable finish time of the service. It could be a set time (At) or a length of time after the job is ordered (After Order Time).

  - After Order Time is often used for jobs that do not have a preset execution start time, but the duration of the execution should be consistent. For example, jobs to be manually ordered or dynamically ordered based on events

  - Our value: We give 07:50am in reference to the average finish time estimated by Forecast

- **Service Alerting Rules**: A set of event to be detected, corresponding actions to be performed, and the event's severity. Possible events are:

- **Job failure on service path**: If any failed jobs are predecessor of the BIM job, they will be detected and the corresponding action will be triggered.

- **Service is late**: BIM monitors all jobs on the services path and constantly recalculate the estimated completion time of the service based on the already completed jobs' end time, current executing job's start time, and average run statistic in conjunction to waiting for execution jobs' average statistic (statistics can be collected and used based on periods, that is, statistics for weekends, end of month, end of year, or any other user defined time periods). If the calculation shows that any job completed late or has been executing for too long has caused the service to not complete on time, a corresponding action will be triggered.

- **Job ran too long**: If any job on the service path has been running for longer than its average running time, the corresponding action will be triggered.

- **Job finished too quickly**: If any job on the service path finished quicker than its average running time, the corresponding action will be triggered.

  Available actions are:

  ○ **Shout actions**: Shout to ECS (EM Alert window), e-mail, Remedy*, and SIM**.

  ○ **Active environment actions**: Force a job into AJF, force a job ok, rerun a job, kill a job, and set an Autoedit variable.

  ○ **BIM actions**: Increase the Service must complete by time, that is, increase the deadline of the service and still consider the service as on time

  Our values:

  ○ **On Event: Job failure on Service path, Do Action: Return, Job to be rerun: The problematic jobs.**

  ○ **On Event: Service is late, Do Action: Shout (to EM Alert window), Severity: Urgent, Message: as default.**

  ○ **On Event: Job ran too long, Do Action: Shout (to EM Alert window), Severity: Urgent, Message: as default.**

- **Job Run-Time Tolerance**: Allow an amount of tolerance when BIM decides whether an individual job is running too long or finished too quickly. The time tolerance can be defined in:

  ○ **Percentile Rage (default method)**: The number of standard deviations of job runs. Three selections are (confidence high to low), 2--95.44%, 3--99.73%, 4--99.99%.

  ○ **Average runtime:** Percentage of the runtime or a fixed amount of minutes in which the job can finish early or late but can still be considered as on time.

  ○ Our value: default value – 3 standard deviations of job runs – 99.73%

*Remedy is BMC Software's incident management product

**BMC Service Impact Manager

After the BIM job is created, we can duplicate it for the maintenance job flow that belongs to `ctm-demo-linux-02` with the job name `BIM-DAILY_MAINT-LINUX-02` and the service name `Daily Maintenance for applications on LINUX-02`. Once we have moved the second BIM job into the SMART table/sub table – `BIM-DAILY_MAINT-LINUX-02`, we can go ahead and link each BIM job to the last job of the corresponding job flow – `BACKUP_MainFS-LINUX-01/2`.

Monitoring services

Once the jobs are uploaded and ordered into AJF, all predecessors of the BIM job will be marked with a special BIM icon. Those marked jobs are a part of a service. As soon as all predecessors of the BIM job are finished, the BIM job itself will execute as a dummy job. Before it starts execution, we can still hold the job instance and modify the service configuration.

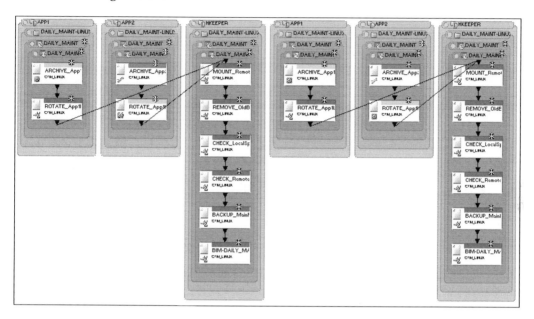

We can view each individual service's status by clicking on the BIM shortcut icon or select **Tools | Service Monitor**. Because we forced the job execution around 10:15pm, BIM will report that each service is late and provide the name of the problematic job. However, it will still give the progress of the service and an estimated completion time. This warning will not show up if we defined the service as HHMM after order time.

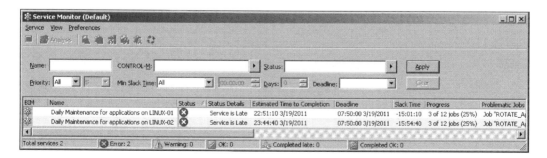

If we log in to the BIM Web Interface now, we would see the same service status and warnings.

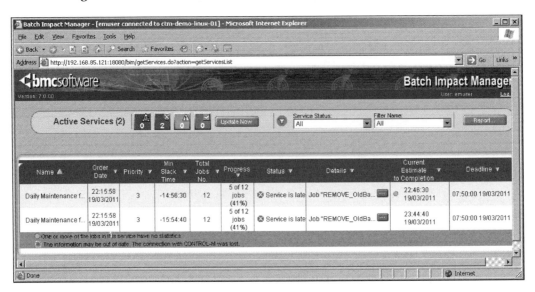

Furthermore, we can open **Business Service Analysis ViewPoint**, located under the EM GUI client's **File** drop-down menu. This special view point allows us to view detailed information about a particular service and perform What-if scenarios on associated SMART table or jobs to see the estimated impact in the form of a mini Control-M/Forecast for the near future of a batch service. It analyzes the active jobs environment, based on the what-if scenarios we applied, and provides estimations. In this case, we can find out what is the best solution to the problem that provides minimal impact to the system before applying it. The analyzing includes showing us how a potential solution will impact other batch services, which may not be the ones that currently have a problem.

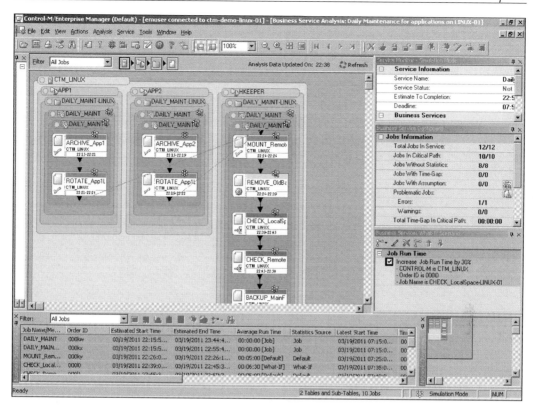

With **Business Service Analysis ViewPoint**, we can also perform normal GUI actions, such as kill, rerun, or bypass a job. We should keep in mind that these normal GUI actions will affect the actual job's status, and should not be confused with What-if scenarios.

The **Business Service Analysis List** window, located at the lower-left corner of the ViewPoint, gives us an estimated start/end time and statistical information of each job within the service. We can apply a number of different filters to limit the display, such as display jobs with time-gap, jobs with assumptions, problematic jobs, and so on.

Control-M reporting facility

We have been monitoring active jobs, viewing archived jobs, forecasting the future, as well as managing batch flows as services. What else can we do, or rather, what else needs to be done in order to have our future batch environment under total control? Well there are many things we can do, but one of the must-haves is a reporting tool for us to spot trend and problems among the huge amount of data. Reports of the batch environment are like financial statements of a company; they tell us what we have in the system and how they are running.

Type of reports

In Control-M, reports are generated by the dedicated GUI Client application, that is, Reporting Facility. After clicking on the **Reporting Facility** icon, we will be asked for the same login as we did for Control-M/EM and Control-M Desktop. By clicking on **File | New | Ad Hoc Report** or the **New Report** shortcut icon, we will have a selection of different report types.

Report types offered by Reporting Facility are fixed, in other words, we cannot create our own report types. However, for each report type, we can define filter rules to limit what data is to be displayed in the output. Defined filter rules can be saved as report templates which can be re-used later on to generate new reports in interactive or batch mode. These report types are grouped into five categories:

- **Definition**: Statistic job/table/condition definition-related information.
    - Jobs/table definitions: Statistic job/table definitions that meet the filter rules.
    - Link definition: Dependencies between jobs that meet the filter rules. A filter can be applied to a condition or job, or both.
    - Manual definitions: Detect in-conditions that meet the filter rules that do not have the matching out-conditions defined in other jobs. A filter can be applied to a condition or job, or both.

- **Active**: Information extracted from the current active environment or from an active environment in the past (archived net).
    - Active jobs: Active job instances that meet the filter rules.
    - Active links: Dependencies between active jobs that meet the filter rules. A filter can be applied to a condition or job, or both.
    - Prerequisite condition report: Conditions have been generated and meet the filter rules (condition name and date).

- Control/quantitative resources in the active environment: Resource properties, current usage, and status.

- Manual/missing conditions in the active environment: Detect in-conditions that meet the filter rules that do not have the matching out-conditions defined in other active jobs. A filter can be applied to a condition or job, or both.

- **General**: All other Control-M-related information.

    - EM alerts: Alerts generated in the EM Alert window that match the time frame and the filter rules. The report is displayed in both, a graphical and text format.

    - EM auditing history: EM activities auditing records over a time frame and matches the filter rules (EM auditing needs to be enabled for data collection).

    - Extreme peaks usage: Indicates the highest/lowest/average number of running jobs (and date occurred) of each particular task type, node ID, and application type on the given Control-M/Server over the specified time period.

    - Workload distribution: Daily Control-M/Server active job statistics over the specified time period.

    - Managed servers: Specifications of (connected) machines that have Control-M application installed over the specified time period.

- **BMC Batch Impact Manager**: Service-related reports, only available if BIM is installed.

    - History: Service statistics (order time, target completion time, actual completion time, and so on) over the specified time period (one or many services can be included in the report).

    - SLA Analysis: Execution status of the selected service over the specified time period (only one service can be included in the report).

    - Detailed: Detailed information of the selected service over the specified time period (only one service can be included in the report).

    - Job-Services: Service name of the selected job that is currently in the active environment (either all jobs or one job to be selected).

    - Service-Jobs: All jobs under the selected service that are currently in the active environment (either all services or one service to be selected).

- **Forecast Analysis**: Job execution-related reports, only available if Forecast is installed.
  - ° Execution: Job statistic information for jobs that met the filter rules over a specified time period in the past.
  - ° Workload: Graphical display of a number of jobs running over a time period on a particular day and each job's statistic.
  - ° Trend Analysis: Graphical display of the number of submitted jobs each day over a time period or on a particular day of each week/month.

Creating a report

A report can be generated by selecting the desired reporting type followed by specifying filters, displaying rules, and report style. General Displaying rules* are fields to be displayed, grouping methods, and result sorting rules. For selected filter rules, we can leave the value as a parameter to be imputed by a user every time before the report is generated. For fields to be displayed, we should keep in mind the length of each file because the report always has limited width (presented, by default, in Letter size and Portrait orientation).

 Displaying rules may not be relevant to some report types.

We will generate the following reports for our environment:

- **Manual definitions**: Daily report to detect any jobs' in-conditions created by users that haven't got the matching out-condition from other jobs. This will allow us to detect potential job delay due to missing conditions.

- **EM alerts**: Weekly report to find unhandled alerts.

- **Execution**: Weekly report to find job failure rate, so we can target the problematic jobs and make improvements.

- **Quantitative resources in the active environment**: We run this report a few times a day to randomly check the resource usage in the active environment. Based on this report, we can identify resource shortage, therefore, we can re-arrange jobs or add more resources as per the requirement.

- **Workload**: Daily report to find the executing peak of the day. Use this report in conjunction with the quantitative resource report to find out if the executing peak reaches any resource bottleneck.

- **SLA Analysis**: Weekly reports to find out if any services have missed their SLA during the last week. Identify service delay trends, combined with other reports to find the root cause and solution.

- **Trend Analysis**: Monthly report to detect the number of jobs run per day over the last month.

Once a report is generated, we can save the report in the Crystal Reports format (**"File | Save/Save as**) or export (**File | Export**) it into the MS Excel, MS Word, Acrobat PDF, HTML 4.0, XML, CSV (Comma Separated Values), or TTX (Tab Separated Text) format. We can also save the current report format as a template (**File | Export**) for reuse at a later day.

Created templates are showing on the home page of the Reporting Facility. We have the choice to run, edit, delete, or duplicate the report at any time. The process of editing a report is the same as generating a new report.

Automated reporting

As Control-M experts, we don't want to get stuck in front of the Reporting Facility every day to run reports, that is, just imagine we need to run the quantitative resource report every 15 minutes manually to spot a resource shortage issue. Control-M is provides us with methods which automate the report creation process.

The emreportcli utility

The emreportcli utility is located under the `<EM home>\bin\` directory. It allows us to generate fresh reporting data from existing templates. We can run the utility from the command line or run it as a job. This utility is only available in Control-M/EM (complete installation or client only) and is installed in MS Windows environments because it relies on Reporting Facility in the backend.

The basic syntax is:

```
emreportcli -u <EM GUI username> -p <EM GUI password> -s <EM server
hostname> -template <template name> [-template_path <template path>]
-output_file_type <file type> -output_file_path <output file path>
[-param <param name>=<param value>]
```

OR (using a password file):

```
emreportcli -pf <password file> -s <EM server hostname> -template
<template name> [-template_path <template path>] -output_file_type
<file type> -output_file_path <output file path> [-param <param
name>=<param value>]
```

The value for output file types are: EXCEL, EXCEL_DO, DOC, PDF, HTML, XML, CSV, and TABBED. EXECL_DO means data only, does not include report title and column names.

We can also specify all the template name/paths, output file type/paths, and params in an XML argument file and replace the five arguments with:

```
-arg <XML file name and path>
```

A sample XML argument file is provided with the EM installation – <EM home>\ Data\Reporting\sample_args.xml, and a full list of parameters are provided under a .dtd – <EM home>\Data\Reporting\emreportcli.dtd.

But before we start to create the first reporting job, let's have a look at the other option so we can decide which way is more convenient for producing our report.

Reporting job

In Control-M/EM version 6.4.01, a new job type, Control-M Report, was introduced. Thanks to this feature, we are now able to define reporting job parameters in GUI without worrying about all the command line arguments. The reporting job also relies on the reporting facility, and therefore can only be scheduled on a computer with Control-M/EM (Server or Client) installed.

The parameters for the Reporting job form are very similar to what were required for the emreprotcli utility. The only difference is that with reporting jobs, we are allowed to save the output to file or sysout.

For example, we created a cyclic job that runs every 15 minutes to report quantitative resource usage in the active environment. The required job parameters worth mentioning are:

- General=>File Path: C:\Program Files\BMC Software\Control-M EM 7.0.00\Default\bin
- Report=>Output file: Full path of the file. We can include variables that are to be resolved at the job's runtime, such as: {date}, {time}, and {counter}.
- Report=>Parameter: We defined one parameter in the report template. It is called Resource Name, with value DISK_IO.

- Execution=>Node ID/Group: `ctm-demo-win-01`

- Execution=>Rerun Information: Cyclic, rerun every 15 minutes

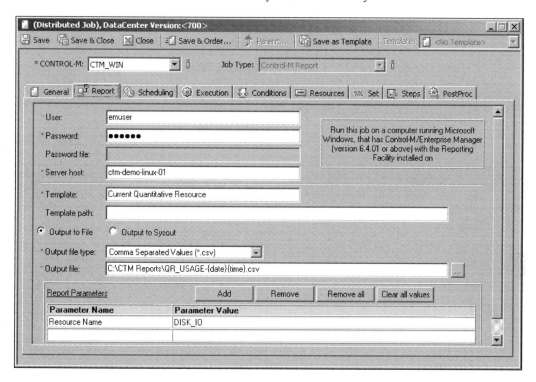

Once the job is scheduled, the execution will each time generate a new report file under the specified path with the current date and time as part of the filename.

Normally, we would group all reporting jobs into the same job group or smart table, at the same time, having housekeeping jobs to archive and clean old reports.

Summary

We should be proud of ourselves because, by now, we have pretty much mastered most of the major features of Control-M.

In this chapter, we added more jobs to Control-M by bulk load jobs from the crontab. We transformed our file processing job flow from time-based scheduling into event-driven scheduling and improved some part of the job flow by using additional Control Modules. After we defined the jobs, we revisited the Control-M/EM GUI client to discover more GUI features, such as advanced functionalities offered in ViewPoints and archived ViewPoints. We also had a look at how to use BIM and Forecast to proactively monitor jobs and estimate potential impacts by creating What-if scenarios. Towards the end, we visited the Reporting Facility, had a look at each available report type, and discussed how to automate reporting.

So is that all there is? Well, there is definitely a lot more to learn in the Control-M space. In the next chapter, we will be looking at how to become a real Control-M expert, that is, we will have a look at advanced administration topics.

7
Beyond Everyday Administration

Security, high availability, and performance have always been the three never-ending topics for all large-scale software platforms since the beginning of modern computing history; Control-M is not an exception. A normal Control-M technical person would know how to install, configure, and maintain Control-M components. But as we saw in the earlier chapters, those were not rocket science. By taking some time to learn how to secure the environment, identify problems, and perform fine tuning, we will standout from the crowd and get into the game of experts.

The second last chapter of the book is dedicated to topics that will allow us to have the potential to become Control-M SMEs. We will first introduce some handy command-line utilities, followed by a look at the security-related features in Control-M, and selectively use them to secure our environment. Then we will look at topics around high availability in detail by implementing Control-M mirroring and failover. Finally towards the second half of the chapter, we will step into the most interesting parts—fine tuning Control-M.

By the end of this chapter, you will be able to:

- Know that the command-line utilities are available and understand how to use them
- List different security features of Control-M, able to choose the appropriate approach and method to secure the environment
- Implement Control-M mirroring and failover
- Have a practical understanding of Control-M tuning and best practices

GUI alternative—command-line utilities

There's no doubt about the rich GUI features provided by Control-M/EM.
However, at the same time we may wonder, when Control-M/EM is down or the
communication between Control-M/EM and Control-M/Servers is interrupted,
how can we monitor and manage active jobs? Fortunately, there are a number
of handy command-line utilities provided by Control-M/Server that allow us to
bypass Control-M/EM to monitor and perform actions that directly affect the active
environment and job/table definitions stored in Control-M/Server database.

These utilities can be used in interactive mode from the command line as well as
running in batch mode when scheduled as Control-M jobs. Apart from using the
utilities as an alternative way to monitor and manage the active environment, a lot
of users leverage the features of these utilities to make the job scheduling much more
flexible and dynamic.

Control-M/Server utilities

On Control-M/Server, utilities are stored under `<Control-M/Server home dir >/
ctm_server/exe_<os type>` directory. Since the utilities are compiled executables,
the directory name is different for installation on different types of operating
systems. In our RHEL environment, it is called `exe_RedHat`. The following are the
utilities that can be used to manage active environment and job/table definitions
stored in Control-M/Server database.

	Utility name	Description
Affecting the active environment	ctmpsm*	For monitoring and performing functions that affect the active environment (provides both menu and command-line interfaces)
	ctmorder	Orders or forces job(s) into the active environment
	ctmcreate	Creates once-off job instance directly into the active environment
	ctmkilljob	Terminates a job, similar to the kill feature in Control-M/EM GUI
	ctmwhy	Displays missing prerequisites of jobs in "waiting for submission" status, similar to the "why" feature in Control-M/EM
	ctmlog	Displays, experts, deletes Control-M log (ctmlog/ IOALOG) from Control-M/Server database
	ctmruninf	Displays and deletes job execution statistical data from Control-M/Server database

	Utility name	Description
	Ctmstats	Displays and deletes job execution statistical average data from Control-M/Server database
	Ctmrpln*	Lists the days that the job is defined to be scheduled. Similar to the **Forecast** button in Control-M Desktop
	ctmcontb	Lists, adds, and deletes conditions
	ctmldnrs	Detects and creates manual conditions (that is, list/add jobs' in-conditions in the active environment that do not have matching out-conditions)
	ctmstvar	Displays the value of an Autoedit variable or function
	ctmvar	Displays, creates, and modifies global and SMART table level Autoedit variables
	ecactltb	Displays control resources and their status
	ecaqrtab	Lists, adds, deletes, and modifies quantitative resource
	ctmshout	Sends message to the specified user or shouts the destination
Affecting job/table definitions	ctmdeftab	Creates a new SMART table definition
	ctmdefsubtab	Creates a new Subtable definition (within a specified SMART table)
	ctmdefine	Adds a job definition into a table, SMART table, or Sub-table
	ctmexdef	Exports job processing definitions from the Control-M/Server database to an ASCII file
	ctmcalc_date	Calculates the date that a job will be ordered after adding or deducting the number of days on top of the original scheduling date we specified

Since the directory is included in the Control-M/Server user's PATH environment variable, we can execute these utilities from any directory as long as we log on as the Control-M/Server user (for Windows environments, they are included in SYSTEM path therefore, they can be invoked by any user from any directory). We can see the list of command-line arguments for each utility by executing the utility with an invalid argument, for example, ctmvar-abc.

*Also available in command-line interactive mode

These utilities do not offer the best-looking user interface, but they could be the "life saver" in emergency situations. For example, a job needs to be confirmed at 9:00 a.m. to trigger the reconciliation job flow but at that time the GUI server is down. By using the `ctmpsm` utility, we are able to confirm the job directly from Control-M/Server. More likely the administrator will be the person to execute these kind of tasks, simply because the normal operators do not have access to the Control-M/Server machine due to security reasons.

Control-M/Agent utilities

Control-M/Agent also offers some of the utilities we just discussed. In this case, users can utilize features provided by the utilities without requiring access to Control-M/Server. This also allows the utilities to be part of a job that runs on the Agent machine. In fact, Control-M/Agent doesn't hold the real executable files. As we introduced in *Chapter 2, Exploring Control-M*, each of the utilities offered by Control-M/Agent is just a link, in the backend each utility triggering is converted into a request and gets sent to Control-M/Server for execution.

The server utilities available on the Control-M/Agent side are: *ctmpsm, ctmorder, ctmcreate, ctmkilljob, ctmcontb, ctmstvar, ctmvar, ecaqrtab, ecactltb, ctmshout, ctmdefine, ctmdeftab, ctmdefsubtab.*

Later in this chapter, we will see utilities such as `ctmlog` and `ctmstats` being used for general housekeeping. Some of the utilities will also be utilized to achieve complex scheduling requirements in *Chapter 8, Road to Workload Automation*.

Using `ctm utils`, agent or server, means these actions won't be audited in EM audit, but they are recorded in `ctmlog`, and even if they are in em audit they will be logged against the server user and not the em user who issued them.

Securing the environment

Batch scheduling platform is unlike normal application software, where anyone in the organization can access and have a play with. Tasks executed within can be dealt with confidential data, therefore, sensitive to the public. Also, because of the nature of cross-platform scheduling, once someone has access to it, the person potentially will be able to execute any scripts or commands on any machine as per the owner's requirements— the owner literally has the control of the whole environment. As such, security becomes one of the biggest concerns of centralizing batch scheduling. For organizations such as financial institutions, the secure level of the batch scheduling platform can be even more important than its general functionality. Fortunately, Control-M comes with comprehensive security features to give us the peace of mind, as well as allow our batch environment to meet compliance and auditing requirements.

The security facilities offered by Control-M are multidimensional among all three infrastructure layers—Control-M/EM, Control-M/Server, and Control-M/Agent. The reason we say it is multidimensional is because each facility focuses on a different aspect to make sure the environment is totally secure. These dimensions are:

- User authentication and privilege
- Job ordering, submission, and execution
- Inter-component communication
- Auditing

Normally it is not necessary to apply all security features; depends on the site requirement. As Control-M administrators, we should—based on the requirements in reality—look at each option and decide the best combination. Implementing unnecessary security can increase the ongoing administration workload. It also makes the Control-M environment more complicated and increases the running overhead.

User authentication: External authentication

We talked about how to define additional GUI users and groups in *Chapter 5, Administrating the Control-M Infrastructure*. By default, the login credentials we created for each user is managed within Control-M/EM—passwords are encrypted and stored in the database. Each time when users log on to the GUI, the username and password entered will get passed to the GUI server for internal authentication.

Control-M is also able to allow GUI user authentication against external mechanism, such as using the organization's centralized LDAP server or other third-party authentication applications. By using external authentication, users are able to use their normal staff login credentials to access Control-M, therefore saving their effort on remembering the additional set of username and passwords and improving security. On the Control-M administrator's side, this mechanism saves us the effort of managing user password policies (for example, complicity and expire date settings), all we need to do is map GUI users to their corresponding credentials on the external authentication server and let Control-M/EM talk to it at the backend to authorize each login request. From the management and compliance point-of-view, external authentication ensures that user policy for Control-M is in complete sync with the company's general user policy and since procedures around this are all done outside Control-M, they are all compliant to the company's user access procedures.

For LDAP type authentication, Control-M supports Microsoft AD (Active Directory) and other compatible technologies such as iPlanet (Sun Java System Directory Server). In order to activate LDAP authentication, we need to follow three steps:

- Configure LDAP parameters in CCM
- Modify existing users to authenticate with LDAP and/or
- Associate Control-M/EM GUI user groups with LDAP groups

Use our environment as an example; we can configure Control-M/EM to authenticate against the MS Windows 2003 Active Directory running on host `ctm-demo-win-01`.

Configuring LDAP parameters

The LDAP parameters are to be configured in CCM, from **Tools | Control-M/ EM System Parameters | LDAP**. We need to select **Enable LDAP Authentication** checkbox and enter the following configuration parameters:

- **LDAP Directory Server Type**: **Active Directory** and **iPlanet** are the two available server types, by default. We can create new types by adding the server attributes into the configuration file `DirectoryServiceType.cfg` located under `<EM home dir>/ctm_em/etc`.
  - ° Our value: **Active Directory**
- **LDAP Directory Search User**: The user (in distinguished name) that is used to run the search action during each user log on. We can leave it blank if the LDAP servers support anonymous user search.
  - ° Our value: **administrator@ctm-demo.ctmexperts.com**
- **LDAP Directory Search Password**: LDAP directory searches user's password (select **Edit Password** checkbox to enable the field).
- **Transmission Protocol**: Communication protocol used between Control-M/ EM and LDAP server. The available choices are TCP and SSL.
  - ° Our value: **TCP**
- **Server Hostname and Port**: The LDAP server's hostname and the port listened by LDAP service. The default port number will be used if the **Port** field is left blank. The default value depends on which communication protocol is selected, for TCP the default port number is 389 and for SSL it is 636. We can specify multiple entries to include the backup LDAP server. Control-M will always establish connection with the first available one (top to bottom).
  - ° Our value: **ctm-demo-win-01.ctm-demo.ctmexperts** with port number 389

- **LDAP Directory Search Base**: The starting domain distinguished name for the user search. The default value (when left blank) is the search user's domain. Multiple entries are allowed.

  ° Our value: **ctm-demo.ctmexperts.com**

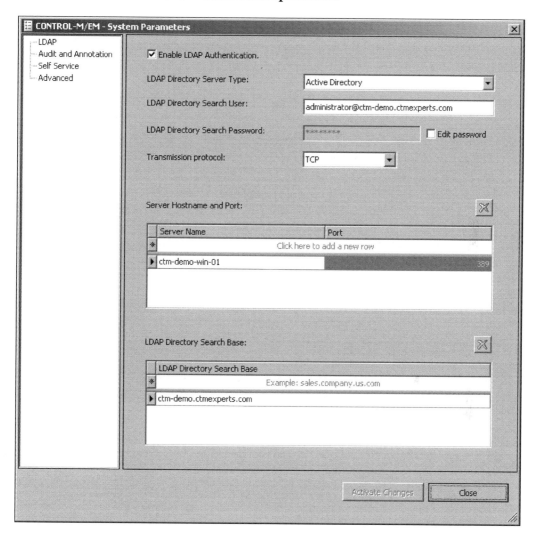

Once done with entering the parameters, we can click on the **Activate Changes** button to enable the LDAP authentication. CCM should respond with a pop-up window saying **GUI Server/GAS/BIM/CMS LDAP authentication is enabled successfully** and the component refresh is done automatically at the same time.

Converting existing GUI users to authenticate with LDAP

For user accounts defined prior to enabling LDAP, we can map each of them to the corresponding LDAP credentials without redefining the account.

We have introduced the **User Authorizations** window in *Chapter 5, Administrating the Control-M Infrastructure*. If we reopen it now, we will see there's a new field called **LDAP User and Domain** under the **General** tab. This is the place where we map the user to its LDAP credentials. Depending on the configuration on LDAP server side, the value can be specified in `user@domain`, `DOMAIN\user`, or `cn=xxx,dc=xxx, dc=xxx` format.

The **User LDAP Authentication Only** checkbox in the **General** tab forces the user to use LDAP credentials to log on. For normal users, we would keep this option checked otherwise it defeats the purpose of LDAP authentication. We have to allow at least one user to be able to authenticate both way; so in case the LDAP server isn't available, someone can still log on to Control-M. It is the so-called emergency user. As common sense, a sufficient level of privilege should be given to these users to allow them manage accounts during emergency or perform GUI actions on behalf of others.

For example, we have a user called **bruce** existing in both Control-M EM and LDAP. We can force the user to authenticate against its LDAP credentials by specifying **bruce@ctm-demo.ctmexperts.com** in **General/LDAP User and Domain** and tick **General/Use LDAP Authentication Only** (EM authentication password field will gray out).

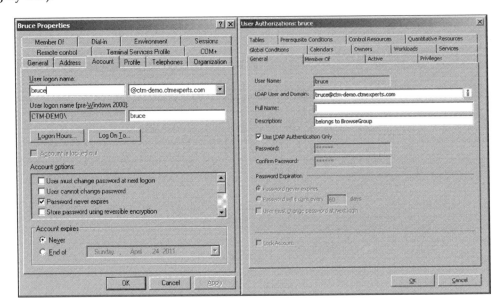

Associating EM user groups with LDAP groups

Frequently defining and managing individual users in Control-M can be very time consuming. Control-M version 7 has made an improvement by allowing us to directly associate LDAP groups with Control-M/EM user groups. By doing so, all users within the LDAP group will automatically have access to Control-M and inherit privileges of the associated Control-M user groups.

Let's take our environment as an example. We need to provide Control-M GUI browse access to users within LDAP group **AppOwners**. Instead of identifying and adding each user of the group into Control-M authorization and assigning them the same privileges, we can link the LDAP group to the existing Control-M/EM group **BrowseGroup**. This is done by adding **LDAP Groups Reference** from Control-M/EM GUI Client's **Authorizations | Group Authorizations | Browse Group** (or the desired group) | **LDAP Groups**. Once we enter the group name **AppOnwers** as a new row, users within the group will be able to log on to GUI with their LDAP login credentials. We will notice that when this kind of user is logged on, the username will be displayed with the full domain name on the top of the GUI window, for example, `Jason@ctm-demo.ctmexperts.com connected to ctm-demo-linux-01`.

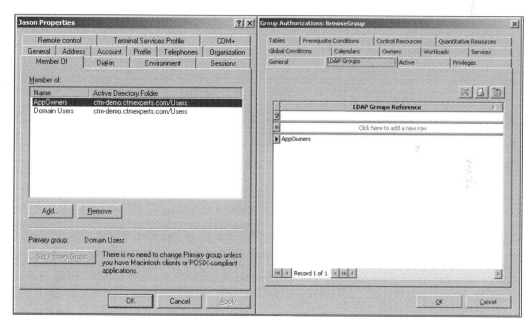

This method can save the Control-M administrators a lot of effort in dealing with individual users. However, by doing so, we are fully relying on LDAP to perform authentication. In other words, no users within these groups are able to log on to Control-M/EM in the event of a LDAP service outage. For such reasons, we still have to define individual user accounts (emergency users), so at least a small amount of users are still able to log on during the outage. Another scenario that involves creating individual user accounts is that when the specific privileges required by a user isn't allowed to be applied at the group level. The user can still be part of the Control-M/EM group, but the user has to be defined individually so the rules can be applied only at the user level.

User privilege: Control-M/Server security

Control-M/Server security is another layer of security on top of Control-M/EM GUI user authorization but only focuses on:

- Which EM users are able to perform action on job and calendar definition stored in Control-M/Server database
- Which EM users are able to perform action on objects within the active environment (for example, active jobs, conditions, quantitative, and control resources)
- Which OS users are able to execute Control-M/Server utilities

Control-M/Server security is "turned off" by default and we would normally consider that the Control-M/EM level security is sufficient. Users enable Control-M/Server security primarily to prevent the communication between Control-M/EM and Control-M/Server from being hacked—in case someone managed to manipulate the user action messages sent from Control-M/EM to Control-M/Server, therefore able to perform unauthorized actions on job/calendar definitions or affect the active environment. It also eliminates unauthorised use of active environment-related Control-M/Server utilities from the command-line or via Control-M jobs.

Control-M/Server security is to be enabled from `ctmsys` Control-M/Server utility, and user's/group's entries can be configured via CCM or from `ctmsec` Control-M/Server utility. Once Control-M/Server security is turned on, for every new Control-M/EM user created, the privileges for that user will need to be defined in Control-M/Server security. Otherwise, users will not be able to perform any of the actions mentioned earlier even if they already have the privilege in Control-M/EM authorization. In Control-M/Security, the privilege can also be defined at the group level and this allows the users under it to inherit the privileges.

The reason we double-quoted the word "turned off" is because Control-M/Server actually checks its security definitions even if `ctmsec` is off. The way it works is when `ctmsec` is off, any user not defined in Control-M/Server security is allowed to do everything and any user that is defined is allowed to do only what is defined. Therefore, in some degree we still have limited security even with security off.

Defining group-level security

In CCM, we go to **Tools | Security | Control-M/Server Security** to define the privileges of each Control-M/EM user and group. The privileges are categorized into three tabs—**Table**, **Authorized AJF**, and **Entities**. Use the user **bruce** as an example; since he's a member of the Control-M/EM BrowseGroup, we can create an entry for his group first and then create a user entry for him and relate back to the group.

In the configuration window, we first need to choose the Control-M/Server instance (we choose: **CTM_WIN**), followed by clicking on the down arrow next to the **+** sign and select **Group (Ctrl+G)**. In the **New Group** pop-up window, we enter the Control-M/EM group name (we enter: **BrowseGroup**) and a short description. We will notice that the group entry has an icon different to normal users. While it is highlighted, we will define the following privileges for the group:

- **Table**: All tables (*) with **Read** as **Yes**, rest as **No**. This will allow users within the group to be able to load all job tables of Control-M/Server CTM_WIN (that is, perform **download** action in **Table Manager**), but not able to perform **upload**, **delete**, or **order** action.

- **Authorized AJF**: All owners (*) and all nodes (*) with **Why, Sysout, Log, Statistics** as **Yes**, rest as **No**. It means the user within the group will be able to perform **Why**, view **Sysout**, **Log**, and **Statistics** from GUI or utility on all jobs belonging to Control-M/Server CTM_WIN no matter who is the job owner and which node the job is defined to run, but not any other actions.

- **Entities**: None. This means the user will not able to add, edit, or delete any calendar, condition, log, control or quantitative resource in Control-M/Server CTM_WIN.

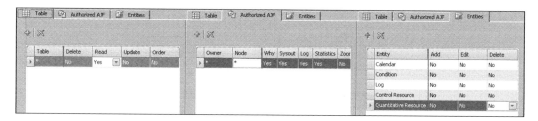

Once we are happy with everything, simply click the **Apply** button to save the changes and repeat the steps for Control-M/Server CTM_LINUX.

Defining user-level security

If we choose **Add User** from the **+** sign's drop-down menu (*Ctrl+U*), we will be asked the group name the user will belong to. A user does not have to be part of a group, but by doing so we can save some time on defining and modifying rules that are common among multiple users.

Items defined with **default** will inherit the group-level privileges, which means any changes in the group will be applied to the user. Control-M will reject the action if **default** is selected but the user doesn't belong to any group. In our case, we will add user **bruce** under the **BrowseGroup** with all items set to **default**.

For our Control-M/Server CTM_LINUX, we will use the **ctmsec** command-line menu to define the user **bruce**. The look and feel of **ctmsec** utility is different to CCM but the concepts are similar. Once we get into the main menu by running `ctmsec` command as Control-M/Server OS user, we select **User Maintenance** | **Add User** to create the new user and assign it to a group. Then we have to go through each of the three authorization categories to set the user privileges.

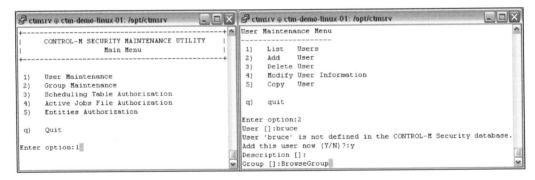

In Unix/Linux environments, the Control-M/Server OS user is predefined by default in Control-M/Server security, otherwise once the security is turned on, we will not to be able to run active environment-related utilities from the command line. Privileges also need to be defined for each job owner who's going to run Control-M/Server utilities from the Agent side.

Enabling Control-M/Server security

In order to activate Control-M/Server security for CTM_LINUX, we need to log on to each Control-M/Server and enable it from the `ctmsys` utility. For Unix/ Linux machines, we run the utility as Control-M/Server OS user, for MS Windows machines we can run it as any user because the utility's home directory has been included in the system PATH environment variable during installation (or we can locate it from `<CTM/Server home dir>\ctm_server\exe`).

In the **System Maintenance Utility Main Menu** we select **2) System Parameters** then change the value of **5) Full Security** from **N** (unrestricted) to **Y** (restricted). The change will take effect imminently; cycling the Control-M/Server is not required.

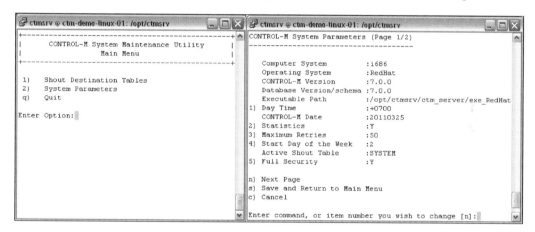

In the existing environment, it is better to define each user and group in Control-M/ Server security first. Otherwise, any actions of the user will be blocked as soon as we enable **Full Security** from **ctmsys**. When switching back from **Full Security** (also known as back to unrestricted mode), users that are already in Control-M/Security will still be limited by the privilege definitions until we remove their entries.

Control-M returns a message for each blocked action. In GUI, we would see something such as **Request rejected by Data Center CTM5323 SECURITY PROTECTION VIOLATION**. For command-line utilities, we would see something like **Security check failed. User *** not allowed to ***.**

Job ordering and submission: User exit

Control-M/EM authorization and Control-M/Server security can lock down user actions effectively but not necessarily means the environment is 100 percent secure. Think about situations where a user can define jobs to run as root on machine A; even though Control-M/Server security does not allow him to directly order the job that has the Owner **root** onto host A, the user can still manage to make the job active in other ways, such as ordering via the user daily SYSTEM. Once the job is ordered, it is out of the hand of Control-M/EM authorization and Control-M/Server security.

Control-M/Server provides a facility called User Exit that can help us to ease this security concern. User Exit is a mechanism used for filtering and modifying information at Control-M/Server's certain action points before the information gets processed. There are six types of user exits in total, each one of them is in-charge for a different action point.

- **CTMUE101**: Job ordering User Exit, executed before each job is ordered
- **CTMUE102**: Job Submission User Exit, executed before each job is submitted for execution
- **CTMUE103**: Before NDP User Exit, executed before NDP starts
- **CTMUE104**: After NDP User Exit, executed after NDP ends
- **CTMUE105**: Before User Daily User Exit, executed before user defined user daily job
- **CTMUE106**: After User Daily User Exit, executed before user-defined user daily job

We will use the most common one, **CTMUE102**, as an example to explain and demonstrate how it works. By enabling the user exit, each time during job submission a flat text file that contains the job definition will be passed to the User Exit. The User Exit will then execute a script defined by the user and take the text file as an input (first argument). In the script, we can scan the text file (for example, use Unix/Linux `sed` command) to look for matching strings and perform modifications (or perform any actions we want). Once the script execution is completed, Control-M will use the modified text file to continue with the process.

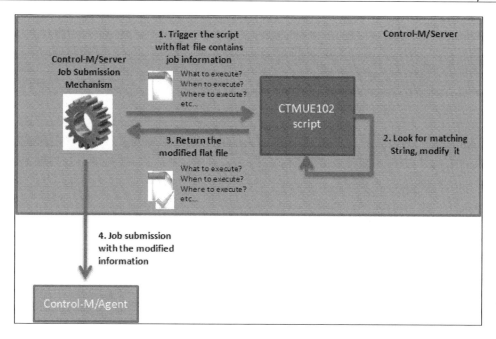

In order to enable CTMUE102 in our environment, we need to perform the following tasks:

- Backup and open Control-M/Server's `config.dat` file under `<Control-M/Server home dir>/ctm_server/data` directory.

- Set the following three parameters in the `config.dat` file**:
    - ○ Make sure the value of `CTM_PRM_ENABLE_UE` is set to `Y` (by default). This will enable User Exit facility.
    - ○ Define parameter `CTM_PRM_ENABLE_UE102` with value `Y`. This will enable CTMUE102.
    - ○ (Optional) Define the maximum time each time Control-M/Server waits for the User Exit to complete by adding the parameter `CTM_PRM_TIMEOUT_UE102` with a value (in seconds). If the parameter is not defined, default value 20 (seconds) will be used.

- Define the script*** to be triggered by the User Exit under `<Control-M/Server home dir>/ctm_server/ue_exit`. The script has to be named `ctm_exit102.sh`. The script name format can be modified by defining `CTM_PRM_SCRIPT_UE102` in the `config.dat` file. If the parameter is not defined, the default format `ctm_exit102.sh` will be used.

*For MS Windows, the time is measured in units of milliseconds.

**Restarting Control-M/Server or issuing IPC refresh command to all processes (that is, `ctmipc -dest ALL -msgid CFG`) is required for the change to take effect.

***For sample of the script and sample text file of each user exit, please see Control-M Administrators Guide Appendix B – Exits.

Job execution: Control-M/Agent security

From a job's lifecycle point-of-view, the last layer of security is at the job execution host level. The limitation is referring to whether or not a job owner is allowed to execute the job on a given host. In addition, there's also a limitation on the Control-M/Server utilities that a Control-M/Agent can trigger.

Security for Windows Control-M/Agents

For Windows Control-M/Agents, all jobs run as the Agent service's running account by default. In other words, no matter which owner we specify in the job definition, Control-M/Agent will ignore it and always execute the job as the user of the Agent service. This can create a security concern because whoever submits jobs to the Windows machine will potentially have control of everything (that is, run jobs with the maximum Windows privilege). The way to eliminate this potential security issue is to enable the **Logon as User** feature.

Logon as User forces job processes to run as the owner defined in their job definition, similar to the way that Unix/Linux Agent submits jobs. However, that doesn't mean the job will be executed as whatever the owner defined in the job; each eligible job owner's login credentials need to be entered into Control-M prior to the job's execution—just like how we define Agentless job owners.

Logon as User can be set from CCM by right-clicking on the **Agent** and going to the **Security** tab under **Properties** or by running `ctmwincfg` utility (execute `ctmwincfg` command from the Windows command line). If the Control-M/Agent is running on Windows Vista or Windows 2008, we first have to modify the Agent service to run as **This Account**. In our case, it is not necessary because the test machine `ctm-demo-win-01` is running on Windows 2003. Regardless of the need, our Agent service has already changed the log in status to **This Account** while configuring the Agentless job execution in *Chapter 5, Administrating the Control-M Infrastructure*.

Before setting the value of **Logon as User** to **Y**, we should first identify each job owner and define them in CCM's **Tools | Security | Owners Authentication Settings** and make sure each of the owners have been granted with **Logon as a batch job privilege** in Windows. Failure to do so, will cause the job to fail with one of the following error messages.

```
TEST-01 - Log                                                              _ □ ×
  Close    Find...   A Fonts...
----- Message -----
ORDERED JOB:439; DAILY FORCED, ODATE 20110326
SUBMITTED TO ctm-demo-win-01
FAILED TO SUBMIT JOB TEST-01. Message from Agent follows
The agent works in 'Logon As User' mode but the password for job owner 'APP1' is not defined.
ENDED NOTOK
JOB STATE CHANGED TO Analyzed
JOB STATE CHANGED TO Post processed
RERUN BY USER emuser
SUBMITTED TO ctm-demo-win-01
FAILED TO SUBMIT JOB TEST-01. Message from Agent follows
The 'Logon as a batch job' privilege has not been granted to the user: 'APP1'
ENDED NOTOK
JOB STATE CHANGED TO Analyzed
JOB STATE CHANGED TO Post processed
```

If the job owner is a local user of the job execution host, we would define the owner as it is in both **Owners Authentication Settings** and the job definition's **Owner** field. If the job owner is a domain user, we have to define the owner in the `<domain name>\<username>` format in both. Alternatively, we can hard code the domain name in Control-M/Agent by specifying a value in the **Logon domain** field under the **Security** tab of Agent properties in CCM or via **ctmwincfg | 2. Logon Domain**. However, this is not recommended by the BMC Software.

Security for Unix/Linux Control-M/Agents

As we introduced in *Chapter 2, Exploring Control-M*, Unix/Linux Control-M/Agent processes are running as the root user by default. This was one of the security concerns for many customers until LINUX/Unix Agents were allowed to run as non-root in the release of Control-M version 7. A lot of users at that time chose to use User Exit 102 as a workaround—filter jobs submitted with owner as **root**, replace the owner with an invalid user on the machine to let the job script fail.

Starting from Control-M version 7, we have the choice to run Agent processes as a non-root user. Just like how the Windows Agent's **Logon as User** works, when the Unix/Linux Agent is running in non-root mode, we have to define each job owner's username and password into **Owners Authentication Settings** before the job can run; except if the job owner is the same user as the one under which the Agent processes are running.

In order to set our Control-M/Agent running on `ctm-demo-linux-02` into non-root mode, we need to define each job owner in CCM's **Owners Authentication Settings** first and then execute `<control-m/agent home dir>/ctm/scripts/set_agent_mode` script as root to enable non-root mode.

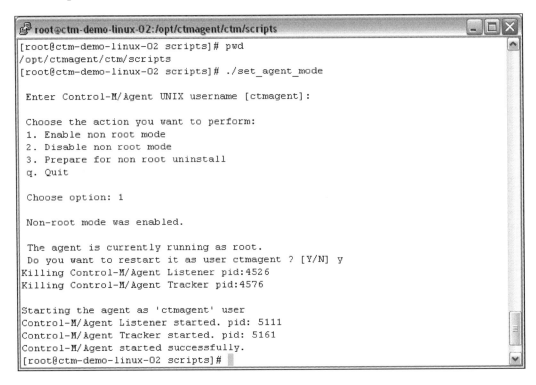

Now if we run a job without defining its owner, the job will fail with the following message:

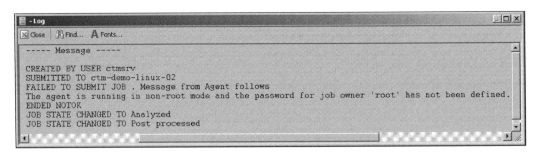

Control-M/Server utility authorizations

Control-M/Server security can limit the user access to a range of Control-M/Server utilities, including some utilities available to be invoked from the Agent side. However, it cannot limit which Agent machine the request is coming from. That is, as long as the defined user exists on a Control-M/Agent host, those utilities are allowed to be invoked from that machine by that user. This may not be secure enough because in general cases, Control-M/Agents installed across the organization are more likely to run as the same user. For example, if we define a user **ctmagent** that is allowed to order jobs in Control-M/Security, any machine with Control-M/Agent installed under the same user will be able to order jobs by executing `ctmcreate` or `ctmorder`.

Control-M/Server has a security mechanism specifically designed to limit which Control-M/Server utilities can be invoked from Control-M/Agent and which Agents are allowed to. By default, this mechanism allows any connected Agents to invoke all Agent-side Control-M/Server utilities.

Again, we use `ctm-demo-linux-02` as an example. In order to selectively limit the utility access from this agent host, we need to create a flat text file with a list of allowed utilities and save it as the agent name in uppercase under the directory `<control-m/server home dir>/ctm_server/data/AGPERMIT_UTILS`. For the very first time, we can create the file by copying the template file `AGUTILS_PERMIT` from `<control-m/server home dir/ctm_server/data/AGDEFS>` and then remove unwanted utilities from the list—the template file contains all unities available to Control-M/Agent. Once the file is created, we need to recycle Control-M/Server or run the ICP refresh command for it to take effect.

For example, once we create the file for Agent `ctm-demo-linux-02` and remove `ctmcreate` from the list, the utility execution on `ctm-demo-linux-02` will fail with an error.

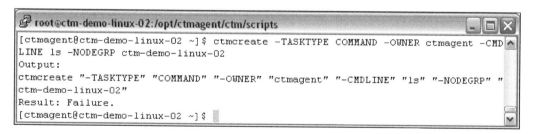

```
root@ctm-demo-linux-02:/opt/ctmagent/ctm/scripts
[ctmagent@ctm-demo-linux-02 ~]$ ctmcreate -TASKTYPE COMMAND -OWNER ctmagent -CMD
LINE ls -NODEGRP ctm-demo-linux-02
Output:
ctmcreate "-TASKTYPE" "COMMAND" "-OWNER" "ctmagent" "-CMDLINE" "ls" "-NODEGRP" "
ctm-demo-linux-02"
Result: Failure.
[ctmagent@ctm-demo-linux-02 ~]$
```

Inter-component communication—firewall

Once the Control-M environment becomes stable, we can start to lock down the firewall ports. Recall the review we did on the Control-M firewall requirements prior to installation, there are two areas where we can bring in a bit of customization—communication ports between Control-M/EM server components and GUI clients, communication between Control-M/Server and Agents. Firewall can also exist between Control-M/EM and Control-M/Server, but apart from the port requirements we mentioned earlier there's not much we can customize, therefore it will not be discussed in this section.

Between Control-M/EM server components and GUI clients

At the moment, on `ctm-demo-linux-01` our Control-M/EM server components—except CORBA naming server—are listening on random ports (by default). At the point of startup, each of the components will notify the CORBA naming server which port number has been selected to listen. CORBA naming server will keep the information in its registry and provide to each GUI client upon connection request. In such a case, all ports between Control-M/EM server components and GUI clients need to be open because we simply don't know which ports the server components will use.

Control-M provides us the option to limit the listening port of server components to a range of ports. The range size should be slightly larger than the number of existing server components in the following cases:

- When we want to run multiple server components—when we run two or three GUI Servers for performance reasons—if all ports in the range are already used by other server components, the additional GUI Servers will not be able to start.

- Another application on the Control-M/EM server host started using the port we specified before our server component had started. So a bigger range allows the server component to select another port.

The recommended port range size should be at least 20, however bear in mind that all these ports need to be opened in the firewall for incoming connections so the larger the range the higher the risk.

The range of ports can be set using the `orbconfigure` utility which is located under `<em home>/ctm_em/bin` (xWindow session is required for Unix/Linux installations). All we need to do is set the **Setup Listen Ports** to **Range** and define the lower and higher port range. The lower port range needs to be a value between 1024 and 65535, the higher port range needs to be a value higher than the lower range value and lower than 65535. The `orbconfigure` utility in fact makes modification to the configuration file `<em home dir>/ctm_em/etc/domain/config.xml`. It is important to back up the file before committing any changes in the utility. Direct modification to the file is not recommended.

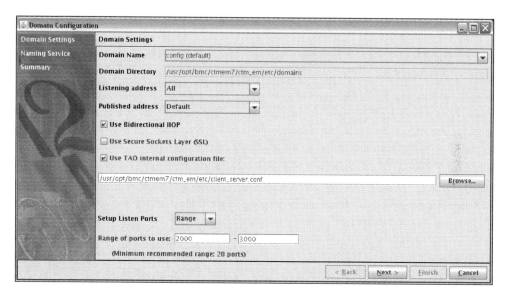

Once the port range is defined, we need to recycle Control-M/EM components and go ahead to lock down the firewall ports between Control-M/EM server components and GUI client machines to the defined range plus 13075 (the default naming server port) and any additional ports required.

Between Control-M/Server and Agents

Connection between Control-M/Server and Agents are set to transient, by default, during installation. With transient connection, Control-M/Server talks to Control-M/Agents on the **Server-to-Agent** port and Control-M/Agents talk to Control-M/Server on the **Agent-to-Server** ports. Sometimes the Agent is outside the company's firewall, like in a DMZ; and firewall rules don't allow applications in DMZ to initiate connection with machines in the company's normal network. Hence, in such cases, the Agent wouldn't be able to send back job status updates. By using a persistent connection, which is initiated by the server and stays open, Agent will be able to send updates back to Control-M/Server via the existing connection.

Persistent mode can be set via CCM or using the `ctmagcfg` utility provided with each Control-M/Agent. For example, in order to change `ctm-demo-linux-02` from transient mode into persistent mode from CCM, we need to:

- Right-click the Control-M/Agent entry in CCM and go to **Properties**
- In **Properties**, go to **Persistent Connection** tab and set the **Persistent Connection** value to **Yes**

After we click on **OK**, the setting will get pushed from CCM to Control-M/Agent via Control-M/Server's CA process. The Control-M/Agent will automatically switch to persistent mode within a short time.

In case the Agent hasn't been defined or the Agent is not reachable by the Control-M/Server, we need to set the persistent mode by logging in to the Agent machine and running the `ctmagcfg` utility. In the `ctmagcfg` utility, we go to **7. Advanced Parameters** and set **5) Persistent Connection** to **Y**. We have to save the changes after returning to the main menu; again the Control-M/Agent will automatically switch to persistent mode.

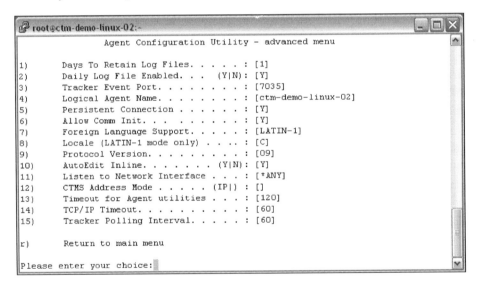

In theory, a persistent connection provides better communication performance than a transient connection because for each request there's no need to wait for the creation of a new session. When SSL mode is used, a hard-shake is required for each connection establishment, which is very costly. Persistent connection can also improve the connection performance in this scenario because only one handshake is needed while establishing the connection. Due to these factors, we can see that many users chose to use persistent connection even when there were no firewall rules blocking the Agent side.

In such cases, we can turn on the **Allow agent to initiate connection** option so the Agent will be able to initiate a connection if and when it needs to. In reality, it would be rare that an Agent would start a connection. The only time this can happen is when the persistent connection is closed for any reason; while it was closed a job ended, and so Agent could initiate a new connection back to the server in order to update the job status in real time. If this option was off, the Agent would have to wait for the server to start a new connection, which would only be the next time it needed to submit a job or during the `track_all`, which only happens every 15 minutes by default.

Inter-component Communication—SSL

There is a huge amount of information related to setting up Control-M with SSL. To talk about it in detail, we have to have a dedicated chapter. Instead, we will have an overview of the technology and discuss the important knowledge points.

Normal communication among Control-M components rely on TCP/IP network, which means they are not secured. There are chances that hackers can manipulate the information during the time it is being transferred between Control-M components or they can pretend to be the sender or receiver of the information. The risk exists in any TCP/IP communication between Control-M components as well as Control-M and other applications.

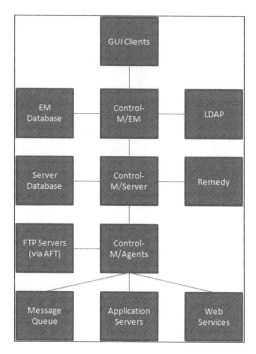

In order to eliminate such security risk, Control-M offers SSL communication between components. In SSL communication mode, the message between the components is encrypted during transit. Each component keeps its own private key and distributes the public key to the components that they will be communicating with, so the destination components will be able to decrypt the message that was encrypted by the sender prior to transfer.

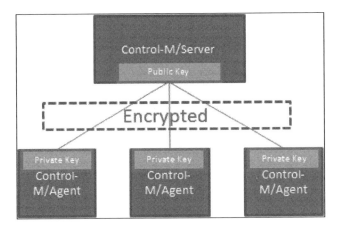

SSL communication mode can be enabled on:

- Between Control-M/EM GUI client and server components
- Control-M/EM API
- Between Control-M/EM and LDAP server
- Between Control-M/EM gateway and its associated Control-M/Server's CE process
- Between Control-M/EM CMS and every connected Control-M/Server's CA process
- Batch Impact Manager
- Between Control-M/Server and Agents

Implementing SSL

The three core components required for implementing SSL are: certificates, certificate requests, and public-private key pairs. These components are to be generated and managed from CCM or using the `sslcmd` utility.

In CCM, we can generate component certificates form **Tools | Security | Manage SSL | Generate Component Certificates**. It is the simple way of implementing SSL in comparison to the `sslcmd` utility because it is based on the built-in OpenSSL utility that provides the certificate and signs the keys automatically for us. All we need to do is enter the certificate authority information and specify which Control-M components the certificates will be generated for. Control-M will then generate the key package for us and provide an executable for distributing the package to each Control-M component.

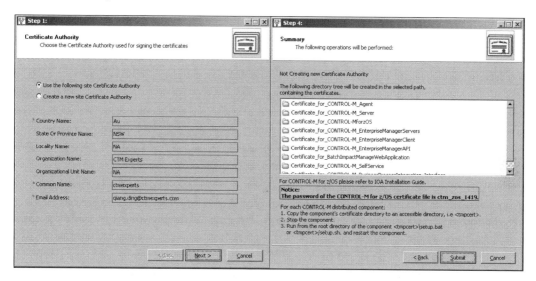

Some organizations may choose to use the hard way to generate SLL key packages—using the `sslcmd` utility. This is because they wanted to use certificate from their trusted provider, such as VeriSign (Symantec). The utility is menu-driven, which provides us with everything that is needed to create a key package. The sequence of generating a key package is:

- Request a trusted root authority certificate (CA) from a certificate signing authority (CSA), the CA will be used across the entire environment

- Once the CA is ready, run the `sslcmd` utility with a key database name and provide password at the prompt—`sslcmd -k <key file name>` (for the first time running the utility, the key database will be created)

- Add the CA by using the utility's option 2—**Add CA**

- Generate a public-private key pair by using the utility's option 1—**Generate key**

- Generate a certificate signing request by using the utility's option 3—**Generate CSR**

- Submit CSR to the CSA for signing
- Once the CSR request comes back with the digital certificate, come back to the utility and add the certificate by using the utility's option 4—**Add cert**
- Export the signed key pair using the utility's option 17—**Export key pair**
- Distribute the key pair to other components

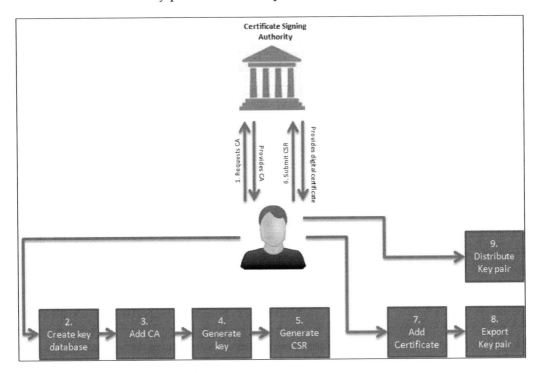

Once the keys are distributed, we can go ahead to enable the SSL communication between the components.

Auditing

So far, we have been talking about preventing security risks. But no matter how much we secure the environment, it is always good to keep a history of user activities. When there's an issue, we can use the information to track down the problem. Such information can also be required for auditing purposes—SOX and compliance regulations.

Enabling and configuring auditing

Auditing feature is provided since Control-M version 6.4.01. Once it is enabled, we can select activities at the Control-M/EM level such as ordering a job, hold/free jobs, lock/unlock tables to be audited (auditing information is stored in the Control-M/EM database). Control-M version 7 has made enhancements by adding the **Audit annotation** option. With this feature, users will be prompted to enter the purpose and justification of each action they perform, and Control-M/EM will record the information in its database.

Auditing and annotation can be enabled in CCM from **Tools | System Configuration | Control-M/EM System Parameters | Audit and Annotation**. Once we enabled them*, we can select the category to be audited and prompt for annotation. Within the same configuration panel, we can also set whether or not to allow Control-M/EM to automatically clean up auditing information (default: on), and if so, how many days to retain the information (default: 1 day).

*Audit has to be enabled in order to use annotation.

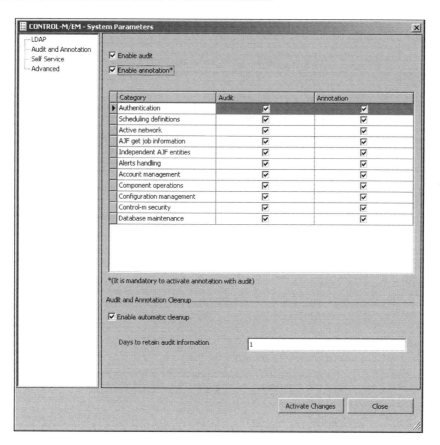

Once the changes are saved, the audit context of GUI Server, GAS, and CMS will get refreshed automatically. Now, if we go back to CCM and try to perform an action on any component, an **Audit Annotation** window will pop up and we have to enter the information before the action takes effect. The information we entered will get stored and can be selected by clicking on the down arrow, so we don't need to reenter the same annotation repeatedly for the same actions. If multiple items are selected for the same action, the user will only be prompted once for annotation.

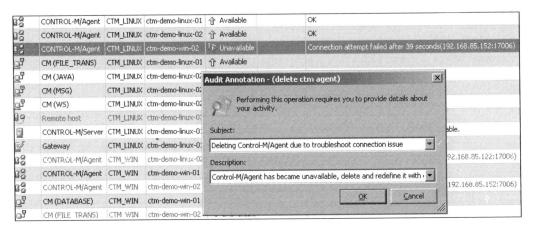

Producing auditing report

Auditing related data, stored in Control-M/EM database, is to be viewed via the reporting facility. The auditing report type is located under the general category. We can define the time frame, select audit type and audit operation to be shown on the report, and create filters from fields that are available in the reporting data.

Once the report is saved as a template, we can schedule the report as a job to run at a fixed interval according to the **Days to retain audit information** value (that is, run the report before the automatic cleanup happens).

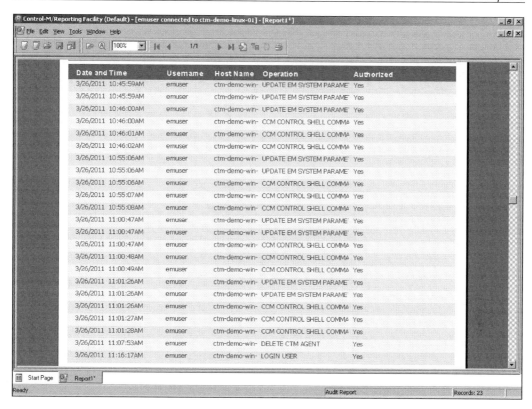

Control-M mirroring and failover

Moving on from the topic of security, now let's have a look at how to use Control-M mirroring and failover to prevent Control-M outages that are caused by major operating system problem or hardware failures.

We have discussed the concept and options available to build a high availability Control-M environment in *Chapter 3, Building the Control-M Infrastructure*. Based on what we know so far, we will create a mirroring database and failover standby for our Control-M/Server running on `ctm-srv-uat-01`. In this section, we will be focusing on the manual way to trigger failovers. The steps we are going to perform can be automated by using integration provided with BMC PATROL KM for Control-M or other third-party applications to call the related Control-M/Server scripts.

Pre-implementation tasks

In order to use Control-M mirroring and failover to achieve application-level HA, we need to install another Control-M/Server and database on a separate host as the standby. The two machines should be identical or at least offer similar performance and capacity, and located in different geographical location with a stable network connection between them. During events of outage, based on the scenario we either let the primary Control-M/Server to use the mirrored database or in case of a total failover we let it use the standby Control-M/Server.

In order for the solution to work smoothly, there are a number of configuration items that need to be matched between the two Control-M/Servers, and some additional configurations are required for the secondary Control-M/Server to communicate with Control-M/Agents and Agentless remote hosts.

Installing and configuring the secondary Control-M/Server

For our environment, we decided to install a new Control-M/Server on host `ctm-demo-linux-02` as a standby for existing Control-M/Server running on `ctm-demo-linux-01`. To have a successful implementation, we should have the following list ready before starting the installation:

- The standby host (`ctm-demo-linux-02`) must meet all Control-M/Server pre-installation requirements
- The standby host should have the same firewall configuration as the primary host (`ctm-demo-linux-01`), to allow communication with Control-M/EM and Control-M/Agents
- The primary Control-M/Server needs to have access to the standby host's database listener port (firewall configuration).

Since the installation process has no difference to a normal Control-M/Server installation, we will skip the details in this section. However, while installing the secondary Control-M/Server, we need to make sure the following are the same as the primary Control-M/Server:

- System date and time
- Control-M/Server Database size
- Server-to-Agent port number and default Agent-to-Server port number (default: 7005 and 7006)
- Control-M/Server CA port number (default: 2369)
- Control-M/EM port number (default: 2370 and 2371)

After the installation, we need to configure the following items to match the settings of the primary Control-M/Server:

- Security related (if applicable)
  - ○ User Exit settings (parameters in `config.dat` file and script in `<Control-M/Server home dir>/ctm_server/ue_exit`)
  - ○ SSL configurations (under `<Control-M/Server home dir>/ctm_server/data/SSL`)
  - ○ Agent-side Control-M/Server utility privileges (files under `<Control-M/Server home dir>/ctm_server/data/AGPERMIT_UTILS`)

- Others (if applicable)
  - ○ Time zone file (content of `<Control-M/Server home dir >/ctm_server/data/TimeZone.dat`)
  - ○ Remedy settings (under `<Control-M/Server home dir >/ctm_server/data/Remedy`)

In our environment, we have already got a Control-M/Agent running on `ctm-demo-linux-02`. We can shut down that Agent and use the default one that came with the secondary Control-M/Server instead. The existing Agent on `ctm-demo-linux-02` needs to be shut down before the installation starts (to release the 7006 Server-to-Agent port), otherwise the default Agent will be automatically configured with a different Server-to-Agent port number.

Configuring Control-M/Agents

For security reasons, Control-M/Agents are designed to only allow job submission from specified Control-M/Server hosts. The eligible Control-M/Server's hostname is entered during Agent installation as the only Primary Control-M/Server host. Other Control-M/Servers will not be able to communicate with the Agent. If they send a discovery request to the Agent, the Agent will return with an error message **Control-M/Server is not authorized**. When implementing failover Control-M/Server, we need to make sure all Control-M/Agent hosts that are known by the primary Control-M/Server can also work with the secondary Control-M/Server. In order to achieve this, we can define the secondary Control-M/Server as the Agent's **Authorized Control-M/Server Hosts**.

Use the existing Agent on `ctm-demo-win-02` as an example; we can add the secondary Control-M/Server (on host `ctm-demo-linux-02`) as its **Authorized Control-M/ Server** by visiting the Agent's properties from CCM (right-click on the agent and select **Properties**). In the **Properties** window, we enter the secondary Control-M/Server hostname into the **Authorized Servers** field after the existing value and with a comma between the two (without space)–**ctm-demo-linux-01,ctm-demo-linux-02**. By doing so, the Control-M/Agent will allow job submission from `ctm-demo-linux-02` during failover. We had to enter the value manually. The secondary Control-M/Server is not defined in CCM and therefore it is not shown in the down arrow. It will take a few minutes for the change to take effect once it is submitted.

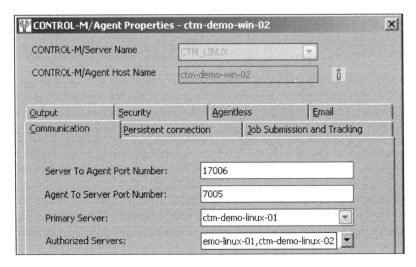

Any Control-M/Server stored in the **Authorized Control-M/Server Hosts** list will be able to submit jobs to the Agent. If the Control-M/Server host added to the **Authorized Control-M/Server** field is not a failover of primary, the Control-M/ Agent will technically allow job submissions from the Control-M/Server if other settings such as connection type and port numbers are also matching. However, this is not allowed because Control-M/Agent is designed to work with one Control-M/ Server at a time and the additional authorized server has to be a failover of the primary (that is, using the same database data). Otherwise, the Control-M/Agent may get confused during job tracking when jobs sent from different Control-M/ Servers have the same job Order ID.

Testing the secondary Control-M/Server

Before the mirroring is initialized, the secondary Control-M can be freely switched on and off. It doesn't take too much effort to execute a test job on-the-fly by using the `ctmcreate` utility just to make sure the secondary Control-M/Server is able to submit jobs and track jobs. Once the mirroring is initialized, all data stored in the secondary Control-M/Server's database will be replaced with the primary Control-M/Server database's data.

We run the `ctmcreate` utility (as Control-M/Server user) with minimal parameters to create a job that runs the `ls` command as the Control-M/Server user (because we didn't specify table, application, and group name; Control-M/Server will generate the job with its default values).

- `ctmcreate –JOBNAME test -TASKTYPE COMMAND -OWNER ctmsrv -CMDLINE ls -NODEGRP ctm-demo-linux-02`

Since this Control-M/Server is not accessible from GUI, we can track the job's execution outcome by using the `ctmpsm` utility. In the utility, we go to 1) List All to display the details of active jobs. We should see our job **test** with **STATE Post proc** and **STATUS OK**. We can view the job's **Sysout** by entering letter **J** followed by the job's order ID.

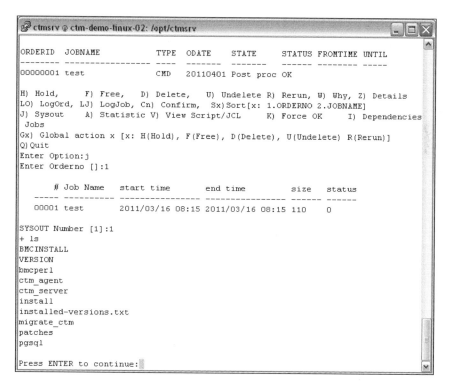

Initializing mirroring and failover

Once all pre-requisites are met and the secondary Control-M/Server is confirmed OK, we can go ahead and shut down the secondary Control-M/Server's CA process and server processes by running the `shut_ca` and `shut_ctm` utilities from the command line. We can double confirm the processes are down by running the `ps -ef | grep ctmsrv` command and make sure the PostgreSQL database processes are still running. The secondary Control-M/Server needs to be set to the **Initialize Failover** state before we initialize mirroring. This is done by going to **ctm_menu** | **3 - Database Mirroring** | **6 - Initialize Failover**. This step will backup some default data from the Control-M/Server database, which will be used if failover is ever started.

Now, come back to the primary Control-M/Server, we first use the same method to shut down its CA process and server processes (or change the desired state of the Control-M/Server to down from CCM). Then start the `ctm_menu` utility from the command line as a Control-M/Server user to configure mirroring.

In `ctm_menu`, we select **3 - Database Mirroring** | **2 - Initialize Mirroring**. The utility will ask if we want to build the mirror database from scratch or copy to an existing database. Since there is a database with the same structure that has already been created by the secondary Control-M/Server installation, we can select **Copy to an existing database** and enter the secondary Control-M/Server's database parameters. By doing so, all data in the secondary Control-M/Server's database will be overwritten.

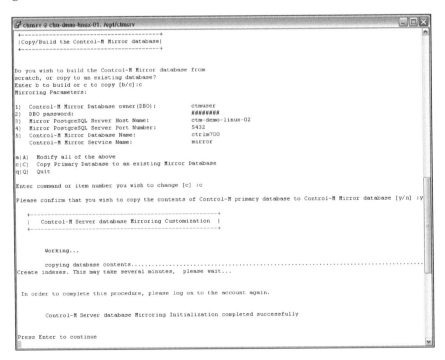

Once the initialization process is completed, we need to log off and log on the primary Control-M/Server's user account for the environment variables to take effect.

We can check the mirroring status at any time from **ctm_menu | 3 - Database Mirroring | 1 - Check Mirroring Status**. The possible outputs are: **Mirroring is enabled**, **Mirroring is damaged**, and **Mirroring is disabled**. Of course, our expected output is the first one. In order to re-initialize mirroring, the mirroring status has to be damaged or disabled.

 With **Build the mirror database from scratch** option, we are required to enter two additional parameters: database SA password and database directory full path.

We are now safe to start the primary Control-M/Server processes together with the CA process. When the mirroring is enabled, starting the secondary Control-M/Server is strictly prohibited. To avoid starting the processes by mistake, we can rename the start_ca and start_ctm scripts and rename them back when failover is required.

Switching to mirroring and failover

During an emergency, if the problem is only related to the primary database we can continue using the primary Control-M/Server with the mirrored database. If the problem is affecting the entire system of primary Control-M/Server, we should then consider performing the Control-M/Server failover.

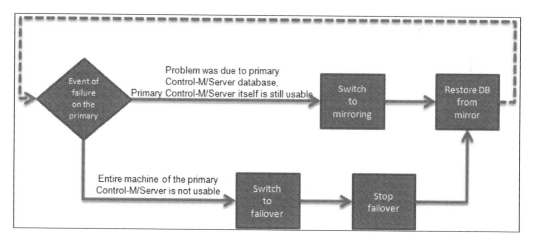

Switching over to mirroring

Switching over to mirroring database requires the following steps:

- Shut down primary Control-M/Server's CA and server processes by issuing the `shut_ca` and `shut_ctm` commands.

- In the primary Control-M/Server's `ctm_menu`, select **3 - Database Mirroring | 4 – Use Mirror Database**, enter **Y** to confirm.

- Log off and log on the primary Control-M/Server user and restart CA and the server processes. Once the primary Control-M/Server is started successfully, it will run with the mirrored database.

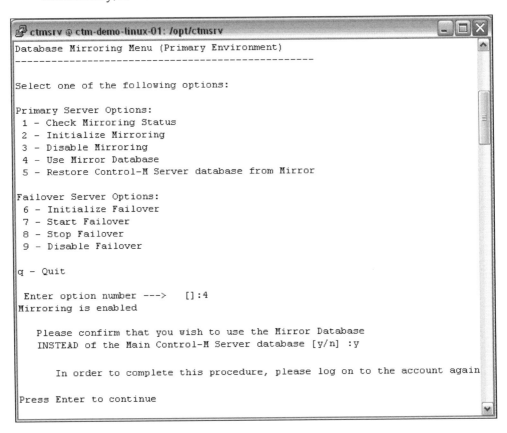

Switching over to failover

Switching over to failover Control-M/Server and mirrored database requires the following steps:

- Check and make sure the primary Control-M/Server's CA and server processes are down by using the `ps -ef` command or `show_ca` and `show_ctm` commands, if not shut them down by issuing the `shut_ca` and `shut_ctm` commands.

- In the secondary Control-M/Server's `ctm_menu`, select **3 - Database Mirroring** | **7 - Start Failover**, enter **Y** to confirm.

- Log off and log on the secondary Control-M/Server user and restart the CA and server processes. Once the secondary Control-M/Server is started successfully, it will take over job submission and track from where the primary Control-M/Server left off.

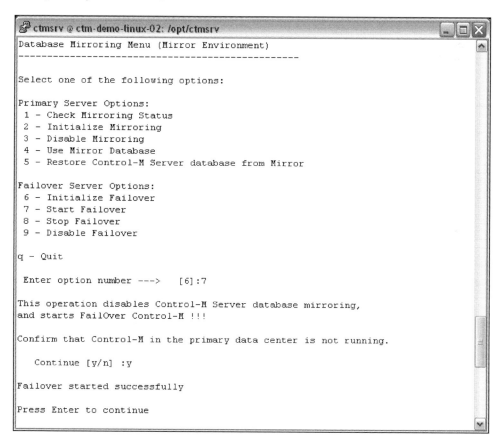

```
ctmsrv @ ctm-demo-linux-02: /opt/ctmsrv
Database Mirroring Menu (Mirror Environment)
-----------------------------------------------

Select one of the following options:

Primary Server Options:
 1 - Check Mirroring Status
 2 - Initialize Mirroring
 3 - Disable Mirroring
 4 - Use Mirror Database
 5 - Restore Control-M Server database from Mirror

Failover Server Options:
 6 - Initialize Failover
 7 - Start Failover
 8 - Stop Failover
 9 - Disable Failover

q - Quit

 Enter option number --->   [6]:7

This operation disables Control-M Server database mirroring,
and starts FailOver Control-M !!!

Confirm that Control-M in the primary data center is not running.

   Continue [y/n] :y

Failover started successfully

Press Enter to continue
```

In order for us to be able to monitor and interact with jobs during failover, we need to modify the datacenter parameter to allow the gateway to talk with Control-M/ Server on `ctm-demo-linux-02`. Back to CCM, in the datacenter's properties, we need to update the **Communication Host** to the secondary Control-M/Server hostname.

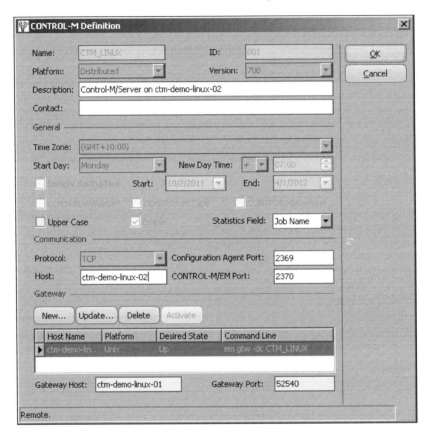

Recovering from mirroring and failover

Once the problem on the primary Control-M/Server host is fixed, we need to convert back from the mirroring database to primary database or disable failover on the secondary Control-M/Server. This should be done as soon as the primary host is ready because there is no data redundancy when running off the mirrored database.

Recovering from mirroring

If the primary Control-M/Server is running with the mirrored database, the following steps are required to convert back to the primary database:

- Shut down primary Control-M/Server's CA and server processes by issuing the shut_ca and shut_ctm commands.

- In the primary Control-M/Server's ctm_menu, select **3 - Database Mirroring | 5 - Restore Control-M Server database from Mirror**, enter **Y** to confirm.

- Log off and log on the primary Control-M/Server user and restart CA and server processes. Once the primary Control-M/Server is started successfully, it will run with the primary database again (with mirroring enabled).

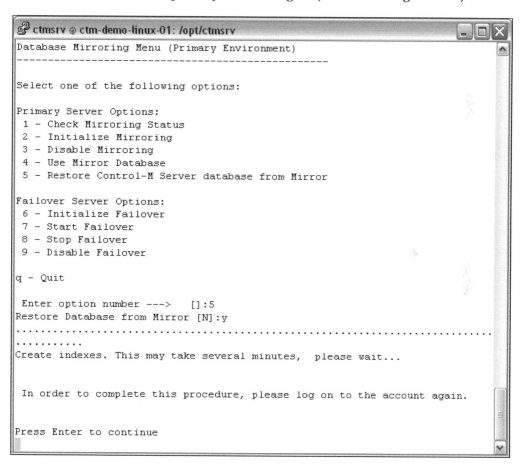

Recovering from failover

If the secondary Control-M/Server is currently active, the following steps are required to stop failover and convert back to the primary Control-M/Server and database:

- Shut down secondary Control-M/Server's CA and server processes by issuing the shut_ca and shut_ctm commands.

- In the secondary Control-M/Server's ctm_menu, select **3 - Database Mirroring | 8 - Stop Failover**, enter **Y** to confirm.

- In the primary Control-M/Server's ctm_menu, select **3 - Database Mirroring | 5 - Restore Control-M Server database from Mirror**, enter **Y** to confirm.

- Log off and log on the primary Control-M/Server user and restart CA and server processes. Once the primary Control-M/Server is started successfully, it will run with the primary database again (with mirroring enabled).

- In CCM, change the datacenter's **Communication Host** back to the primary Control-M/Server's hostname.

Perfecting Control-M

As passionate Control-M administrators, we just cannot leave the Control-M running in production with all the default settings; we will try our best to figure out the configurations and tunings that can be done to make it close to perfect in every aspect. People may argue that it is something good to have but not 100 percent necessary in reality. Well, it may not be necessary for a site that only runs the same 200 jobs everyday, but it definitely makes noticeable difference if it is a reasonable sized environment with a large amount of users and running complex batch flows.

Talks around Control-M best practices and fine tuning can go pages after pages. In this section, we will be focusing on two major topics—housekeeping and NDP turning, plus highlighting some worth-to-consider features.

Housekeeping

If we walk to an existing Control-M customer site, it is guaranteed that we will see a small group of jobs running daily to perform all kinds of housekeeping activities for Control-M itself. It is important to have these jobs running especially for large and busy sites, as unofficial statistics show, a noticeable amount of Control-M issues were simply caused by a lack of housekeeping.

The housekeeping jobs are grouped into the following categories:

- Active environment related
- Database related
- Filesystem related
- Component status checking

Active environment-related housekeeping

We need to perform a number of necessary activities daily to maintain the active environment. In minimum, these activities are Control-M job statistic average calculation, historical statistic average cleaning, and job condition cleaning. There are also other activities carried out by NDP by default, which will be talked about in the NDP tuning section.

Statistic average calculation

Control-M/Server records the statistics of every job's successful execution, including its start time, finish time, duration, and CPU time. Control-M/EM gets a copy of the data and automatically compiles statistic average for each job, therefore we can see each job's average elapsed time from the GUI (right-click on a job and select **Statistics**) and estimate the **Total runtime for path** in the **Critical Path** feature. The calculation results are also used by EM components, such as BIM and Forecast for their internal calculation.

Apart from facilities on the EM side, Control-M/Server itself may also need to access the statistic average data such as when job contains When Exectime +/-n% in PostProc. However, Control-M/Server doesn't automatically perform the calculation and cannot go to EM to request the information.

ctmjsa is a Control-M/Server utility that calculates the average runtime and standard deviation for each job (also known as statistic summary) based on the available data within the date range we specified in the command-line arguments, for example ctmjsa <from date> <to date> (the date is in yyyymmddhhmmss format). By leveraging the excellent scheduling feature of Control-M, we can define the utility as a command job to be executed right after NDP each day. However, instead of specifying the date range in the command line, we normally would run the utility as ctmjsa "*" for calculation based on all available data. In this case, we will not miss out any jobs that did not have statistical data within the specified date range (that is, all execution dates of the job were outside the range).

Historical statistic average cleaning

Once we have the statistical average calculation job scheduled, every time it executes a new result will be inserted into the Control-M/Server database for each job included in the calculation (that is, replacing the pervious calculation result, if any). For jobs that no longer run, its average data will be stored forever even though the job definition itself was removed from Control-M.

Control-M provided a utility called `ctmstats` for deleting (and listing) statistic average historical data. The utility allows us to specify the date range for the data to be deleted, for example, `ctmstats –delete <from date> <to date>` (the date is in yyyymmddhhmmss format). When scheduled as a job, we can use the Autoedit facility to calculate the `from date` and `to date` and then pass the two values to the utility as arguments. For example, if we want to remove any statistic average data that is older than 30 days, we can perform the calculation in an Autoedit variable—`%%TEMPVARIABLE = %%$CALCDATE %%$DATE -30` and including the "hhmmss" within another variable using the `.` string concatenation operator— `%%TODATE = %%TEMPVARIABLE.000000`. As such, we can specify the command line of the job as `ctmstats –delete 20000101000000 %%TODATE` (we define a date before Control-M/Server was built as the `from date`, in this case we guarantee all historical statistic average data before the `to date` is removed). This job can be scheduled either before or after the new statistic average calculation job (that is, use job condition to build the dependency). In best practice, we might want to make sure that the yearly jobs' average statistical data is not removed before the job's next execution; as such we would specify the date range to allow anything older than 1 year + 31 days to be removed.

Job condition cleaning

Upon a job's successful execution, out-condition(s) defined in the job will be generated and stored in Control-M/Server database for its dependent jobs to use. These conditions will only get removed 1 day less than 1 year later from the day they were added. Speaking from experience, letting old conditions stay in the active environment not only takes up a lot of database space, more importantly it may cause the gateway download to fail if the amount is too large. For our peace of mind, it is worth remembering to clean out old conditions regularly.

 If a gateway download fails, it will repeat the download process again and again until it is successful. During the download, the Control-M/Server is in suspended mode, therefore no jobs can be scheduled.

Like what we did in our file processing job flow, by defining used conditions as the dependent jobs' out-condition with a - sign, they will get removed as soon as the dependent job ends as OK. This way of defining jobs is the best practice but may not be suitable for all situations, such as we don't know which dependent job should be deleted, the condition when it is required by more than one jobs at different times or on different days.

The `ctmcontb` utility we mentioned at the beginning of the chapter can be defined as a daily job for deleting old conditions. The syntax of the command for such action is `ctmcontb -DELETEFROM <condition name> <from date> <to date>`. When we scheduled it as a daily-housekeeping job, we can specify * as the `condition name` argument therefore, all conditions within the date range will be deleted rather than an individual one. For the date range, because condition's date only has date and month (without year), for best result we would specify the `from date` as tomorrow's date and `to date` as a date in the past (that is, today's date minus the number of days we want to keep). By doing so, the utility will perform two deletions, one from `tomorrow` to 1231 and one from 0101 to `date in the past`.

Again we can use the Autoedit facility to calculate the value of `from date` and `to date`. For example, if we want to keep two days worth of conditions, we can calculate the date range based on the job's `odate`:

```
%%TEMPTOMORROW = %%CALCDATE %%ODATE +1
%%TEMPPAST = %%CALCDATE %%ODATE -2
```

And then use the `%%SUBSTR` Autoedit function to remove the year digits from the string:

```
%%TOMORROW = %%SUBSTR %%TEMPTOMORROW 3 4
%%PAST = %%SUBSTR %%TEMPPAST 3 4
```

Finally, the job command will be:

```
ctmcontb -DELETEFROM "*" %%TOMORROW %%PAST
```

The number of days to the conditions should be based on how jobs are designed in Control-M. On one hand, we need to make sure the date range is big enough to cover the requirement of all jobs—we do not want to delete a number of conditions from (dated) 2 days ago and find out that there are jobs ordered today which still require them as in-conditions. On the other hand, we should build standards to make sure jobs are not designed to have in-conditions that are extremely old—maybe there's a reason behind it, but is it reasonable and what would be an alternative way to achieve it?

To get the full benefit of this daily housekeeping job, it is recommended to run the job before NDP, so the gateway download after NDP will only download minimal number of conditions. This can shorten the download time and reduce the chance of download failure. Scheduling job before NDP can be achieved simply by giving the job a `From time`. The job start time should be early enough so it can finish well before NDP starts (for example, starts 1 hour prior to NDP). Letting the job (utility) to run during NDP can cause serious problems to Control-M/Server; it is worthwhile to build a late shout into the jobs, so when it is delayed someone can be notified and can kill the job before NDP starts.

For environments that have been running for a while but never had condition cleaning, it is safer to run the utility from the command line and delete old conditions month-by-month. After scheduling it as a job and running it for a while, we can adjust its start time based on the job's statistic average.

Exporting Control-M/Server Log (IOALOG/ctmlog)

By default, Control-M/Server logs (IOALOG/ctmlog) older than two days are removed automatically during NDP. For most users they would like to keep the data much more than two days in case it is needed for troubleshooting or future reference. Control-M/Server allows us to increase the number of days `ctmlog` is to be kept, however it is not efficient to store such static data in the database for too long. Also, given that the amount of `ctmlog` generated per day can be surprisingly huge if the number of daily jobs and/or number of executions of each job is large.

Rather than keeping weeks and months worth of `ctmlog` in the database, we can dump the log in to text files by using the `ctmlog` utility. With the utility, we are required to provide the timeframe of the `ctmlog` to be exported together with the output filename and path. The syntax for such purpose is `ctmlog list <from date> <from time> <to date> <to time> <file name and path>` (the date is in yyyymmdd format and time is in hhmm format). We can define the job to run daily around quite a period before NDP to export portion of `ctmlog` that is going to be deleted on that day. For example, if the Control-M/Server is currently set to delete `ctmlog` order than two days*, we would define the job to export `ctmlog` created two days ago, before it gets cleaned during NDP.

*We will look at how to change the parameter value in the next section.

Same as what we did earlier, the utility's arguments `from date` and `to date` can be calculated by Autoedit facilities. We can also include the date as part of the export file name. For example, the variable and the job command line can be:

```
%%EXPORTDATE = %%$CALCDATE %%$DATE -2
ctmlog list %%EXPORTDATE 0000 %%EXPORTDATE 2359 ~/OURSTUFF/ctmlog_
export/logdump_%%EXPORTDATE.txt
```

Database-related housekeeping

There are a number of checking, optimizing, and backup-related activities recommended to be performed regularly for Control-M databases. Users selectively choose the ones that fit their purpose to be included as part of the daily housekeeping jobs.

Control-M/Server database statistics calculation

Control-M/Server comes with a utility called `ctmdbopt` for calculating database table and index statistics. The accuracy of the statistics is critical for database performance because it is what the database optimizer uses for optimizing queries. Data within Control-M/Server database can be dynamic, therefore it is recommended to run the utility once a day.

The utility doesn't require any parameters. We can simply schedule it as a command job to run before and after NDP each day. For extremely busy Control-M/Servers, the user may decide to run the utility many times a day as a cyclic job.

Control-M/Server health check

We can perform Control-M/Server database checking regularly by running the `ctmdbcheck` utility. The syntax of the utility for PostgreSQL database is `ctmdbcheck <general threshold%>` (the `general threshold` argument is optional). The utility will check the database status, its size and data usage. If the database's usage is over the general threshold specified, a message will be displayed similar to **Warning: DB is more than x% full**. The `ctmdbcheck` utility is not recommended to run during a busy time. If we want to check the database usage more frequently, we can use the `ctmdbspace` utility as an alternative. This utility only checks the database usage without worrying about the status. The syntax goes like this `ctmdbspace -limit <amount>`. The utility will end with non-zero return code, if the database usage is higher than the limit amount specified. For databases with auto-grow data files, we can check the disk space directly by using `ctmdisksapce` utility. The syntax of the command is `ctmdiskspace -limit <amount> {%|K|M} -path <path to be checked>`.

For Control-M/Servers that have database mirroring configured, we can run the `ctmcheckmirror` utility to detect the status of mirroring. The output of the utility indicates if mirroring is enabled, disabled, or damaged.

These utilities can be triggered at regular intervals by the Control-M/Server Watchdog facility. In order to use this feature, we need to enable it by specifying a set of WD user exit parameters in Control-M/Server's config.dat configuration file. In fact, there are three WD user exits that are enabled by default — ctmdiskspace, ctmdbspace, and a perl script that backs up nodes status parameters. A WD user exit template is provided within the config.dat file; we can simply copy and modify the template within the config.dat file to create additional WD user exits. Another parameter called WD_ERROR_HANDLER_SCRIPT_FILE defines how an error should be handled, by default it points to a script that comes with the Control-M/Server installation that performs a shout to the Control-M/EM alert window. We can create our own script and get the parameter re-pointed (modifications to the config.dat file requires Control-M/Server reboot or IPC refresh).

 On Control-M/EM, we can check the database free space by using the db_check_space utility.

Some users may want to schedule these health-checking utilities as Control-M jobs instead of getting better visibility of their execution. In this case, we can disable the corresponding WE user exit and depend on the utility's output warning message to define the Step code within the job and perform the Do statement (for example, send e-mail or force a job) when the specific string is detected in the job sysout.

Control-M/Server database hot backup

Control-M/Server provides two utilities for database backup — ctmdbbck and ctm_backup_bcp. We will focus on the first utility, because it allows backup to happen while Control-M/Server is running, so it is called hot backup. With the second utility, we can only run it when Control-M/Serve and CA processes are down, therefore hard to be automated as a job.

The ctmdbbck utility has two pre-requisites when used with PostgreSQL database. First, the PostgreSQL database must be owned by the Control-M/Server. Second, database archive mode must be set to **On** in order to enable hot backup.

Database archive mode can be enabled from **ctm_menu** | **2 - Database Menu** | **1 – Management** | **3 - Set Database Archive Mode**. We need to set the value of the parameter to **ON**, specify the archive directory (the directory has to be empty), and then restart the database server to let the change take effect.

Once the database archive mode is enabled, we can go ahead to define the job to trigger the `ctmdbbck` utility. The syntax for the utility is `ctmdbbck -p<SA password> -d<backup directory> -m H`. The `-m H` means the backup will be performed in hot backup mode. The `-p<SA password>` argument can be replaced with `-f<password file name and path>` so we don't have to show the database SA password in the job. For example, `ctmdbbck -f/opt/ctmsrv/OURSTUFF/ ctmdbbck.cfg -d/opt/ctmsrv/OURSTUFF/ctmdbbck_data/ -m H`. Before the backup utility gets triggered, we need to make sure the backup directory is empty; and after the backup is completed successfully, we would move the backup dump file to a remote location and at the same time delete database archive files that are more than one day old to free up disk space. The utility also provides us the option to specify `-m C` for a cold backup.

Data backup by `ctmdbbck` can be restored by `ctmdbrst` utility. `ctmdbrst` also requires the database to be owned by Control-M/Server. The restore operation can be performed in hot and cold mode and the command syntax is the same as `ctmdbbck`. The utility will restore the database to the state when the backup takes place, after that we can apply each archive log generated after the backup to let the database go back to the state right before the failure occurs.

Control-M/EM data backup

In some way, we could say the data stored in Control-M/EM database is not considered as critical as Control-M/Server. This is true if we are referring to the active environment because Control-M/Server holds the real status of the active environment in AJF; if the information is lost, we simply don't know where the job executions are upto and potentially have to reload all jobs for that New Day and start from the beginning (this can be a disaster event). Whereas with Control-M/EM, if the active environment data is lost, we can simply force a gateway download to build a new Active Net. However, apart from the active environment, other information stored in Control-M/EM may not be retrieved from Control-M/Server and they are extremely critical. Think about user authentication definitions, job statistics stored by forecast, auditing data, alerts, defined viewpoints and filters, and so on. And last but not the least, users may decide to store unfinished job drafts in EM without uploading to the Control-M/Server.

Well, there are indeed more moving parts for us to worry about, however luckily Control-M/EM provides features within the `em util` to look after all our backup needs mentioned earlier.

The em util utility allows us to export/import information stored in Control-M/EM database into/from an ASCII file. The export/import can be done for each specific data type (for example, job definition, calendar, user authorization, and so on) or all types at once. The utility arguments can get very complicated, so rather than going into the details we will look at the basic usage—export/import all data types into a file. The syntax for such purpose is em util -D <database> -U <username> -P <password> [-export | -import] -type all -file <filename and path>. The -D <database> is the target database name, the -U <username> -P <password> are the DBO username and password. For example, em util -D ctm-demo-linux-01 -U emuser -P Passw0rd -export -type all -file /opt/ctmem/OURSTUFF/em_backup/em_backup.dat. With this utility, we can also replace the -U <username> -P <password> with -pf <password file name>.

When the password file is used, both username and password are required to be specified in the file in the following format:

```
user=<username>
password=<password>
```

We can also perform database hot backup and restore on EM, if database archive mode is turned on. The utility to perform these tasks are—DBUHotBackup and DBUHotResotre. On the other hand, cold backup and restore can be performed by utility DBUColdBackup and DBUColdRestore. These tasks can also be performed in command-line interactive mode via em_database-menu utility.

Filesystem-related housekeeping

Control-M/EM stores general log files in its ~/ctm_em/log directory. Control-M/Server stores log files for the current active Control-M/Server processes in ~/ctm_server/proclog directory and moves them into ~/ctm_server/proclog.save each time during restart. Similar to Control-M/Server, Control-M/Agent stores all log files in its proclog directory (standalone Control-M/Agent: ~/ctm/proclog, default Agent on Control-M/Server: ~/ctm_agent/proclog). These directories can build up after a while and the log file size can be large if process debugging has been turned on previously*. Too many files in these directories can use up the disk space and may even cause Control-M application to behave strangely. Even debug logs are rotated automatically and there are parameters that can be set to control the size and number of generations of the debug log. The size of these logs can still be large and the last set of files, before debugging was turned off, will not be removed automatically.

It is good to have checking mechanism (for example, using BMC Patrol) to ensure there are not too many files in these directories. A more proactive way would be using Control-M jobs to remove or archive files that are older than x days from these directories, but at the same time we should ensure the files that we are deleting are old enough and not still being accessed by active processes.

For Control-M/EM, we can pay more attention to gateway logs because a new gateway log gets generated for each datacenter every time when a new download is performed (format of the log file: `gtw_log.<datacenter name>.<date>.<#of download>`). For other components, a new log only gets generated when the process is restarted.

For Control-M/Server's `proclog` directory, it is important to keep the `SYSTEM_LOG` file and all process log files (format of the log file: `<process name>.<process id>.log`) untouched, but we can freely remove or archive logs generated by utilities and any log files within the `proclog.save` directory. (Alternatively, we can manually clean these files via **ctm_menu | 9. Troubleshooting | 11. Erase proclog Files**.)

For Control-M/Agents, there are log files generated for each process and utilities, such as `AG/AS_<process id>.log` process logs, `shut_ag_<process id>`, or `ag_ping_<process id>` utility logs, we can simply schedule jobs to clean the aged ones.

Component status checking

Control-M/EM's Configuration Server and Agent provide status checking and automatic restart for Control-M/EM components. Control-M/Server also has the CA process to work with Control-M/EM to check and maintain the state of Control-M/Server. The questions are, what if the Configuration Server and Agents are down? Who will be monitoring them and maintaining their status? In fact, there are many components that are not covered but Control-M provides utilities for the checking. These components are databases, Naming Server, Control-M/EM Configuration Server (CMS), Control-M/EM Configuration Agent, and Control-M/Server Configuration Agent (CA).

Control-M/Server database checking is done by `ctmdbcheck` utility that we discussed earlier. For Control-M/EM, we have already used the utility in the pervious chapter—`check_server`. This tiny utility returns **ok** if the database is running or returns **not_ok** if the database is not running. This utility may not be very useful if the Control-M/Server shares the database with Control-M/EM, simply because it is impossible for Control-M/Server to submit the checking job if the shared database is down.

For the other three Control-M/EM components, the corresponding utilities are as follows:

- Naming server: `check_ns_daemon`
- Control-M/EM Configuration Server (CMS): `check_cms`
- Control-M/EM Configuration Agent: `check_config_agent`

For Control-M/Server CA process the checking utility is `show_ca`.

NDP tuning

As we mentioned in the earlier chapters, Control-M/Server stays in suspended mode while NDP is running, and no job can be scheduled during this period. Depending on the size of the environment, the time can go from 1-2 minutes to more than 10 minutes. As the number of jobs starts to grow and the environment becomes busier, the duration is likely to increase.

In a small environment with statistics jobs, this daily process gap may not cause any significant impact. However, in busy environments that already have a tight batch processing window, this may create a rappel effect that can potentially cause job delays. More importantly, as event-driven scheduling becomes common, users are expecting an instant response to the event they triggered. With this processing gap, such a response may get delayed or events are missed out (if jobs are not designed to cope with this processing gap).

It is the Control-M administrator's responsibility to make this outage as short as possible. In order to do that, we will have to perform tunings on each Control-M/Server's NDP and that begins with understanding what is exactly happening during NDP.

Things happening during NDP

Control-M/Server performs a series of housekeeping tasks during NDP to refresh itself to be ready for the New Day. When we talked about *Lifecycle of a job* in *Chapter 4, Create and Manage Batch Flows with Control-M GUI*, we have already introduced two tasks performed during NDP—active job ordering and cleaning. In addition to those two tasks, Control-M/Server also performs `ctmlog` (IOALOG) cleanup, job statistics cleanup, old conditions deletion, as well as removing of old `sysouts` on each connected Control-M/Agent.

Throughout the day, the Control-M/Server CE process will regularly check the system time with the New Day time set in Control-M/Server. Once the system time matches the New Day time, the CE and CS processes will perform the NDP tasks in the following sequence:

- CE: Suspend Control-M/Server processes
- CE: Send stop-link signal to Control-M/EM
- CE: Update Control-M Date to the new system date
- CE: Remove old `ctmlog`
- CE: Remove old Job statistic information
- CS: Send Sysout cleanup trigger to each connected Control-M/Agent
- CE: Delete conditions
- CS: Active job ordering
- CS: Active job cleaning
- CE: Send start-link signal to Control-M/EM
- CE: Start Control-M/Server processes
- CS/CE: AJF download to Control-M/EM

The steps mentioned earlier are recorded in `ctmlog`.

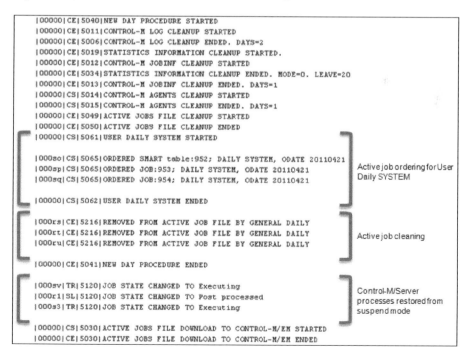

Removing old ctmlog

Control-M/Server CE process performs `ctmlog` cleaning according to the value set in `Maximum Days Retained by CONTROL-M Log` parameter. Any log entries older than the specified number of days will be removed during the cleaning process.

The parameter can be set from **ctm_menu | 5 – Parameter Customization | 5 - Parameter Customization | 3 - System Parameters and Shout Destination Tables | 2) System Parameters | n) Next Page | 6) Maximum Days Retained by CONTROL-M Log" or "ctmsys | 3 - System Parameters and Shout Destination Tables | 2) System Parameters | n) Next Page | 6) Maximum Days Retained by CONTROL-M Log**

Removing old job statistic information

There are two options on how Control-M/Server performs job statistic record cleaning:

- **Method 1:** Deletion based on the number of statistic records to be kept for each job (default: 20 records), for example, if a job has 25 statistical records, the latest 20 records will be kept regardless how old these records are
- **Method 2:** Deletion based on the number of days of statistic information to be kept for each job (default: 20 days), for example, if a job has 25 records and all of them are more than 20 days old, all 25 records will be removed

The cleaning method is decided by the parameter `RUNINF_PURGE_MODE`. By default the parameter's value is set to `0` for Method 1. In order to switch to Method 2, we need to add the parameter into Control-M/Server configuration file—`config.dat <control-m/server home>/ctm_server/data/config.dat` with a value `1`—`RUNINF_PURGE_MODE 1` (recycle Control-M/Server or IPC refresh is required).

The number of records to be kept for Method 1 is controlled by the `RUNINF_PURGE_LIMIT` parameter. Default value is 20—last 20 records are kept for each unique job. In order to increase or decrease the value, we need to add the parameter into Control-M/Server's configuration file, for example `RUNINF_PURGE_LIMIT 25` (range 1 - 2^31). If Method 2 is used, the number of days of statistical information to be kept is according to the value of the `Maximum Days Retained by CONTROL-M Log` parameter.

Sending Sysout cleanup trigger

Job sysout cleaning is according to the `Maximum Days to Retain Sysout Files` parameter. Control-M/Server CS process initiates the trigger to all Control-M/Agents defined under the Control-M/Server, Agents that are available at the time will receive the trigger and perform the cleaning. By default, any job sysout that is older than one day will be removed.

The parameter can be set from **ctm_menu | 5 – Parameter Customization | 5 - Parameter Customization | 3 - System Parameters and Shout Destination Tables | 2) System Parameters | n) Next Page | 6) Maximum Days to Retain Sysout Files** or **ctmsys | 3 - System Parameters and Shout Destination Tables | 2) System Parameters | n) Next Page | 6) Maximum Days to Retain Sysout Files**.

Deleting conditions

By default, conditions that exist in the active environment with date matching the coming Control-M date will be removed (control-M date + 1). This ensures that jobs are only to be triggered when their in-conditions are newly generated rather than by the old condition in the AJF that matches the job's in-condition's name and date.

For example, if the coming Control-M date is 11/12/2011, the newly ordered job B with in-condition name A-ENDEDOK and date odate will only get triggered if job A with the same odate ended ok and posted its out-condition A-ENDEDOK. The condition's date will be resolved to 11/12, therefore job B will be triggered. However, in case these two jobs ran last year on the same day and the condition hasn't been removed, job B will get submitted as soon as it is ordered.

After active job cleaning and ordering

We are already familiar with the details of active job cleaning and ordering from *Chapter 4, Create and Manage Batch Flows with Control-M GUI*. So let's have a look at what will happen after these two activities.

Once active job ordering is completed, the NDP of the day is considered as finished. Imminently, all Control-M/Server processes will be wakening up and start to perform its usual tasks—submit jobs, update resources, add/remove conditions, track job status, and so on. A Start-link signal will be sent to Control-M/EM at the same time to re-establish the connection.

Once the connection is re-established, Control-M/Server will send a download request to Control-M/EM to re-synchronize the active environment. The corresponding Control-M/EM gateway will convert the pervious Active Net into Archived Net and create a new (Active) Net to hold data of the new active environment. On the Control-M/Server side, all processes will go into suspend mode again until the download is complete.

Shortening NDP

Now we are familiar with the tasks performed during NDP, so how can we shorten the duration to allow Control-M/Server spend less in the suspend mode and therefore reduce the impact to active jobs? Optimizing the database is one way, but wouldn't it be good if we can take some of the tasks out from NDP and perform them while Control-M/Server is running as normal? Well, that is absolutely possible.

Among those tasks, we will be looking at how to remove old job statistic information and order new jobs outside NDP. Before we talk about these two, let's have a look at why other tasks are to be kept in NDP.

- **Remove old ctmlog**: We don't need to worry too much about this one, as it doesn't take very long to execute. This is because each day's ctmlog is stored in a separate database table (that is, CMR_IOALOG_n). Therefore, Control-M/Server cleans them by quickly truncating the table rather than doing row deletion.

- **Send Sysout cleanup trigger**: On Control-M/Server side, it only sends out the request then imminently continues onto the next task; the real work is performed by each Control-M/Agent.

- **Delete conditions**: The condition deletion housekeeping job we defined earlier would have removed the coming day's conditions prior to NDP.

- **Active Job Cleaning**: This step has to be performed during NDP, but usually it doesn't take too long to run.

Removing old job statistic information outside NDP

We are allowed to perform remove old job statistic information task outside NDP. In order to do so, we first need to add parameter STATISTICS_CLEANUP_IN_NEWDAY into Control-M/Server's configuration file config.dat with value N, for example, STATISTICS_CLEANUP_IN_NEWDAY N. Once Control-M/Server is restarted or IPC is refreshed after the change, job statistic information cleaning will no longer happen during NDP.

Performing the cleaning outside NDP is done by the utility ctmruninf. The utility offers two deletion methods—delete and purge. With the delete option, the utility removes any job statistic information within the date range we specified (in yyyymmddhhmmss format). Whereas the purge option is the same as the default way of cleaning during NDP. It is based on the number of statistical records to be kept that was specified in the parameter RUNINF_PURGE_LIMIT (default: 20 records).

Schedule a job to trigger `ctmruninf -purge` once a day before NDP is equivalent to the cleaning process during NDP. However, in best practice, we would schedule two jobs in the following way to get the best result:

- Run `ctmruninf -purge` many times a day (for example, define as a cyclic job to run every one hour).

- Run `ctmruninf -delete <from date> <to date>` before NDP (for example, clean anything more than 13-months old).

Cyclic jobs that run frequently will produce a large amount of statistical information. The extra amount of information doesn't provide any benefit, but takes up a lot of database space. By running the purge job many times a day, we can keep the volume down. It is especially useful for large sites with huge number of cyclic jobs (for example, think if 5,000 out of the total 35,000 jobs are cyclic jobs, each of them runs every 5 minutes on an average).

By running the purge job, we will keep each job's statistic information down to the `RUNINF_PURGE_LIMIT`. However, this will never delete the statistic information for jobs that no longer run. If the environment's job turnover is large, (that is, always retire old jobs and create new jobs for execution) we will have a lot of irrelevant job statistic information that stays in the Control-M/Server database forever. By running a deletion with a date range (that is, 60 days or 90 days old), statistic information associated to jobs that are no longer run will always be removed after a certain number of days.

Ordering jobs outside NDP

By taking job ordering outside of NDP, we can significantly shorten the duration of NDP especially when the number of jobs is large. It also effectively reduces the length of post-NDP gateway download time simply because there will be much fewer items in the active environment that are to be downloaded.

Recall what we have discussed in *Chapter 4, Create and Manage Batch Flows with Control-M GUI*, Control-M has two ways to automate job ordering. One is via the user daily SYSTEM, which is performed during NDP. The other method is by running `ctmudly` utility after NDP for user-defined user dailies.

In order to use `ctmudly` utility to order jobs, we need to:

- Define job tables with a user daily name other than SYSTEM

- Schedule command job to run `ctmudly` at the desired time with an argument that indicates the user daily name

- Schedule command job to run the `ctmudchk` utility to check if all jobs within the user daily that are eligible to run on that day have been ordered successfully

- Define the `ctmudly` job's table as user daily `SYSTEM`

Use our `DAILY_MAINT` job table as an example; we first load up the table in Control-M Desktop to change the table's user daily name from `SYSTEM` to `DAILYMAINT` (user daily name as to be equal or less than 10 characters). Once the job table is written to EM and uploaded to Control-M/Server, we can open a new Workspace to define the `ctmudly` job.

The basic syntax of `ctmudly` for job ordering is `ctmudly -DAILY_NAME <user daily name>`. During execution, the `ctmudly` utility examines the scheduling criteria of each job within the tables that have the matching user daily name (that is, multiple job tables can have the same user daily name) and order those jobs that are eligible to run on that day with the original scheduling date (odate). For our `DAILY_MAINT` job table we would specify the command line as `ctmudly -DAILY_NAME DAILYMAINT`.

We can customize the scheduling date in the `ctmudly` command by using the argument `-odate <date>` (the date is in yyyymmdd format) and define when the job should run in the argument `-odate_option {value_date|run_date}`.

With the `run_date` option, the ordered jobs will only run when the specified job scheduling date comes, for example, `-odate 20110601 -odate_option run_date` means the job will get ordered with scheduling date 20110601 regardless of the actual Control-M date, but will stay in AJF with `wait for ODATE` state and only begin to run when that day comes.

With the `value_date` parameter, the ordered jobs will ignore what their scheduling date is and start to run on the date that they are ordered. For example, `-odate 20110601 -odate_option value_date` means the job will get ordered with scheduling date 20110601 and begins to run on that day (if other pre-requisites are met).

The `ctmudchk` utility should be scheduled to run right after the `ctmudly` job to check the user daily. We have options either to list unordered jobs or try to reorder them on the spot. It is not necessary but gives us a peace of mind— it ensures all jobs to be ordered are ordered. The syntax for this utility is `ctmudchk -DAILY <user daily name> -ACTION <LIST | ORDER>`. This utility also allows the `-ODATE` and `-ODATE_OPTION` argument to decide how the missing jobs are to be ordered.

Once we have the `ctmudly` job and the `ctmudchk` job defined, we need to specify its job table as user daily `SYSTEM` so it can be ordered during NDP. In reality, instead of defining all jobs into one user daily, users normally group jobs into multiple user dailies, for example, according to the application name of the jobs.

Other configurations items

In this section, we will highlight some small configuration items that Control-M administrators should be aware of. In fact, there are a lot more parameter items within each of the Control-M component. We cannot cover everything in this section but this will at least help you get an idea and focus on the most necessary ones.

Control-M/EM: MaxOldDay and MaxOldTotal

The `MaxOldDay` parameter determines how many days of archived nets for each datacenter are to be stored in Control-M/EM database (default: two days). By having a larger number, the users will be able to view more historical Viewpoints but the downside is that it can take up a lot of database space, especially when the number of datacenter is large (imagine 30 days of archived Viewpoints for 15 datacenters equal to 450 sets of archived nets stored in Control-M/EM database all the time). When we change the value of this parameter, we also should consider changing Control-M/Server's `Maximum Days Retained by CONTROL-M Log` and `Maximum Days to Retain Sysout Files` parameters accordingly, therefore when the user is in the archived Viewpoint he/she is also able to view the job's `sysout` and `log`.

The `MaxOldTotal` parameter determines the total number of archived nets to be held by Control-M/EM for each datacenter (Default: 4). Apart from the downloading that happens after each day's NDP, Control-M/Server may trigger downloads during any time of the day under special circumstances. It is not something that should happen, but may happen when:

- The link between Control-M/Server and EM has been broken for a period of time, (Control-M/Server or gateway was shutdown or the network between the two was down). During that time, Control-M/Server has accumulated too many updates yet to be sent to Control-M/EM. As such, Control-M/Server decided to trigger a download to re-sync the whole active environment.

- A user can manually trigger a `force download` from **ctm_menu | 9 – Troubleshooting | 16 - Force Download**.

The value of `MaxOldTotal` should always be larger than `MaxOldDay`. Otherwise, if a download is triggered for a datacenter during the middle of the day, the oldest archived net for that datacenter will be replaced.

These two parameters are to be changed from **CCM | Tools | System Configuration | Control-M/EM System Parameters | Advanced**.

Control-M/EM: Default AverageTime

Sometimes we might have new jobs included in the BIM or Forecast calculation that has no statistical information. By default, Control-M gives these jobs a default average run time of 5 minutes. This value is global to the entire Control-M environment and is determined by the Control-M/EM parameter `DefaultAverageTime` (in HH:MM format). We can change the default average to a more realistic value (for example, 1 minute) to make the calculation more accurate.

This parameter is also to be changed from **CCM | Tools | System Configuration | Control-M/EM System Parameters | Advanced**. If BIM is installed, there are two of these parameters one with Type **BIM** and one with type **general**.

Control-M/Server: New Day Time

Control-M/Server New day time is to be changed from Control-M/Server utility `ctm_menu` or `ctmsys` — **ctm_menu | 5 – Parameter Customization | 5 - Parameter Customization | 3 - System Parameters and Shout Destination Tables | 2) System Parameters | 1) Day Time" or "ctmsys | 3 - System Parameters and Shot Destination Tables | 2) System Parameters | 1) Day Time**.

The date is to be specified in HHMM format, with a + or - sign at the beginning. The + sign means the Control-M date will always be behind the actual calendar date, that is the Control-M date will be updated to the current calendar date after NDP. For example, if we set to +0700, from 07:00:00 a.m. on the 20th of January to 06:59:59 a.m. on the 21st of January, the Control-M date will stay as the 20th and only get updated after NDP at 07:00:00 a.m. on the 21st of January. With the - sign it is the opposite way; Control-M date will always be in front of the actual calendar day. For the same example, if we set to -0700, from 07:00:00 a.m. on the 20th of January to 06:59:59 a.m. on the 21st of January, the Control-M date will be the 21st and will get updated to 22nd after NDP at 07:00:00 a.m. on the 21st of January.

It is common to see users use the + sign for their New Day time. The change takes effect as soon as we exit the menu options back to the command line.

Control-M/Server: Simple Mail Transfer Protocol parameters

Control-M has the feature to send out e-mail notifications. In order to enable this feature, we need to configure the mail server parameters. It is to be configured via **ctm_menu | 5 - Parameter Customization | 6 - Simple Mail Transfer Protocol Parameters**.

In the settings, we are required to enter:

- **SMTP Server (Relay) Name**: Name of the SMTP server
- **Sender Email**: E-mail address of the sender
- **Port Number**: SMTP server port number
- **Sender Friendly Name**: Alias name of the sender that appears on the e-mail
- **Reply-To Email**: Reply address of the sent e-mail (the sender's e-mail address is used by default)

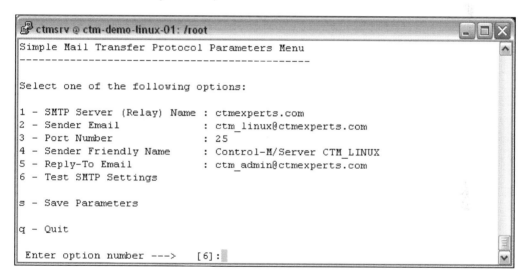

Once the parameters are saved, we will be able to define the e-mail addresses in the Control-M jobs to be the notification delivery destination.

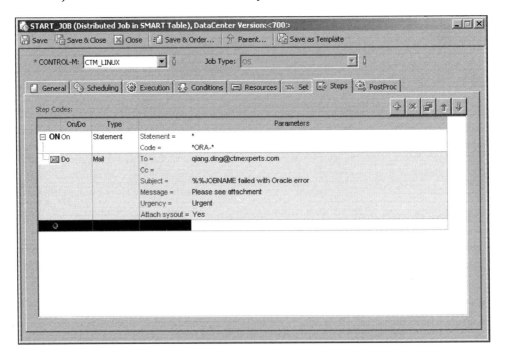

Control-M/Server: shout destination tables

In our previously defined jobs, we used ECS as the only shout destination. We can also define our own shout destinations for each Control-M/Server from **CCM | Tools | Alerts | Shout Destinations Manager**.

A shout destination table is a collection of shout destinations. For each Control-M/ Server, we are allowed to define multiple shout destination tables but only one can be active at any given time. Within each shout destination table, we can create different shout destinations with logical names. The available types are:

- **User:** Control-M GUI user.
- **Mail:** E-mail address.
- **Console**: System console.
- **Log**: Control-M/Server log (ctmlog/IOALOG).
- **Program**: A script or a program.
- **Control-M/EM**: Control-M/EM Alert Window.
- **Terminal:** Unix/Linux terminal.

There's also an **Address** field to be specified for each shout destination. The selections are **Server** and **Agent**. By selecting **Server**, the shout will be performed on the Control-M/Server. Whereas when **Agent** is selected, the shout will be performed on the job's execution agent. For example, **Destination: terminal** with **Address: Agent** means the shout will appear on the Control-M/Agent machine's terminal session.

It is recommended that you define each user's e-mail as shout destination rather than specify the e-mail address in the job directly. In this case, if the person left or had a job role change, we only need to change the destination once rather than modify each associated job.

Summary

By now, we have the full potential to become a real Control-M expert. The reason we say "potential" is because real-world experience is rather critical for mastering any skill.

In this chapter, we again focused on the administration side of Control-M but in more depth. We started with looking at command-line utilities that can be used to affect the active environment. More importantly, we reviewed different security options provided by Control-M, as well as a demonstration of Control-M mirroring and failover. Once we had secured the environment, we took one step further by perfecting the Control-M environment.

As people always say, "*once things on hand are perfectly done, a new door will open up in front*". We have come a long way from planning and building the Control-M environment, to building all different kinds of job flows, to securing and perfecting the environment. We have done an excellent job and it is now time to progress into the golden age—workload automation.

8
Road to Workload Automation

Welcome to the final chapter of this book. People buy books all the time, but don't always make it to the last chapter. I am impressed you are still reading. Assuming you did not jump from the first chapter, by now you must be able to confidently design and build a simple Control-M environment, schedule jobs to meet business requirements as well as manage the environment and identify areas for improvement. By acquiring all this knowledge and skill, we are technically qualified to enter into the Golden Age, that is, Workload Automation.

In this chapter, we have to get back from administration to scheduling. We will be using Control-M add-on features to enhance the file processing batch flow to make it true real-time parallel processing and meet the expectation of loosely-coupled integration with external applications. This is followed by enhancing the overall processing performance by using node group technology and making it more flexible and dynamic with the workload automation approach. Finally, we will enter into the ideal world, that is, break the physical machine limitations by taking our file processing workload into the cloud.

By the end of this chapter, you will be able to:

- Integrate Control-M with external applications by using features from Control-M Business Process Integration Suite.
- Perform parallel processing and dynamic scheduling.
- Master the Control-M node group technology, and define and manage workloads.
- Use the Control-M for Cloud control module to integrate Control-M with virtual machine resources.

Integrating Control-M with business processes

In *Chapter 6, Advanced Batch Scheduling and Management*, we modified our original file processing job flow from the traditional fixed-time batch processing mode into event-triggered processing by using Control-M's built-in file watch mechanism. By doing so, generated source files get processed immediately, rather than having to wait for the next batch window and the amount of data to be dealt with is significantly reduced for each processing cycle. As a result, a dedicated batch window is no longer necessary and, from the business point of view, the processed data can get delivered to down flow clients in real-time.

As we are just about to sit back and relax, the IT architect in charge of enterprise integration delivers bad news that moving the processing away from Control-M is being considered for the following reasons:

- The current file watch mechanism requires an external system to generate the flag file. This is fine for Control-M but does not offer any reusability for other systems. Therefore, it doesn't fit into their big picture of enterprise integration, which is based on the so-called SOA design principles. Their intention is to re-design file processing purely to be web service-driven. In which case, it can be invoked by external systems through a standard interface and can be assembled along with different business processes according to dynamic business requirement.

- Currently, the processed records are archived into files and database tables. Control-M silently does the work in the background as the source file comes. External applications that need to process the information have no idea when the processing starts and completes. Therefore, even the mechanism is considered as real time processing, but doesn't mean the processed information will be delivered to its clients in real time.

- The processing has been modified into event triggering, but still is only able to process one set of files each time. In other words, it cannot perform multiple sets of source files in parallel during peak time and take full advantage of the high performance computing resource.

Today, this kind of request is becoming more and more frequent for certain types of processing. Instead of reinventing the wheel, we can sit down with the IT architect and application owner to look at how to achieve what they want by making minimal modification to the existing design, based on what Control-M is capable of. The bottom line is, some people can get really excited by new technologies but we need to remind them to keep calm and think about the implications of such dramatic changes, such as the challenges those in operations will face with the new tool, and the hidden cost and risk of a complete migration, especially for large and complex systems.

After analyzing their requirements in detail and re-visiting what Control-M can offer, we came up with the following improvement proposal, based on Control-M's standard features and the add-on component we implemented earlier, that is, Business Process Integration Suite.

- Throw away the current file watch mechanism. Utilize Control-M Business Process Integration interfaces to allow the file processing job flow to be exposed to external systems through Web Services. In this case, without knowing the internal details of the file processing, and without modifying anything on Control-M side, any other system can easily invoke the file processing using the standard SOAP request or even integrate it into their business rules using BPEL.

- Modify the current job design. Instead of processing a set of source files each time, a new instance of the file processing job flow gets invoked by external request to process a single source file. The source file name is to be specified as part of the request. Each job flow instance only gets executed once to process the submitted source file (that is, no more cyclic). However, multiple job flow instances can run concurrently to process different source file processing requests that were generated around the similar time.

- For records generated on the Linux side, we will push them into a message queue. In this case, the down flow client (that is, message consumer) can get the process records instantly. If the consumer isn't available at the time the message is sent, the queue will maintain the message until the consumer is available again. From a Control-M point of view, we don't need to worry which consumer receives the processed records and what they will do with it. Alternatively, we can push records to a message topic; by doing so, whoever requires the information can subscribe to the topic and get the information in real time.

- For records generated on the Windows side, after inserting the data into a database Web Services get triggered so that whoever needs the information will get notified and thus can immediately access the database to retrieve the data.

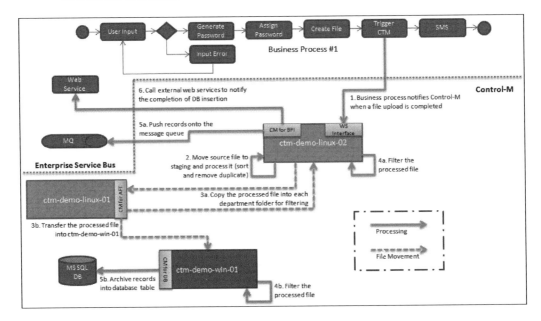

Sounds exciting? Let's get our hands dirty!

Building the environment

In order to have a fully workable testing environment, we need some third-party software packages installed and configured to interact with Control-M. The ones we selected here are all downloadable from the Internet and are relatively easy to install. More experienced users can use tools of their own choice as long as they are compatible with each other and, more importantly, supported by Control-M Business Process Integration Suite.

 For compatibility information, please check the latest release notes of Control-M BPI Suite.

The selected tools are:

- **OpenESB 2.3:** A Java-based open source Enterprise Service Bus platform based on GlassFish Open Source Java application server. In our demo scenario, it will be used for hosting web services.

- **NetBean IDE 6.9.1:** An integrated software development environment that came with the OpenESB installation for designing and deploying applications (in our case, the web application) into OpenESB.

- **JBoss AS 6:** Open Source Java EE-based application server provides us a message queue destination.

- **soapUI 3.6.1:** An Open Source Web Service GUI testing tool. We use it to test our Control-M BPI web service interface.

> Please note that message queue and web services features come with both OpenESB and JBoss. In a real-world scenario, it is more likely that an organization has a single platform. Two different distributions of Java application servers are used in this book because we want to experience the different options. Again, people may argue that there are better ways to archive the file processing requirements, but the primary goal of the book is to demonstrate the features of Control-M in the simplest way.

We have to implement these software packages on a machine that is reachable by Control-M hosts on the network. To make our life easier, we will let them share the existing virtual machines with our Control-M environment.

Machine type	Hostname	Component installed	Default listening ports
Windows	`ctm-demo-win-02`	OpenESB	TCP port 4848 for admin console, and TCP port 8080 for web services access
Windows	`ctm-demo-win-02`	NetBean IDE	NA
Linux	`ctm-demo-linux-02`	JBoss AS	TCP port 8080 for admin console, and TCP port 1099 for message queue access
Windows	`ctm-demo-win-01`	soapUI	NA

We will not go through the details of the installation in this book, the installation should be straightforward and a large amount of installation- and configuration-related information can be found online. The demos we are using here are all based on default installation parameters.

The OpenESB installation contains both GlassFish server and NetBean IDE. After installation, we can start the OpenESB GlassFish server through the NetBeans IDE **Services** window. OpenESB web admin console is accessible from `http://ctm-demo-win-02:4848/`, once the server is successfully started.

JBoss AS doesn't require installation, once the downloaded folder is placed into the desired directory, `chmod`, the `./bin/run.sh` command turns into owner executable and runs it as root, with arguments `-Djboss.as.deployment.ondemand=false` `-b 0.0.0.0` to start the service. The first argument is telling JBoss AS to not use on-demand JMX and JBossWS consoles deployment, to reduce server boot time. The second argument is telling JBoss AS to bind the service onto all available network interfaces. For example:

- `# pwd`
- `/usr/java/jboss-6.0.0.Final/bin`
- `# ./run.sh -Djboss.as.deployment.ondemand=false -b 0.0.0.0`

Once the command is executed, we can access its admin console through `http://ctm-demo-linux-02:8080/admin-console/`. We will notice that some of the features listed on the admin console web page are similar to what we have seen in OpenESB.

The soapUI installation, just like any other Windows application installation, doesn't require any additional configuration or customization.

Interacting with BPI interfaces

For now, let's leave the new toys for a while and go back to the Control-M side to explore the BPI interfaces. In this section, we will configure the BPI interfaces to allow external applications to order Control-M jobs through web services.

Technical background

Control-M BPI interfaces allow external applications to send requests to Control-M to trigger a number of actions that normally happen at a fixed time or have to be performed manually through GUI. Majority of the available request types are related to the active environment, such as order/force jobs, hold/free/re-run/kill/force ok jobs, track job execution, add/remove conditions, create/delete job definitions, upload scheduling tables, and so on. By having such powerful features, Control-M is able to offer more options when it comes to handling external events and, therefore, bridge the gap between batch processing and real-time systems.

Having said that, there are other ways available within Control-M to achieve a similar outcome, such as using Control-M command line utilities or EMAPI. In fact many Control-M sites today are using command line utilities to make their batch environment more event-driven. The most popular ones are `ctmcontb` (add, remove conditions), `ctmorder` (order jobs into the active environment), `ctmcreate` (directly create jobs in the active environment). EMAPI is not widely used in normal environments, because it involves some degree of in-house software development and consequently requires ongoing maintenance.

The reason we decided to use the BPI interfaces for the file processing scenario is that it has encapsulated the complicity on the Control-M side by providing standard web service and a messaging interface for external systems to interact with. This is in line with the loosely-coupled, service-oriented enterprise integration big picture. By using these two interfaces, during interaction, external systems do not need to know the details of how the requests are handled on the backend by Control-M. Furthermore, in order for us to submit requests through the BPI interface, we do not need to leave any footprint on the Control-M environment and do not need to hardcode anything into the external systems either. Another good reason is that requests through BPI are now audited as part of Control-M/EM Auditing and controlled by Control-M/EM security. Using Control-M command-line utilities means the audit record will show that Control-M performed the action, rather than the actual requester. In order to limit what the utility can do, we have to have Control-M/Server security turned on, rather than BPI using Control-M/ security, which provides much more granularity.

Unlike the normal control modules, the BPI interface can be installed standalone, without a Control-M/Agent installation. Though, in our case, we installed the BPI interface in the Agent home directory on `ctm-demo-linux-02`, as part of the CM for BPI installation.

Defining an account

In the backend, the BPI interface, in fact, communicates with Control-M/EM through EMAPI. When a request gets initiated by an external application, the BPI interface will process the request and trigger the Control-M/EM's EMAPI to perform the action. Upon completion of the action, the EMAPI sends a response back to the BPI interface, and then the BPI interface will translate the request into standard message format (web service or messaging) and route it to the external application that initiated the request.

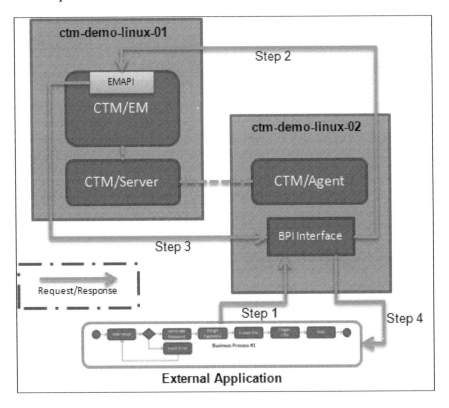

Not hard to figure out, in order for a request to be delivered and auctioned, we need to somehow inform the BPI interface which Control-M/EM we are going to communicate with; we also need to provide it with appropriate EM GUI user login credentials. Account utilities for these two interfaces are provided with the installation. They are located in the `<installation directory>/bin` directory and are called `ctmmsgapiacc` (for the messaging interface) and `ctmwsapiacc` (for the web services interface). In our environment, it is under the `/opt/ctmagent/CTM_BPI_ interface/bin` directory on `ctm-demo-linux-02`.

These utilities are GUI tools that require an X window session. In order to run them, we need to have the X window server running on the machine or on our workstation. We need to set the DISPLAY environment variable first, before running the utilities. In our case, we will set point DISPLAY to our workstation (where X window server is running) and invoke the `ctmwsapiacc` utility (so that we can use the web services interface).

```
root@ctm-demo-linux-02:~
[ctmagent@ctm-demo-linux-02 bin]$ pwd
/opt/ctmagent/CTM_BPI_interface/bin
[ctmagent@ctm-demo-linux-02 bin]$ ls
ctmmsgapiacc   show_ctmmsgapi   start_ctmmsgapi   stop_ctmmsgapi   upgrade_ifc.sh
ctmwsapiacc    show_ctmwsapi    start_ctmwsapi    stop_ctmwsapi
[ctmagent@ctm-demo-linux-02 bin]$ setenv DISPLAY 192.168.85.204:0.0
[ctmagent@ctm-demo-linux-02 bin]$ ./ctmwsapiacc
```

In the Web Service Account Management GUI window, once we navigate to **File | New Account** or click on the **New Account** icon, a pop-up window will ask for the following information:

- **General** tab - **Account Name**: Give a meaningful name to identify the account.
  - ° Our value: **FILE_PROCESSING**
- **General** tab - **Transport Protocol**: Can be HTTP or HTTPS.
  - ° Our value: **HTTP**
- **General** tab - **URL of Endpoint**: Where the web services will be published. Normally it is published with the default URL plus the account name we given.
  - ° Our value: `http://ctm-demo-linux-02:6060/ctmbpi/FILE_ PROCESSING`
- **EM Servers** tab - **Control-M/Enterprise Manager Configuration**: Which CTM/EM to connect. It requires the EM version, hostname and naming server port number for submitting requests (that is, it connects to Control-M/ EM through a GUI server as well as the GAS, for some requests).
  - ° Our value: **EM Version – 6.3.01** (this value is used for EM version 6.3.01 and above), EM Host – `ctm-demo-linux-01`, EM Port – 13075, GAS and GUI Server: `ctm-demo-linux-01` (address that is published in naming server)

- **EM Servers** tab - **Requests Authentication**: User credentials for logging on Control-EM in order to interact with EMAPI.
  - ○ Our value: **Automatic Sign In** – ticked (therefore avoid the need to include a user token for each request), EM User – emuser, EM Password - <the password> (For audit and security purposes it would be better to have a dedicated user. That way we know what it has done (audit) and can control what it is allowed to do (security). In a real scenario, we would probably have a few users, for different applications, making requests to the web Service interface).
- **EM Servers** tab - **Retries Configuration**: How many connection retries (to EM) should be performed and time between retries. Increase these values if getting timeout errors while submitting requests.
  - ○ Our value: keep the default value unless you face connection problems in the future.

After we click on the **Apply** button at the bottom right corner, the utility will ask if we want to activate the account. Once it is activated, we will be able to click the **Validate…** button at the bottom left corner to test the account. If all details are correct, we should see a dialog box that says **Account test completed successfully**. And, once we close the **New Account** window, we should see that a new entry has been created with the status **Up**.

Triggering job ordering

We don't have the file processing job flow ready to be ordered by web services yet. However, there's no problem with ordering any existing job flow from web services. Our file processing job flow is not ready because we still have to make modifications to it to allow parallel processing. Before we start modifying the job flow, let's give the BPI interface a try first. Please keep in mind that, for what we want to do with the BPI interface (that is, ordering jobs), we do not need to test it with specific jobs; if it works with a testing job, it should work with our real job flow too, given that security settings on the Control-M/EM allow it.

The BPI interface allows us to order individual jobs or many jobs within the same SMART table. As we will be ordering jobs at SMART table-level, we are going to simulate the scenario by creating two dummy jobs with minimal scheduling definitions in a SMART table under datacenter `CTM_LINUX`. The two jobs are called `TEST-01` and `TEST-02` and are stored under the same SMART table, called `TEST`. Once we have the job defined, written to EM database, and successfully uploaded to Control-M/Server, we can go ahead and create a new project in soapUI to perform the ordering.

Creating a project in soapUI

When creating a new project in soapUI, we are required to enter a new project name and the initial WSDL location. We can find the WSDL file `EMAPI.wsdl` under `<Agent Home Directory>/CTM_BPI_Interface/conf/6.3.01`. Once the WSDL file is copied over to the local drive and selected for the new project in soapUI, we will see a list of items showing up in the tree view under the project name we have given. These items are the available operations we can send to Control-M. We can create a new request by right-clicking on an item and selecting **New request**. In our case, we will create a request called **TEST** under operation **order_force**.

By double-clicking on the request we will see the SOAP message template showing up in a new window that appears on the right hand side. In that SOAP message, we need to specify the details of the job or table we would like to order. In our case, we can safely delete most of the lines that have `<!--Optional:-->` written above and only specify values for the following fields:

```
<soapenv:Envelope xmlns:soapenv="http://schemas.xmlsoap.org/soap/
envelope/" xmlns:sch="http://www.bmc.com/ctmem/schema630">
   <soapenv:Header/>
   <soapenv:Body>
      <sch:request_order_force>
         <sch:user_token>?</sch:user_token>
         <sch:force_it>yes</sch:force_it>
         <sch:control_m>CTM_LINUX</sch:control_m>
```

```
            <sch:table_name>TEST</sch:table_name>
            <sch:odate>ODAT</sch:odate>
        </sch:request_order_force>
    </soapenv:Body>
</soapenv:Envelope>
```

We do not need to specify anything for `user_token` because, during account creation we chose **Automatic Sign In**; however, we cannot remove the line from our SOAP message because it is not an optional field (the `?` character can be kept or removed). For the `force_it` field, we specified `yes` because we want to force the jobs into active environment (that is, we did not define any scheduling criteria during creating the SMART group and jobs).

Sending SOAP request to the web services

Before we click on the green **Run** button on the top, we need to make sure that:

- The web service interface has already been started. We can check its status by logging on to the Agent machine and issuing `show_ctmwsapi` command-line utility under the `<BPI home dir>/bin` directory. If the web services interface is not running, we can start it by issuing the command `start_ctmwsapi`.

- In soapUI, make sure the `endpoint` of the request is pointed to the URL defined during account creation. In our case, it is `http://ctm-demo-linux-02:6060/ctmapi/FILE_PROCESSING`.

```
root@ctm-demo-linux-02:/opt/ctmagent/ctm/scripts
[ctmagent@ctm-demo-linux-02 bin]$ pwd
/opt/ctmagent/CTM_BPI_interface/bin
[ctmagent@ctm-demo-linux-02 bin]$ ./show_ctmwsapi
CONTROL-M Business Process Integration Interface - Web Services server is not running.
[ctmagent@ctm-demo-linux-02 bin]$ ./start_ctmwsapi
Starting CONTROL-M Business Process Integration Interface - Web Services server...
nohup: appending output to `nohup.out'
.\c
.\c

CONTROL-M Business Process Integration Interface - Web Services server started successfully. PID: 7717
[ctmagent@ctm-demo-linux-02 bin]$
```

Once the request is executed from the EM GUI client, we should see both the jobs appear in the active environment. On the soapUI side, it should display the SOAP reply from Control-M in XML format, which indicates that two jobs, together with the SMART table, are ordered. The SOAP reply should look like this:

```
<SOAP-ENV:Envelope xmlns:SOAP-ENV="http://schemas.xmlsoap.org/
soap/envelope/">
    <SOAP-ENV:Body>
        <ctmem:response_poll_order_force xmlns:ctmem="http://www.
bmc.com/ctmem/schema630">
```

```
            <ctmem:status>OK</ctmem:status>
            <ctmem:jobs>
                <ctmem:job>
                    <ctmem:status>OK</ctmem:status>
                    <ctmem:job_data>
                        <ctmem:order_id>00023k</ctmem:order_id>
                        <ctmem:job_name>TEST</ctmem:job_name>
                        <ctmem:ret_text>Job ordered</ctmem:ret_text>
                    </ctmem:job_data>
                </ctmem:job>
                <ctmem:job>
                    <ctmem:status>OK</ctmem:status>
                    <ctmem:job_data>
                        <ctmem:order_id>00023l</ctmem:order_id>
                        <ctmem:mem_name>TEST-01</ctmem:mem_name>
                        <ctmem:job_name>TEST/TEST-01</ctmem:job_name>
                        <ctmem:ret_text>Job ordered</ctmem:ret_text>
                    </ctmem:job_data>
                </ctmem:job>
                <ctmem:job>
                    <ctmem:status>OK</ctmem:status>
                    <ctmem:job_data>
                        <ctmem:order_id>00023m</ctmem:order_id>
                        <ctmem:mem_name>TEST-02</ctmem:mem_name>
                        <ctmem:job_name>TEST/TEST-02</ctmem:job_name>
                        <ctmem:ret_text>Job ordered</ctmem:ret_text>
                    </ctmem:job_data>
                </ctmem:job>
            </ctmem:jobs>
        </ctmem:response_poll_order_force>
    </SOAP-ENV:Body>
</SOAP-ENV:Envelope>
```

We will leave soapUI as it is for now and come back to it again when the file processing job flow is ready to be ordered.

Taking parallel processing to the next level

Now let's take a look at how to enable true parallel processing by allowing multiple identical file processing job flow instances to run concurrently to process different source files.

Merging the two file processing job flows

Currently, the file processing job flow is across two datacenters. We did this on purpose, previously, because we wanted to experience how global conditions work. To reduce confusion, from here on we will avoid the need for global conditions by combining all jobs into datacenter CTM_LINUX. This involves disassociating Control-M/Agents installed in ctm-demo-win-01 with datacenter CTM_WIN and associating them with datacenter CTM_LINUX, as well as updating the CONTROL-M field for all file processing job definitions into CTM_LINUX.

To redirect the Control-M/Agent, first we will disable the CTM_WIN Control-M/ Server from CCM by changing its **Desired State** to **Down**. Then, we will add ctm-demo-linux-01 into the **Authorized Control-M/Server Host** list of Control-M/ Agents running on ctm-demo-win-01. If we want to keep the CTM_WIN Control-M/Server running, we have to remove hostname ctm-demo-win-01 from the agent's **Authorized Control-M/Server Host** list to avoid potential job submission from two Control-M/Servers occurring at the same time. To bring the Agent alive in CTM_LINUX, we can either manually define it from CCM to make it appear under CTM_LINUX immediately or leave it for Control-M to discover automatically when a job is submitted. We do not need to worry about the Control-M/Agent on ctm-demo-win-02 because we have already installed a second Control-M/Agent on the host (instance: ctmagent2) to talk with the CTM_LINUX Control-M/Server.

For the job definition, we need to perform the following steps to bring them across to the CTM_LINUX datacenter:

- Load the AdvancedJobs SMART table and jobs from both datacenter CTM_LINUX and CTM_WIN into an empty Control-M/Desktop local workspace.

- Perform Find-and-Update to convert CONTROL-M jobs into datacenter CTM_LINUX and the Node ID/Group from blank* into ctm-demo-win-01. In **Find and Update** define Find as CONTROL-M, like we did in CTM_WIN. With Update CONTROL-M, assign CTM_LINUX and with Update Node ID/Group, assign ctm-demo-win-01.

- Remove DETECT_SourceFile job since the filewatch is no longer required. Also remove JOIN_SourceFiles job because, for each request there is only going to be one file processed.

- Combine the scripts of SORT_JoinedFile and REMOVE_Duplicate into one job called PROCESS_SourceFile.

- Create a condition between MOVE_SourceFiles and PROCESS_SourceFile.

- Perform Find-and-Update to remove cyclic definition within each job – in **Find and Update** define Find CONTROL-M like * with Update Cyclic assign FALSE.

- Remove the global condition prefix from the condition names between job FILETRANS_ProcessedFILe_LIN02toWIN01 and FILTER_Records_department-04/5/6.

- Delete the CLEAR_Staging job. In the coming section we will be talking about the changes in the filesystem directory structure clean staging right after each execution of the job flow is no longer required.

We need to update the jobs' Node ID/Group field because we originally left the field blank, so, the jobs will be running on the Windows Control-M/Server's default Agent. Since the job submissions are done by the Linux Control-M/Server, if we keep the field blank, these jobs will be submitted to the default Agent of the Linux Control-M/Server.

The JOIN_Records_department-01/2/3 jobs on the Linux processing side are to be removed from the processing flow. Instead, very soon, we will define message queue jobs, which will provide the processed records for the down flow systems in real time.

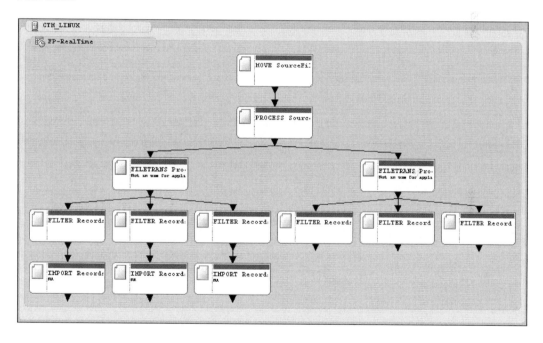

Before we move on to the next step, let's update the SMART table name into FP-RealTime and group name into ForthDemo. Let's also save it as a job draft or XML file, in case we lose it.

Enabling parallel processing

One of the most powerful features of Control-M is to allow identical job flow instances to run concurrently, without interfering with each other. By having this ability, the job execution host's machine resource can be utilized much more efficiently, thereby possibly reducing the total processing time during peak periods.

If we set up our file processing job flow to be able to have multiple instances running in parallel without interfering each other, we can potentially have hundreds and thousands of incoming files at the same time to process different source files, as long as the job execution machine can handle the actual processing workload. Earlier versions of the job flow can only process one set of source files at a time; even if the machine is only five percent utilized, other arriving source files still have to queue up and get processed in a first-come-first-serve fashion.

Adding table ID into condition names

Right now if we pick a job flow and order it twice into the active environment, we will notice from the GUI that the two job flow instances will be inter-connected in Control-M. Let's say the job flow has job **A** followed by job **B** linked below it. With multiple instances, if any **A** job finishes, all job **B** instances will get triggered because they are all defined with the same in-condition name and date, which will match up with the out-condition produced by the completed job **A** instance. As we can see at this stage, the parallel processing is not going very far.

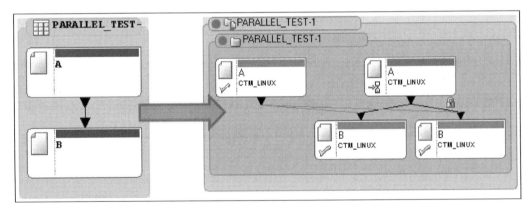

Not hard to imagine, the workaround to this behavior is to isolate the instances and somehow force jobs to only inter-connect to each other within their own instance. As we discussed in the earlier chapters, Control-M's SMART table has most of the properties a job would have, including an **Order ID**. This **Order ID** is given when the SMART table is ordered. If the same SMART table gets ordered many times, each of them will have a unique **Order ID**. For each SMART table instance, its **Order ID** gets stored within a table-level autoedit variable `%%TABLE_ID`. This variable is accessible by all jobs within the table instance. What does this mean to us? Well, we can let Control-M distinguish which instance a condition belongs to by embedding `%%TABLE_ID` in condition names. During runtime, the variable name will be converted into `Order ID*` of the SMART table instance to which the condition belongs. For example, a SMART table containing job definition with condition called `A-%%TABLE_ID-ENDED` got ordered twice with **Order ID 2898** and **2901**. As a result, the same condition in two instances will be converted into **A-2899-ENDED** and **A-2901-ENDED**.

[Order ID is resolved in base 10 format.]

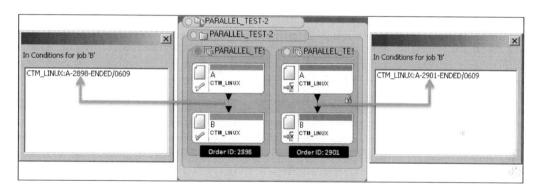

By including this **Order ID** as part of the condition name of all jobs within a SMART table, we will be able to have multiple identical job flows existing and running in the active environment concurrently, without having them inter-connected to each together. In addition, different SMART table instances are displayed separately in Active Environment.

The fastest and easiest way to update our file processing job flow is to export the entire job flow definition into a XML file, open it in a text edition and replace `-ENDED` with `-%%TABLE_ID-ENDED`. Once done, reopen the XML file in Control-M/ Desktop. Or, we can use the Control-M Desktop Find and Update feature's `Replace Substring` function to update all **In Conditions** and **Out Conditions** in two different update criteria.

Modifying the filesystem directory structure and job scripts

Modifying the file processing mechanism to be capable of parallel processing only at the Control-M level sometimes may not enough. Take our file processing job flow as an example; let's review how files are currently processed at the filesystem level. Recall what we have done in *Chapter 6, Advanced Batch Scheduling and Management*.

- Control-M's filewatch facility picks up the flag file, use the flag file's filename as an index to move the set of source files (that is, all files belonging to the set have the same prefix) into the staging directory.

- Control-M joins the source files into a single temporary file, sorts the records, and then removes any duplicate entries.

- The temporary file gets duplicated into each department folder on both Linux and Windows machines.

- After processing, files under the staging folder get removed.

As we can see, at the moment, if we let Control-M run multiple file processing job flows at the same time, the temporary file created by different job flow instances will overwrite each other during processing. To avoid this problem, we let the temporary file to be created with the source file's filename as prefix. In this case, the job flow instance will create a unique temporary file each time so nothing will get overwritten during parallel processing. For example, `SOURCE_CSV_SORTED.csv` will become `<source file name>-SOURCE_CSV_SORTED.csv`.

The filewatch was used to capture the source file name; we may wonder, after it is removed, how Control-M can know which source file is to be processed? Well, by using web service to order the job flow, the requester can specify the source file name as a SMART table-level Autoedit variable. In such cases, all jobs within the SMART table will be able to share the information, and accessibility is limited within the SMART table instance. We will name to this variable `%%SOURCEFILE_PREFIX`. For script jobs, we can pass the value to the script by associating the variable with a parameter Autoedit variable (that is, `PARM1` or `PARM2`). For command jobs, we can invoke the variable directly by including the it as part of the command line (for example, `echo %%SOURCEFILE_PREFIX`). For AFT jobs, we can include it as part of the job definition in the **Source File** field of the **FILE_TRAN** tab (for example, `/home/file_tran/staging/%%SOURCEFILE_PREFIX-SOURCE_CSV_NO-DUPLICATE.csv`).

In summary, we will be required to perform the following modifications to our jobs:

Tab	Field	Value
General	Job Name	`MOVE_SourceFiles`
General	Task Type	**Job**

General	Embedded Script Content	`#!/bin/sh`
		
		`mv /home/file_tran/source/$1.csv / home/file_tran/staging`

General	Description	**Move the source file specified in %%SOURCEFILE_PREFIX from source directory into staging directory**
Execution	Node ID/Group	`ctm-demo-linux-02`
Set	PARM1	`%%SOURCEFILE_PREFIX`
General	Job Name	`PROCESS_SourceFile`
General	Task Type	**Job**

General	Embedded Script Content	`#!/bin/sh`
		
		`sort /home/file_tran/staging/$1.csv > /home/file_tran/staging/$1-SOURCE_ CSV_SORTED.csv`
		
		`cat /home/file_tran/staging/$1- SOURCE_CSV_SORTED.csv
			uniq -u > / home/file_tran/staging/$1-SOURCE_ CSV_NO-DUPLICATE.csv`

General	Description	Sort records in the source file, remove duplicates
Execution	Node ID/Group	`ctm-demo-linux-02`
Set	PARM1	`%%SOURCEFILE_PREFIX`

General	Job Name	`FILETRANS_ProcessedFile_LIN02toWIN01`
		
		`FILETRANS_ProcessedFile_LIN02toLIN02`

General	Task Type	**Job (AFT CM)**
FILE_ TRANS	Source File Location	`/home/file_tran/ staging/%%SOURCEFILE_PREFIX-SOURCE_ CSV_NO-DUPLICATE.csv`
General	Description	**Transfer processed source files to each department directory**
Execution	Node ID/Group	`ctm-demo-linux-01`

Tab	Field	Value
General	**Job Name**	`FILTER_Records_department-01`
		`FILTER_Records_department-02`
		`FILTER_Records_department-03`
General	**Task Type**	**Job**
General	**Embedded Script Content**	`#!/bin/sh`
		`cat /home/file_tran/dest/$1/$3-SOURCE_CSV_NO-DUPLICATE.csv	grep "$2" >> /home/file_tran/dest/$1/$3-$1.csv`
		`rm /home/file_tran/dest/$1/$3-SOURCE_CSV_NO-DUPLICATE.csv`
General	**Description**	**Filter the file according to department name**
Execution	**Node ID/Group**	`ctm-demo-linux-02`
Set	**PARM1**	`<department name as sub-directory name>`
	PARM2	`<department name as search keyword>`
	PARM3	`%%SOURCEFILE_PREFIX`
General	**Job Name**	`FILTER_Records_department-04`
		`FILTER_Records_department-05`
		`FILTER_Records_department-06`
General	**Task Type**	**Job**
General	**Embedded Script Content**	`find %2 c:\file_tran\dest\%1\%3-SOURCE_CSV_NO-DUPLICATE.csv >> c:\file_tran\dest\%1\%3-%1.csv`
		`echo 'y'	del c:\file_tran\dest\%1\%3-SOURCE_CSV_NO-DUPLICATE.csv`
General	**Description**	**Filter the file according to department name**
Execution	**Node ID/Group**	`ctm-demo-linux-02`
Set	**PARM1**	`<department name as sub-directory name>`
	PARM2	`"<department name as search keyword>"`
	PARM3	`%%SOURCEFILE_PREFIX`

Tab	Field	Value
General	**Job Name**	`IMPORT_Records_department-04`
		`IMPORT_Records_department-05`
		`IMPORT_Records_department-06`
General	**Task Type**	**Job (Database CM)**
General	**Database Query Content**	`INSERT HISTORY_WIN`
		`FROM '%%IMPORT_FILE'`
		`WITH`
		`(`
		`FIRSTROW = 2,`
		`FIELDTERMINATOR = ',',`
		`ROWTERMINATOR = '\n'`
		`)`
		`GO`
General	**Description**	**Join records into a history file**
Execution	**Node ID/Group**	`ctm-demo-win-01`
Set	**DIRNAME**	`<department name as sub-directory name>`
	FILENAME	`%%SOURCEFILE_PREFIX -<department name>.csv`
	IMPORT_FILE	`C:\file_tran\ dest\%%DIRNAME.\%%FILENAME`

For job `FILTER_Records_department-04/5/6`, in order for its Windows script to resolve the department name keyword properly, we need to double quote the value of the `PARM2` Autoedit variable in the **Set** tab.

For job `IMPORT_Records_department-04/5/6`, when specifying the `IMPORT_FILE` Autoedit variable in the **Set** tab, we need to add a concatenate operator . in between `%%DIRNAME` and `\%%FILENAME`. This will avoid the two variables being resolved incorrectly because, without the `".",` Control-M will mistakenly try to resolve the two variables together as a single variable under a SMART table (that is, resolve `%%DIRNAME\%%FILENAME` as `%%\<SMART_table_name>\<var_name>`).

Updating the quantitative resource

After the Windows jobs have been brought over to CTM_LINUX datacenter, we need to modify the quantitative resource **DISK_IO** to be host-specific. By only increasing the quantity of **DISK_IO** resources, we cannot guarantee the resource will be evenly distributed between the Windows and Linux hosts during job submission. In our case, we will replace **DISK_IO** with **DISK_IO_WIN** and **DISK_IO_LINUX**, with a quantity of **10** each.

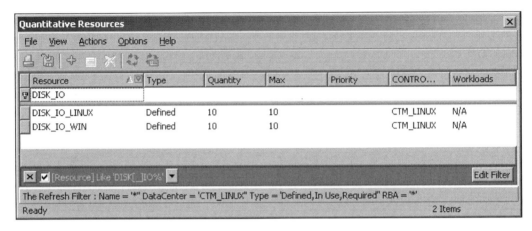

Once the old resource **DISK_IO** is removed and the new resources are created, we need to reflect the change to each job either by updating the definitions one-by-one, manually, or performing mass updates.

Implementing control module for BPI jobs

The last part of this implementation is to define the CM for BPI jobs, which includes a web service job and a number of message queue jobs. The web service job is in charge of triggering a web service, which will notify the external system that the processing (on the Windows Agent side) has completed and new records have been inserted into the MS SQL database. The set of message queue jobs is designed to push each record from the processed file (on the Linux Agent side) into a message queue so that down flow systems subscribed to the queue can get the record as soon as it is processed.

Technical background

In today's IT environment, the Java application server is commonly used as the foundation behind real time enterprise integration. There are many commercial and open source enterprise integration productions that are built on this software framework to provide functionalities such as XSLT (XML transformation), WS (web service), JMS (message queue), BPEL (orchestration), database/filesystem binding, and so on. These building blocks together become the so-called **Enterprise Service Bus** (ESB) that offers a centralized communication hub with standard interface for applications to work with each other in a loosely-coupled fashion (that is, eliminates direct function calls between applications). It allows rapid integration by encapsulating the details and complexity of individual components residing in each involved application.

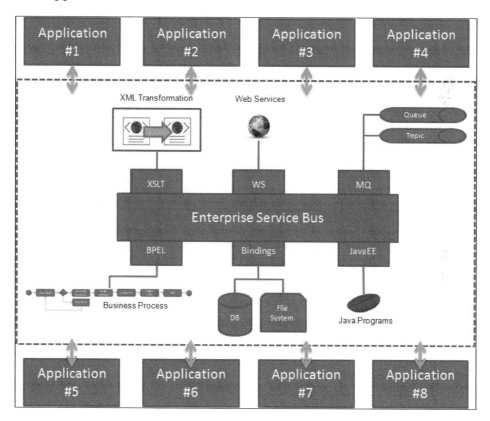

CM for BPI is all about extending Control-M's scheduling capability to to include the ability to submit Java, web service, and message queue jobs, thereby allowing Control-M to have full integration with the real time world.

Defining accounts

CM for BPI components are used for Control-M to communicate with the external application in a standard and loosely-coupled fashion. For such communication, appropriate information should be supplied, such as account definitions prior to any job submission.

Web service account

Control-M uses the standard way to invoke web service, that is, by knowing the web service through its WSDL (Web Services Description Language) document. During account creation, all it requires are the WSDL's source type and the actual location. A valid WSDL source could be an UDDI (Universal Description Discovery and Integration) repository, a published web service URL, or a WSDL file stored on the local filesystem of the Agent machine. In the real world, normally the WSDL information is supplied by the external application owner; behind the scenes, it gets generated during the web application's development phase.

In our case, we have a pre-defined web application project called PROFILE_LOAD in NetBeans IDE, and the WSDL was created as part of it. The project has to be deployed as a web application into the GlassFish Enterprise Server (that is, our OpenESB running on ctm-demo-win-02). Once it is deployed successfully, we should be able to test the WSDL from a web browser (for example, http://ctm-demo-win-02:8080/PROFILE_LOAD/PROFILE_LOADService?wsdl).

Getting back to Control-M, we can define the account from CCM by right-clicking on the **CM (WS)** entry of host `ctm-demo-linux-02` and select **WS Account Management**. In the **Account Management** window, we will add a new account with the following parameters:

- **Account Name**: Name of the account that will be used in job definitions.
    - ○ Our value: **PROFILE_LOAD**
- **WSDL Source**: How the WSDL is provided, can be UDDI, Web Service URL, or a WSDL file on the local drive.
    - ○ Our value: **Web Service URL**
- **WSSDL Location**: Physical location of the WSDL.
    - ○ Our value: `http://ctm-demo-win-02:8080/PROFILE_LOAD/PROFILE_LOADService?wsdl`

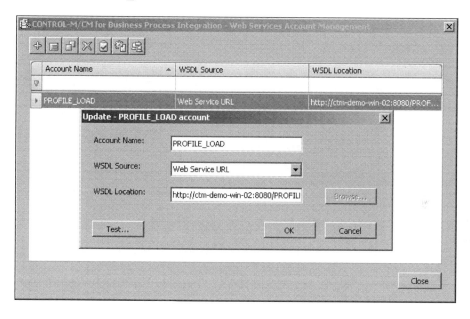

One thing we need to make sure is that the machine that runs the CM has to have access to the application server machine that holds the web service. In our OpenESB environment the TCP port for such communication is **8080** (default). We can verify the connection by clicking on the **Test...** button.

Message queue account

The message queue BPI component supports many types of messaging server providers, which includes JBoss, SAP Netweaver, Weblogic, Wesphere 5.0/6.0/6/1/7(MQ), as well as generic JMS servers. In our case, we are using JBoss AS 6.0.

Creating an account for message queue is a bit more complicated than for web service. Before defining the account in CCM, we need to make sure the machine that runs the CM has a JRE (Java Runtime Environment) and the JBoss message queue client Jar files installed.

In our environment, the account can be defined from CCM by right-clicking on the **CM (MQ)** entry of host `ctm-demo-linux-02` and selecting **Messaging Account Management**. In the **Account Management** window, we will be required to enter:

- **General/Account Name**: Name of the account that will be used in job definitions.
- Our value: **PROFILE_QUEUE**
- **General/Messaging Server**: Supported messaging server vendor and versions.
- Our value: **JBOSS (JMS)**
- **Runtime Environment/JRE Home Path**: Full path to the JRE's bin directory on the machine where the CM is installed. The JRE has to be the Oracle (Sun) Java with version 1.4.2 or above (that is, cannot be the default GNU Java that comes with Linux installations).
- Our value: `/usr/java/jre1.6.0_25/`
- **Messaging Server/JNDI Service Parameters**: The machine's host and port number that runs the JNDI service. Normally, JNDI runs on the same machine where the messaging server is running. The default port is 1099.
    - ○ Our value: `ctm-demo-linux-02`, Port 1099 (these values will be translated into `jnp://ctm-demo-linux-02:1099/`
- **Messaging Server/Required Client Jars**: Where the client JAR files are located. These files are used for the message queue BPI component to communicate with the message queue server.
- Our value: Root directory – `/usr/java/jboss-6.0.0.Final/client`, client Jars, that is, `$CLINET_DIR$/jbossall-client.jar"`
- **Messaging Server/Connection Factories**: If the JNDI parameters are correctly provided, we will be able to browse queue and topic connection factories defined within the messaging server.

- Our value: a connection factory created by default within Jboss AS 6 – `XAConnectionFactory`

- **Queue Parameters/Destination Queue Definitions**: The destination type can be either a queue or a topic. The queue name can be entered or selected by JNDI browsing; together, enter the message's priority (0-9), expiration time (in seconds) and correlation ID prefix (optional).

- Our value: **Type – Queue, Queue/Topic name - queue/DLQ, Message priority - 4, Message expiration time – 0** (never), **Correlation ID prefix - NULL**

- **Queue Parameters/Reply Queue Definition (optional)**: Ticked if requires a reply message from a queue. It is supplied in either text or binary format. When ticked, the reply queue name (can be selected by JNDI browsing) and the timeout for waiting on such a reply are also to be specified.
  - Our value: Not ticked. Our job will just push the message to the queue without the need for any reply.

- **Queue Parameters/Override options**: Specify which parameters are to be overridden in message queue job definitions.

- Our value: **NULL**

- **Predefined Messages/Predefined Messages (optional)**: Message to be pushed to the queue can be specified as part of each job definition or predefined in this section. Predefined messages can be shared among all jobs that use the same account. In order to create a predefined message, the physical file (`.txt` or `bin` file) contains the actual message and a name to be specified; the name will be used later on in job definition to associate to the actual file.
  - Our value: **NULL**. We will be using the Autoedit variable to store the content of the message

After all settings are entered and saved, we can click on the **Test…** button to verify the account.

Creating jobs

Once the accounts are defined and tested, we can go ahead with re-loading our DynamicFileProcessing SMART table from the EM database into Control-M/Desktop and start adding the new jobs.

Web service job

We will be creating the web service job first, since it is the simple one. For the new job, we need to make sure Job Type **WS** is selected in order for the **WS** tab to appear in the job editing form. The job parameters we need to enter are listed as follows:

- **Account**: We can choose the account we defined earlier by clicking on **Select Account**. In order for the available accounts to load up, we need to make sure the job's execution Node ID/Group is set to the host where the CM for BPI is installed (for example, in our case it is `ctm-demo-linux-02`).
    - Our value: **PROFILE_LOAD**

- **Business**: Select the business that is registered in the UDDI server. This parameter is valid only if UDDI is selected as the WSDL source.

- Our value: **NULL**

- **WSDL**: The WSDL location (when WSDL source is set to Local FileSystem or Web Service URL). The predefined WSDL location is selectable if the account was properly loaded and accessible.
    - Our value: `http://ctm-demo-win-02:8080/PROFILE_LOAD/ PROFILE_LOADService?wsdl`

- **Service**: Available services offered by the web service (that is, defined in the WSDL) to be consumed by the job.
    - Our value: **PROFILE_LOADService**(Port:PROFILE_LOADPort)

- **Operation**: Available operation (that is, defined in the WSDL) to be performed by the job.
    - Our value: **NOTIFIER**

- **Input Parameters (optional)**: Click on the **Load Parameters** button to load up available parameters described in the WSDL. Once a parameter is loaded, we can specify the value in the **Value** field below. A web service may not necessarily require a parameter.

- Our value: **Name – NOTIFIER.NEWDATA, Value – TRUE**

- **Use Parameters from input file (optional)**: This option is ticked if we would like to let Control-M to load the input parameters in from an XML file instead of define them one-by-one in the job.

- Our value: **NULL**

- **Add SOAP header from file (optional)**: This option is ticked if we would like Control-M to use our predefined SOAP header during invoking the web service each time.

- Our value: **NULL**

- **Output Parameters (optional)**: If the web service produces output, Control-M allows the value to be saved into an Autoedit variable or a file.

    ○ Our value: **NULL**. For us, the output value is not required, but we still can view the value from the job's sysout (that is, it is a part of the job's sysout by default).

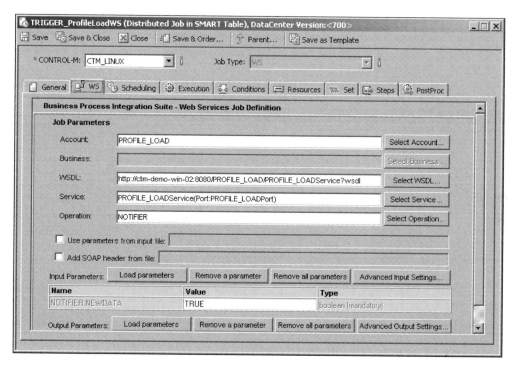

Once the job definition is saved, we will link it after the three IMPRT_Records_ department-04/5/6 jobs. In this case, the web service will be triggered as soon as the database insertions are completed for all three departments. Job TRIGGER_ ProfileLoadWS will have 3 in conditions with AND relationship between them.

Message queue jobs

The message queue job itself does not require as much detail as the web service job. However, in our file processing job flow, we have to implement extra jobs in addition to the message queue job itself to get the concept working. The idea is that we want to push one record to the message queue each time, until all records have gone through. We will have three cyclic jobs after each FILTER_Records_ department-01/2/3 job to do the work for us.

- The first job will read the first line of the filtered records file and assign the text into a SMART table-level Autoedit variable.

- The second job is the message queue job, which will push the value of the Autoedit variable into PROFILE_QUEUE.

- The third job will remove the first line from the filtered records file and perform a do-condition during post processing to re-trigger the first job, so the first job can read the next line, which has just became the first line of the file after the deletion. This job also does a line count each time after the removal. If there's only one line left in the file, in addition to performing the do condition, it will stop the cycle. In such a case, the first job and second job will still get triggered to process the last line of the file but will no longer be triggered after that.

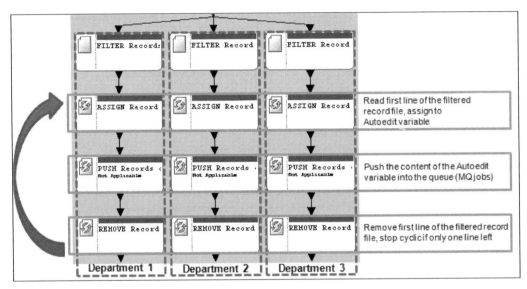

The details of each job are as follows:

Tab	Field	Value
General	Job Name	ASSIGN_Record_department-01
		ASSIGN_Record_department-02
		ASSIGN_Record_department-03
General	Task Type	Command

Tab	Field	Value
General	Embedded Script Content	`ctmvar -ACTION SET -var "%%#\` `FP-RealTime\D01" -varexpr` `"`head -1 /home/file_tran/` `dest/%%DIRNAME/%%FILENAME`"` `ctmvar -ACTION SET -var "%%#\` `FP-RealTime\D02" -varexpr` `"`head -1 /home/file_tran/` `dest/%%DIRNAME/%%FILENAME`"` `ctmvar -ACTION SET -var "%%#\` `FP-RealTime\D03" -varexpr` `"`head -1 /home/file_tran/` `dest/%%DIRNAME/%%FILENAME`"`
General	Description	Read first line of the filtered records file and assign the text into a SMART table-level Autoedit variable
Execution	Node ID/Group	ctm-demo-linux-02
Set	DIRNAME	\<department name\>
	FILENAME	%%SOURCEFILE_PREFIX -\<department name\>.csv
Conditions*	IN Conditions	FILTER _Records_department-0x-%%TABLE_ID-ENDED OR REMOVE_Record_department-0x-%%TABLE_ID-ENDED
Condition*	OUT Condition	ASSIGN_Record_department-0x-%%TABLE_ID-ENDED (+) FILTER_Records_department-0x-%%TABLE_ID-ENDED (-) REMOVE_Record_department-0x-%%TABLE_ID-ENDED (-)
General	Job Name	PUSH_Records_department-01 PUSH_Records_department-02 PUSH_Records_department-03
General	Task Type	CM (MQ)
MSG	Account	PROFILE_QUEUE

Tab	Field	Value
MSG	Use free test message	%%D01
		%%D02
		%%D03
General	Description	Push the content of SMART table-level Autoedit variable %D01 into the queue
Execution	Node ID/Group	ctm-demo-linux-02
Condition*	IN Conditions	ASSIGN_Record_department-0x-%%TABLE_ID-ENDED
Condition*	OUT Conditions	PUSH_Records_department-0x-%%TABLE_ID-ENDED (+)
		ASSIGN_Record_department-0x-%%TABLE_ID-ENDED (-)
General	Job Name	REMOVE_Record_department-01
		REMOVE_Record_department-02
		REMOVE_Record_department-03
General	Task Type	Command
General	Embedded Script Content	`sed 1d /home/file_tran/ dest/%%DIRNAME/%%FILENAME -i; wc -l /home/file_tran/ dest/%%DIRNAME/%%FILENAME`
General	Description	Remove first line of the
Execution	Node ID/Group	ctm-demo-linux-02
Set	DIRNAME	<department name>
	FILENAME	%%SOURCEFILE_PREFIX-<department name>.csv
Steps*		"Statement *, Code *
		Do Condition: REMOVE_Record_department-0x-%%TABLE_ID-ENDED, ODAT, +
Steps*		Statement wc -l*, Code 1 *
		Do Stop Cyclic (stop cyclic when keyword "1 " is returned by the "wc -l" command)
Conditions*	IN Conditions	PUSH_Records_department-0x-%%TABLE_ID-ENDED
Conditions*	OUT Conditions	PUSH_Records_department-0x-%%TABLE_ID-ENDED (-)

Character x in condition names is replaced by department ID 1, 2, or 3.

Updating the quantitative resource

Since our job flow is designed to be able to run as multiple instances concurrently, the new jobs we just defined together with the AFT and database jobs also need to have a quantitative resource defined in order for Control-M to limit the number of concurrent running instances for each job type. The following resource definitions will be added to our job definitions:

Job name	Resource name	Quantity required
FILETRANS_ProcessedFile_LIN02toWIN01	**AFT**	1
FILETRANS_ProcessedFile_LIN02toLIN02	**AFT**	1
ASSIGN_Record_department-01/2/3	**CTMUTILITY**	1
PUSH_Records_department-01/2/3	**MQ**	1
REMOVE_Record_department-01/2/3	**DISK_IO_LINUX**	1
IMPORT_Records_department-04/5/6	**DB**	1
TRIGGER_ProfileLoadWS	**WS**	1

On the other hand, we need to define these resources with the maximum quantity value from the Control-M/Enterprise Manager GUI client. We will give quantity **10** for each of the new resource types (that is, **AFT**, **MQ**, **DB**, **CTMUTILITY**, and **WS**) and keep DISK_IO_LINUX as it is.

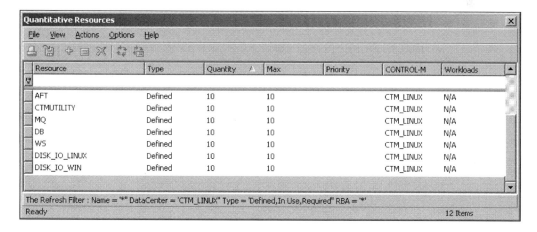

Before we ordering the job flow, make sure the SMART table has been written to the EM database, as well as uploaded to the Control-M/Server database. We don't need to define any user daily to this job table because it will be ordered on demand, rather than for a regular time each day.

End-to-end testing

Now, let's do some end-to-end testing to experience the beauty of parallel processing.

First of all, we make sure the source files are loaded into the source directory (`/home/file_tran/source`) on host `ctm-demo-linux-02` and we will randomly select a number of source files to be used for the testing.

Open soapUI, load up the WSDL and locate the `order_force` operation. In the XML file, enter the following items:

- `user_token`: NULL
- `control-m`: CTM_LINUX
- `table_name`: FP-RealTime
- `odate`: ODAT
- `wait_for_odate`: no
- `autoedit_assignment`
    - name: SOURCEFILE_PREFIX
    - value: `<name of the source file>`

A sample SOAP message could be like this:

```
<soapenv:Envelope xmlns:soapenv="http://schemas.xmlsoap.org/soap/
envelope/" xmlns:sch="http://www.bmc.com/ctmem/schema630">
    <soapenv:Header/>
    <soapenv:Body>
        <sch:request_order_force>
            <sch:user_token></sch:user_token>
            <sch:force_it>no</sch:force_it>
            <sch:control_m>CTM_LINUX</sch:control_m>
            <!--Optional:-->
            <sch:job_id></sch:job_id>
```

```
        <!--Optional:-->
        <sch:job_name></sch:job_name>
        <sch:table_name>FP-RealTime</sch:table_name>
        <!--Optional:-->
        <sch:table_library></sch:table_library>
        <sch:odate>ODAT</sch:odate>
        <!--Optional:-->
        <sch:wait_for_odate>no</sch:wait_for_odate>
        <!--Optional:-->
        <sch:with_hold></sch:with_hold>
        <!--Optional:-->
        <sch:autoedit_assignments>
            <!--1 or more repetitions:-->
            <sch:autoedit_assignment>
               <sch:name>SOURCEFILE_PREFIX</sch:name>
               <sch:value>SOURCE_CSV_01ac</sch:value>
            </sch:autoedit_assignment>
        </sch:autoedit_assignments>
        <!--Optional:-->
        <sch:scheduling_group_info>
            <sch:into_group></sch:into_group>
            <!--Optional:-->
            <sch:group_id></sch:group_id>
            <!--Optional:-->
            <sch:allow_dup></sch:allow_dup>
        </sch:scheduling_group_info>
        <!--Optional:-->
        <sch:max_returned_nodes></sch:max_returned_nodes>
      </sch:request_order_force>
   </soapenv:Body>
</soapenv:Envelope>
```

Within a few seconds, we will be getting a SOAP reply with a Job ordered message for each job along with their Order IDs. If we switch to the Control-M/EM GUI client now, we would see the job flow instance appear in the Active ViewPoint. You will notice that the number of concurrent jobs on either the Linux or Windows side will be limited to maximum 10 by the quantitative resource DISK_IO_WIN/DISK_IO_LINUX we set earlier. The department flow on the Windows side will always finish quicker than on the Linux side as the message queue cyclic jobs take more time to push through the messages. We can push through a few more through soapUI, just to make sure the parallel processing really works.

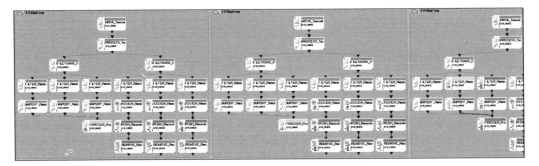

Now, if we randomly click on a job and go to its **Set** tab, we will notice the SMART table-level Autoedit variable %%SOURCEFILE_PREFIX appears with the value given during job ordering. If we click on a web service job and select **View Sysout**, we will see the web service's return message in the sysout file.

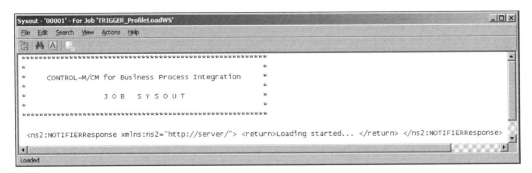

If we view a sysout of a message queue job, we will see the actual message that was pushed to the queue, together with its time stamp.

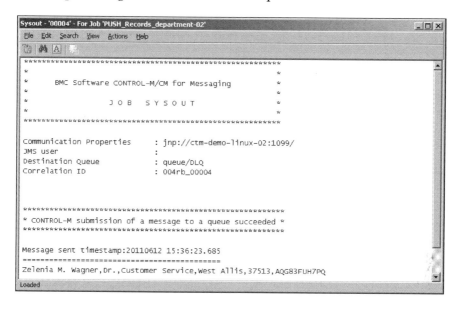

On the other hand, we can monitor the number of messages being pushed into the queue from **JBoss AS 6 Admin Console**.

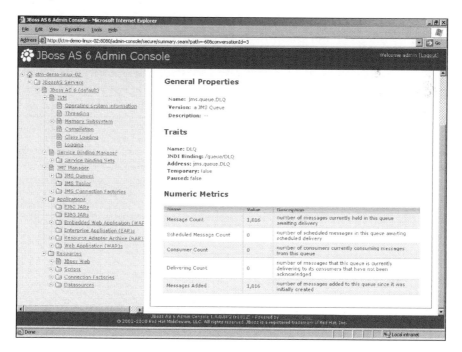

At the filesystem level, we see that all the temporary files in `staging` and `dest` directory are created with the source file name as their prefix. In addition, in each `ctm-demo-linux-02` department directory, we should see each of the filtered record files reducing in size as the processing goes; this is because our message queue cyclic job flow removes one record from the file after each insertion.

Managing batch jobs as workloads

The jobs we have been running so far are designed to be submitted onto a predefined host for execution; this is the so-called **static scheduling**. There is nothing wrong with it and, in fact, this is how batch processing happened originally, right back to the OS built-in scheduling tool (for example, CRON) days. It is absolutely fine if there is only a handful of non-critical jobs running on fixed dates at fixed times. However, as we progress into event triggering, the batch workload no longer stays the same and becomes subject to a number of external events, generated at a given time. Peak periods are hard to predict. Too many events generated around the same period can overload the job execution machine and thereby delay the delivery of processing outcome. On top of that, an outage may not be affordable for critical processing requests due to the business's real time expectation.

As famous American investor and author Robert Kiyosak, said, "Inside every problem lies an opportunity"; Control-M, a state-of-the-art batch scheduling tool, took one step further in version 7 by putting the workload automation concept into reality. As we discussed during *Chapter 3, Building the Control-M Infrastructure*, workload automation is the beginning of the Golden Age. A well-organized batch environment should fully utilize workload automation features offered by Control-M to optimize their batch execution, thereby ensuring SLA and reducing administrational overhead. In this section, we will be using the workload automation features provided within Control-M to modify our file processing job flow to become more flexible and resource-aware.

There are two parts in this section. In part one, we will modify some of our file processing jobs to let them run in node groups; thus, the processing requests can be shared among many hosts and each job execution is no longer subject to the availability of a particular host, that is, we avoid a single point of failure. In part two, we will introduce the workload concept in greater detail and limit the file processing job flow's executions at the workload level in conjunction with quantitative resource usage, as well as become able to freely shift the execution of the entire workload from one job execution host/group to another.

Running jobs in node groups

The new file processing job flow calls to action both the IT architects and the software developers. They are all excited by what Control-M can offer. As we are just about to sit back and have a cup of skinny latte, an e-mail marked as critical from the application owner appears in our inbox. To cut a long story short, they have been constantly experiencing delays with the new file processing mechanism; other applications running on the machine have also had significant performance issues since the new mechanism was put into use. They suspect the performance bottleneck is Control-M!

As passionate Control-M administrators, we do not allow such assumptions unless there's a reliable artifact. We start the investigation by running Control-M reports and compare the results against the resource usage (for example, CPU, RAM, and disk I/O) on each job execution host. What we find out is, even though we have limited the concurrent number of running FILTER_Records* jobs by the DISK_IO_WIN and DISK_IO_LINUX quantitative resource, the amount of processing happening during peak periods constantly causes the two job execution hosts' CPU and RAM usage to reach 100 percent while the actual disk I/O still has plenty capacity.

We outlined the issue to the application owners and explained to them that in order to increase processing performance we need to allow more processing to happen at the same time. However, it doesn't make any sense unless more machine resources are provided to support the additional number of running jobs. We explained to them that Control-M is capable of balancing the workload onto multiple job execution hosts by using its node group technology.

Technical background

Node group, in fact, is not brand new technology. It was introduced as a standard feature of Control-M many versions back and has been widely used since. In order to use the technology, we need to specify the number of hosts that must be part of a node group and update the job's execution **Node ID/Group** with the node group name.

The key functionalities offered by node group technology are listed as follows:

- Load balancing: Group a number of job execution hosts as a resource pool and select which host to execute the next job by, on a round-robin basis (hosts within the node group can be Control-M/Agent hosts and/or Agentless hosts).

- Provide high availability for job execution at the Control-M level: If one or more hosts within the node group have became unavailable, Control-M will ignore these hosts during job submission and route all jobs onto hosts that are still available within the node group.

- Reduce the effort of administration: When the job execution hosts are changed, simply update the node group's associated nodes. The job definition can stay unchanged with the same node group name.

In Control-M version 7, a new feature was introduced on top of what has been described in the preceding list. The new feature allows nodes within the node group only to be available at a particular time period or under a certain condition. It also allows node restrictions to be set based on the job execution host's max CPU utilization and max number of concurrent jobs.

Creating node groups

Node groups can be defined in CCM through **Tools | Node management | Nodes Manager** or through Control-M/Server **ctm_menu | Option 6 - Node Group**. For our file processing job flow we will be using CCM to define two node groups, one called FP_LINUX and one called FP_WIN.

In **Node manager**, make sure the **Control-M/Server** field on top is selected to reflect CTM_LINUX and then press the **+** sign within the **Node Groups** tab to bring up the **New Node Group** pop-up window. When creating a new node group, we will be asked for the following information:

- **Node group name**: Where the name of the node group is given. Later on it will be defined into each job's **Node ID/Group** field to replace the specific node name.
    - Our value for 1st node group: FP_LINUX.
    - Our value for 2nd node group: FP_WIN.

- **Application type**: Node groups are application type-specific. If we want to have a node group for running jobs of a particular CM, the corresponding application type needs to be selected during node group creation. For example, a node group with application type OS will not be able to run CM for AFT jobs even if every node within the group has CM for AFT installed.

- ○ Our value for both node groups: `os`. For the file processing job flow we will only convert the selected script jobs and command jobs to be running on these node groups; CM jobs will stay as they are.

- **Associated nodes**: Define which Control-M/Agents and/or Agentless hosts are going to be part of the node group. Each node can belong to more than one node group.

    - ○ Our value for 1st node group: `ctm-demo-linux-02` and `ctm-demo-linux-03`.

    - ○ Our value for 2nd node group: `ctm-demo-win-01`, `ctm-demo-win-02`, and `ctm-demo-win-03`.

- **Participation definitions (optional)**: Availability of an individual node to the node group based on date/time or the existence of a job condition.

    - ○ Our value for 1st node group:

- `ctm-demo-linux-02` is available everyday between 9:00pm to 6:00am. Outside the time frame, this host is dedicated for CM for BPI jobs, WS Interface requests, and processing outside Control-M such as to handle OpenESB activities.

- `ctm-demo-linux-03` is available everyday from 3:00am to 1:00am. During the 2 hour gap each day, the machine will be dedicated for housekeeping jobs and patching activities.

    (As such, the two nodes can cover each other's outage and provide 24/7 processing).

    - ○ Our value for 2nd node group:

- `ctm-demo-win-01` is available when condition REPORTING-OK with Date ODAT exists. (There is a reporting job running on this host daily. When the job starts, the REPORTING-OK condition will be removed; when the job finishes, the condition will be re-added. By doing so, the node will be not available for the node group when the database backup job is running and will become available again as soon as the reporting job is complete).

- `Ctm-demo-win-02/3` are available 24/7 for the node group.

Multiple participation rules can be defined to the same node.

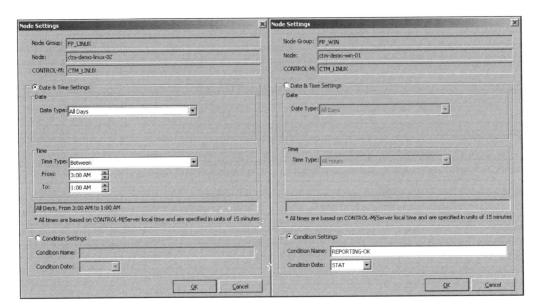

After creating the node groups, we will also define some node restrictions for each individual job execution host. The restrictions are applied to all jobs running on the host, not at the overall node group level. It is to be set by pressing the + sign under the **Node Restrictions** tab. We will apply the following restrictions to each node:

Node(s)	Max CPU Utilization (%)	Max Concurrent Jobs
ctm-demo-linux-02	50	150
ctm-demo-win-01	50	100
ctm-demo-win-02	50	100

The reason we limit Max CPU Utilization of `ctm-demo-linux-02` and `ctm-demo-win-01/2` to 50% is because there are other major applications running on these hosts: JBoss on `ctm-demo-linux-02`, MS SQL on `ctm-demo-win-01`, and OpenESB on `ctm-demo-win-02`. By setting the hard limit, Control-M jobs will never be able to take over the entire machine's CPU resource even during peak time period. We also set **Max Concurrent Jobs** on these hosts to **150/100**. If either one of the limits is reached, Control-M will stop the pending job submissions on these hosts, for jobs that are eligible for submission will stay in waiting for resource state until either the CPU usage is reduced or other jobs are completed. The same node restrictions can be set to more than one nodes within one definition by using * in the node name. However, node restrictions cannot be set to Agentless remote hosts, and Max CPU Utilization is available to version 7 Control-M/Agents only.

Making necessary changes to the environment and jobs

After the node groups are defined, we need to modify the **Node ID/Group** field of each OS and command type jobs in our file processing job flow to reflect the name of the group. We also need to make modifications to the job scripts and the environment so the same processing outcome can be produced no matter which host of the node group the job is submitted to.

The big picture

For jobs that are not based on their previous step's output data, it is not hard to get them to run in a node group. All we need to do is modify the job's **Node ID/Group** from the specific node name into the node group name. However, the story becomes a bit more complicated when it comes to our file processing scenario due to the fact that jobs within the flow are interrelated at the data level, that is, each processing step within the job flow is going to make further modifications to the output file of the pervious step. When these jobs are defined to be submitted to node group, we never know which node the next job will be submitted to because the selection of the job execution host is round-robin based. If the job is submitted to a host different from the one in the previous step, it will not be able to access to the output file produced by the pervious step, which is located on a different host.

To overcome this issue, we made the `file_tran` directory on both the `ctm-demo-linux-02` and `ctm-demo-win-01` into shared drives for other hosts to access. To keep the environment simple, NFS is used on the Linux side and normal Windows shared drive is used on the Windows side. In real world scenarios, better technology may be used to archive high performance and comprehensive security.

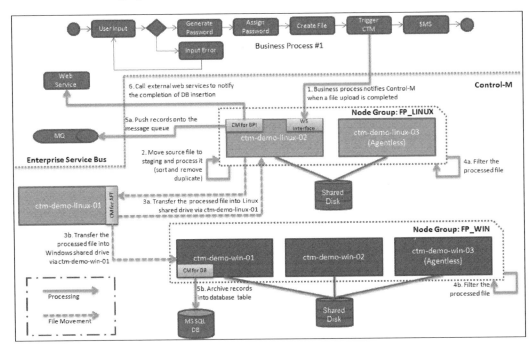

For Linux host `ctm-demo-linux-03`, the directory is permanently mounted by root under `path /home/file_tran`, which is the same as the original path on `ctm-demo-linux-02`. For Windows hosts `ctm-demo-win-02` and `ctm-demo-win-03`, the directory `C:\file_tran` is to be mapped as network drive Z during each job execution.

Making changes to jobs and scripts

Modifications to job definitions on the Linux side are very straightforward. All we need to do is update the **Node ID/Group** field of the following jobs into `FP_LINUX`:

- `MOVE_SourceFiles`
- `PROCESS_SourceFile`
- `FILTER_Records_department-01/2/3`
- `REMOVE_Record_department-01/2/3`

Because the jobs will be running as owner file_tran, we need to make sure the user has been created on Agentless job execution host ctm-demo-linux-03. On the Control-M side, we will enable Agentless job submission by defining job owner file_tran with SSH key authentication in **Owners Authentication Settings (CCM | Security | Owners Authentication Settings)**. At the same time, the SSH public key needs to be populated into the user's ~/.ssh/authorized_keys file.

For Windows jobs, the situation is a little bit tricky. We still have to begin by updating the **Node ID/Group** field of the jobs that are to be running in the node group from its current single node value into node group FP_WIN. These jobs are: FILTER_Records_department-04/5/6.

At the moment, FILTER_Records_department_01/2/3 are all running under owner SYSTEM. When node group is introduced, these jobs can potentially be running on the Agentless remote host ctm-demo-win-03. As such, we have to define a domain user that can be used across all three hosts, for example, CTM-DEMO\file_tran. This user needs to be added into the **Owners Authentication Settings** for WMI access to ctm-demo-win-03 and updated to each job definition's owner field.

In order for each job to access the shared drive, we will be using net use command at the beginning of each job script to connect the remote drive. For example, the command to connect network drive is: net use z: \\ctm-demo-win-01\file_tran /USER:CTM-DEMO\file_tran <user password>. The file path within each command line of the scripts also needs to be updated from c:\file_tran\dest\... into z:\dest... to reflect the new drive name and directory. The network drive Z also needs to be mounted onto ctm-demo-win-01 even if the actual files are located within the host itself otherwise, when the job is submitted to ctm-demo-win-01, we will get **Z drive path not found...** type error message.

Making changes to quantitative resources

The performance issue raised earlier was due to too many jobs being allowed to run concurrently, thereby causing the job execution machines' CPU and RAM usage to hit 100 percent during peak period. With the additional machine resources, we now have the luxury of keeping the limit the same or even of increasing it. However, we have to somehow make sure job submission on each node of the node group is well balanced. Simply increasing the quantity of DISK_IO_WIN and DISK_IO_LINUX will not be the ideal, because, in case any hosts within the node group become unavailable, all jobs will be submitted to the rest of the available hosts and therefore may overload these machines even more.

To implement resource load balancing in Control-M, we can define machine-specific quantitative resources using the format `<resource name>@<node name>`, followed with specifying `<resource name>@` within each job definition. By doing so during job submission, Control-M will decide which quantitative resource to deduct based on the job's actual execution node. In our file processing job flow, we will define a new resource for each node that has common prefix `FP@` with quantity of **6**.

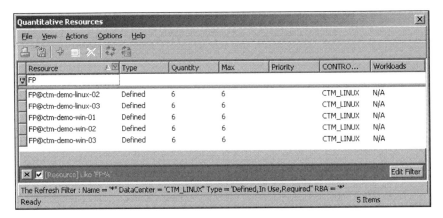

On the other hand, we will set the following jobs to require `1x FP@` for execution:

- `MOVE_SourceFiles`

- `PROCESS_SourceFile`

- `FILTER_Records_department-01/2/3`

- `REMOVE_Record_department-01/2/3`

- `FILTER_Records_department-04/5/6`

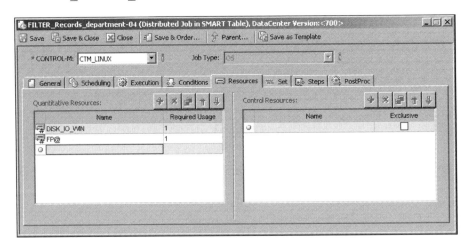

For `DISK_IO_WIN` and `DISK_IO_LINUX`, even we are not sure which host the jobs will be running on; having these two common resources among all jobs still makes perfect sense as the real disk I/O overhead will all come down to the same shared drive, no matter which host the job is submitted to. According to our earlier investigation the disk I/O usage hasn't reached its capacity, therefore, it is safe for us to increase `DISK_IO_WIN` and `DISK_IO_LINUX` quantitative resources to allow more concurrent running jobs. For now, we will increase `DISK_IO_WIN` to **18** and `DISK_IO_ LINUX` to **12**.

Again, before we go ahead and order the job, we will rename the SMART and group name. This time, we will call the SMART table `FP-LoadBalancing` and group name `FifthDemo`. We also need to update the command line of job `ASSIGN_Record_ department-01/2/3`, that is, the argument of the `ctmvar` utility needs to reflect the new SMART table name in order to assign the group level Autoedit variable. The new command line will be, for example, for job `ASSIGN_Record_department-01`: `ctmvar -ACTION SET -var "%%#\FP-LoadBalancing\D01" -varexpr "`head -1 /home/file_tran/dest/%%DIRNAME/%%FILENAME`"`.

Putting into action

When ordering the job flow from soapUI, we need to make sure the new SMART table name is specified in the SOAP message `<sch:table_name>FP-LoadBalancing</sch:table_name>`. The behavior of our file processing job flow will not change a lot after adding the node group execution. In the active job environment, if we click on a running or completed job instance that is defined to run on node group, we will notice that, in addition to the **Node Group** name, the selected **Node ID** for job execution is also displayed under the **Execution** tab.

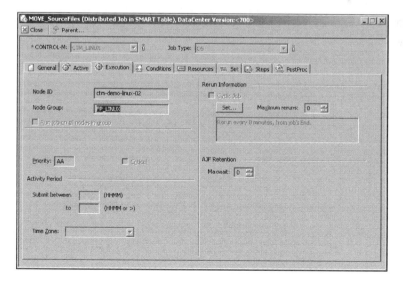

The actual job execution **Node ID** is also displayed in the `ctmlog` of each job, together with the resolution of the FP@ resource.

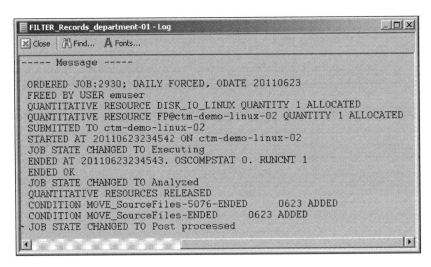

Due to the participation rules we defined earlier, we will notice that between 6:00am and 9:00pm each day all jobs defined to run under node group FP_LINUX will only be submitted to node `ctm-demo-linux-03`, and between 1:00am to 3:00am each day all these jobs will only be submitted to `ctm-demo-linux-02`. Also notice that node `ctm-demo-win-01` will only be available in node group FP_WIN when the condition **REPORTING-OK** exists in the active environment.

Defining and managing workloads

Since the file processing job executions are distributed onto multiple hosts, the processing performance has improved significantly and the job execution machines are no longer getting hammered during peak periods. While we are enjoying good feedback from the application owner, a meeting request from the MSSQL DBA group comes to our inbox. Basically, they are investigating the issue of database overnight backup taking too long and they want to know if it is anyhow related to jobs triggered from Control-M.

Again, we run some reports from Control-M's Reporting Facility to compare with the statistics of the backup tasks. We notice that the performance issue started roughly at the same time when our file processing job execution went into parallel processing. On some days, the backup will slow down when there are many `IMPORT_Records_department-04/5/6` MSSQL database jobs running during the backup period (between 2:00am to 3:30am); otherwise, the backup will complete on time, as expected. We summarize our investigation to the DBAs and explain to them that before they came to us we even didn't know at exactly what time the backups are running and what the impact will be if they get delayed. We promise them we will resolve the issue if they agree to let Control-M schedule their database backups. After a Control-M overview presentation, the DBAs are happy to give us a chance.

Technical background

The problem described in the previous section has always been common. By letting Control-M schedule those database backup jobs, we can use quantitative resources to control the number of executions between the database import jobs of the file processing job flow and the MSSQL database backup jobs. Based on our current knowledge of Control-M, there are two approaches to it. One way is to manually update or schedule a Control-M job* before the backup job starts to modify the amount of quantitative resource DB to 0. In this case, newly-ordered database import jobs of the file processing job flow will be in waiting for resource state until the resource DB gets added back after the backup completes. Alternatively, we can set up the database jobs to have the same DB resource but with higher priority so, when their start time is reached, the DB resource will be assigned to them, rather than to others. However, due to the dynamic nature of our file processing job flow, the database import jobs may get submitted right before the backup jobs' start time (that is, taking all available DB resources) and finish 15 to 30 minutes later (that is, to release the resource). Therefore, with this approach we cannot be a hundred percent sure the backup jobs will get the resource right at the time when they are meant to be started.

 Schedule a Control-M job to run the **ecaqrtab** utility to update the resource DB's usage.

As we can see, the two methods are both complex and may not be reliable. However, with workload automation, we don't need to do any of the above; at the same time, we are able to manage the situation effectively. In Control-M version 7, we are allowed to group together into workloads any jobs that share common characteristics and dynamically apply restrictions on them or route the execution onto a different node/node group, without the need for modifying job definitions. In terms of restrictions, we can define resource allowance for jobs in the workload or specify the total number of running jobs. The workload rules can be applied to any jobs based on filter rules and can be changed at any time.

Let's forget about our file processing job flow for now and use a simple scenario to understand the concept further. Say we have 6 jobs running in our Control-M. We group these jobs based on their functionality into three workloads.

- **Workload #1**: **Job A** and **B**: Each of them requires 40xWL (QR) to run. They normally start after 3:00 and finish around 6:00 each day.

- **Workload #2**: **Job C, D,** and **E**. These jobs are dynamically ordered (that is, they can have multiple instances running in the active environment) and can happen at any time of the day. Each of them requires 1xWL (QR) to run, except **Job E**.

- **Workload #3**: **Job F**. This job is also dynamically ordered, but only allowed to execute between 17:00 and 3:00 on weekends. If any instances are ordered during the week, they have to wait until the coming weekend for execution. Each of them requires 2xWL (QR) to run.

In **Workload Management**, we first group them together by applying filters and then apply rules to each of them.

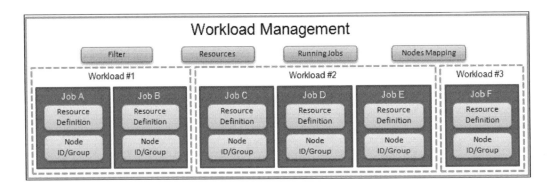

The rules we apply are based on quantitative resource allowance. According to the requirement, we have the following resource allocation of the common resource WL:

- **Workload #1**: Allowed to have 80 of resource WL between 3:00 to 6:00 each day, which will be enough for the two jobs to run.

- **Workload #2**: Allowed to have 50 of resource WL on Saturday and Sunday, between 17:00 and 3:00.

- **Workload #3**: Allowed to have 100 of resource WL at all times, except the time periods specified above; that is, during workload #1's period, it will have 20 of resource WL and during workload #2's period, it will have 50 of resource WL.

We also can define a restriction for **Workload #3**, so that, on each Sunday between 11:00 to 12:00 no jobs are running, in order to allow machine patching. We are using running jobs restriction here because restricting WL to 0 during the period will not stop job E's submission (that is, it doesn't require resource WL).

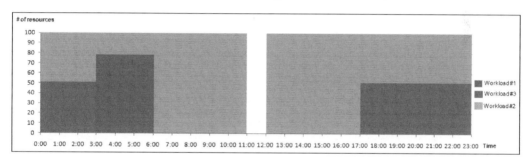

Alternatively, if we want, node mapping rules can be applied to any of the workloads so the jobs within will be routed to different execution environments, given the secondary node has been pre-set up for the jobs to execute.

By having workload management features, we are able to achieve all these complex tasks without touching the job definitions at all.

Defining workloads

Now that we've got the basic idea, let's look at our file processing job scenario and define a number of workload restrictions to eliminate the database backup performance issue as well as making general improvements.

Workload settings are to be defined from the Control-M/Enterprise Manager GUI client or **Desktop | Tools | Workload Management | Workload Manager**. In Workload Manger, we can create a new workload by going to **Actions | New Workload** or simply clicking on the + sign.

In the new **Workload** pop-up window, we begin with giving a name and description to the workload; in our case, we will call our first workload **WL_FP-LoadBalancing**, with description **File processing workload**. We also need to at least specify one filter attribute to define which jobs are going to be part of the workload. Wildcards can be used within the filter definition; as usual, * represents one or more characters and ? represents one character. In addition, , can be used to specify when there are more than one items in one field; for example, to include multiple datacenters in the filter we can specify CTM_LINUX, CTM_WIN. In our case, we are going to specify the **CONTROL-M** field as CTM_LINUX and set the table field to FP-LoadBalancing.

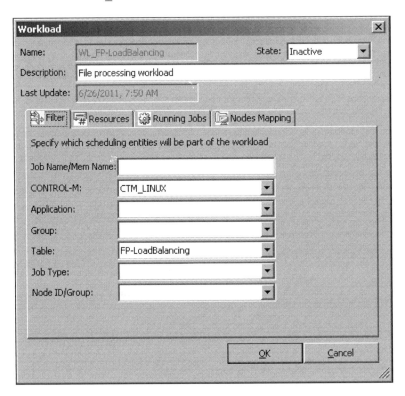

The **Resources** tab is where we can define resource allowance for the workload. After clicking on the **+** sign, a blank **Period Definition** window will pop up for us to define the new rules. In our case, two rules will be defined; one is to limit the DB resource usage during the database backup; the other one is to limit the CTMUTILITY resource usage after NDP. The workload settings are as follows:

- Rule #1: To limit the number of running IMPORT_Records_ department-04/5/6 jobs down to 3, during database backup running period.
  - **Control-M**: CTM_LINUX, **Quantity**: 3, **Resource**: DB

     ○   **Date Type: All Days**

     ○   **Time Type**: Between **2:00AM** to **3:30AM**

- Rule #2: To limit the number of running `ASSIGN_Record_department-01/2/3` jobs down to 1 after NDP, since there will be Control-M/Server housekeeping utilities running after NDP and we want to control the number of concurrent running utilities and give priority to the housekeeping ones.

     ○   **Control-M**: `CTM_LINUX`, **Quantity: 1**, **Resource: DB**

     ○   **Date Type: All Days**

     ○   **Time Type**: Between **7:00AM** to **7:15PM**

In each definition, the minimal resource quantity is 1 and the time is to be specified in units of 15 minutes based on the local time of the Control-M/Server machine.

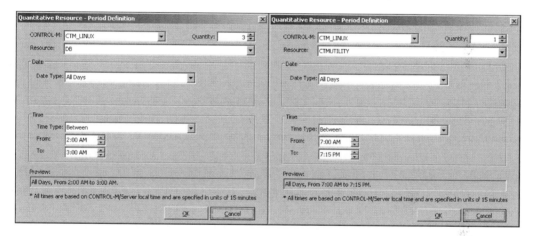

Now we move onto the next one, that is, **Running Jobs**. In this tab, we will define a rule to stop all jobs within the workload during regular machine patching period, which happens on each Sunday between 12:00am to 1:00am. The rule will have **Running Jobs** with value **0**, **Data Type** as **Every (periodic day of week)**, **Sunday**, and **Time** as **Between 12:00am to 1:00am**.

The second workload we are going to define is specifically for the AFT jobs. The objective is that so we can map the AFT jobs' execution from the defined host `ctm-demo-linux-01` into `ctm-demo-win-01` when needed, but without the need for modifying the job definitions. The workload settings are as follows:

- **Name**: WL_AFT

- **Description**: AFT workload

- **Filter**: We want to include all file transfer jobs within datacenter CTM_LINUX
    - ° **CONTROL-M**: CTM_LINUX
    - ° **Job Type**: FILE_TRANS
- **Nodes Mapping**:
    - ° **CONTROL-M**: CTM_LINUX
    - ° **Node Groups/Node IDs**: ctm-demo-linux-01
    - ° **Map To**: ctm-demo-win-02

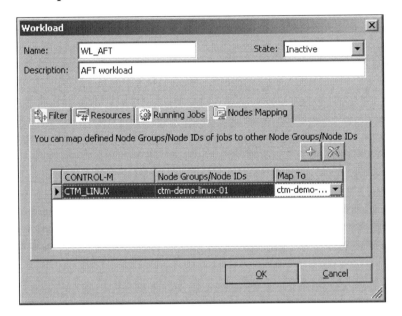

For the first workload we defined, we can enable it by selecting **Active** from the **State** drop-down menu. But for the second workload, we will keep it set to **Inactive** until we want to shift the workload onto ctm-demo-win-02.

Putting into action

The workloads we defined are now shown in the **Workload Manager** but, at this stage, they are not known by the Control-M/Server yet. Synchronization can be done by clicking on the **Apply** or **Refresh** (*Ctrl + R*) button. By doing so, workload settings will be duplicated to all Control-M/Servers regardless of what the filter definitions are. Once the synchronization is successful, the workload settings will take effect immediately.

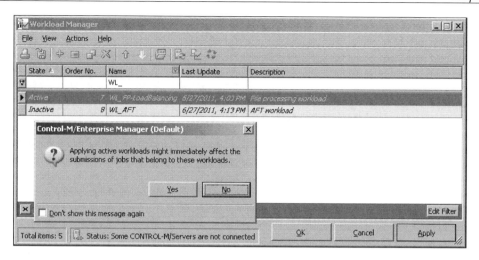

We are able to see active workloads from the Control-M/Enterprise Manager
GUI client or **Desktop | Tools | Workload Management | Workload Monitor**.
Workload Monitor displays each workload's status and the overall status, including,

- **Wait Nodes**: The number of jobs that cannot be submitted for execution due
  to node restrictions set in Node Manager or due to the job execution Agent
  not being available at that time.

- **Wait Resources**: The number of jobs that cannot be submitted for execution
  because the required resource isn't available (that is, resource usage has
  reached resource limitation in the workload settings).

- **Wait Workloads**: The number of jobs that cannot be submitted for execution
  due to **Running Jobs** restrictions set in the workload.

- **Running Jobs**: The number of jobs that are currently running in the workload.

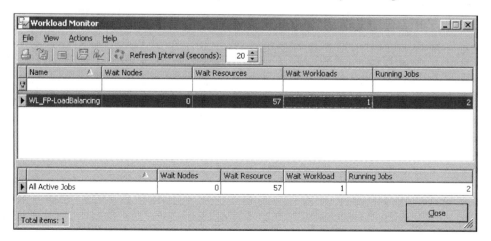

If we check the active environment around 2:00am to 3:00am while there are new file processing job flow instances constantly getting ordered and the `WL_FP-LoadBalancing` workload is active, we should only see maximum 3 `IMPORT_Records_department-04/5/6` jobs running concurrently, because the DB resource is limited by the workload settings during that time period. The same goes for `ASSIGN_Record_department-01/2/3` jobs; there should only be 1 job instance running between 7:00am to 7:15am. If we do a **why** on those waiting for resource jobs, we should see a message similar to **Workload 'WL_FP-LoadBalancing limits the quantitative resource 'xxx' – needed 1 free 0**. When we check the active environment on Sunday between 12:00am to 1:00am, we should see no file process job instances are running at all due to the workload's **Running Jobs** restriction. The output of **why** on those jobs will be **Workload 'WL-FP-LoadBalancing' – Reached Max Jobs policy limit of 0**.

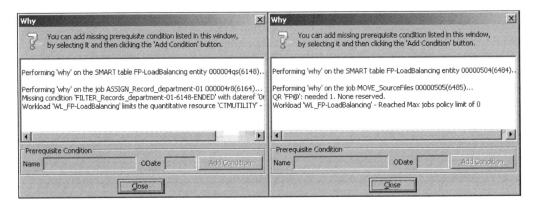

Before we activate the `WL_AFT` workload to test Nodes Mapping, we need to make sure the AFT accounts in `ctm-demo-linux-01` are also defined in `ctm-demo-win-02` in exactly the same way and `ctm-demo-win-01` has network connectivity with all the hosts specified in the accounts. Similarly for other CM jobs, such as BPI or Database, we need to make sure the same accounts are defined and valid on both hosts. For normal OS jobs, we need to make sure the host to be mapped has the necessary environment for the job to execute.

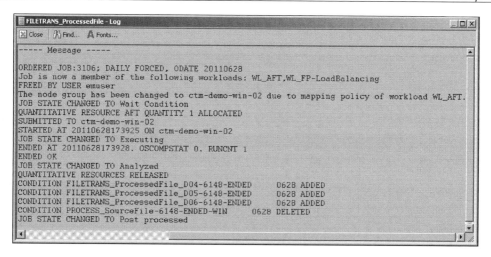

Node mapping activities are recorded in the job log as **The node group has been changed to xxx due to mapping policy of workload xxx**. Once we make the workload inactive or delete the mapping rule from the workload settings, submissions of the jobs under the workload will resume to its normal execution host, that is, originally defined in the job definition.

Into the Cloud

We came a long way to get to where we are standing right now. Finally, this is the time to expand our scheduling into the cloud by using Control-M for Cloud Control Module. In this section, we are going to introduce two cloud environments, that is, a public cloud based on Amazon EC2 and a private cloud based on VMware ESX/ESXi.

Amazon EC2, that is, Elastic Compute Cloud is one of the most popular public clouds out on the market that offers on-demand virtual computing resources and charges machine usage based on hourly rate. VMware, of course, is the most well known virtual machine platform software vendor. In our example, we will register an Amazon EC2 account and have a local VMware ESX/ESXi environment.

Once the two environments are configured, we will be taking the Filtering records part of our file processing job flow into the private/public hybrid cloud. In this case, we not only free up the resource on the existing hosts (that is, `ctm-demo-linux-02` and `ctm-demo-win-01/2`), but, more importantly, we can dynamically allocate virtual machine resources for job execution based on the actual processing needs at different time periods of the day.

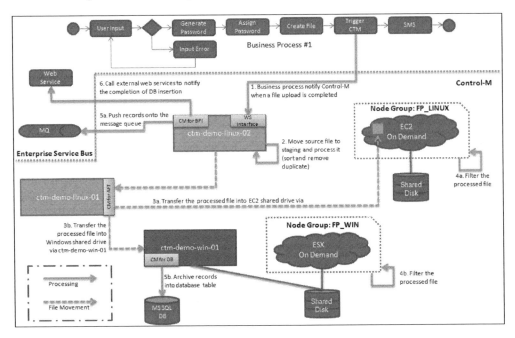

From Control-M point of view, we will have two new node groups; one contains the **EC2** Control-M/Agent hosts and the other one contains the **ESX** Agentless remote hosts. The filter records jobs will be re-directed onto these two node groups accordingly. The nodes within these node groups are not static. We will have Control-M for Cloud jobs running a number of times a day to acquire or release virtual resources from these two environments. The time for such jobs to be triggered is based on the statistics collected for the file processing job flow. By doing so, during file processing off-peak hours, the VMware ESX/ESXi machine can dedicate its processing power to other virtual machines and, on the other hand, the **EC2** virtual machine instances can be closed to avoid unnecessary usage cost.

In order to allow nodes within the cloud to receive and process the processed incoming file, we will have a new shared drive in EC2 public cloud for virtual machines within the cloud to access (that is, replacing the NFS drive on `ctm-demo-linux-02`). Virtual machines within our **ESX** private cloud will have access to the existing shared drive on `ctm-demo-win-01`.

Technical background

Control-M for Cloud, released in April 2011, became the newest Control Module at the time of writing this book. It was made available so that Control-M is able to bring workload execution into the cloud and, therefore, able to dynamically utilize the virtual resources based on actual needs at a given time. By doing so, the batch environment is able to handle peak processing periods and meeting future growth without the need of physically provisioning new server resources. Tapping into the cloud environment also improves the batch applications' uptime (that is, without the need for having outages for hardware maintenance) and makes high availability become simple to achieve.

Control-M for Cloud has the ability to interact with Amazon EC2 and VMware (ESX and ESXi). The idea behind it is that tasks such as provisioning or terminating virtual machine resources in the public/private resource can be automated in conjunction with the real-time status of batch execution. Examples are:

- For event trigger batch workloads, when the peak period starts, Control-M is able to detect it. Therefore, trigger Control-M for Cloud jobs to acquire more machine resources to be added into the jobs' node group for processing. And once the new event generation starts to quiet down, Control-M will detect such trends and shut down the unutilized virtual machine resources by running the corresponding Control-M for Cloud shut-down jobs.

- Another scenario could be that a workload is predefined to run on a number of physical machines. During scheduled hardware maintenance, we can simply switch the workload's execution from the physical machine into virtual by running Control-M for Cloud jobs to provision the virtual resource followed by a workload node mapping from the physical resource into virtual.

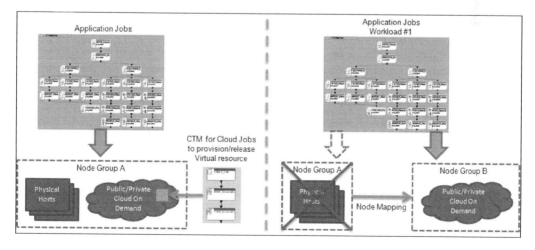

The supported VMware ESX versions are (at the time the book was written), ESX 3.5, 4.0, and 4.1; ESXi 4.0 and 4.1, vCenter Server 4.0 and 4.1, VirtualCenter 2.5.

> In reality, we will see more private clouds that are driven by the organization's internal virtual infrastructure are used, than Amazon EC2 (at least, at the time of writing this book). However, Amazon EC2 can be a perfect environment for running development or testing tasks, which requires large computing capacity, but only for a short period of time. It saves the organization time and the expense of acquiring physical machines or increasing virtual infrastructure capacity just for occasional tests or computing tasks.

Apart from directly interacting with public and private clouds, Control-M for Cloud also has the ability to work with BMC BladeLogic. Bladelogic is also an automation tool, but its focus is at the datacenter and infrastructure management level. It centralizes and automates the configuration changes (that is, patching and snapshot) of physical/virtual server, network, database, and application, which used to be performed manually; it has the ability to manage cloud lifecycle, interacts with CMDB, and provides overall dashboard view, analysis, and reporting. By allowing integration of the two automation tools, we can bring those management tasks into Control-M to work in harmony with our existing application batch workload. As a result of the integration, the tools have the ability to build dependencies between them, pass variables, and control execution by using resources and workload settings. Typical scenarios can be:

- Without the integration:
    - The maintenance team needs to apply a patch on 100 servers that require application restart or system offline.
    - The maintenance team defines the task in Bladelogic for each server and contacts the owner of the affected application for change approval.
    - The application owner cannot determine when will be the right time or if there's enough time in a given window for such a task.
    - After deep analysis of the application's batch behavior and a long negotiation between the two, the application team approves the change request, the maintenance is scheduled for 09:00pm, 05/01/2010.
    - At 09:00pm, 05/01/2010, the maintenance task starts on time but, for some reason, it is running longer than usual. The application team has no visibility of it and therefore becomes a bit panicky. They keep calling the maintenance team to find out whether it will complete within the planned outage window.

- ○ Finally, the maintenance task is completed, but the maintenance team, for some reason, does not inform the application team in time for them to manually start the application batch execution. As a result, the some critical jobs miss SLA and impact the business.

- Now, with the integration:

  - ○ For the same maintenance task, the maintenance team defines the task in BladeLogic for each server and defines corresponding jobs in CONTROL-M.

  - ○ The maintenance team then contacts each application owner for change approval.

  - ○ The application owner exports a job execution history report of the application batch from CONTROL-M, trying to find a good time window for such task. Then they open CONTROL-M Forecast to simulate the application batch execution together with the maintenance tasks and put in **What if** scenarios to estimate the impact of unexpected errors and delays.

  - ○ The application quickly finds the best time window, thus approving the change request. The maintenance is scheduled for 09:35pm, 05/01/2010.

  - ○ At 09:35pm, 05/01/2010, the Control-M for Cloud BladeLogic jobs reserve all quantitative resources that are also used by the application batch (that is, so the application jobs will be in waiting for resource state) and start execution.

  - ○ For some reason, the jobs are running longer than expected. A BIM alert imminently comes up; both the maintenance team and application owner get an e-mail notification.

  - ○ The maintenance team gets onto the system to troubleshoot the problem straightaway; at the same time, the application owner looks into information provided by BIM to find out how the delay will affect their batch. Based on updated estimation of the maintenance task's completion time, they try to analyze the impact by using the **What if** feature in BIM and communicate with the business.

- ° After the maintenance task is completed, the application jobs are imminently triggered by in-conditions produced by the maintenance tasks. Eventually, the SLA is met and the business is happy.

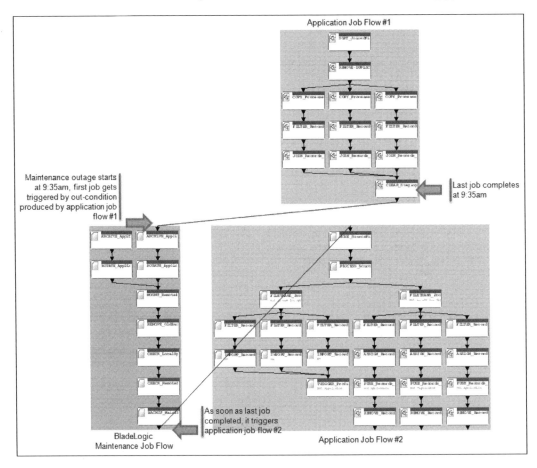

[In this book, we will focus on Amazon EC2 and VMware part of Control-M for Cloud.]

Defining accounts

Like any other CM job, in order to use Control-M for Cloud, we need to begin with defining accounts so Control-M will know whom to talk to and with what kind of user credentials.

With each Amazon EC2 account, apart from the normal username and password login, there is also an access key created by default. It contains an **Access Key ID** and a **Secret Access Key**. This access key is used for secure REST or Query protocol requests to AWS service API, which is how Control-M for Cloud interacts with EC2. New access keys can also be created and we can select which one is to be active or inactive. Defining an EC2 account in Control-M is just a matter of entering the **Access Key ID** and **Secret Access Key** during a new account definition through **Account Management** (accessed by *right clicking* on the CM).

Creating a VMware account is also not complicated. Because Control-M for Cloud interacts with VMware ESX/ESXi through web services, the VMware server host name, server port and path are required together with a username and password. The default server port **80** and service path /sdk are used by leaving the two **Use Default Port** and **Use Default Service Path** options ticked. If SSL is used on the ESX/ESXi server, we need to get the SSL certificate from the server and import it into our Control-M for Cloud installation. For ESX/ESXi, we can find the file from /etc/vmware/ssl/rui.crt. We need to copy the file into our Control-M for Cloud machine, rename the file into <esx/esxi server name>.cer, and run the following command to import:

 During import, enter password **changeit** and enter **Y**.

```
<CTM/Agent home dir>\CM\CLOUD\JRE\bin\keytool -import -file <esx/esxi
server name>.cer -alias <esx/esxi server host name> -keystore <CTM/
Agent home dir>\CM\CLOUD\JRE\lib\security\cacerts
```

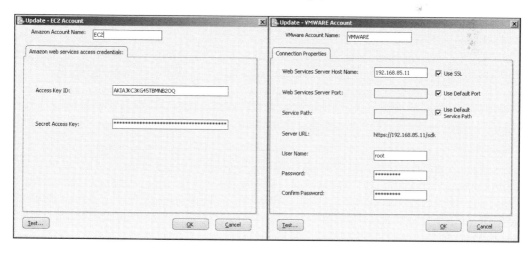

Once the accounts are created, we can press the **Test...** button to verify the definitions and press **OK** to save them.

```
SSL mode can be disabled for Control-M for Cloud by modifying the CM
container configuration file and restarting the CM. The configuration
file is called cm_container_conf.xml and is saved under \CM\CLOUD\
data. All we need to do is find the line <IgnoreSSL>N<IgnoreSSL> and
replace the N with Y. Once the change is saved, restart the CM by
issuing command <CTM/Agent home dir>\CM\CLOUD\ctmcloudcontainer stop
from the command line (that is, restart is automatic).
```

 If Control-M for Cloud is installed on a Unix or Linux machine, we need to make sure the certificate file `cacerts` has owner write permission.

Defining jobs

Control-M for Cloud VMware job has the ability to automate general VMware tasks including the following:

- **Power tasks**: Power On/Off, Suspend, Reset, Reboot Guest, Shutdown Guest, and Standby Guest.
- **Snapshot tasks**: Take Snapshot, Revert to Snapshot, Remove Specific/ All Snapshot.
- **Configuration tasks**: Clone Virtual Machine, Deploy from (Machine) Template, Reconfigure Virtual Machine, Migrate Virtual Machine.

A typical scenario to use VMware jobs would be to define VMware job to take snapshot of a job execution machine. Once the snapshot is taken, it triggers a BladeLogic job to perform patching to the machine. If the patching is not successful, revert to snapshot that was just taken. If the patching is successful, continue to application batch and, at the same time, clone the virtual machine. For each cloned virtual machine, reconfigure its number of CPUs, memory size, and disk size according to needs.

Another scenario where we can use VMware jobs together with BladeLogic jobs would be to define a VMware job to migrate virtual machines from physical ESX/ ESXi host A to B, followed by a BladeLogic job to perform physical server A reboot. After rebooting, deploy a test virtual machine on server A from a template and run test jobs. If the test jobs are all completed successfully, they can then migrate from virtual machine B back to A.

In this section, we will not demonstrate the VMware jobs; instead, we will focus on the EC2 jobs that will enhance our file processing on the Linux side. The features of EC2 jobs are not as fancy as the VMware ones. With EC2 jobs, we can create a virtual machine instance from **AIM** (**Amazon Inventory Management**), and perform start, stop, reboot, or terminate on existing instances. For each new machine instance created from AIM, we can choose to launch it into predefined VPC (Virtual Private Cloud) and define its security properties, including which set key pair is to be used and which security groups it should be part of. We can also define which Node Group the newly-created machine instance should be part of; in this case, as soon as the instance is up and running it will become part of the node group for job execution.

Modifying the file processing job flow

In EC2, we will have one Linux virtual machine permanently running to handle processing requests during off-peak and, at the same time, hosting the shared drive. The shared drive will have exactly the same folder structure as before, so we don't have to change the job scripts and the file transfer rules. Having said that, we still need to update the AFT job's account details to allow file transfer from ctm-demo-linux-02 into the EC2 virtual machine.

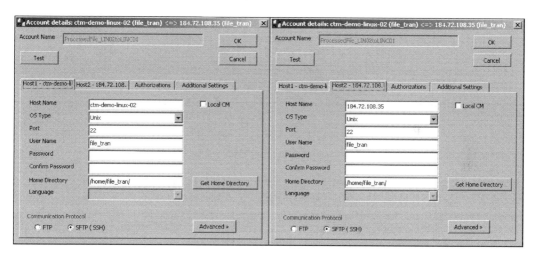

Later on, we will update the Node Group FP_LINUX with EC2 virtual machines. In this case, the execution of job MOVE_SourceFiles and PROCESS_SourceFiles needs to be taken out from the Node Group FP_LINUX and put pack into ctm-demo-linux-02. This can be done by simply updating the **Node ID/Group** field of the two jobs. Because these jobs are no longer participating in load balancing, their quantitative resource FP@ needs to be updated. We have to update it at the job-level with resource name FP_ctm-demo-linux-02, as well as add the actual quantitative resource with a quantity of **6**.

We also need to create a new quantitative resource DISK_IO_EC2 and update it into all jobs that will be running in the cloud (that is, to replace DISK_IO_LINUX).

 Each virtual machine on EC2 has to have Control-M/Agent installed in order for job ASSIGN_Record_departmenet-01/2/3 to run ctmvar utility, otherwise we could run them as Agentless remote hosts and schedule jobs through SSH.

Before we write the job flow back to Control-M/EM, let's do a mass update to modify the SMART Table named FP-Cloud and Group name SixthDemo.

Defining CM for Cloud jobs

We will define five CM for Cloud jobs, in total, to be triggered under different conditions to start predefined virtual machine images. Two out of the five will be triggered during week days, one at 9:00am and one at 12:00pm. Each of them will start five EC2 instances. There's one job that only runs on the weekend at 11:00am. This job will start three EC2 instances. The remaining two jobs are manual confirmation jobs to be ordered each day, but only to be triggered by the user if additional machine resources are required.

Week days		Weekends and public holidays	Manual	
1st Batch	2nd Batch	1st Batch	1st Batch	2nd Batch
9:00am	12:00pm	11:00am	NA	NA
4	5	3	3	3

We will create a new SMART Table called EC2_Manager with application name EC2 and group name EC2_StartStop. In this SMART Table, we will have three Rule-Based Calendars defined, that is, WEEKDAYS, WE&PH (weekend and public holidays), and ALL (for manual jobs).

Use the week day 1st batch starting job, that is, START_EC2-WEEKDAYS-B1 as an example; we first have to select **Job Type** as **AmazonEC2** and select **Node ID/Group** as the host where Control-M for Cloud Control Module is installed (in our case, it is ctm-demo-win-02). In the **AmazonEC2** job tab, we will select the predefined account and select the Operation **Start**, followed by adding the instance IDs. Before saving and closing the job definition, we also need to set its start time to 9:00am and optionally add Post Processing definitions for event notification or automated rerun and so on.

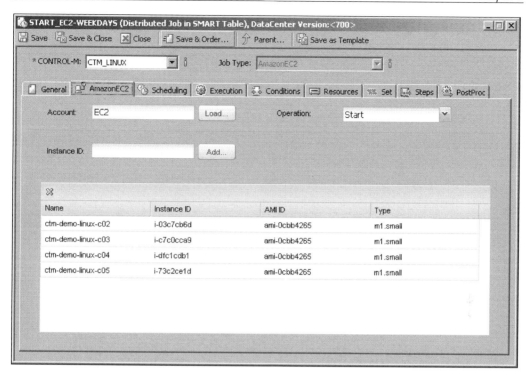

On the other hand, we need to define jobs to close off the running instances each day when the off-peak period starts. To make it simple, we will create one job, that is, STOP_EC2-ALL to close off all instances and let it run every day at the same time. For instances that never got started (manual confirmation instances), the job will detect their status is already **stopped** and leave them that way.

There can be chances of the EC2 instances being told to stop by the STOP_EC2_ALL job when jobs are running on them. To avoid this, we can define the DISK_IO_EC2 quantitative resource into STOP_EC2_ALL with maximum quantity and mark the job as critical. In this case, when the job's start time is met it will start to reserve the resource until it reaches the maximum quantity (that is, which means all running jobs are completed) then it will get submitted to stop the EC2 instances, followed by releasing the resource. By doing so, we will have a processing gap of a few minutes each day, but it is better than the risk of killing running jobs.

End-to-end testing

Because we are using predefined EC2 machine instances, we need to prediscover these machines as Control-M/Agents and manually add each of these machines into Node Group FP_LINUX, as well as define quantitative resource FP@xxx, for each host. After that, we can start sending job processing requests and watch the job flow running.

After a successful execution of the START_EC2-WEEKDAYS job from the EC2 web console, we should see each corresponding instance's status become **Running** and also see the Control-M/Agent status in CCM become **Available**. The job's sysout should show something similar to the following screenshot:

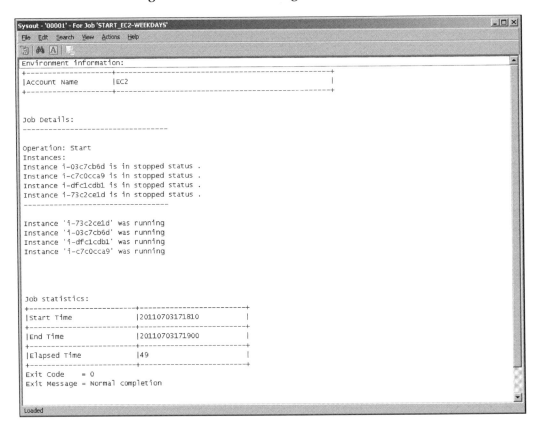

From the job execution point of view, everything should be transparent, that is, Control-M/Server will realize there are additional machines within the Node Group that have become available and will therefore start to use them for job execution.

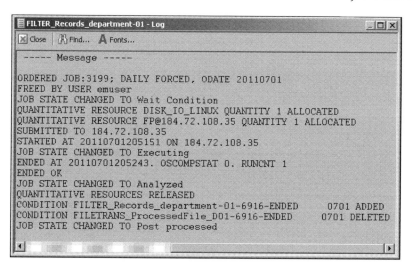

Once the STOP_EC2-ALL job is executed, the additional agents will become unavailable and all further job submission will back onto the constant running EC2 instance. It is good practice to disable these Agents once the machine instances are down. If they remain unavailable, Control-M/Server will continually try to ping them every two minutes (by default). This can take up a lot of resources from Control-M/Server if the number of unavailable Agents is large and can potentially reduce its job-tracking performance. So, after the STOP_EC2-ALL job, we can set another job that triggers the ctm_agstat utility to disable these Agents. Consequently, we are required to run another job that triggers ctm_agstat utility to re-enable these Agents after each time the machines' instances are started (that is, change the Agent status from **Disabled** to **Available**).

Summary

Look back what we have achieved on this journey: we started with building a Control-M environment from scratch to making workload automation a reality and, finally, taking the processing into close. We should be impressed by what we did!

In this chapter, we made a number of improvements to our file processing job flow from both the integration and performance aspects by using the cutting-edge Control-M add-on features. These include enabling the job flow to have exposure to external applications by using the BPI web service interface, integration with ESB with BPI web service and message queue jobs, rendering the processing truly parallel, and implementing load balancing. Towards the end, we turned our processing flow into workloads and tapped into the power of Cloud computing to for limitless processing.

This is not the finish line; this is the only the beginning! As long as we remain consistently focused, we can become real Control-M experts and will be able to build a perfect Control-M environment and lead it into the Golden Age.

Index

Thank you for buying
BMC Control-M 7: A Journey from Traditional
Batch Scheduling to Workload Automation

About Packt Publishing

Packt, pronounced 'packed', published its first book "Mastering phpMyAdmin for Effective MySQL Management" in April 2004 and subsequently continued to specialize in publishing highly focused books on specific technologies and solutions.

Our books and publications share the experiences of your fellow IT professionals in adapting and customizing today's systems, applications, and frameworks. Our solution based books give you the knowledge and power to customize the software and technologies you're using to get the job done. Packt books are more specific and less general than the IT books you have seen in the past. Our unique business model allows us to bring you more focused information, giving you more of what you need to know, and less of what you don't.

Packt is a modern, yet unique publishing company, which focuses on producing quality, cutting-edge books for communities of developers, administrators, and newbies alike. For more information, please visit our website: www.packtpub.com.

About Packt Enterprise

In 2010, Packt launched two new brands, Packt Enterprise and Packt Open Source, in order to continue its focus on specialization. This book is part of the Packt Enterprise brand, home to books published on enterprise software – software created by major vendors, including (but not limited to) IBM, Microsoft and Oracle, often for use in other corporations. Its titles will offer information relevant to a range of users of this software, including administrators, developers, architects, and end users.

Writing for Packt

We welcome all inquiries from people who are interested in authoring. Book proposals should be sent to author@packtpub.com. If your book idea is still at an early stage and you would like to discuss it first before writing a formal book proposal, contact us; one of our commissioning editors will get in touch with you.

We're not just looking for published authors; if you have strong technical skills but no writing experience, our experienced editors can help you develop a writing career, or simply get some additional reward for your expertise.

HP Network Node Manager 9: Getting Started

ISBN: 978-1-849680-84-4   Paperback: 584 pages

Manage your network effectively with NNMi

1. Install, customize, and expand NNMi functionality by developing custom features

2. Integrate NNMi with other management tools, such as HP SW Operations Manager, Network Automation, Cisco Works, Business Availability center, UCMDB, and many others

3. Navigate between incidents and maps to reduce troubleshooting time

4. Screenshots and step-by-step instructions to customize NNMi in the way you want

Cacti 0.8 Beginner's Guide

ISBN: 978-1-849513-92-0   Paperback: 348 pages

Learn Cacti and design a robust Network Operations Center

1. A complete Cacti book that focuses on the basics as well as the advanced concepts you need to know for implementing a Network Operations Center

2. A step-by-step Beginner's Guide with detailed instructions on how to create and implement custom plugins

3. Real-world examples, which you can explore and make modifications to as you go

Please check **www.PacktPub.com** for information on our titles

Made in the USA
Lexington, KY
01 July 2014